Programming VB.NET: A Guide for Experienced Programmers

GARY CORNELL AND JONATHAN MORRISON

Apress™

Programming VB.NET: A Guide for Experienced Programmers

ISBN (pbk): 1-893115-99-2

Printed and bound in the United States of America 12345678910

Editorial Directors: Dan Appleman, Gary Cornell, Jason Gilmore, Karen Watterson

Technical Reviewers: Ken Getz, Tim Walton

Managing Editor and Production Editor: Grace Wong

Copy Editors: Steve Wilent, Tracy Brown Collins

Compositor: Susan Glinert Stevens

Artist: Allan Rasmussen

Indexer: Valerie Haynes Perry

Cover Designer: Karl Miyajima

Marketing Manager: Stephanie Rodriguez

Distributed to the book trade in the United States by Springer-Verlag New York, Inc.,175 Fifth Avenue, New York, NY, 10010

and outside the United States by Springer-Verlag GmbH & Co. KG, Tiergartenstr. 17, 69112 Heidelberg, Germany

In the United States, phone 1-800-SPRINGER, email orders@springer-ny.com, or visit http://www.springer-ny.com.

Outside the United States, fax +49 6221 345229, email orders@springer.de, or visit http://www.springer.de.

For information on translations, please contact Apress directly at 901 Grayson Street, Suite 204, Berkeley, CA 94710.

Phone 510-549-5930, fax: 510-549-5939, email info@apress.com, or visit http://www.apress.com.

The source code for this book is available to readers at http://www.apress.com in the Downloads section.

Dedication

To the people at Apress: the best group of people I can ever imagine working with.

Contents at a Glance

Contents

Chapter 4 Classes and Objects (with a Short Introduction to Object-Oriented Programming) 97

Chapter 5 Inheritance and Interfaces 177

Chapter 6 Event Handling and Delegates 237

Chapter 7 Error Handling the VB .NET Way: Living with Exceptions 265

Acknowledgments

ONE OF THE BEST PARTS of writing a book is when the author gets to thank those who have helped him or her, for rarely (and certainly not in this case) is a book solely the product of the names featured so prominently on the cover. First and foremost, I have to thank my friends and colleagues at Apress, but especially Grace Wong, whose efforts to get this book out under quite stressful conditions was nothing short of amazing! I would also like to thank Steve Wilent, Tracy Brown Collins, Susan Glinert Stevens, Valerie Haynes Perry for all their efforts on my behalf.

Next, Ken Getz did an amazingly thorough job of reviewing this book under terribly tight constraints. He caught dozens of obscurities and helped me avoid dozens of false steps (any errors that remain are solely my responsibility!). Karen Watterson and Tim Walton made comments that were very useful as well. Rob Macdonald, Carsten Thomsen, and Bill Vaughn all helped me to understand how ADO .NET relates to classic ADO. Thanks also go to my friend Dan Appleman—suffice it to say that not only have I learned an immense amount about *every* version of Visual Basic from him, but his general guidance on so many things have helped me over many difficult spots during these stressful times. While my friend Jonathan Morrison had to step away from this project before it could be completed, his insights into VB were very helpful as I worked to finish this book.

Finally, thanks to all my family and friends who put up with my strange ways and my occasionally short temper for lo so many months.

Gary Cornell
Berkeley, CA
September 2001

About This Book

THIS BOOK IS A COMPREHENSIVE, hands-on guide to the Visual Basic .NET programming language addressed to readers with some programming background. No background in Visual Basic is required, however.

While I show you the syntax of VB .NET, this book is not designed to teach you syntax. I have taken this approach because trying to force VB .NET into the framework of older versions of VB is ultimately self-defeating—you cannot take advantage of its power if you continue to think within an older paradigm.

First off, I have tried to give you a complete treatment of object-oriented programming in the context of the VB .NET language. I feel pretty strongly that without a firm foundation here, it is *impossible* to take full advantage of the power that VB .NET can bring to you.

Also, I have tried to cover at the least the fundamentals of *every* technique that a professional VB .NET developer will need to master. This includes topics like multithreading, which are too often skimped on in most books. This does not mean that I cover all the possible (or even the majority of) applications of VB .NET to the .NET platform; that would take a book two or three times the size of this one. This is a book about the techniques you need to master, not the applications themselves. (I have tried to make most of the examples realistic, avoiding toy code as much as possible.)

Finally, since most people reading this book will have programmed with some version of Visual Basic before, I have also tried to be as clear about the differences between VB .NET and earlier versions of VB as I could. However, I want to stress that this book does not assume any knowledge of earlier versions of VB, just some programming experience.

How This Book Is Organized

Chapter 1, "Introduction," explains what is so different about VB .NET. Experienced VB programmers will benefit from reading this chapter.

Chapter 2, "The VB .NET IDE: Visual Studio .NET," introduces you to the Visual Studio .NET Integrated Development Environment (IDE).

Chapter 3, "Expressions, Operators, and Control Flow," covers what I like to call the "vocabulary" of VB .NET. This is the basic syntax for code including variables, loops, and operators.

Chapter 4, "Classes and Objects (with a Very Short Introduction to Object-Oriented Programming)," is the first of the core object-oriented programming chapters. It shows you how to construct objects and use them.

Chapter 5, "Inheritance and Interfaces," covers the other key parts of object-oriented programming in VB .NET: *inheritance* and *interfaces*. This chapter also contains an introduction to the useful .NET collection classes which allow you to efficiently manage data inside a program.

Chapter 6, "Event Handling and Delegates," takes up events and the new .NET notion of a *delegate*. Event-driven programming is still the key to good user interface design, and .NET depends on it just as much as Windows did.

Chapter 7, "Error Handling the VB .NET Way: Living with Exceptions," covers *exceptions,* the modern way of dealing with errors that lets you banish the archaic `On Error GoTo` syntax that has plagued VB since its start.

Chapter 8, "Windows Forms, Drawing, and Printing,," takes up building Windows user interfaces, graphics and printing. Although the browser is obviously becoming more important as a delivery platform, traditional Windows-based clients aren't going away, and this chapter gives you a firm foundation to build them under .NET.

Chapter 9, "Input/Output," presents I/O, with a complete treatment of *streams,* which are at the root of .NET's way of handling I/O.

Chapter 10, "Multithreading," is a concise treatment of the fundamentals of multithreading. Multithreading is an amazingly powerful technique of programming that is nonetheless fraught with peril. I hope this chapter does not just teach you enough "to be dangerous," but rather, enough so that you can use this powerful technique safely and effectively in your programs.

Chapter 11, "A Brief Introduction to Database Access with VB .NET," and **Chapter 12, "A Brief Overview of ASP .NET,"** are very brief introductions to two of the most important applications of .NET: ASP .NET and ADO .NET. Please note these chapters are designed to give you just a taste, and you will have to look at more detailed books to learn how to use ASP .NET or ADO .NET in production-level code.

Chapter 13, ".NET Assemblies, Deployment, and COM Interop," is a brief introduction to what goes on under the hood in .NET that includes a look the idea of assemblies and COM Interop. While I have tried to give you a flavor of these important topics, you will also need to consult a more advanced book to learn more about the topics.

Contacting Me

I would love to hear about your experiences with this book, suggestions for improvements, and any errata you may find. (The current list of errata may be found at the Apress Web site at `www.apress.com`). You can contact me at `gary@thecornells.com`.

Gary Cornell
Berkeley, CA
September 2001

CHAPTER 1

Introduction

WE HOPE THIS BOOK will be useful to experienced programmers of all languages, but this introduction is primarily aimed at Visual Basic programmers. Other programmers can jump to Chapter 2, to begin delving into an incredibly rich integrated development environment (IDE) backed by the first modern fully object-oriented language in the BASIC[1] family. Programmers accustomed to Visual Basic for Windows may need some convincing that all the work they face in moving to VB .NET is worth it. Hence this chapter.

Visual Basic Then and Now

Visual Basic for Windows is a little over ten years old. It debuted on March 20, 1991, at a show called "Windows World," although its roots go back to a tool called Ruby that Alan Cooper developed in 1988.[2]

There is no question that Visual Basic caused a stir. Our favorite quotes came from Steve Gibson, who wrote in *InfoWorld* that Visual Basic was a "stunning new miracle" and would "dramatically change the way people feel about and use Microsoft Windows." Charles Petzold, author of one of the standard books on Windows programming in C, was quoted in the *New York Times* as saying: "For those of us who make our living explaining the complexities of Windows programming to programmers, Visual Basic poses a real threat to our livelihood." (Petzold's comments are ironic, considering the millions of VB books sold since that fateful day in 1991.) But another quote made at Visual Basic's debut by Stewart Alsop is more telling: Alsop described Visual Basic as "the perfect programming environment for the 1990s."

But we do not live in the 1990s anymore, so it should come as no surprise that Visual Basic .NET is as different from Visual Basic for Windows as Visual Basic for Windows Version 1 was from its predecessor QuickBasic. While we certainly feel there is a lot of knowledge you can carry over from your Visual Basic for Windows programming experience, there are as many changes in programming for the

1. Read BASIC as meaning "very readable-with no ugly braces…."

2. Its code name, "Thunder," appeared on one of the rarest T-shirts around—it says "Thunder unlocks Windows" with a lightning bolt image. You may also see a cool screen saver that looks like the shirt.

.NET *platform*[3] using Visual Basic.NET (or VB .NET for short) as there were in moving from QuickBasic for DOS to VB1 for Windows.

The Versions of Visual Basic

The first two versions of Visual Basic for Windows were quite good for building prototypes and demo applications—but not much else. Both versions tied excellent IDEs with relatively easy languages to learn. The languages themselves had relatively small feature sets. When VB 3 was released with a way to access databases that required learning a new programming model, the first reaction of many people was, "Oh great, they've messed up VB!" With the benefit of hindsight, the database features added to VB3 were necessary for it to grow beyond the toy stage into a serious tool. With VB4 came a limited ability to create objects and hence a very limited form of object-oriented programming. With VB5 and VB6 came more features from object-oriented programming, and it now had the ability to build controls and to use interfaces. But the structure was getting pretty rickety since the object-oriented features were bolted on to a substructure that lacked support for it. For example, there was no way to guarantee that objects were created correctly in VB—you had to use a convention instead of the constructor approach used by practically every other object-oriented language. (See Chapter 4 for more on what a constructor does.) Ultimately the designers of VB saw that, if they were going to have a VB-ish tool for their new .NET platform, more changes were needed since, for example, the .NET Framework depends on having full object orientation.

We feel that the hardest part of dealing with the various changes in VB over the years is not so much in that the IDE changed a little or a lot, or that there were a few new keywords to learn, the pain was in having to change the way that you thought about your VB programs. In particular, to take full advantage of VB5 and VB6, you had to begin to move from an *object-based* language with an extremely limited ability to create your own objects to more of an *object-oriented* language where, for example, interfaces was a vital part of the toolset. The trouble really was that many VB programmers who grew up with the product had never programmed using the principles of object-oriented programming before. When classes were introduced in VB, most VB developers had no idea what a class really was—never mind why they would ever want to use one.

Still, even with the limited object-oriented features available to you in VB5 and 6, when you learned how to use them they made programming large projects easier. For example, you could build reusable objects like controls, or on a more prosaic level, you could do neat things to help make maintaining your programs easier. You could also banish the `Select Case` statement from maintenance hell.

3. Microsoft takes the word platform seriously. It even calls Windows a platform.

What we mean is that instead of having to write code that worked more or less like this:

```
Select Case kindOfEmployee
Case Secretary
   RaiseSalary 5%
Case Manager
  RaiseSalary 10%
Case Programmer
   RaiseSalary 15%
Case Architect
   RaiseSalary 20%
'etc
End Select
```

which was a pain to maintain because whenever you added a new type of employee you had to change all the corresponding `Select Case` statements, the *compiler* could do the work for you. This was finally possible because starting with VB5, you could use the magic of *interface polymorphism* (see Chapter 5 for more on this) and write code like this:

```
For Each employee in Employees
  employee.RaiseSalary
Next
```

and know that the compiler would look inside your objects to find the right `RaiseSalary` method.

Classes let you create VB apps in a much more efficient and maintainable manner. Whether you stick with VB5 or shift to VB .NET we cannot imagine writing a serious VB app without them.

The .NET Mentality Shift

What does all of this have to do with .NET? Quite a lot. You see, .NET is going to change the way you design your applications as much as the introduction of classes to VB changed the best way to build your VB5 or 6 applications. And just as we VB programmers suffered through the change from the classless to class-enabled incarnations of VB, so will we feel some pain in the transition to .NET![4]

---

4. There is a conversion tool supplied with VB .NET, but we guarantee it will not ease the pain much. Any serious program will not convert well—you're better off redoing them from scratch.

With that in mind, let us look at some of the things to watch out for—or take advantage of—when switching from VB6 to VB .NET.

The Common Language Runtime

Visual Basic has always used a runtime, so it may seem strange to say that the biggest change to VB that comes with .NET is the change to a Common Language Runtime (CLR) shared by *all* .NET languages. The reason is that while on the surface the CLR is a runtime library just like the C Runtime library, MSVCRTXX.DLL, or the VB Runtime library, MSVBVMXX.DLL, it is much larger and has greater functionality. Because of its richness, writing programs that take full advantage of the CLR often seems like you are writing for a whole new operating system API.[5]

Since all languages that are .NET-compliant use the *same* CLR, there is no need for a language-specific runtime. What is more, code that is CLR can be written in *any* language and still be used equally well by *all* .NET CLR-compliant languages.[6] Your VB code can be used by C# programmers and vice versa with no extra work.

Next, there is a common file format for .NET executable code, called *Microsoft Intermediate Language* (MSIL, or just IL). MSIL is a semicompiled language that gets compiled into native code by the .NET runtime at execution time. This is a vast extension of what existed in all versions of VB prior to version 5. VB apps used to be compiled to p-code (or pseudo code, a machine language for a hypothetical machine), which was an intermediate representation of the final executable code. The various VB runtime engines, interpreted the p-code when a user ran the program. People always complained that VB was too slow because of this,[7] and therefore, constantly begged Microsoft to add native compilation to VB. This happened starting in version 5, when you had a choice of p-code (small) or native code (bigger but presumably faster). The key point is that .NET languages combine the best features of a p-code language with the best features of compiled languages. By having all languages write to MSIL, a kind of p-code, and then compile the resulting MSIL to native code, it makes it relatively easy to have cross-language compatibility. But by ultimately generating native code you still get good performance.

---

5. Dan Appleman, the wizard of the VB API, intends to write a book called something like *The VB .NET Programmers Guide to Avoiding the Windows API.* The .NET Framework is so full-featured that you almost never need the API.
6. Thus, the main difference between .NET and Java is that with .NET you can use any language, as long as you write it for the CLR; with Java, you can write for any platform (theoretically at least—in practice there are some problems) as long as you write in Java. We think .NET will be successful precisely because it leverages existing language skills.
7. Actually, this was not the bottleneck in a lot of cases. People can only click so fast and compiled code was irrelevant in most UI situations.

Completely Object Oriented

The object-oriented features in VB5 and VB6 were (to be polite) somewhat limited. One key issue was that these versions of VB could not automatically initialize the data inside a class when creating an instance of a class. This led to classes being created in an indeterminate (potentially buggy) state and required the programmer to exercise extra care when using objects. To resolve this, VB .NET adds an important feature called *parameterized constructors* (see Chapter 4).

Another problem was the lack of true *inheritance*. (We cover inheritance in Chapter 5.[8]) Inheritance is a form of code reuse where you use certain objects that are really more specialized versions of existing objects. Inheritance is thus the perfect tool when building something like a better textbox based on an existing textbox. In VB5 and 6 you did not have inheritance, so you had to rely on a fairly cumbersome wizard to help make the process of building a better textbox tolerable.

As another example of when inheritance should be used is if you want to build a special-purpose collection class. In VB5 or 6, if you wanted to build one that held only strings, you had to add a private instance field that you used for the *delegation* process:

```
Private mCollection As Collection 'for delegation
```

Then you had to have `Initialize` and `Terminate` events to set up and reclaim the memory used for the private collection to which you delegated the work. Next, you needed to write the delegation code for the various members of the specialized collection that you wanted to expose to the outside world. For example:

```
Sub Add(Item As String)
  mCollection.Add Item
End Sub
```

This code shows delegation at work; we delegated the `Add` method to the private collection that we used as an instance field.

The sticky part came when you wanted a `For-Each`. To do this you had to add the following code to the class module:

```
Public Function NewEnum As IUnknown
  Set NewEnum = mCollection.[_NewEnum]
End Function
```

and then you needed to set the Procedure ID for this code to be –4!

---

8. Inheritance is useful , but you should know that this is not the be-all, end-all of object-oriented programming, as some people would have you believe. It is a major improvement in VB .NET but not *the* major improvement.

(Obviously, "and then magic happens" is not a great way to code. With inheritance, none of this nonsense is necessary.) In VB .NET you just say

```
Class MyCollection
   Inherits Collection
```

and you get a `For Each` for free (see Chapter 5).

Automatic Garbage Collection: Fewer Memory Leaks

Programmers who used Visual Basic always had a problem with memory leaks from what are called *circular references.* (A circular reference is when you have object A referring to object B and object B referring to object A.) Assuming this kind of code was not there for a reason, there was no way for the VB compiler to realize that this circularity was not significant. This meant that the memory for these two objects was never reclaimed. The *garbage collection* feature built into the .NET CLR eliminates this problem of circular references using much smarter algorithms to determine when circular references can be "cut" and the memory reclaimed. Of course, this extra power comes at a cost, and Chapter 4 will explain the advantages and disadvantages of automatic garbage collection.

Structured Exception Handling

All versions of Visual Basic use a form of error handling that dates back to the first Basic written almost 40 years ago. To be charitable, it had problems. To be uncharitable (but we feel realistic), it is absurd to use `On Error GoTo` with all the spaghetti code problems that ensue in a modern programming language. Visual Basic adds *structured exception handling* (see Chapter 7) the most modern and most powerful means of handling errors.

True Multithreading

Multithreaded programs seem to do two things at once. E-mail programs that let you read old e-mail while downloading new e-mail are good examples. Users expect such apps, but you could not write them very easily in earlier versions of VB. In Chapter 10 we introduce you to the pleasures and pitfalls of this incredibly powerful feature of VB .NET.

Why You Will Need to Learn a Whole Lot of New Concepts to Use VB .NET

You may be tempted to think that you can use the conversion tool and a little bit of fiddling to move your VB programs to VB .NET. Do not go down this path. To really take advantage of VB .NET, you need to understand object-oriented principles and how the .NET Framework works. Note that we do not mean you have to memorize the many, many thousands of methods that are in the .NET Framework. However, in order to read the documentation or to take advantage of the IntelliSense feature of the IDE, you really do need to understand how the .NET "ticks." To use the various Windows and Web form designers in the IDE, you really have to understand these issues.

The best way to help you see the massive changes that have come is to compare the code you saw when you activated a button in earlier versions of VB. All you needed to code (and all you saw as a result) was code inside a `Button1_Click` event procedure.

Fair warning: if you add a button to a form in VB .NET, you will get a *lot more* code generated by the VB .NET IDE. One of the main purposes of this book is to show you why all this extra code is worth understanding—and of course, how to understand it as easily as you can the simple `Button1_Click` of yore.

Here is the code you get (luckily most is automatically generated for you) for adding a button to a form and having it display a message box when you click on it.. (The circled numbers in the code are not from the IDE—they are pointers to where the concepts relevant to that block of code are explained in this book):

```
❶ Public Class Form1
❷     Inherits System.Windows.Forms.Form

❸ #Region " Windows Form Designer generated code "

❹     Public Sub New()
❺         MyBase.New()

        'This call is required by the Windows Form Designer.
❻         InitializeComponent()

        'Add any initialization after the InitializeComponent() call

    End Sub
```

```
    'Form overrides dispose to clean up the component list.
(7)   Protected Overloads Overrides Sub Dispose(ByVal disposing As Boolean)
        If disposing Then
            If Not (components Is Nothing) Then
                components.Dispose()
            End If
        End If
        MyBase.Dispose(disposing)
    End Sub
(8) Friend WithEvents Button1 As System.Windows.Forms.Button

    'Required by the Windows Form Designer
    Private components As System.ComponentModel.Container

    'NOTE: The following procedure is required by the Windows Form Designer
    'It can be modified using the Windows Form Designer.
    'Do not modify it using the code editor.
(9)   <System.Diagnostics.DebuggerStepThrough()> Private Sub _
InitializeComponent()
    Me.Button1 = New System.Windows.Forms.Button()
    Me.SuspendLayout()
    '
    'Button1
    '
    Me.Button1.Location = New System.Drawing.Point(109,224)
    Me.Button1.Name = "Button1"
    Me.Button1.Size = New System.Drawing.Size(200, 48)
    Me.Button1.TabIndex = 0
    Me.Button1.Text = "Click me!"
    '
    'Form1
    '
    Me.AutoScaleBaseSize = New System.Drawing.Size(5,13)
    Me.ClientSize = New System.Drawing.Size(292, 266)
    Me.Controls.AddRange(New System.Windows.Forms.Control() {Me.Button1})
    Me.Name = "Form1"
    Me.Text = "First Windows Application"
    Me.ResumeLayout(False)

  End Sub

 #End Region
```

```
❿   Private Sub Button1_Click(ByVal sender As System.Object, _
ByVal e As _ System.EventArgs) Handles Button1.Click
     MsgBox("Welcome to Visual Basic .NET!")
   End Sub
⓫  End Class
```

❶ Classes are explained in Chapter 4.

❷ The keyword `Inherits` is discussed in Chapter 5, and Windows Forms are discussed in Chapter 8.

❸ The new IDE has the ability to define collapsible regions (Chapter 2).

❹ The constructor `New` is explained in Chapter 4.

❺ This is based on inheritance, which is explained in Chapter 5.

❻ This is explained in the Windows Forms chapter (Chapter 8)

❼ This is explained in the Inheritance chapter (Chapter 5), but the key idea of a `Dispose` method is explained in Chapters 4 and 5.

❽ Events are explained in Chapter 6. Event handling for GUI applications is covered in Chapter 8.

❾ All the important code in this sub is explained in Chapter 8.

❿ This is also explained in Chapter 8.

⓫ This is explained in Chapter 4.

Should You Use C# and Not Bother with VB .NET?[9]

There is certainly something to be said for switching to C#.[10] Most of the .NET Framework is written in it, so one can argue that C# *is* the .NET language. Although C# is a wee bit more powerful than VB .NET, 99 percent of programmers will never use its extra features.

But for those who have never programmed in a C-style language, C# will look strange and might be harder to learn than VB .NET. Besides, there are some definite pluses to VB .NET over C#. Here is our top five countdown:

5. **Inclusion of many of the familiar VB/VBScript functions** such as `Mid`, `Sin(x)` instead of `Math.Sin(x)`, or `FormatNumber` instead of the more cryptic and often harder to use functions in the .NET Framework.

9. Dan Appleman has a e-book that goes into this question at some length (available at `www.desaware.com`). Still, if you are browsing this chapter in a bookstore trying to decide, we hope the following are sufficient reasons for choosing VB .NET.

10. We are writing a book tentatively entitled *C# for the Experienced (VB) Programmer* for those who want to do this, but VB remains *our* first love, which is why we wrote this book first.

4. **Readability**. VB .NET uses human-readable words for everything. For example, C# uses a "**:**", and VB .NET uses "inherits" or "implements." C# uses words like `abstract`, `sealed`, and `virtual`, while VB .NET uses `MustInherit`, `NotInheritable`, `Overridable`, `Overrides`, `Shadows`. Which are clearer to you—even without knowing what the terms mean?

3. You still have **background compilation** of your code. This means you get immediate feedback from the compiler. (This is much better than simply parsing your code, as is done in C#.)

2. VB .NET is **case insensitive and has a smart editor** that changes the case to reflect your declarations. C#, like all languages in the C family, is case sensitive, which, for those inexperienced with case-sensitive languages, is guaranteed to drive you nuts.

and the #1 reason in our opinion is:

1. **It still looks pretty much like Visual Basic 6, the most popular programming language in the world!**

CHAPTER 2

The VB .NET IDE: Visual Studio .NET

IF YOU ARE ACCUSTOMED TO using an earlier version of VB, then the .NET IDE (integrated development environment)—Visual Studio .NET—will look somewhat familiar. The concept of a rapid application development (RAD) tool with controls that you to drag onto forms is certainly still there, and pressing F5 will still run your program, but much has changed and mostly for the better. For example, the horrid Menu Editor that essentially has been unchanged since VB1 has been replaced by an in-place menu editing system that is a dream to use (see Chapter 8).

Also, VB .NET, unlike earlier versions of VB, can build many kinds of applications other than just GUI-intensive ones. For example, you can build Web-based applications, server-side applications, and even console-based (in what looks like an old-fashioned DOS window) applications. Moreover, there is finally a unified development environment for all of the "Visual" languages from Microsoft. The days when there were different IDEs for VC++, VJ++, Visual InterDev, Visual Basic, and DevStudio are gone. (Actually, Visual Interdev is now subsumed into VS .NET.) Another nice feature of the new IDE is the customization possible via an enhanced extensibility model. VS .NET can be set up to look much like the IDE from VB6, or any of the other IDEs, if you like those better.

The purpose of this chapter is to give you an overview of the IDE, not to bore you to death with details. The best way to get comfortable with the IDE is to use it, working with the online help as needed. We suggest skimming this chapter and returning to it for reference as needed. Also, note that the parts of the IDE that are connected with specific programming elements such as GUI design are covered in greater depth in later chapters.

> **NOTE** *If you have never used Visual Basic, you may need to read this chapter more closely.*

Getting Started

Users of earlier versions of VB (like us, for example) will probably want the IDE to resemble and work like the traditional VB6 IDE as much as possible. You can do this by selecting Visual Basic Developer from the Profile dropdown list on the My Profile link on the VS home page, as shown in Figure 2-1.

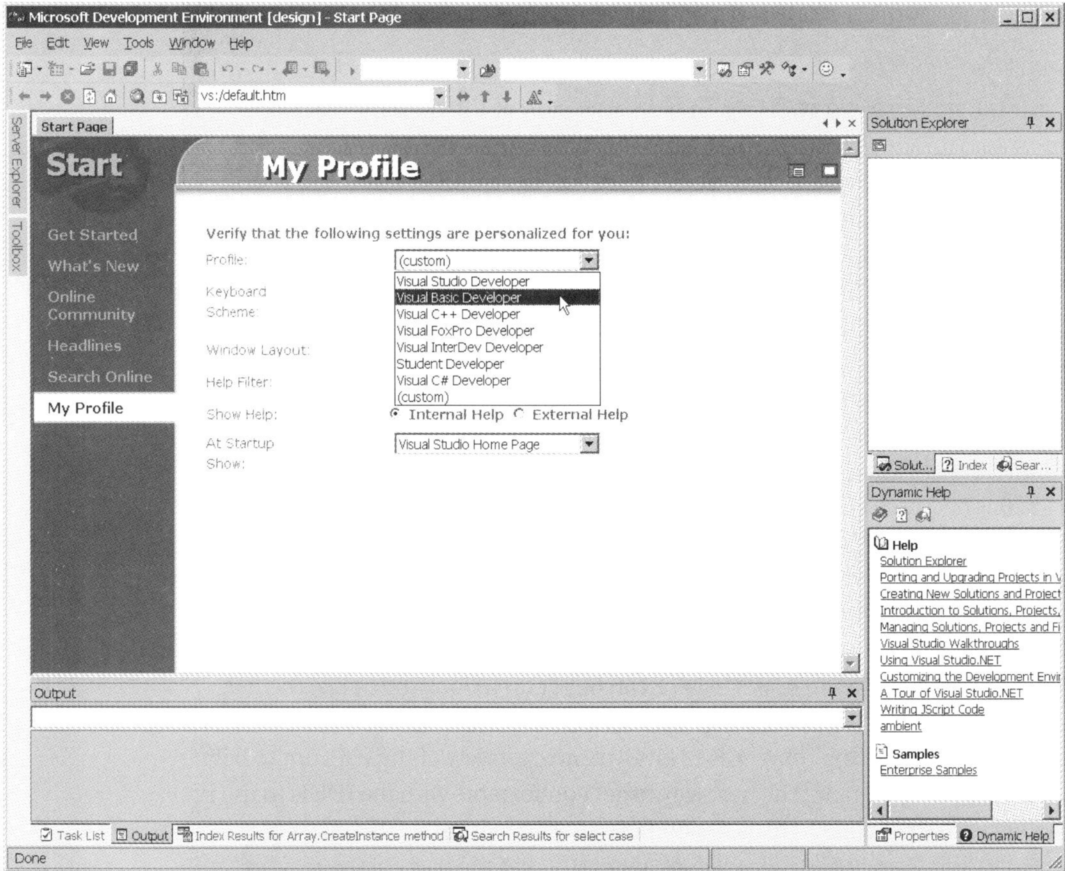

Figure 2-1. Visual Studio home page

Notice that you can also customize the keyboard and the window layout for the IDE, and that you can save these in different profiles. You can always change your profile by going to Help|Show Start Page and then choosing My Profile.

In VB .NET, every project is part of what Microsoft calls a *solution*. You cannot do anything in the VB .NET IDE without your code being part of a specific solution. Think of a solution as the container that holds all information needed to compile your code into a usable form. This means a solution will contain one or more projects; various associated files such as images, resource files, *metadata* (data that describes the data in your program), XML documentation; and just about anything else you can think of. (People coming from VB5 or 6 should think of a solution as analogous to a program group.) Although solutions are cumbersome at first, and in all honesty are always cumbersome for small projects, once you get used to using solutions, enterprise development will be much easier. This is because with a solution-based approach you can more easily dictate which files you need to deploy in order to solve a specific problem.

Creating a New Solution

The first step in creating a new solution is to select File|New. At this point you have two choices: create a New Project or a Blank Solution. Note that even when you choose New Project, you get a solution. The difference is that the VS .NET IDE builds a bunch of bookkeeping files and adds them to the solution container if you choose a specific type of project. (The kind of files you get depends on what kind of project you choose.)

Most of the time you will choose New Project. When you do so, you will see a dialog box like the one shown in Figure 2-2, where we scrolled roughly halfway through the list of possible projects. This dialog box shows the many different kinds of projects VB .NET can build. (As we write this, there are ten types.) These project templates work in much the same way as templates did in VB6. For example, they often contain skeleton code but always contain bookkeeping information such as which files are part of the solution.

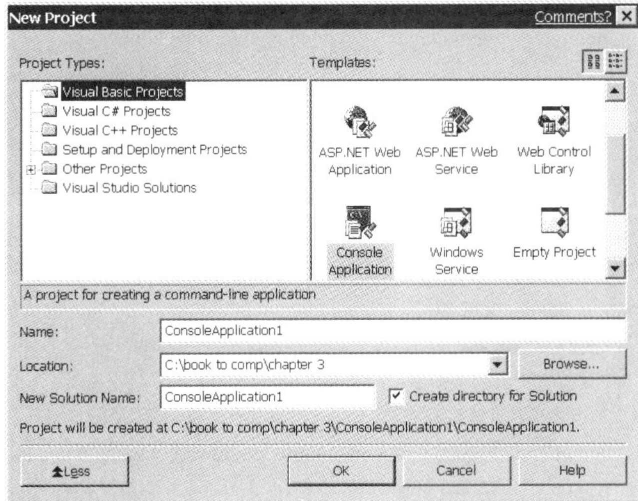

Figure 2-2. New Project dialog box

NOTE *In order to focus on the new features of the VB .NET language instead of getting bogged down in the complexities of GUI applications under .NET, we will only build console applications in the first part of this book. These are text-based applications that write and read to, what is for all practical purposes, a DOS window (they read from standard in and write to standard out).*

Since we scrolled down the New Project Dialog box, the icon for a Console Application is actually shown in Figure 2-2. Notice that when you choose Console Application (or any item but the last one, New Project in Existing Solution) from the New Project dialog, you are not asked if you want to create a solution. This is because, when you create a new project outside of an existing solution, the IDE creates the basic structure of a solution for you. (Most .NET programmers put each solution in a separate directory whose name matches the name of the solution, and this is the default behavior for solutions created in the IDE.)

We named this sample solution vb_ide_01, but any legal filename is acceptable. So, if you prefer spaces or capital letters in your solution names, that is fine. Of course, like everything in the Windows file system, case is ignored (but retained for readability). By making sure that the Create Directory for Solution box is checked, the IDE will automatically create a subdirectory for the solution using the name of the solution in the home directory you specify. In this case, our choices led to a directory named `C:\vb net book\Chapter 2\vb_ide_01`. At this point, your IDE should look similar to Figure 2-3.

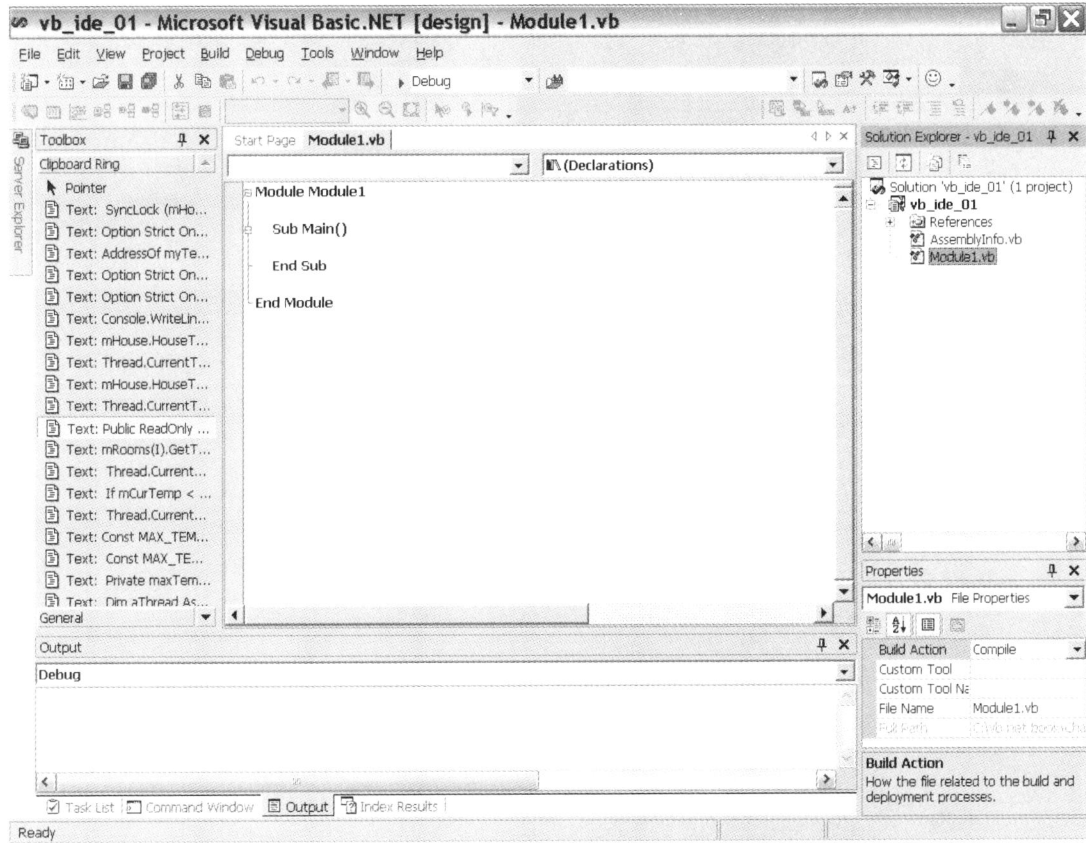

Figure 2-3. The basic Visual Studio IDE

> **TIP** *Remember that the IDE has context-sensitive help. For example, Figure 2-4 shows you roughly what you will see if you hit F1 when the focus is in the Solution Explorer. There is also a "Dynamic Help" (use Ctrl+F1) feature that automatically monitors what you are doing and attempts to put likely help topics into focus. Figure 2-5 shows the list of dynamic help topics you see when you are starting to work with a project. The downside to dynamic help is that it is CPU intensive. Once you get comfortable with the IDE, you might want to turn it off to improve performance.*

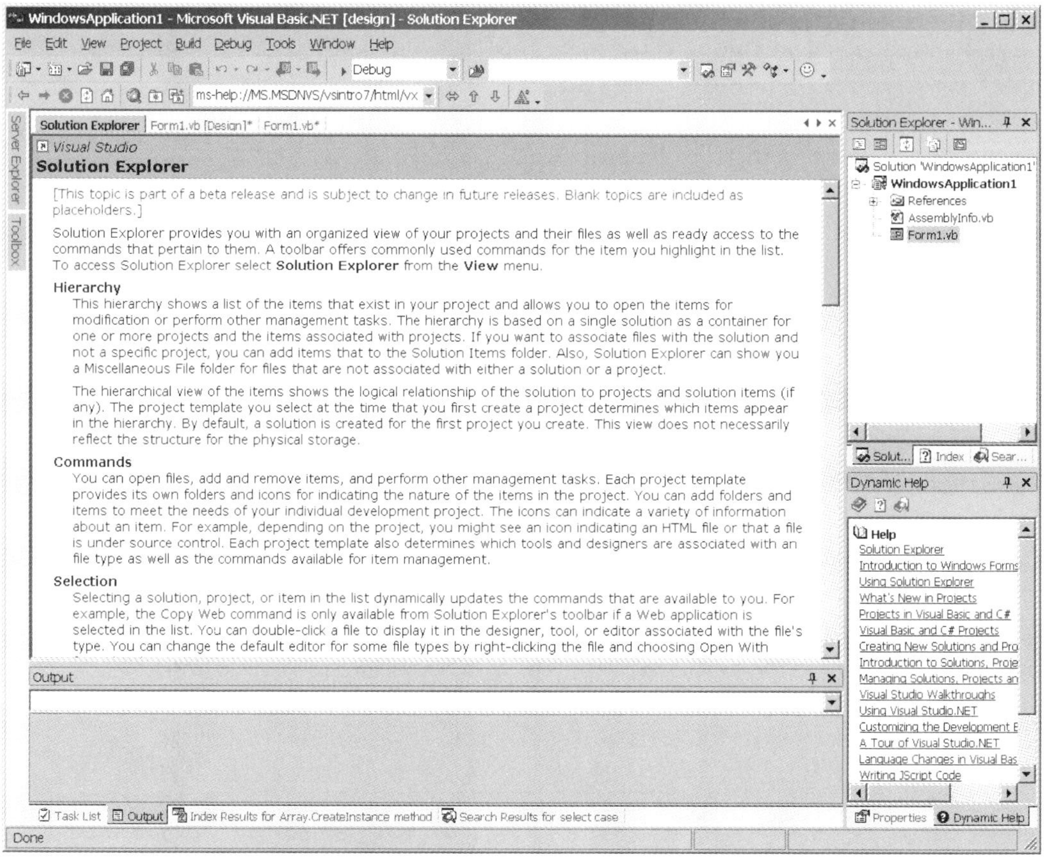

Figure 2-4. Context-sensitive help at work

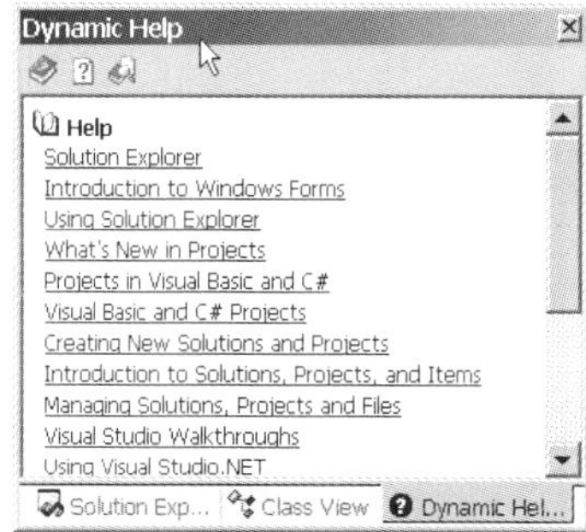

Figure 2-5. Dynamic help at work

The View menu on the main menu bar is always available to bring a specific window of the IDE into view (and into focus). Note that all windows on the IDE can be dragged around and actually "free float." Interestingly enough, these are not MDI (multiple document interface) child windows that must live inside a parent window—you can move any window in the IDE outside the main window.

Another cool feature is that if you dock a window and it completely overlaps an existing window, you are not as lost as you sometimes were in VB6. The reason is that you automatically see the hidden windows as tabs. As an example, notice where the cursor is pointing in Figure 2-6. To reveal one of the hidden windows simply click and drag on the tab for that window. To recombine windows—for example, to preserve real estate—simply drag one on top of the other. The use of tabs in this way is a welcome change from the VB6 IDE, where overzealous docking occasionally caused the IDE to become practically unusable, forcing you to tweak the Registry in order to get things back to normal. Also note the use of tabs in the main window gives you another way to access the IDE Start page.

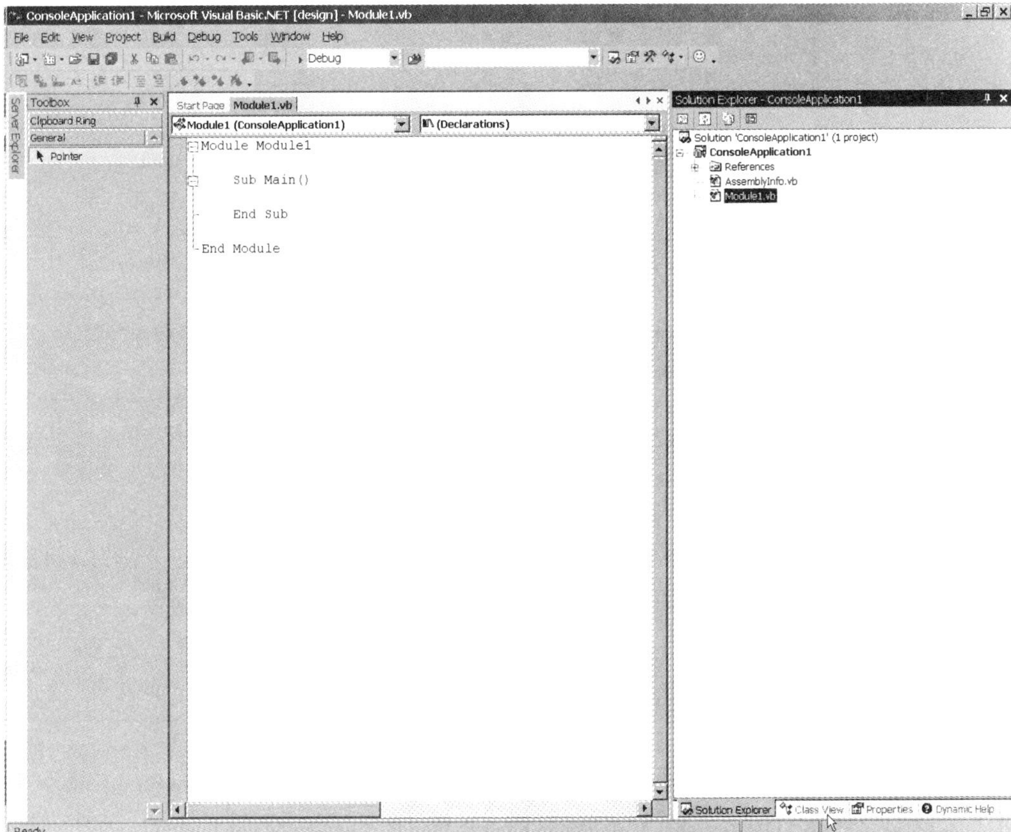

Figure 2-6. Docked windows with tabs

A Tour of the Main Windows in the IDE

We cover the basic windows in this section and address specialized windows, such as the ones for debugging, later in this chapter or in subsequent chapters. Before we go any further, however, we want to remind you that in the VS .NET IDE, as with most modern Windows applications, you get context menus by right clicking. We strongly suggest that you do a little clicking to become comfortable with each context menu. For example, the context menu available in the editor is shown in Figure 2-7.

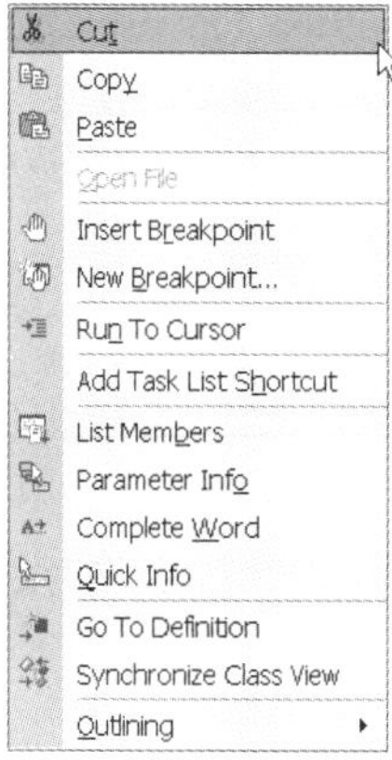

Figure 2-7. The editor context menu

As you can see, this context menu makes a mixture of editing tools and debugging tools available.

Next, the various icons on the menu bars have tool tips.[1] A few of the icons have little arrows on them indicating they actually serve as mini menus. For example, the second item (Add New Item) has a list of the items you can add to a solution, as you can see in Figure 2-8.

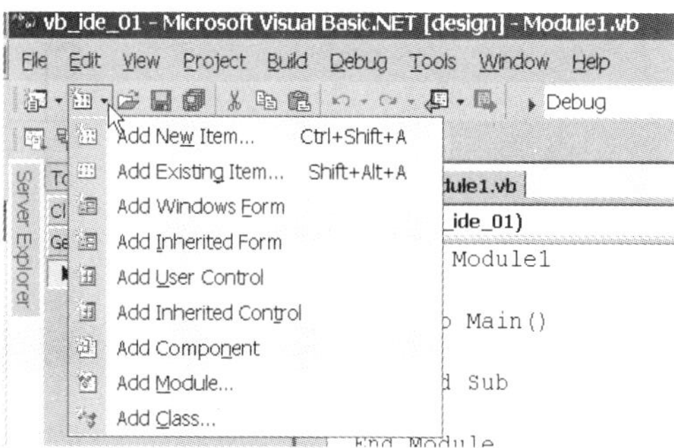

Figure 2-8. Icon mini menus

---

1. It has struck us, from time to time, that the need for tool tips shows that GUIs have their limitations. We wonder if the next trend in UI design will be to have these things called *words* on buttons dispensing with the icons completely??

TIP *If you are accustomed to using the incredibly useful Comment Block and Uncomment Block tools introduced in VB5, they are again available. Only now, thankfully, these default to being available in the standard toolbars that show up in the IDE as opposed to being on the Edit toolbar, where they were relegated to obscurity in VB6.*

The Toolbox is used mostly for GUI applications (Chapter 8), but it also holds the new Clipboard Ring that we describe in the next section. You can also store code fragments directly on the Toolbox. We cover these features in the next section too.

The Editor

The code editor has all the features you might expect in a program editor, such as cut, paste, search, and replace.[2] You access these features via the usual Windows shortcuts (Ctrl+X for cut, Ctrl+V for paste, and so on). If you like icons, you have them as well, on the context menu inside the Code window or the Edit menu. Check out the Edit menu for the keyboard shortcuts or look at the Help topic on "Editing, shortcut keys" for a full list. The shortcut Ctrl+I activates an incremental search facility, for example.

NOTE *Certain options, such as Option Explicit, are now the defaults and do not show up in your Code window as they did in VB6. (Although we still have a habit of putting them in to make sure!) See the next chapter for more on these options.*

You also have the amazingly useful IntelliSense feature, which tells you what methods are available for a given object or what parameters are needed for a function, as you can see in Figure 2-9. You usually see IntelliSense at work when you hit the ".", which is ubiquitous in accessing functionality in Visual Basic.

2. You can even automatically add line numbers by working with the dialog box you get by choosing Tools|Option|Text Editor

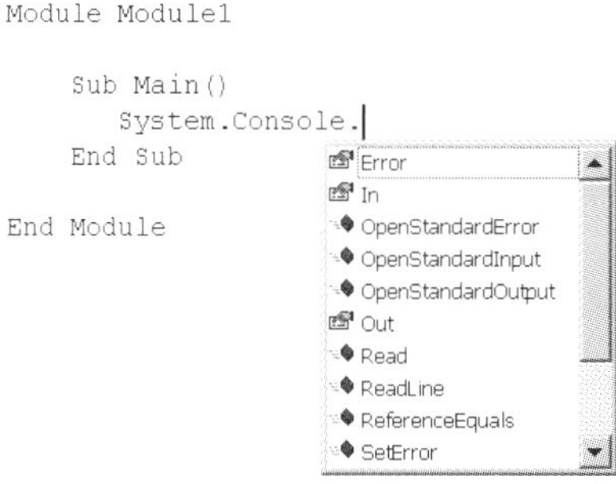

Figure 2-9. IntelliSense at work

You usually get the global features of the editor by working with the Tools|Options dialog box and choosing the Text Editor option, as shown in Figure 2-10. This Options dialog box is quite different from its counterpart in earlier versions of VB6, so we suggest exploring it carefully. To set tab stops, for instance, click on the Text Editor option as shown in Figure 2-10. Once you do that, you can either set tabs on a language-by-language basis or solely for VB. You can also change how the indentation of the previous line affects the next line from None to Block (where the cursor aligns the next line with the previous line) to a Smart setting (where the body of a loop is automatically indented) as good programming style would indicate. (You can select tabs and apply smart formatting after the fact using Ctrl+K, Ctrl +F or via the Edit|Advanced|Format Selection option. Note that when you are using Smart Tabs, selecting a region and pressing Shift+Tab (to manage indents) also reformats.)

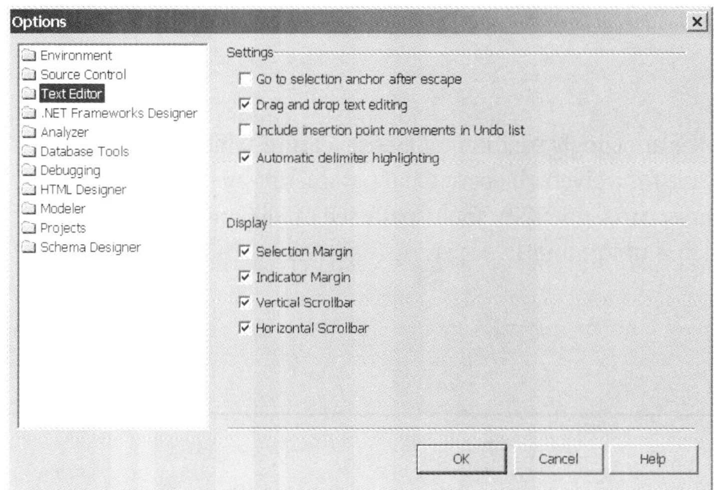

Figure 2-10. The Options dialog box

One neat new feature in the Editor is the ability to "collapse" regions of code so that all you see is the header. Notice the lines of code in Figure 2-11 with the + signs next to them. Clicking on one of these would expand the *region,* as it is called in VS .NET. Hovering the mouse over the ellipses (the three dots) would show the collapsed code. The Edit|Outlining submenu controls this feature.

```
Public Class Form1
    Inherits System.Windows.Forms.Form

#Region " Windows Form Designer generated code "

    Public Sub New()...

    'Form overrides dispose to clean up the component list.
    Public Overrides Sub Dispose()...

    'Required by the Windows Form Designer
    Private components As System.ComponentModel.Container

    'NOTE: The following procedure is required by the Windows Form Designer
    'It can be modified using the Windows Form Designer.
    'Do not modify it using the code editor.
    Private Sub <System.Diagnostics.DebuggerStepThrough()> InitializeComponent()...

Private Sub Form1_Load(ByVal sender As System.Object, ByVal e As System.EventArgs) Handles MyBase.Loa

#End Region

End Class
```

Figure 2-11. Collapsed regions in the editor

TIP *You can create your own named regions as well by simply mimicking what you see in Figure 2-11. Place a* `#Region "NameOfRegion"` *at the beginning of the block you want to potentially collapse, and place a* `# End Region` *line after it.*

There are a few other nifty features of the VS .NET editor that will be new to experienced VB programmers, and we take them up next.

TIP *The online help topic called "Editing Code and Text" and its various links are particularly useful for learning how to use the editor in the IDE. There are quite a few very useful rapid navigation features available, for example.*

The Clipboard Ring

You now have the ability to collect multiple items in a *Clipboard Ring* (Office 2000 and Office XP have similar features). Whenever you cut or copy text, it goes into the Clipboard Ring that is available on the Toolbox. You can see what is in the ring by clicking the Clipboard Ring tab on the Toolbox. The ring holds the last fifteen pieces of text that you cut or copied. To use the Clipboard Ring:

- Use Ctrl+Shift+V to paste the current item into the current document.

Repeatedly pressing Ctrl+Shift+V lets you cycle through the Clipboard Ring. Each time you press Ctrl+Shift+V, the previous entry you pasted from the Clipboard Ring is replaced by the current item.

Code Fragments

You can store any piece of code for instant reuse in the Toolbox. (Most people use the General tab for this, but you can easily create your own tab by right-clicking and choosing Add Tab from the context menu.) Storing code can be incredibly useful since it is very common to repeatedly use the same code fragment inside programs, and it is time consuming to constantly retype it. You store code fragments by highlighting them and dragging them to the Toolbox (see Figure 2-12). The fragments remain in the Toolbox until you delete them using the context menu. To reuse code, simply drag a fragment back to the correct insertion point in the Code window, or select the insertion point first and then double-click on the code fragment.

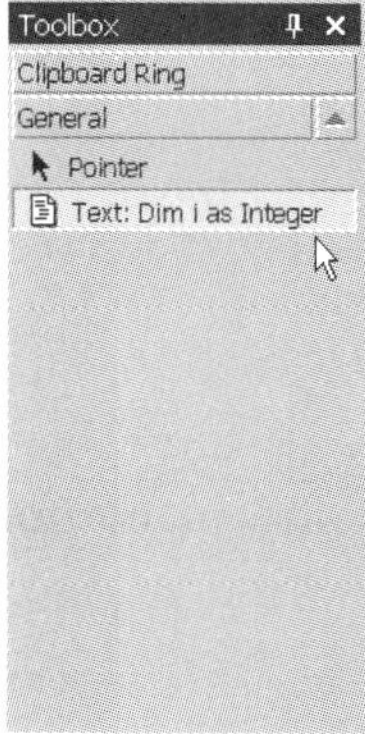

Figure 2-12. Code stored in the Toolbox

Task List and TODO, HACK, and UNDONE Comments

Visual Studio now comes with a Task List feature that it inherited from Visual InterDev and Visual J++. The idea is that you can list in a comment what you need to do using special keywords right after the comment symbol. The built-in task comments include TODO, HACK, and UNDONE. These comments will then show up in the Task List window, which you display by choosing View|Other Windows|Task List (or Ctrl+Alt+K). An example is shown in Figure 2-13.

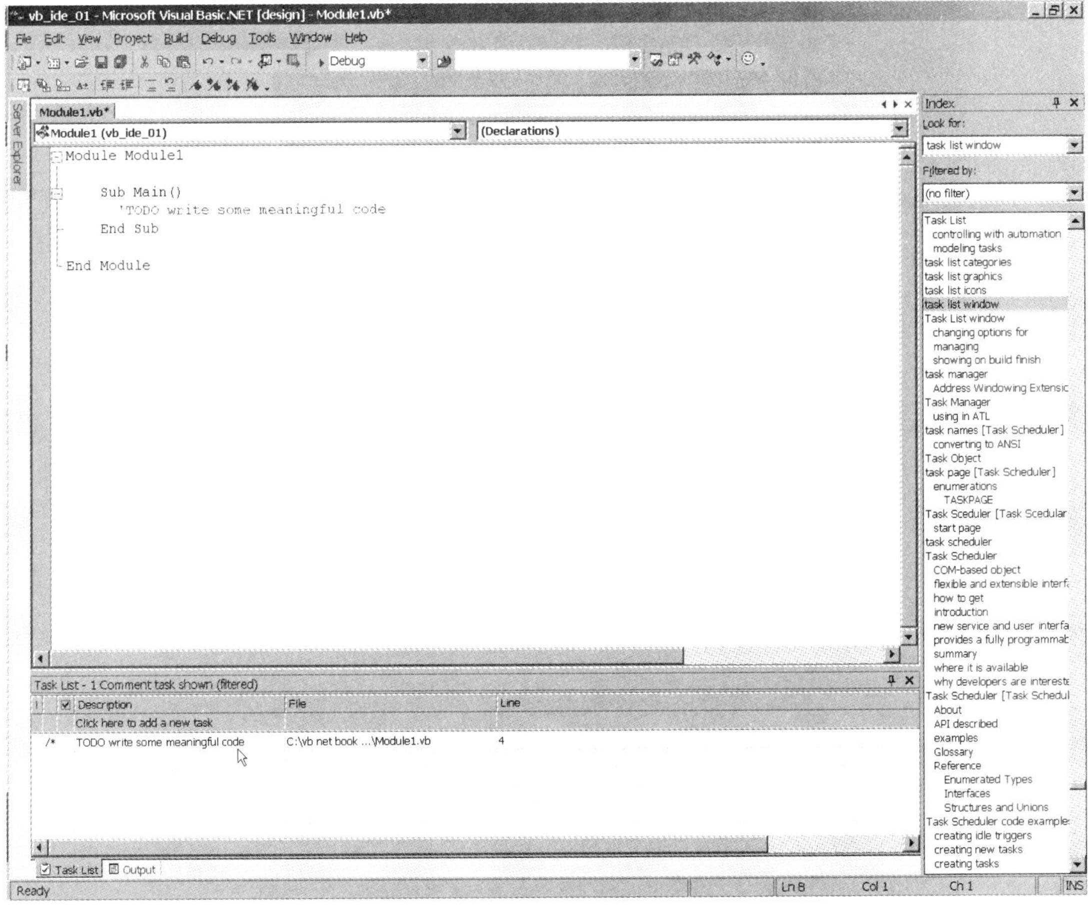

Figure 2-13. Task List at work

You can set up a custom keyword for use in the Task List such as "FOR_KEN" if it is code that Ken needs to look over. (Note that no spaces are allowed in Task keywords, hence the underscore). To set up a custom keyword for the Task List:

1. Select Tools|Options|Environment|Task List.
2. Enter **FOR_KEN** for your custom token (this enables the Add button).
3. Select the priority level.
4. Click Add and then OK.

The Solution Explorer

The Solution Explorer window, shown in Figure 2-14, lets you browse the files that make up your solutions. The default name of the solution is the same as the first project created in it. As you can see in the Solution Explorer window, we also have a project named vb_ide_01, which contains a file named Module1.vb.

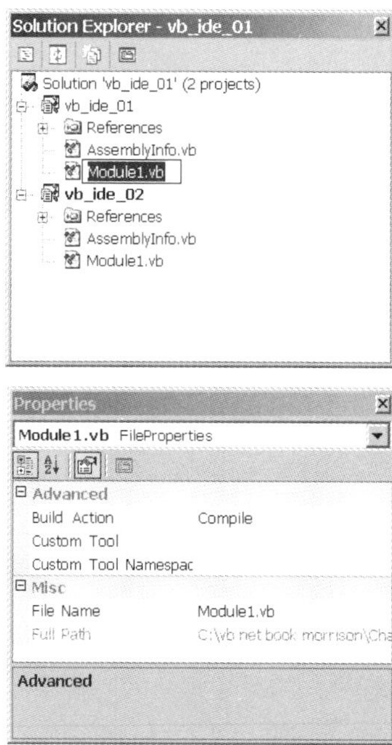

Figure 2-14. Solution Explorer and Properties windows for File Properties

Note that in VB .NET, the .vb file extension is what is used for *all* VB .NET files, regardless of their type: no more .frm, .bas, or .cls files. One important feature is unchanged however: .vb files are still text files, just as in VB6. (And, in fact, the free .NET SDK comes with a standalone VB compiler that compiles VB programs that you can write with a text editor.)

NOTE *Later in the book you will see how the IDE deals with designing forms and how it knows which parts of a file are visual and which parts are not. For now, you need only know that all VB .NET files end in .vb.*

TIP *You can create an empty solution without first creating a project by choosing the Visual Studio Solutions|Blank Solution option from the New Project dialog box. Using this option is the easiest way to create a solution when you do not want the solution to have to have the same name as one of the projects.*

Properties Window

The Properties window in VS .NET (also shown in Figure 2-14) is now much more than the place where you go to set properties of controls. The item you select determines what the Properties window shows. The combo box at the top of the Properties window describes the item you are working with. To edit a property, click in the cell to its right and start typing. The usual Windows editing shortcuts work within the Properties window.

As you can see in Figure 2-14, the Properties window now lets you set the properties of the Module1.vb file. You can also use it to set the properties of designers such as the ones you use for building Web applications or server-side solutions.

ICON	DESCRIPTION
	Displays a Property Page for the property if one is supplied. (As in VB6, Property Pages are an aid to setting more complicated properties.)
	Gives an alphabetical list of all properties and property values arranged by category. Categories can be collapsed or expanded at will.
	Sorts the properties and events.
	Displays the properties for an object. When you are dealing with objects that have events associated with them, you can see them here as well.

References and the Reference Window

If you look at the list of files in the Solution Explorer, you can see that there is a branch of the Solution Explorer tree named References that holds a list of the current assemblies you can use. (Think of an assembly as being analogous to a DLL. Chapter 13 has a lot more about assemblies.) Think of the References dialog box in a VB .NET solution as being analogous to the References dialog box you used to import COM libraries into your VB6 project.) Visual Studio always includes a reference to the basic .NET assemblies needed for any project, and they are the ones currently listed in the Solution Explorer. If you expand the tree by clicking on the + icon, you should see something similar to Figure 2-15. Notice that almost all of the assemblies that Visual Studio is referencing are named `System.<Something>`.

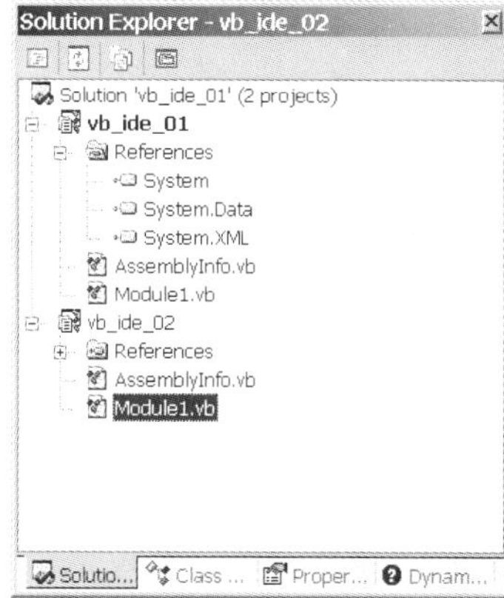

Figure 2-15. Drilling down in the Solution Explorer

Now right-click on the References branch of the Solution Explorer tree and choose Add Reference. (You can also choose Project|Add Reference.) You will see a dialog box like the one pictured in Figure 2-16. Notice that you can add three types of references: .NET, COM, and Projects.

> **NOTE** *Yes, you can use traditional COM components in your .NET apps and thus use ActiveX controls, including ones you may have built yourself. This is done through the magic of "interop"; see Chapter 13. However, just because you can do something does not necessarily mean that you should do it. Using COM components in .NET applications adds significant overhead to your application.*

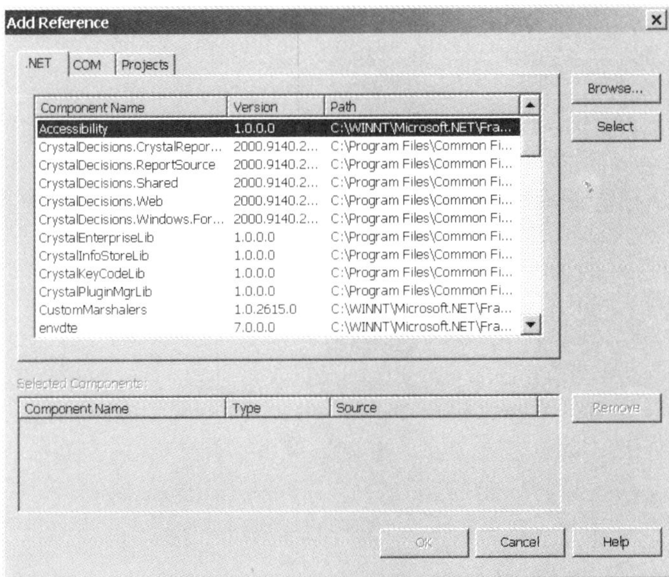

Figure 2-16. The Add Reference tabbed dialog box

Output Window and Command Window

The Output window (choose View|Other Windows or Ctrl+Alt+O) displays status messages. When you (try to) build a solution (see the section on this later in this chapter) this where you see the results of the compilation process, both good and bad.

The Command window (choose View|Other Windows or Ctrl+Alt+A) is analogous to VB6's Immediate window and remains useful when debugging (more on this later). Unfortunately we think it fair to say that the Command window is much less useful than the Immediate window was in VB6, mostly because it does not supply real IntelliSense, nor does it work at design time. (IntelliSense does work in a very limited way when you use the Command window but only for menus and macros, and not for objects or while debugging.)

However, the Command window has gained the ability to interact with the IDE environment. You can actually issue commands like this:

```
File.AddNewProject
```

which brings up the New Project dialog box (although we are not sure why anyone would do this).

The Command window has two modes: Command and Immediate. You switch back and forth between them by typing either a greater-than sign (>) followed by `cmd` into the window or typing `immed` into the window (without the greater-than sign). You can navigate through the Command window using the following keystrokes:

NAVIGATION MOVEMENT	COMMAND
Move through the list of previously entered commands.	Up Arrow or Down Arrow
Scroll up the window.	Ctrl+ Up Arrow
Scroll down the window.	Ctrl+ Down Arrow

TIP *You can copy part or all of a previously issued command to the current action line by scrolling to it, highlighting it, and then pressing Enter.*

Working with a Solution

Let us return to the simple vb_ide_01 you saw earlie in this chapter. Even for this simple a solution , the folder containing the vb_ide_01 solution (which you can view via Windows Explorer) has quite a few files and folders that were created automatically. Here is a list of everything in our folder; yours should be similar although not identical.

```
943 AssemblyInfo.vb
     <DIR>          bin
               79 Module1.vb
     <DIR>          obj
           1,354 vb_ide_01.sln
           7,168 vb_ide_01.suo
           3,008 vb_ide_01.vbproj
           1,643 vb_ide_01.vbproj.user
           6 File(s)         14,195 bytes
```

As you can see, there are two subdirectories named `bin` and `obj` that are used for compiled code, plus the four files that make up the solution. The `bin` directory contains the compiled code. The `obj` directory contains a subdirectory for debugging code. The `Module1.vb` file contains the source code. In this case, all you would see if you looked at it in a text editor is the following (we will explain how to put meaningful code into the file in the next chapter):

```
Module Module1
   Sub Main()
   End Sub
End Module
```

The `vb_ide_01.sln` file is the equivalent of the .vbp project file from VB6. It contains all the bookkeeping information needed to compile your solution. For example, this file contains information about all of the projects and files in the solution. It will look something like this when viewed in a text editor:

```
Microsoft Visual Studio Solution File, Format Version 7.00
Project("{F184B08F-C81C-45F6-A57F-5ABD9991F28F}") = "vb_ide_01", _
"vb_ide_01.vbproj", "{F40E94D3-09CA-4E17-9DEA-7A514E991F93}"
EndProject
Project("{F184B08F-C81C-45F6-A57F-5ABD9991F28F}") = "vb_ide_02", _
"..\vb_ide_02\vb_ide_02.vbproj", "{926DC073-167F-49D0-8A30-AF27E27BA2B4}"
EndProject
Global
GlobalSection(SolutionConfiguration) = preSolution
        ConfigName.0 = Debug
        ConfigName.1 = Release
    EndGlobalSection
    GlobalSection(ProjectDependencies) = postSolution
    EndGlobalSection
    GlobalSection(ProjectConfiguration) = postSolution
        {F40E94D3-09CA-4E17-9DEA-7A514E991F93}.Debug.ActiveCfg = Debug|.NET
        {F40E94D3-09CA-4E17-9DEA-7A514E991F93}.Debug.Build.0 = Debug|.NET
        {F40E94D3-09CA-4E17-9DEA-7A514E991F93}.Release.ActiveCfg = Release|.NET
        {F40E94D3-09CA-4E17-9DEA-7A514E991F93}.Release.Build.0 = Release|.NET
        {926DC073-167F-49D0-8A30-AF27E27BA2B4}.Debug.ActiveCfg = Debug|.NET
        {926DC073-167F-49D0-8A30-AF27E27BA2B4}.Debug.Build.0 = Debug|.NET
        {926DC073-167F-49D0-8A30-AF27E27BA2B4}.Release.ActiveCfg = Release|.NET
        {926DC073-167F-49D0-8A30-AF27E27BA2B4}.Release.Build.0 = Release|.NET
    EndGlobalSection
    GlobalSection(ExtensibilityGlobals) = postSolution
    EndGlobalSection
    GlobalSection(ExtensibilityAddIns) = postSolution
    EndGlobalSection
EndGlobal
```

The file named vb_ide_01.vbproj, which is actually written in XML, contains information about the project, including descriptions of properties. These can usually be changed by choosing Project|Properties or by right-clicking on the project name in the Solution Explorer.

> **NOTE** *XML is actually omnipresent throughout .NET. Wherever possible, items built with .NET are described (and even transported over the Web) via XML.*

Here is what a project file looks like in text form. Notice the constant repetition of the keyword Assembly. We explain the other important keywords used here, Imports and Namespaces, in Chapter 4:

```
<VisualStudioProject>
    <VisualBasic
        ProjectType = "Local"
        ProductVersion = "7.0.9148"
        SchemaVersion = "1.0"
    >
        <Build>
            <Settings
                ApplicationIcon = ""
                AssemblyKeyContainerName = ""
                AssemblyName = "vb_ide_01"
                AssemblyOriginatorKeyFile = ""
                AssemblyOriginatorKeyMode = "None"
                DefaultClientScript = "JScript"
                DefaultHTMLPageLayout = "Grid"
                DefaultTargetSchema = "IE50"
                DefaultServerScript = "VBScript"
                DefaultSessionState = "True"
                DelaySign = "false"
                OutputType = "Exe"
                OptionCompare = "Binary"
                OptionExplicit = "On"
                OptionStrict = "On"
                RootNamespace = "vb_ide_01"
                StartupObject = "vb_ide_01.Module1"
```

```
>
    <Config
        Name = "Debug"
        BaseAddress = "0"
        DefineConstants = ""
        DefineDebug = "true"
        DefineTrace = "true"
        DebugSymbols = "true"
        Optimize = "false"
        OutputPath = "bin\"
        RemoveIntegerChecks = "false"
        TreatWarningsAsErrors = "false"
        WarningLevel = "1"
    />
    <Config
        Name = "Release"
        BaseAddress = "0"
        DefineConstants = ""
        DefineDebug = "false"
        DefineTrace = "true"
        DebugSymbols = "false"
        Optimize = "false"
        OutputPath = "bin\"
        RemoveIntegerChecks = "false"
        TreatWarningsAsErrors = "false"
        WarningLevel = "1"
    />
</Settings>
<References>
    <Reference Name = "System" />
    <Reference Name = "System.Data" />
    <Reference Name = "System.XML" />
</References>
<Imports>
    <Import Namespace = "Microsoft.VisualBasic" />
    <Import Namespace = "System" />
    <Import Namespace = "System.Collections" />
    <Import Namespace = "System.Data" />
    <Import Namespace = "System.Diagnostics" />
</Imports>
```

```
            </Build>
            <Files>
                <Include>
                    <File
                        RelPath = "AssemblyInfo.vb"
                        BuildAction = "Compile"
                    />
                    <File
                        RelPath = "Module1.vb"
                        SubType = "Code"
                        BuildAction = "Compile"
                    />
                </Include>
            </Files>
        </VisualBasic>
    </VisualStudioProject>
```

The file named `vb_ide_01.suo` is a binary file that contains user settings for the solution, such as current breakpoints and open documents. If you delete the .suo file, you will lose these cached settings, but it will not break the solution. The analogous `vbproj.user` file is for user settings at the project level, such as how and where to start it, and whether it should be compiled for debugging. Notice how it, too, is written in XML.

```
<VisualStudioProject>
    <VisualBasic>
        <Build>
            <Settings
                OfflineURL = "/vb_ide_01_Offline"
                ReferencePath = ""
            >
                <Config
                    Name = "Debug"
                    EnableASPDebugging = "false"
                    EnableASPXDebugging = "false"
                    EnableUnmanagedDebugging = "false"
                    EnableSQLServerDebugging = "false"
                    StartAction = "Project"
                    StartArguments = ""
                    StartPage = ""
                    StartProgram = ""
                    StartURL = ""
                    StartWorkingDirectory = ""
                    StartWithIE = "false"
                />
```

```
            <Config
                Name = "Release"
                EnableASPDebugging = "false"
                EnableASPXDebugging = "false"
                EnableUnmanagedDebugging = "false"
                EnableSQLServerDebugging = "false"
                StartAction = "Project"
                StartArguments = ""
                StartPage = ""
                StartProgram = ""
                StartURL = ""
                StartWorkingDirectory = ""
                StartWithIE = "false"
            />
        </Settings>
    </Build>
    <OtherProjectSettings
        CopyProjectDestinationFolder = ""
        CopyProjectUncPath = ""
        CopyProjectOption = "0"
        ProjectView = "ProjectFiles"
    />
  </VisualBasic>
</VisualStudioProject>
```

Adding Projects to a Solution

Adding an existing project to a solution is easy. With the preceding solution still open, simply select File|New|Project. You should see the now-familiar New Project dialog box, but if you look closely at Figure 2-17, you will see that two radio buttons have been added that let you choose whether to Close Solution or Add to Solution. If you choose Close Solution, you get a new project within a new solution as before. But if you choose Add to Solution, the IDE adds the new project to the already open solution.

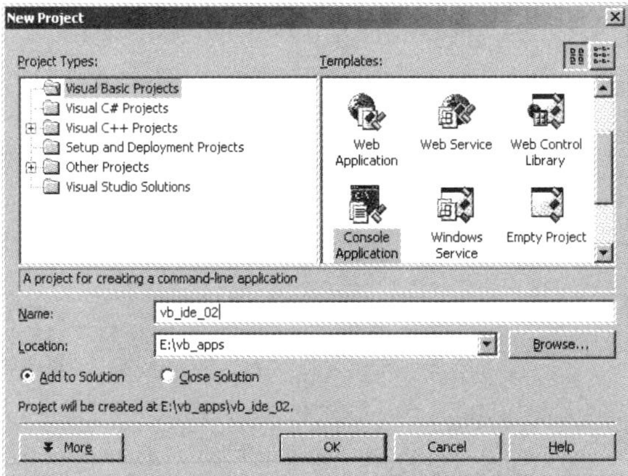

Figure 2-17. Adding to an existing solution

Suppose you choose Add to Solution and then select Console Application as before. At this point, as you can see in Figure 2-18, a new project named vb_ide_02 is added to our vb_ide_01 solution. So, we have a solution named vb_ide_01, which contains two projects named vb_ide_01 and vb_ide_02, respectively. This is similar to a Project Group in VB6. These multiple projects can interact with each other, and you can use them for testing components; for example, in the IDE.

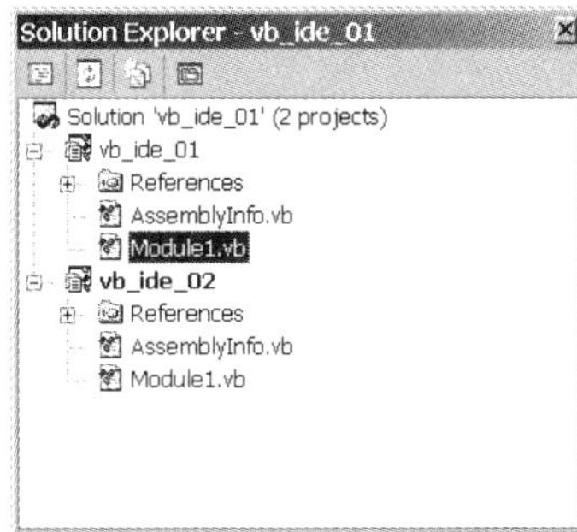

Figure 2-18. Multiple projects, single solution

Compiling

As mentioned in Chapter 1, when you compile .NET code you first get an intermediate language called MSIL, which is then compiled into native code. Suppose we want to create an executable from our solution. In this case, we have two *compilation* units—our two projects. We can create an executable from either project; each project is capable of being independently compiled. The easiest way to do this is to right-click on one of the projects in the Solution Explorer window and select Build or Rebuild from the menu. Choosing Build tells the compiler to compile only those parts of the project that have changed since the last build, while Rebuild recompiles all parts of the project. Using Build is often better, because it is faster than Rebuild. (If you choose F5 to run the project, the project gets Built, not Rebuilt.)

Once the project is compiled, you can see how things went during the build process by looking at the Output window. When we compiled the vb_ide_01 project, we got the output shown in Figure 2-19.

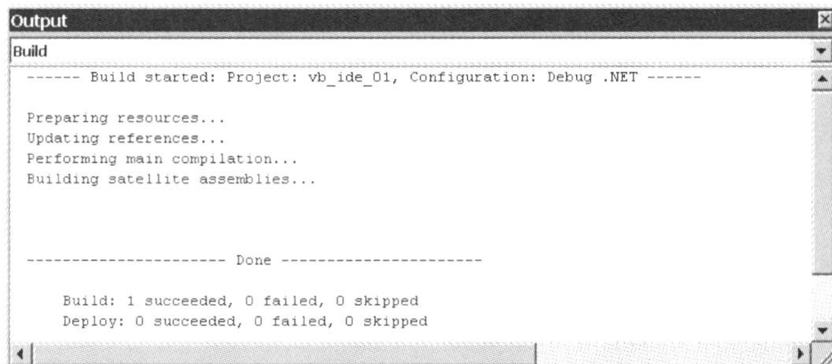

Figure 2-19. Output of a successful build

As Figure 2-19 shows, our project compiled successfully. What happens if things do not go so well? Figure 2-20 shows a build after a bogus function call.

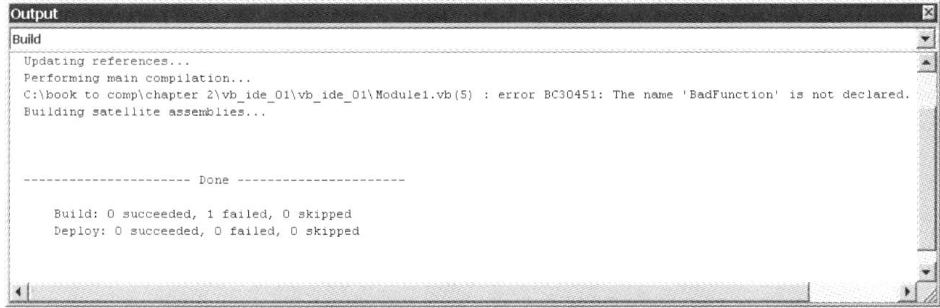

Figure 2-20. Output of an unsuccessful build

Note that because of the background compilation feature of VB .NET you would see a squiggly line under the bad line of code. You can get detailed information in the Output window as well as a task-oriented view of the build errors in the Task List window, as shown in Figure 2-21. This is much more detailed than the output from the VB6 compiler.

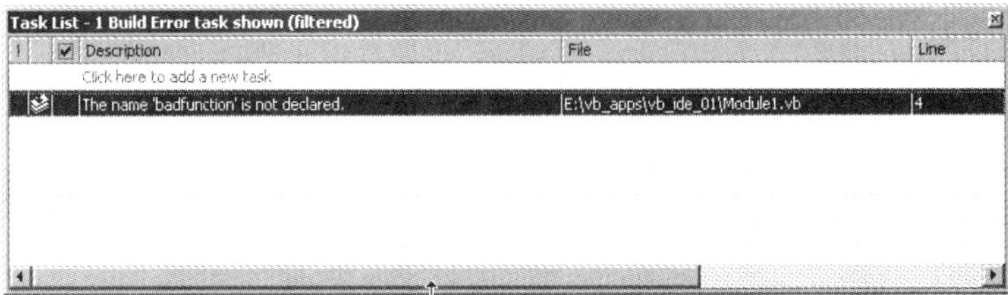

Figure 2-21. Details of a unsucessful build in the Task List window

> **TIP** *If you double-click on any item in the Task List build errors list, you will be taken to the code that caused the error.*

Multiple Compilations

You will occasionally want to build all or some of the projects in a given solution without having to do individual builds of each part. This is where the Build Solution and Batch Build features of VB .NET come into play. When you select Build|Build Solution, *all* projects in the solution will be compiled. We do this when we are close to the end of the development process and getting ready to build all of the projects in our solution for deployment (see Chapter 13 for more on Deployment).

The Batch Build option lets you select which projects in the solution you want to build. This cool feature is especially useful when you are working on one or two projects and you do not want to have to wait for a Build Solution compilation, but also do not want to have to build each project by hand. When we used Build Solution on the vb_ide_01 solution, the Output window looked like Figure 2-22.

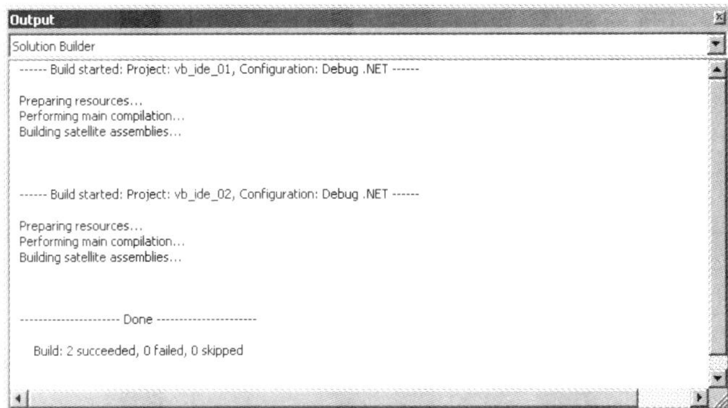

Figure 2-22. Details of a multiple build

In this case, you can see that both of the projects in our solution have been built successfully. Had there been errors in either of the projects in the solution, they would have been tagged in the Output window.

If you choose Select Build|Batch Build, then you will see the dialog box shown in Figure 2-23. If you ever have a solution with several projects and have problems with one or two of the projects, you will really grow to love the Batch Build option.

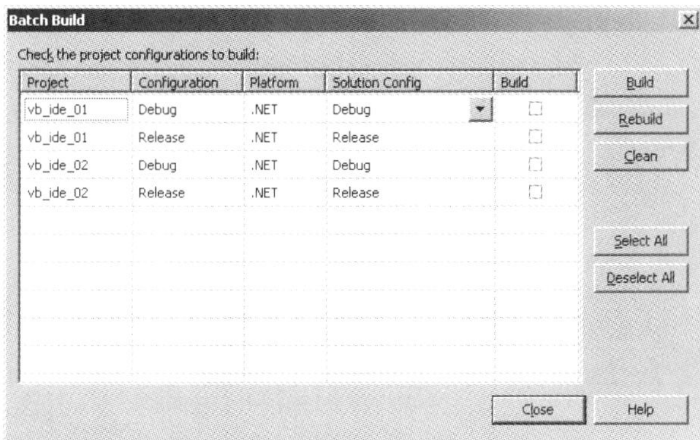

Figure 2-23. Selecting what to build

Most of the general options for compiling a project are available by right-clicking the name of the project in the Solution Explorer and choosing Properties (or Project|Properties). This opens up the Property Pages screen shown in Figure 2-24. We cover the most important ones pertaining to building projects here, but we encourage you to explore all the possibilities available in the Common Properties and Configuration Properties items. For example, you can:

- Set the Application Icon (Common Properties|Build).
- View or change the libraries that are automatically imported (Common Properties|Imports).
- Control various features of the Assembly and Namespace that your project will become part of (Common Properties|General). See Chapters 4 and 13 for more on these important topics.

NOTE *The default names used for the assembly name and root namespace are derived automatically from the name of your solution. These cannot have spaces in them, so VB .NET automatically replaces spaces with underscores.*

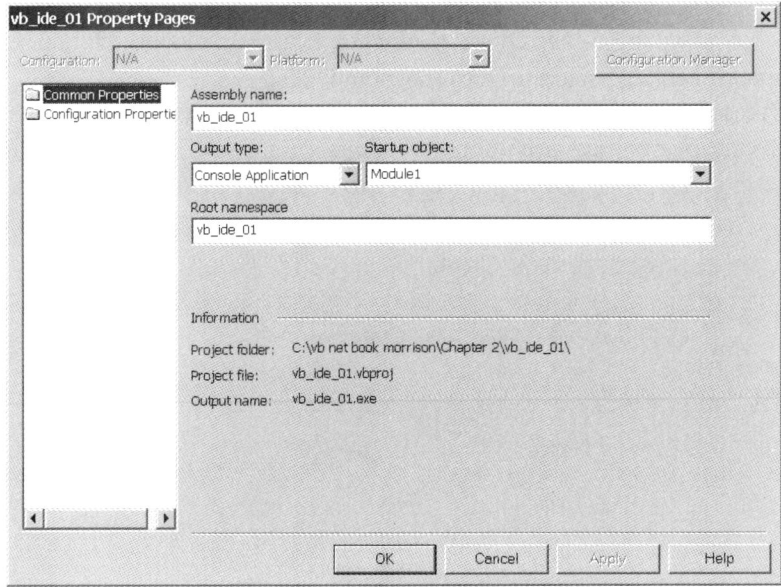

Figure 2-24. Project properties

Build Options

Now that you have seen the different ways to compile projects and solutions, we want to show you the options for compiling an individual project. When you right-click on a project in the Solution Explorer window and choose Properties|Configuration Properties|Build, you see the options that are available to you when you compile. For example, the Debugging option lets you set command-line arguments. Figure 2-25 shows the available build options for our project.

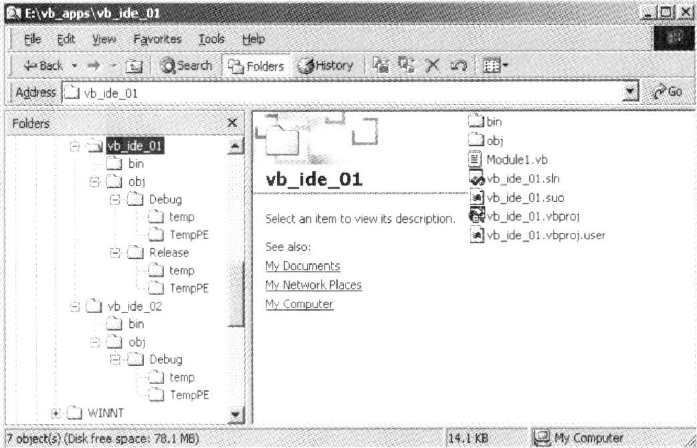

Figure 2-25. Build options

Note how few options there are compared to VB6. This is *not* necessarily a bad thing: the CLR handles a lot of the stuff that you had to worry about in VB6. The main options are that you can choose whether to create debug info (which we cover next), define the `DEBUG` and `TRACE` constants, and whether you want to see warnings.[3] The point of defining the `DEBUG` and `TRACE` constants is similar to VB6: they let you write conditionally compiled code like this:

```
#If DEBUG Then
        Debug.WriteLine("In debug mode")
#End If

#If TRACE Then
        Trace.WriteLIne("Tracing")
#End If
```

Of course, if you have not checked off the `DEBUG` constant, then the line above with `Debug.WriteLine` code does not execute. The same happens to the line that tests the `TRACE` constant.

By clicking on the Optimizations item in the Configuration Properties listbox, you can turn off integer overflow checks—again, not a very good idea. Hopefully, Microsoft will add more optimizations before the final version of VB .NET is released or provide them in service packs.[4]

Debug vs. Release Versions

At the top of the Project Properties|Configuration Properties|Build dialog box is a dropdown listbox called Configuration, with three options: Release, Debug, and All Configurations. Having these settings available is simply a matter of convenience. They let you set different options for different kinds of builds. For example, when you get ready to ship, you may want to change some of the options you previously set for a Debug build. In this case, you choose Release build and reconfigure the options. Clicking the Configuration Manager button lets you set the Build options for multiple projects at once.

3. We cannot imagine a situation when you would disable this option, and offer a free glow-in-the-dark Apress t-shirt for the first rational answer.

4. <advertisement>Remember to register for free electronic updates to this book at `http://www.apress.com</advertisement>`

> **TIP** *Generally, the difference between these two builds will be the inclusion of debugging information or the turning on or off of optimizations. We suggest you do all development under the debug configuration and then build your shipping product under a release build configuration. For example, in a debug configuration you may want to turn on the "Treat warnings as errors" feature. You may want to turn it off in your release configuration.*

Output Files

What do you get when you finally compile a project? Figure 2-26 shows the directory structure generated by the IDE for our vb_ide_01 solution. As we mentioned previously, the source files are kept in the root of the vb_ide_01 folder. The `bin` folder gets the binary output files after compilation—in this case, we get an .exe file and a .pdb file. The .pdb file is the debug info file that gets created whenever you choose to create debugging information via the Project|Configuration Properties|Build dialog box.

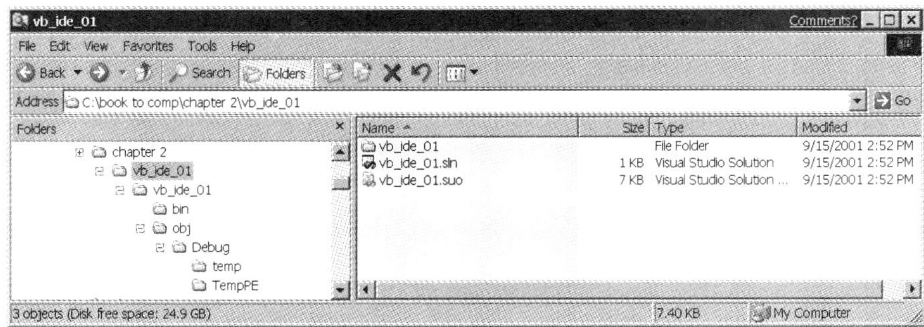

Figure 2-26. Directory structure after a build

Debugging in VB .NET

We cover this important topic in more depth in later chapters when we have some meaningful code to debug. Still, we want to give you a quick overview of the changes and features of VB .NET debugging. Unfortunately, we have to start by saying that the Edit and Continue feature that lets you make changes while a program is stopped in Break Mode and then continue running the program with those changes having gone into effect *is gone in Beta 2*. You can edit at debug time, but those edits will not affect debugging until you recompile Luckily, the various forms of stepping through or breaking your program are still available, such as procedure stepping or conditional breakpoints.

Still, without a doubt, the existence of a common debugger for all of VS .NET, whose power is at the level of the VC++ editor, is one of the greatest improvements in VB .NET over previous versions of VB. You now have much tighter control over all elements of your applications while you are debugging them. You can drill down to the loaded module and thread level.

NOTE *To take advantage of the power of the debugger, you need to make sure the .pdb file is created with Debug Symbols. You do this by making sure "Generate symbolic debug information" on the Build Options dialog box is checked. The .pdb file contains the information necessary for the debugger to know what line you are on in the source code and what the values of your variables are. Without symbolic debug information, you are usually forced to resort to looking at assembly listings to figure out what the heck has gone wrong in your application.*

New Debugger Features

The VB .NET debugger has several features that were not available in VB6. Here is an overview of them.

Memory Window

A Memory window lets you look at a memory address or a variable so that you can see what is actually there, byte by byte. No version of VB prior to VB .NET had this feature, which is amazingly helpful in some situations, such as when you have to go through the low-level code running and try to figure out *exactly* what is going on. You access the Memory window in the IDE by selecting Debug|Windows|Memory|Memory1 (or 2 through 4). When you do this, you will see a window similar to Figure 2-27. When you right-click on the Memory window, you get lots of choices about to display the memory, such as 1-64 byte display, No data display, and Unicode display.

```
Memory 2
Address 0x030d1674                    Cols Auto
0x030D1674  5e 5f 8b e5 5d c3 00 00 1c 45 5e 03 00 00 00  ^_..]....E^....
0x030D1683  00 80 30 ae 02 55 8b ec 50 89 4d fc ff 15 3c  ..0..U..P.M...<
0x030D1692  31 ae 02 8b e5 5d c3 00 00 00 00 00 00 00 00  1....].........
0x030D16A1  00 00 00 24 45 5e 03 00 00 00 00 e8 30 ae 02  ...$E^......0..
0x030D16B0  55 8b ec 83 ec 08 57 56 33 f6 33 ff 90 be e8  U.....WV3.3....
0x030D16BF  03 00 00 33 ff ff 15 40 31 ae 02 90 5e 5f 8b  ...3...@1...^_.
0x030D16CE  e5 5d c3 00 00 00 00 00 00 00 00 00 00 00 00  .].............
0x030D16DD  00 00 00 00 00 00 00 00 00 00 00 00 00 00 00  ...............
0x030D16EC  00 00 00 00 00 00 00 00 00 00 00 00 00 00 00  ...............
0x030D16FB  00 00 00 00 00 00 00 00 00 00 00 00 00 00 00  ...............
0x030D170A  00 00 00 00 00 00 00 00 00 00 00 00 00 00 00  ...............
0x030D1719  00 00 00 00 00 00 00 00 00 00 00 00 00 00 00  ...............
0x030D1728  00 00 00 00 00 00 00 00 00 00 00 00 00 00 00  ...............
0x030D1737  00 00 00 00 00 00 00 00 00 00 00 00 00 00 00  ...............
0x030D1746  00 00 00 00 00 00 00 00 00 00 00 00 00 00 00  ...............
0x030D1755  00 00 00 00 00 00 00 00 00 00 00 00 00 00 00  ...............
```

Figure 2-27. The Memory window

Process Debugging

Every time you debug code you are technically debugging a process (see Chapter 10 for more on processes). Prior to VB .NET, VB never had the ability to drill down into a running process—only the debugger supplied with VC++ could do this. In VB .NET selecting Debug|Processes gives you the dialog shown in Figure 2-28.

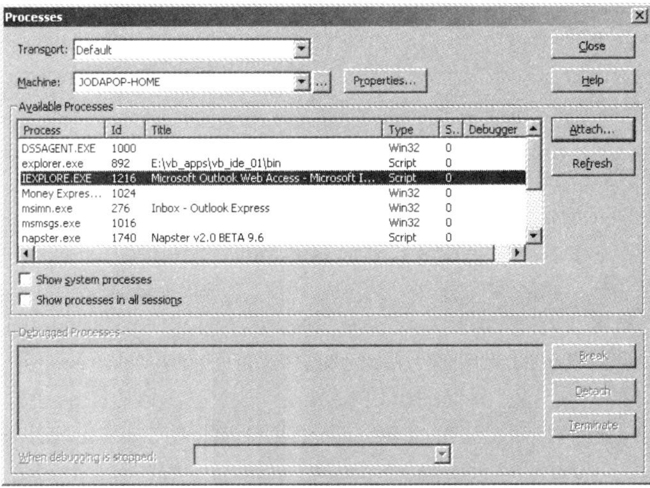

Figure 2-28. Process debugging

To start debugging, select a process from the list and click Attach. Once attached, you select Break to see the current state of the application. If you have not generated debug symbols, you will be looking at a disassembly listing of the code. Also, after you click Attach, you will get a dialog that asks what you want to debug (for instance, native code, CLR code, script, and so on). In most cases, you will want to debug either native code or CLR code. As an example, we started an instance of Notepad.exe and attached it to the VB .NET debugger so we could "debug" it. Figure 2-29 is what we saw.

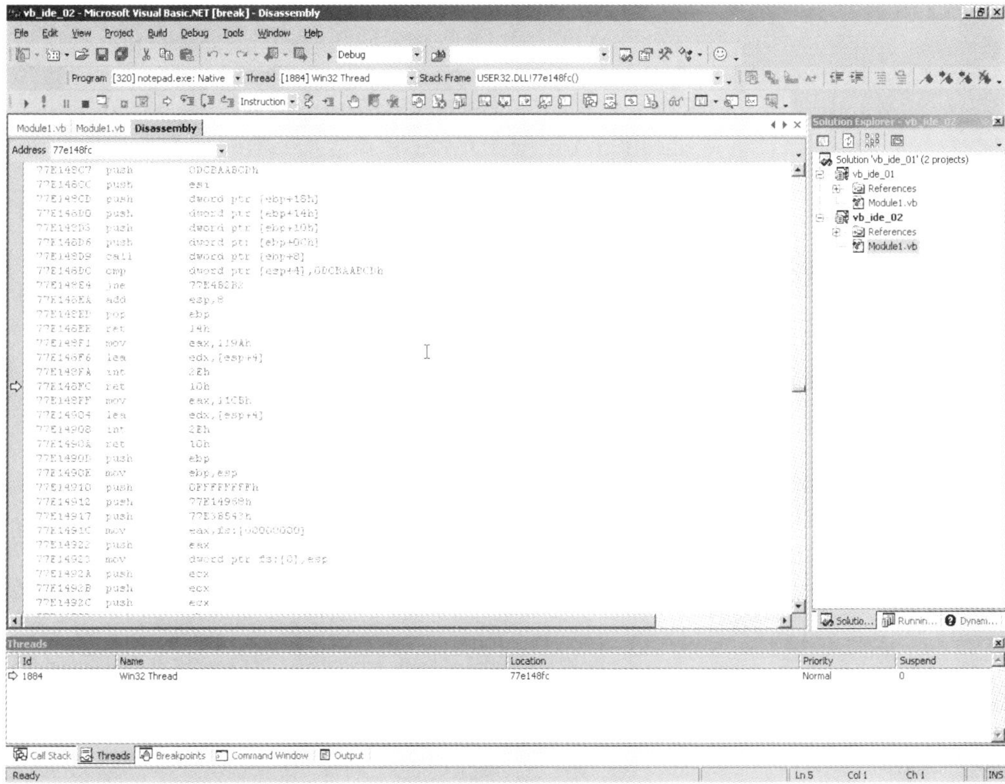

Figure 2-29. Process debugging of Notepad

It is pretty ugly, because we do not have debug symbols for Notepad.exe. If we did have them, we would have seen the source line and function names of the functions that were in call when we stopped the application to look at it in the debugger.

Threads

Another important feature of the VB .NET debugger is the ability to view all running threads for an application. When you are trying to debug multithreaded applications, the ability to switch threads in the debugger is invaluable. We will look a bit more at this feature in Chapter 10, which deals with multithreaded programming.

Exception Flow Management

Exception flow management seems like an esoteric feature until you are stuck in a situation where numerous exceptions (see Chapter 7) occur during the testing cycle. In this case you definitely want to fine-tune what happens when an exception occurs. You manage exception flow by selecting Debug|Windows|Exceptions (see Figure 2-30). This dialog box lets you control what the debugger does when specific exceptions occur For example, suppose you are trying to track down an access violation in your application. You need to:

1. Select the Win32 Exceptions|0xc0000005 exception.

2. Then select the "Break into the debugger" radio button under the "When the exception is thrown" frame.

This triggers the debugger every time a 0xc0000005 access violation occurs. You would then know exactly which line of code caused the access violation to occur.

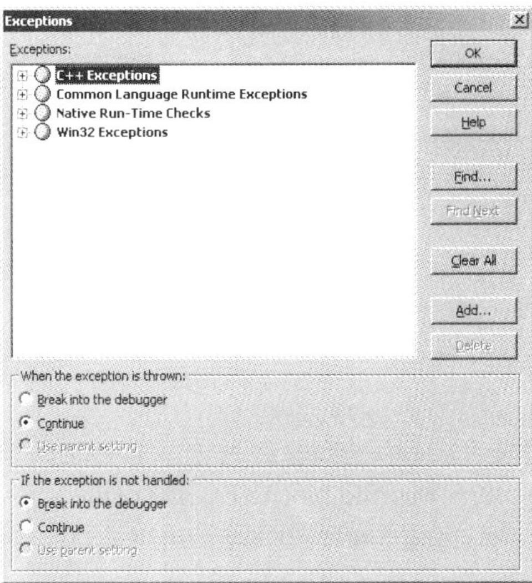

Figure 2-30. Exception management

Debugging Managed vs. Unmanaged Code

Managed code is what .NET calls code that is run through the CLR and is "safe." You cannot use pointers, and you let the CLR manage memory. Unmanaged code (which C# and C++ can build but VB .NET cannot) is code that breaks out of the boundary of the CLR.

When you are working with managed code, some debugging options may be difficult to use. The reason is that the CLR runtime environment optimizes a lot of the code that it runs. This can make it hard for the debugger to build good stack frames (the addresses of all of the functions being called). Also, depending on what you are doing, your code may have been so optimized that the code the debugger shows is hard to relate to your original code. At any rate, these few problems are negligible compared with the benefits of the new debugging environment in VB .NET.

CHAPTER 3

Expressions, Operators, and Control Flow

IN THIS CHAPTER, we will show you what might be called the basic vocabulary of VB .NET. Most of this chapter is simply a quick overview of vocabulary common to all programming languages, such as variables and loops, and the fundamental data types, such as the various kinds of numbers and strings. Readers familiar with VB6 might want to just skim this chapter.

Note that few of the examples in this chapter contain the kind of code you would use in a serious VB .NET program. This is because serious VB .NET programming depends on stamping out cooperating object instances from cookie cutter templates called classes that you build, and we will not be doing any of this until Chapter 4. The reason we chose to cover the basic language constructs first is that, without a basic vocabulary, it is impossible to build anything but the most trivial classes, and the objects they stamp out would be pretty useless. In this chapter, we offer no user-defined classes and hence no user-defined objects, and we show only the simplest uses of the amazingly powerful built-in objects and classes from the .NET Framework.

Ironically, what all this means is that in this chapter we are writing code that, except for some strange (but required) syntax, is fairly close in style to traditional programming from the early days of BASIC (or even from the days of Fortran and COBOL before that). In particular, unlike programs in future chapters, the ones in this chapter have a "top" and a "bottom" and except for the various branches, execution proceeds from top to bottom.

Finally, we want to remind you again that, as we said in the introduction to this book, we are making every effort to write code that looks like native .NET code and avoids the VB6 compatibility layer as much as possible.

Console Applications

Every VB .NET application must have a place to use as an entry point. This *entry point* contains the code that gets executed automatically when the program runs. Any other code that will run would be orchestrated from this entry point. When we start building GUI applications, this can be a startup form just like in VB6. However, as you saw in the introduction to VB .NET in Chapter 1, the code to build a Windows form is tricky and the entry point none too obvious. In this chapter, we build only console applications (an application that writes to a DOS-style console window). And yes, this means VB .NET can easily write traditional console-style applications such as those used for much of server-side scripting.

The entry point for a console application is the `Sub Main` in a module. This is similar to starting a VB6 application from `Sub Main`. For example, if you choose a Console Application from the New Project dialog box, you get a framework for a `Sub Main` in a module as the entry point, as shown here:

```
Module Module1
    Sub Main()

    End Sub
End Module
```

Notice that, unlike in VB6, the module name is given in the first line (shown in the code in bold). Here we accepted the default name of Module1. The custom is that this name matches the name given the file. So, for example, if you changed the line of code to read:

```
Module Test1
```

and tried to run the console application, you would get this error message:

```
Startup code 'Sub Main' was specified in 'Test.Module1',
but 'Test.Module1' was not found
```

To change the name of a module after you created it, follow these steps:

1. Change the name of the module in the code window.
2. Change the name of the module in the Solution Explorer.
3. Right-click the `ConsoleApplication` line in the Solution Explorer and choose Properties.
4. In the dialog box that appears (see Figure 3-1), make sure the Startup Object is set to the name of the module.

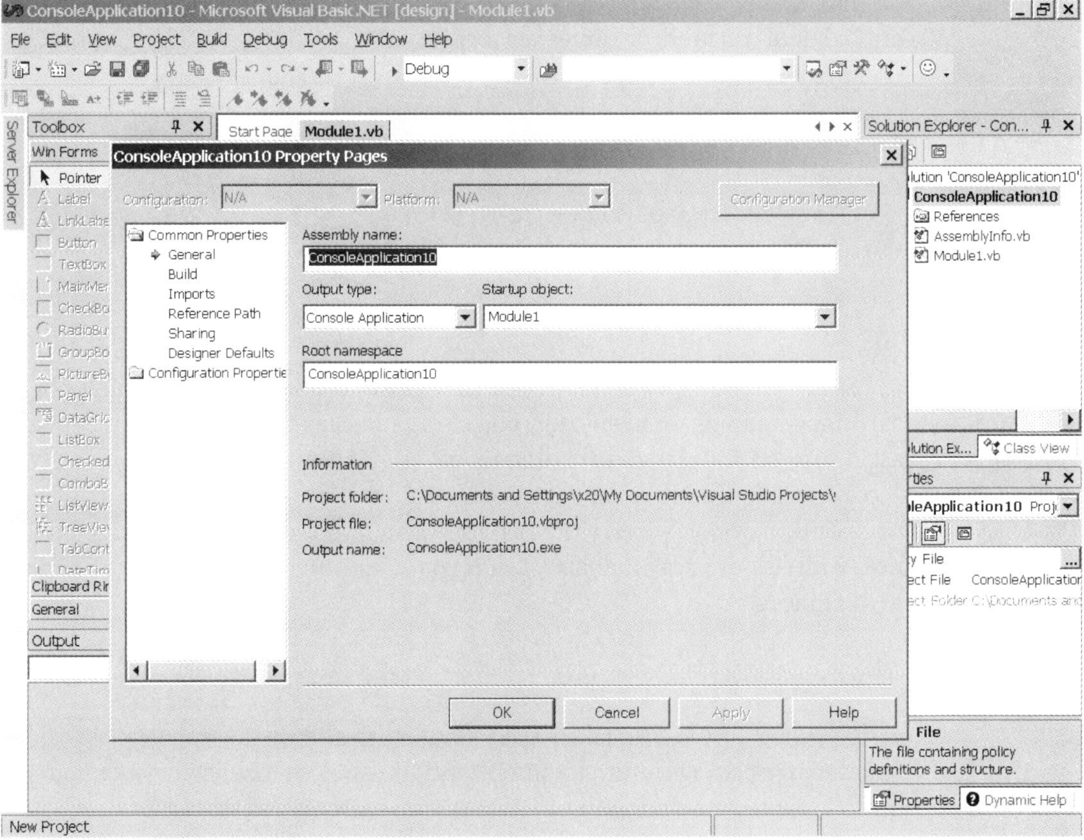

Figure 3-1. The Properties dialog box

As with VB6, you can have multiple modules in a VB .NET program (or *solution*), but only one of them can have a `Sub Main`. The application ends when the `End Sub` of the `Sub Main` is reached. For example, the proverbial "Hello world" program looks like this:

```
Module Module1
  Sub Main()
      Console.WriteLine("Hello world")
  End Sub
End Module
```

and when the program runs within the IDE, you will see (very quickly) a DOS window appear with the words "Hello world" before that console window disappears. (It disappears when the `End Sub` is finished being processed.)

If you add the line that is shown here in bold, the console window will stay around until you press the Enter key (because the `ReadLine()` at least waits for the user to hit the Enter key—more on this useful method later.)

```
Module Module1
  Sub Main()
      Console.WriteLine("Hello world")
      Console.ReadLine()
  End Sub
End Module
```

Simple as these two programs are, they illustrate one of the key features of VB .NET programming (or in any fully object-oriented language for that matter): asking objects and classes to do things. Just as in VB6, the period (".") lets you access a facility of an object or a class when this is permitted. Although you usually work with object instances, as in this case, certain special facilities can also be used with classes rather than the objects you stamp out from a class. For example, in this line:

```
Console.WriteLine("Hello world")
```

we are asking the `Console` class to use its `WriteLine` method that can display text followed by a carriage return (as in VB6, facilities are usually called *methods* in object-oriented programming). `WriteLine` is an example of a shared, or class, method. Shared methods are described in detail in Chapter 4. With the shared `WriteLine` method, the text you want displayed must be surrounded by double quotes and surrounded by parentheses. The line added to the second version of the "Hello world" program uses the `ReadLine` method to wait for the Enter key to be pressed. (The `ReadLine` method is more commonly used together with an assignment to a variable in order to get information from the console—see the following Note.)

NOTE *A couple of subtleties are being pushed under the table here. As we just mentioned, you usually need an actual object instance to use a method of the object. However, as we just said and as you will see in Chapter 4, there is an exception to this rule for certain special class methods called shared methods. Think of shared methods as part of the cookie cutter rather than the cookie. For example, if the cookie cutter kept a counter of the number of cookies being stamped out, this number would be the equivalent of a shared method of the class (the cookie cutter) and not a method of an individual object (the cookies). The other subtlety we are hiding is that* `Console` *is part of the* `System` *namespace, so the complete incantation to use this method is* `System.Console.WriteLine("Hello world")`. *This is unnecessary here for reasons that will be explained in Chapter 4, which covers namespaces in more detail.*

NOTE *Users of previous versions of VB .NET should note that the parentheses are not optional in method calls—they are usually added automatically by the IDE if you forget them, but it is good to get into the habit of remembering. Also the* `Call` *keyword is allowed, but is now somewhat superfluous.*

Statements in VB .NET

If you use a text editor to write a VB .NET program, then you do not benefit from the IntelliSense features built into the editor. Our suggestion is to use the IDE, because the IntelliSense feature is really useful in dealing with a framework as rich as .NET. (Of course, you will need to upgrade from the free .NET SDK to a version of the Visual Studio product.) The IDE editor even corrects some common typos, such as leaving off the `()` in certain method calls.

NOTE *As with all versions of BASIC, unless the text occurs within quotation marks, VB .NET is not case sensitive. Also, white space within a line that is not surrounded by quotes is irrelevant to VB .NET.*

Nonetheless, the VS .NET IDE will try to impose its own conventions on your VB .NET programs. It capitalizes the first letter of keywords and often adds extra spaces for readability. For example, no matter how you capitalize `End SUB`, you will end up with `End Sub`. Methods in VB .NET use the capitalization that is usually called *Pascal casing* (initial caps). The alternative form, `writeLine`, which is not commonly used in .NET for methods, is called *camel casing*. (It is called such because names written using camel casing tend to have a "hump" in the middle, just like a camel.)

Next, statements in VB .NET rarely—if ever—use line numbers, although line numbers are possible, and each statement generally occurs on its own line. Lines can be extended to the next line by using the underscore character (_) as long as the underscore is preceded by one or more spaces. Thus, unless a line ends with an underscore, pressing the Enter key indicates the end of a line. (There is no semicolon statement separator, as in some other languages in the VS .NET family.) You can combine statements on one line by placing a colon (:) between them, but this is rarely done. If you use a line with more characters than can fit in the window, the IDE scrolls the window to the right, as needed.

Comments

As with any programming language, commenting your code is up to you. Comment statements are neither executed nor processed by VB .NET. As a result, they do not take up any room in your compiled code. There are two ways to indicate a comment. The usual way is with a single quote as in the line in bold:

```
Sub Main()
  Console.WriteLine("Hello world")
  'throw away the return value of ReadLine
  Console.ReadLine()
End Sub
```

(Interestingly enough, you can still use the older `Rem` keyword that dates back to the original days of BASIC in the early 1960s!)

When adding comments to the end of a line, it is easier to use the single quotation mark because the `Rem` form requires a colon before it. VB .NET does not have a way to comment out multiple lines except through the comment tool on the toolbar.

> **NOTE** *Unlike C#, which has XML comments built into its parser, it is likely that VB .NET will use an add-in to build XML documentation into your program rather than have it as part of the base parser.*

Variables and Variable Assignments

Variable names in VB .NET can be up to 255 characters long and usually begin with a Unicode letter (see `www.unicode.org` for more on Unicode), although an underscore is also permitted as the first character. After that, any combination of letters, numbers, and underscores is allowed. All characters in a variable name are significant, but as with most things in VB .NET, case is irrelevant. `firstBase` is the same variable as `firstbase`. Assignments are done with an = sign, just as in earlier versions of VB:

```
theYear = 2001
```

> **NOTE** *If you wish to follow the conventions used in the .NET Framework, then your variable names will be quite different than they were in VB6. According to the suggestions contained in the documentation, the prefix-laden Hungarian notation is no longer recommended, and significant variable names—that is, names other than letters such as* `i` *or* `t`*–should be in camel casing rather than Hungarian. Pascal casing was most common in earlier versions of VB.*

You also cannot use names reserved by VB .NET (see Table 3-1 for the current list) for variable names unless you surround them with brackets. For example, `Loop` is not acceptable as a variable name, but `[Loop]` would work—even though there is no good reason to do this. Embedded reserved words work fine. For example, `loopIt` is a perfectly acceptable variable name. VB .NET will underline the keyword and present an error message (via a tooltip) if you try to use a reserved word as a variable name.

Table 3-1. Current VB .NET Keyword List

AddHandler	AddressOf	Alias	And	Ansi
As	Assembly	Auto	Binary	BitAnd
BitNot	BitOr	BitXor	Boolean	ByRef
Byte	ByVal	Call	Case	Catch
Cbool	Cbyte	Cchar	Cdate	Cdec
CDbl	Char	Cint	Class	CLng
Cobj	Compare	Const	Cshort	CSng
CStr	Ctype	Date	Decimal	Declare
Default	Delegate	Dim	Do	Double
Each	Else	ElseIf	End	Enum
Erase	Error	Event	Exit	Explicit

Table 3-1. Current VB .NET Keyword List (Continued)

ExternalSource	False	Finally	For	Friend
Function	Get	GetType	GoTo	Handles
If	Implements	Imports	In	Inherits
Integer	Interface	Is	Lib	Like
Long	Loop	Me	Mod	Module
MustInherit	MustOverride	MyBase	MyClass	Namespace
Next	New	Not	Nothing	NotInteritable
NotOverridable	Object	Off	On	Option
Optional	Or	Overloads	Overridable	Overrides
ParamArray	Preserve	Private	Property	Protected
Public	RaiseEvent	ReadOnly	ReDim	REM
RemoveHandler	Resume	Return	Select	Set
Shadows	Shared	Short	Single	Static
Step	Stop	Strict	String	Structure
Sub	SyncLock	Text	Then	Throw
To	True	Try	TypeOf	Unicode
Until	When	While	With	WithEvents
WriteOnly	Xor			

Literals and Their Associated Data Types

A *literal* is simply a combination of keystrokes that can be interpreted by VB .NET as the value of a primitive type. But types (even primitive ones) are not quite so simple in practice in VB .NET as they were in earlier versions of VB.

Although any program language can interpret data directly, how it interprets the data can be tricky. For example, we all agree that 3 is the number 3 and should be interpreted this way. Well, sort of. What exactly is the number 3 to a computer? How much space does it take up in memory, for example? In theory, you can store the number 3 in two bits of memory, but of course that rarely happens in any modern programming language.

Thus, some analysis by the compiler has to occur, even for literals, and it is best to be as explicit as you can about what you mean and not rely on compiler defaults. Let us take that simple number 3 for example. In VB .NET it can be (among other things):

- A byte: Meaning you are telling the compiler to store it in the smallest possible amount of memory
- A short: This is the old VB6 Integer type
- A .NET integer: This is the old VB6 Long type, meaning the compiler should store it four bytes

Thankfully, it will not *ever* be automatically interpreted as the numeral 3 (unless you overrule the defaults in VB). In VB .NET, strings and numbers are not mixed up by default—see the section on type conversions later in this chapter for more on this.

So, under the hood, things are quite a bit more subtle than saying "It's the number 3." Of course, as with every programming language, VB .NET has ways for you to tell the compiler exactly what you mean. For example, 3I is a literal with value 3 of `Integer` type and the numeral 3—which you get by surrounding the numeral 3 with quotes—is a `String`. (See more on the `String` type in VB .NET later in this chapter—it works quite differently than strings did in earlier versions of VB.)

> **NOTE** *You can think of primitive types as the atomic elements in a language, although in VB .NET they are actually aliases for instances of classes from the System library.*

Variables corresponding to each primitive type hold values of that type. VB .NET defines these primitive numeric types:

- Byte: 1-byte unsigned integer, values from 0 to 255.
- Short: 2-byte signed integer, values from –32,768 to 32,767. This is the old VB Integer. Use an S at the end of the literal to force it to be stored as a short: 237S.
- Integer: 4-byte signed integer, values between –2,147,483,648 to 2,147,483,647. Same as the old VB Long type. You can use an I at the end of the literal to force it to be stored as an integer: 237I .

> **NOTE** *If you leave off an identifier and the number fits into the range for* `Integer`*, it will be stored as an* `Integer`*.* `Integer` *is the default type for literals that fit into the correct range. Also note that* `Integer` *is actually the preferred type for other reasons: on 32-bit processors, it is by far the fastest integral type to process.*

- Long: 8-byte signed integer, values between –9,223,372,036,854,775,808 and 9,223,372,036,854,775,807. No counterpart in earlier versions of VB. Use an L at the end of the literal to force it to be stored as a long: 237L.

> **NOTE** *You can also use the older % and similar identifiers such as & to indicate an Integer or Long—for example,* `1234%` *for a Long. But keep in mind that they mean different things in VB6 and VB .NET, because the Integer data type in VB .NET is like VB6's Long. We strongly recommend not doing this.*

All integral literals can use hexadecimal encoding (base 16) by preceding the literal by a &H. For example, &HF is decimal 15 stored as an Integer because there is no identifier and it certainly fits into the range of integers. Octol (base 8) is also permitted by proceeding the literal by an &O.

The floating-point value types are:

- Single: 4-byte floating point. Use an F to force a literal to be floating point. For example, 1.23F or 3F.

- Double: 8-byte floating point. When you write a literal with a decimal point and leave off the identifier, it will be stored as a Double. This is because it is actually faster than using Single; on 32-bit processors, Double is a native type for the floating point operations. Use a # (or an R) to force a literal to be a Double.

Finally, there is a new type called Decimal that replaces the older Currency type used in earlier versions of VB. Use Decimal for calculations where no round-off error should occur:

- The Decimal type (12-byte decimal value) is guaranteed to have no round-off error in its (rather enormous) range of 28 significant digits. More precisely, the Decimal type is a scaled integer in the range ±79,228,162,514,264,337,593,543,950,335 with no decimal point, but you can scale by as many powers of 10 as you want, as long as the number of significant digits is 28 or less. For example, the smallest number you can represent is ±0.0000000000000000000000000001. Use a D to force a literal to the Decimal data type.

  We obviously recommend using the type identifier for literals so as to avoid confusion and the occasional weird error you can get if you try to multiply two numbers together and the result is too big. For example:

```
Console.WriteLine(12345678 * 4567)
```

  gives the build error:

```
This constant expression produces a value that is not representable in type
 System.Integer.
```

  You will need to write:

```
Console.WriteLine(12345678L * 4567)
```

TIP *If you ever need to know the maximum or minimum values of a type, use the* `MaxValue` *or* `MinValue` *shared methods attached to the type. For example:*

```
Console.WriteLine(Integer.MaxValue)
```

To summarize, Table 3-2 shows how the VB .NET numeric types correspond to those in the .NET Framework, and also what they would be in VB6 if a corresponding type exists.

Table 3-2. Correspondence between Numeric Types

VB .NET TYPE	.NET FRAMEWORK TYPE	VB6 TYPE
Byte	System.Byte	Byte
Boolean	System.Boolean	Boolean
Decimal	System.Decimal	**NONE**
NONE	**NONE**	Currency
Double	System.Double	Double
Short	System.Int16	Integer
Integer	System.Int32	Long
Long	System.Int64	**NONE**
Single	System.Single	Single

Non-Numeric Literals

Non-numeric literals include Boolean, Date, and Char data types. The Boolean data type represents True or False and takes up four bytes in VB .NET, as opposed to two bytes in VB6.

CAUTION *In VB .NET Beta 1, True was +1 (as in other .NET languages). Starting in Beta 2, it goes back to –1. More precisely, in "logical operations" in VB and in conversions to numeric types, True will be –1, not 1. However, when a Boolean in VB .NET is passed out of VB , it is treated as 1 when it is converted to a number in that language. We think this was the wrong decision, because the point of .NET is to have as much cross-language compatibility as possible. As long as you use the built-in constants for True and False, you will be fine. If you use numeric values, you may run into problems!*

The Date data type represents a date and/or a time. As in VB5, you surround a literal that represents a date and time by two #s, as in #Jan 1, 20001#. If you do not specify a time, the date literal will be assumed to be that date at midnight.

> **NOTE** *Dates in VB .NET are no longer convertible to doubles. This means, for example, you cannot perform mathematical operations on dates, such as Today + 1 to get tomorrow's date.*

The Char data type represents a single Unicode character. The Unicode system allows 65,536 characters, which is enough to encompass all known alphabets. Characters are usually surrounded by single quotes followed by a C, as in: "H"C, but if you want to get an actual Unicode character, simply use the `Chr` built-in function. For example, `Chr(&H2153)` is a ⅓ in the Unicode charts, although you may not see it as such on some operating systems when the program runs. Note that if you use one character within quotes without the "C" suffix, you get a String rather than a Char and the two are not automatically convertible (more on Option Strict later in this chapter).

Declaring Variables

The way to declare a variable in VB .NET within a procedure or function is with the `Dim` plus `As` keywords, just as in VB6. You use the equals sign to make the assignment:

```
Dim foo As String
foo = "bar"
```

Note that unless you change the defaults for VB .NET, you must declare a variable before using it. (The optional `Option Explicit` introduced in VB4 is now the default.) In VB .NET, you can initialize a variable when you declare it. For example:

```
Dim salesTax As Decimal = 0.0825D
```

declares a variable called `salesTax` and gives it the initial value .0825 of the new Decimal type. You can also use any valid VB .NET expression to give the initial assignment. For example:

```
Dim startAngle As Decimal = Math.PI
```

gives `startAngle` the built-in value for the mathematical constant π by using a constant built into the `System.Math` class.

If you do not initialize a variable, it gets the default value for the type: numeric types get the value 0 for example. Because VB .NET allows the declare-and-initialize syntax, it makes sense to always initialize rather than rely on default values. For example, consider the following code, which also uses the same `&` that was used in VB6 to concatenate text:

```
Sub Main()
    Dim salesTax As Decimal = 0.0825D
    Dim state As String = "California"
    Console.WriteLine("The sales tax in " & state & " is " & salesTax)
    Console.ReadLine()
End Sub
```

When you run this program, you see:

```
The sales tax in California is 0.0825
```

You can combine multiple declarations on a single line and, for those coming from earlier versions of VB, this does what you expect instinctively. That is:

```
Dim i, j, k As Integer
```

makes `i`, `j`, and `k` all integer variables. Note that you cannot use an initialization when you do multiple declarations on the same line, so lines such as this are not allowed:

```
Dim i, j, k As Integer = 1
```

As in earlier versions of VB, you can still use the type identifier instead of the `As`. For example:

```
Dim i%, myName$
```

makes `i` an `Integer` variable (= old VB Long) and `myName` a `String` variable, but most VB .NET programmers avoid this.

Finally, as all programmers know, naming conventions for variables have also inspired quite a lot of flaming. Many complicated systems of prefixes (usually called Hungarian) exist that indicate, at a glance, the type of a variable. Generally, Hungarian notation is discouraged in the .NET Framework guidelines, and thus seems not to be very common in the .NET code we have seen so far. We will follow this trend and use prefixes only in a very limited way for instance variables.

> **NOTE** *The* `Deftype` *statements, such as* `DefInt`*, are not supported in VB .NET.*

Conversion between Values of Different Types

Most programmers thought that earlier versions of VB were way too permissive when it came to converting between types. This led to the phenomena of "evil type conversion" where, for example, VB6 allowed you to multiply, say, a string of numerals by an integer.

The option you have in VB .NET to make type conversion safe is called `Option Strict`. You can turn this feature on by using:

```
Option Strict On
```

as the first line of code in any program you write. (You can also use the Build tab of the Projects Properties dialog box.) Once you turn this option on (and you should!), VB .NET *requires* you to explicitly make a conversion (sometimes called a *cast*) whenever there is the possibility of loss of information (a *lossy* conversion, to say it in the jargon). For example, when you convert a Single to an Integer, there is the possibility of losing information. On the other hand, if there is no potential of information loss (for instance, from an Integer to a Long or Decimal), VB .NET automatically makes the conversion. The documentation for VB .NET refers to these lossless conversions as *widening conversions.* Table 3–3 lists the permissible widening conversions for basic types.

Table 3–3. Permissible Widening Conversions for Basic Types

TYPE	WIDENS TO
Byte	Byte, Short, Integer, Long, Decimal, Single, Double
Short	Short, Integer, Long, Decimal, Single, Double
Integer	Integer, Long, Decimal, Single, Double
Long	Long, Single, Decimal, Double
Single	Single, Double
Date	Date, String

What is more, if you have the default of `Option Strict` on, then you *cannot* have lines of code like:

```
Dim foo As Boolean
foo = 3
```

which tries to give `foo` the value `True` by assigning to it a non-zero number, as was common in VB6. Instead you *must* use a conversion function to do the conversion:

```
Dim foo As Boolean
foo = CBool(3)
```

Nor will VB .NET automatically convert between characters and a string with one character.

> **CAUTION** *Although we do not recommend it, you can return to the sloppy days of yore by putting the statement*
>
> ```
> Option Strict Off
> ```
>
> *before any other code in the module.*

When it is acceptable to convert the contents of a variable from one type to another, you do the cast with a conversion function such as the `CBool` you just saw. The ones you need are shown in Table 3-4.

Table 3-4. Conversion (Cast) Functions

CONVERSION FUNCTION	WHAT IT DOES
`CBool`	Makes an expression a Boolean.
`Cbyte`	Makes an expression a byte.
`Cint`	Makes a numeric expression an integer by rounding.
`CLng`	Makes a numeric expression a long integer by rounding.
`CSng`	Makes a numeric expression single precision.
`Cdate`	Makes a date expression a date.
`CDbl`	Makes a numeric expression double precision.
`CDec`	Makes a numeric expression of the currency type.
`CStr`	Makes any expression a string.
`CChar`	Converts the first character in a string to a Char.

VB .NET performs numeric conversions only if the numbers you are trying to convert are in the range of the new type; otherwise, it generates an error message.

> **NOTE** *You may be tempted to think of the Char type as an unsigned, short integer (i.e., an integer between 0 and 65535), but you shouldn't. Starting in beta 2, you cannot use a C-conversion function such as* `CInt` *to convert a Char to a number; instead, you must use the built-in function* `Asc`.

For example, in the proverbial Celsius (centigrade) to Fahrenheit converter that follows, we assume that:

1. The user hits the Enter key after entering the text.
2. What he or she enters is picked up in its entirety by the call to `ReadLine()`.
3. The user enters a number, so we can use `CDec` to convert the text entered to a number. (Obviously, a more realistic program would have to parse the data entered before blindly using it.)

```
'Degree converter
Option Strict On
Module Module1
  Sub Main()
    Dim cdeg As Decimal
    Console.Write("Enter the degrees in centigrade...")
    cdeg = CDec(Console.ReadLine())
    Dim fdeg As Decimal
    fdeg = (((9@ / 5) * cdeg) + 32)
    Console.WriteLine(cdeg & " is " & fdeg & " degrees Fahrenheit.")
    Console.ReadLine()
  End Sub
End Module
```

Notice the use of the @ sign to force the calculation to be done for decimals. If you remove it, you will get an error message with `Option Strict` on! (The simple "/" we used for division has a couple of hidden gotchas in VB .NET. See the section on "Arithmetic Operators" for more on them.)

The Object Type (and the Death of Variants)

You may have noticed that we have not mentioned variants. That is because they are gone—and good riddance to them! In VB6, the *variant* data type holds any type of data, is prone to misuse, and is a source of subtle bugs. In VB .NET, every data type is actually a special case of the Object data type—even numeric types such as Integer—making it tempting to think of the Object type as the VB .NET equivalent of variants. Do not. As you will see in Chapters 4 and 5, the Object type is far more important to .NET programmers than variants—and far more interesting. Stay tuned to Chapters 4 and 5 for more on the Object type!

Strings

String variables hold groups of Unicode characters. A string can contain up to about 2 billion (2 ^ 31) Unicode characters. As you have seen, you now assign a string to a variable using double quotes:

```
Dim message as String
message = "Help"
```

and the simplest way to concatenate (join them together) is to use the `&`. The older + will also work, but can lead to major problems if you leave `Option Strict` off, so we do not recommend using a + sign for string concatenation. The older way to identify string variables (which are occasionally still used for temporary variables) is to use a dollar sign (`$`) at the end of the variable name: `aStringVariable$`.

CAUTION *Rather than being base type, strings in VB .NET are instances of the* `String` *class. We offer more on their subtleties in the Chapter 4, but here is a hint of what you need to know to use VB .NET efficiently: every time you make a change to a string in VB .NET, a new string must be created. Because this could cause a big performance penalty whenever a string needs to be repeatedly changed, VB .NET comes with a* `StringBuilder` *class to manipulate strings that require change (such as picking up data from a buffer and stringing it together in a variable).*

NOTE *VB .NET does not support fixed-length strings as did earlier versions of VB.*

String Functions

You have access to all the traditional VB6 string functions, such as `Left`, `Right`, `Mid`, and so on, but note that the versions of these functions that end with $ are now gone. The most important functions in the `String` class that can be used to replace the VB6 string functions are summarized in Table 3-5. (Keep in mind that, if you have to modify a string repeatedly with `Mid`, such as in a loop, you should use the `StringBuilder` class described in Chapter 4.) Note that some of these methods rely on arrays, which we cover later in this chapter.

Table 3-5. String Functions in the VB Compatibility Layer

FUNCTION	DESCRIPTION
`Asc`	Returns the character code corresponding to the first letter in a string.
`Chr`	Converts a number to Unicode.
`Filter`	Takes a string array and a string to search for, returns a one-dimensional array containing all the elements that match the search text.
`GetChar`	Returns a Char representing a character from a specified index in a string. The index for `GetChar` begins with 1. Example: `GetChar("Hello", 2)` returns a Char containing the character "e."
`InStr`	Returns the position of the first occurrence of one string within another.
`InStrRev`	Returns the position of the last occurrence of one string within another.
`Join`	Lets you build a larger string out of smaller strings.
`LCase`	Converts a string to lowercase.
`Left`	Finds or removes a specified number of characters from the beginning of a string.
`Len`	Gives the length of a string.
`LTrim`	Removes spaces from the beginning of a string.
`Mid`	Finds or removes characters from a string.
`Replace`	Replaces one or more occurrence of a string inside another.
`Right`	Finds or removes a specified number of characters from the end of a string.
`RTrim`	Removes spaces from the end of a string.

Table 3-5. String Functions in the VB Compatibility Layer (Continued)

FUNCTION	DESCRIPTION
`Space`	Generates a string of spaces.
`Split`	Lets you break up a string at specified places, such as spaces.
`Str`	Returns the string equivalent of a number.
`StrComp`	Another way to do string comparisons.
`StrConv`	Converts a string from one form to another, such as proper case.
`String`	Returns a repeated string of identical characters.
`Trim`	Trims spaces from both the beginning and end of a string.
`UCase`	Converts a string to uppercase.

Still, it is more in keeping with the flavor of .NET to use the methods and properties of the `String` class built into the .NET Framework, if possible. The most common of these are listed in Table 3-6 (note the lack of "s" in the name of the class).

Table 3-6. Common String Methods in the .NET Framework

MEMBER	DESCRIPTION
`Chars`	Gets the character at a specified position in the string.
`Compare`	Compares two strings.
`Copy`	Creates a new string by copying a string.
`CopyTo`	Copies a specified number of characters from a specified position in this string to a specified position in an array of characters.
`Empty`	A constant representing the empty string.
`EndsWith`	Tells you whether the specified string matches the end of this string.
`IndexOf`	Returns the index of the first occurrence of a substring within the string.
`Insert`	Returns a new string with a substring inserted at the specified place.
`Join`	Lets you join together an array of strings with a specified separator.
`LastIndexOf`	Gives the index of the last occurrence of a specified character or string within the string.
`Length`	Gets the number of characters in the string.

Table 3-6. Common String Methods in the .NET Framework (Continued)

MEMBER	DESCRIPTION
`PadLeft`	Right-aligns the characters in this string, padding on the left with spaces or a specified character to a specified total length.
`PadRight`	Left-aligns the characters in this string, padding on the right with spaces or a specified character to a specified total length.
`Remove`	Deletes the specified number of characters from this string, beginning at the specified location.
`Replace`	Replaces all occurrences of a substring with a different substring.
`Split`	Splits a string into an array of substrings.
`StartsWith`	Determines whether a specified substring starts the string.
`Substring`	Returns a substring from the current string from the position indicated.
`ToCharArray`	Copies the characters in this string to a character array.
`ToLower`	Returns a lowercase copy of this string.
`ToUpper`	Returns an uppercase copy of this string.
`Trim`	Either removes spaces or removes all occurrences of a set of characters specified in a Unicode character array from the beginning and end of the string.
`TrimEnd`	Either removes spaces or all occurrences of a set of characters specified in a Unicode character array from the end of the string.
`TrimStart`	Either removes spaces or all occurrences of a set of characters specified in a Unicode character array from the beginning of the string

CAUTION *Unlike VB6, where most string functions assumed "1" as the first position in a string, the .NET Framework methods use "0" for the first position.*

Because the .NET Framework treats strings as objects, the syntax for using these methods is rather neat: you can actually "dot a string." For example, if you run this program:

```
Sub Main()
  Dim river As String = " Mississippi " one space on left
  Console.WriteLine(river.ToUpper())
  Console.WriteLine(river.ToLower())
  Console.WriteLine(river.Trim())
  Console.WriteLine(river.EndsWith("I"))
  Console.WriteLine(river.EndsWith("i"))
  Console.WriteLine(river.IndexOf("s")) 'REMEMBER 0 based!
  Console.WriteLine(river.Insert(9, " river"))'REMEMBER 0 based!
  Console.ReadLine()
End Sub
```

You will see:

```
MISSISSIPPI MISSIPPI
mississippi missippi
Mississippi Missippi
False
True
3
Mississi riverppi Missippi
```

Formatting Data

All formatting functions return a new string in the format specified. VB .NET has equivalents to the older `Format` functions from VB6 and VBScript, so you can continue to use: `Format`, `FormatNumber`, `FormatCurrency`, `FormatPercent`, and `FormatDateTime`. The last four in particular remain quite convenient for simple formatting. Even so, we often prefer to use the even more powerful formatting capabilities built into the .NET Framework.

The syntax for using the formatting capabilities of the .NET Framework will seem strange at first. Here is an example to get you started:

```
Dim balance as Decimal = 123456
Dim creditLimit As Decimal = 999999
Console.WriteLine("Customer balance is {0:C}, credit limit is {1:C} ", _
balance, creditLimit - balance)
```

gives:

```
Customer balance is $123,456.00, credit limit is $876,543.00
```

If you change the key line in bold to read:

```
Console.WriteLine("Customer credit is {1:C}, balance is {0:C} ", _
balance, creditLimit - balance)
```

you will see:

```
Customer credit is $876,543.00, balance is $123,456.00
```

The idea is that you indicate the variables you want formatted in the order you want them to appear. So in the second example `{1:C}`, the "1" meant format the second variable listed and the `{0:C}` meant format the first variable listed. (The .NET Framework is zero based, of course.) The "C" means format as currency using the current Locale as set in Windows.

Arithmetic Operators

Table 3-7 gives you the symbols for the six fundamental arithmetic operations.

Table 3-7. Arithmetic Operations

OPERATOR	OPERATION
+	Addition
–	Subtraction (and to denote negative numbers)
/	Division (conversion to double—cannot cause a DivideByZero exception—see Chapter 7 for more on exceptions)
\	Integer division (no conversion to double—can cause a DivideByZero exception)
*	Multiplication
^	Exponentiation

> **CAUTION** *The ordinary division symbol (/) gives you a value that is a double, even if the division is perfect. The integer division symbol (\) only returns an integer. This means you will often need to use a conversion function if you're working with decimals or integral types.*

You can see all this using the useful `GetType` method built into .NET, which, when used in a print statement such as `WriteLine`, returns a human-readable form of the type name. For example, if you run this program:

```
Module Module1
  Sub Main()
    console.WriteLine((4 / 2).GetType())
    Console.ReadLine()
  End Sub
End Module
```

you will see:

```
System.Double
```

in the console window.

> **NOTE** `GetType` *is actually a very powerful method that you can use to do reflection. See Chapter 4 for an introduction to reflection.*

Or, for a more serious example of where you need to remember that a / gives you a Double, consider the line in bold in the following simple (but broken) version of the program to convert Celsius (centigrade) to Fahrenheit, where we leave off the @ in the bolded line in order to force the answer to be a decimal.

```
Option Strict On
Module Module1
  Sub Main()
    Dim cdeg As Decimal
    Console.Write("Enter the degrees in centigrade...")
    cdeg = CDec(Console.ReadLine())
    Dim fdeg As Decimal
    fdeg = ((9 / 5) * cdeg) + 32
    Console.WriteLine(cdeg & " is " & fdeg & " degrees Fahrenheit.")
    Console.ReadLine()
  End Sub
End Module
```

The problem is, because of the division symbol, the line in bold makes the `fdeg` variable a Double. This in turn means that with `Option Strict` on, you see this error message at compile time:

```
Option Strict disallows implicit conversions from Double to Decimal.
```

To fix it, *do not* turn off `Option Strict`—it is one of the best features of .NET: no more evil type conversions. Instead, use the @ or rewrite the code with a cast around any of the elements (or the whole thing). For example:

```
fdeg = (CDec(9 / 5) * cdeg) + 32
```

forces the whole result to be a Decimal, because one of the parts is a Decimal. One final point about this simple example: note how we used the `Write` method rather than the `WriteLine` method, because it does not throw in a carriage return-line feed combination. (Also note that in a more realistic program we would have to parse the result, because users rarely enter data correctly.)

Finally, floating-point division now conforms to the IEEE standard, which means that what used to be a divide by zero error is just strange. Here is an example:

```
Sub Main()
  Dim getData As String
  Dim x, y As Double
  x = 4
  y = 0
  Console.WriteLine("What is 4/0 in VB .NET? " & x / y)
  Console.ReadLine()
End Sub
```

gives:

```
What is 4/0 in VB .NET? Infinity
```

Divide 0/0 and you get `NaN` (not a number) as the result.

For integers and long integers, there is one symbol and one keyword for the arithmetic operations unique to numbers of these types, as shown in Table 3-8:

Table 3-8. Unique Integral Arithmetic Operators

OPERATOR	OPERATION
\	Integer division for any integral data type. (This symbol is a backslash).
Mod	The remainder after integer division.

The backslash (\), on the other hand, throws away the remainder in order to give you an Integer if the answer fits into the range of this type. For example, 7\3 = 2I. Because a / gives a Double, use a \ or cast if you want to work with an Integer type.

The Mod operator is the other half of integer division. This operator gives you the remainder after integer division. For example, `7 Mod 3 = 1`. When one integer perfectly divides another there is no remainder, so the `Mod` operator gives zero: `8 Mod 4 = 0`.

Parentheses and Precedence

In performing calculations, you have two ways to indicate the order in which you want operations to occur. Use parentheses and you will not have to remember priority of operations. As with all programming languages, VB .NET allows you to avoid parentheses, provided you follow rules that determine the precedence of the mathematical operations. For example, multiplication has higher precedence than addition. This means 3 + 4 * 5 is 23 rather than 35 because the multiplication (4 * 5) is done before the addition.

Here is the order (hierarchy) of operations:

1. Exponentiation (^)
2. Negation (making a number negative)
3. Multiplication and division
4. Integer division

5. Remainder (Mod) function

6. Addition and subtraction

Operations are carried out in order of precedence. If two operations have the same precedence, they are carried out from left to right.

VB Shortcuts

With VB .NET, Microsoft has adopted some of the shortcuts for combining operators with assignment statements. They have not adopted shortcuts such as the ++ operator, however, which gave C++ its name. These are the VB .NET shortcuts:

SHORTCUT	EQUIVALENT
A *= B	A = A * B
A += B	A = A + B
A /= B	A = A / B
A -= B	A = A-B
A \= B	A = A \ B
A ^= B	A = A ^ B
A &= B	A = A & B (string concatenation)

Math Functions and Math Constants

The built-in functions from VB6 still work, but we prefer to use the ones built into the `Math` class of the .NET Framework. This class also has useful constants such as `Math.PI` and `Math.E`. Table 3-9 summarizes the most useful math functions in the `Math` class. All of these functions are shared, so they belong to the `Math` class and not to an instance of the `Math` class (which turns out not to be creatable anyway—see Chapter 4).

Table 3-9. Shared Math Functions in the `Math` *Class*

MATH FUNCTION	DESCRIPTION
Abs	Returns the absolute value.
Acos	Returns the angle whose cosine is the specified number.
Asin	Returns the angle whose sine is the specified number.
Atan	Returns the angle whose tangent is the specified number.
Ceiling	Returns the smallest whole number greater than or equal to the specified number.
Cos	Returns the cosine of the specified angle.
Exp	Returns e (approximately 2.71828182845905) raised to the specified power.
Floor	Returns the largest whole number less than or equal to the specified number.
Log	Returns the natural logarithm.
Log10	Returns the base 10 logarithm.
Max	Returns the larger of two specified numbers.
Min	eturns the smaller of two numbers.
Round	Returns the number nearest the specified value.
Sign	Returns a value indicating the sign of a number.
Sin	Returns the sine of the specified angle.
Sqrt	Returns the square root.
Tan	Returns the tangent of the specified angle.

Because these are shared methods of the `Math` class, you need to use the "`Math.`" prefix, as in `Math.Log10(10)`, which yields a 1.

> **NOTE** *VB .NET has another useful group of methods for generating various kinds of random numbers. We will look at this group in Chapter 4, when you learn how to create object instances.*

Constants

VB .NET also has the capability to create named constants that allow you to use mnemonic names for values that never change. Constants are declared in the same way as variables, and the rules for their names are also the same: 255 characters, first character a letter, and then any combination of letters, underscores, and numerals. Our convention is to use capitals plus underscores for constants.

Note that in VB .NET, with `Option Strict` on, you must declare the type of constants. So:

```
Const PIE = 3.14159  'won't compile with Option Strict
Const PIE  As Double = 3.14159 'correct but Math.PI is better :-)
```

You can even use numeric expressions for constants, or define new constants in terms of previously defined constants:

```
Const PIE_OVER_2 As Double = PIE / 2
```

And you can set up string constants:

```
Const USER_NAME As String = "Bill Gates"
```

The .NET Framework also has many built-in, predefined global constants that you can use in your programs. Many are similar to the ones that were given using the prefix of `vb` in VB6, but are shared members of various classes and so must be accessed a little differently. You can use `vbCrLf` in VB .NET, for example, as well as the constants built into the `ControlChars` class, such as `ControlChars.CrLf`.

Repeating Operations—Loops

VB .NET, like most programming languages, has language constructs for loops that repeat operations a fixed number of times, continuing until a specific predetermined goal is reached or until certain initial conditions have changed. This involves only minor changes from earlier versions of VB. For one, the `While-Wend` construct is changed—but there is no need for it anyway.

Determinate Loops

Use the keywords `For` and `Next` to set up a loop to repeat a fixed number of times. For example, this code:

```
Sub Main()
   Dim i As Integer
   For i = 1 To 10
      Console.WriteLine(i)
   Next i
   Console.ReadLine()
End Sub
```

prints the numbers 1 to 10 on the console window.

In general, VB .NET first sets the counter variable to the starting value, and then it determines whether the value for the counter is less than the ending value. If the value is greater than the ending value, nothing is done. If the starting value is less than the ending value, VB .NET processes subsequent statements until it comes to the keyword `Next`. (The variable name is optional.) At that point, it defaults to adding 1 to the counter variable and starts the process again. This process continues until the counter variable is larger than the ending value. At that point, the loop is finished, and VB .NET moves past it.

> **TIP** *Although you can use variables of any numeric type for the counters, choose* `Integer` *variables whenever possible. Doing so allows VB .NET to spend as little time as possible on the arithmetic needed to change the counter and thus speeds up the loop.*

You do not always count by 1, the default. Sometimes it is necessary to count by twos, by fractions, or backward. As with all versions of VB, you do this by adding the `Step` keyword to a `For-Next` loop. The `Step` keyword tells VB .NET to change the counter by a specified amount. For example, a space-simulation program would not be complete without the inclusion, somewhere in the program, of this fragment:

```
Sub Main()
   Dim i As Integer
   For i = 10 To 1 Step -1
     Console.WriteLine("It's t minus " & i & " and counting.")
   Next i
   Console.WriteLine("Blastoff!")
   Console.ReadLine()
End Sub
```

When you use a negative step, the body of the `For-Next` loop is bypassed if the starting value for the counter is smaller than the ending value. This is most useful when performing an operation such as deleting items from a list. If you went from 0 to

ListCount, you would run out of items at the midpoint while going from ListCount to 0 while step –1 removes the highest item to the lowest item correctly.

You can use any numeric type for the Step value. For example:

```
For yearlyInterest = .07 To .09 Step .0125D
```

begins a loop that moves from 7 percent to 9 percent by one-eighth-percent increments. Note that we used the Decimal type to avoid any potential for round-off error.

As with earlier versions of VB, VB .NET lets you nest loops to essentially unlimited depths. A fragment such as:

```
Sub Main()
   Dim i, j As Integer
   For j = 2 To 12
    For i = 2 To 12
      Console.Write(i * j & "    ")
    Next i
    Console.WriteLine()
   Next j
   Console.ReadLine()
End Sub
```

gives a somewhat primitively formatted multiplication table. (We used the Write method rather than the WriteLine method in the inner loop because it does not throw in a carriage return-line feed combination.)

Indeterminate Loops

Loops often need to either keep on repeating an operation or not, depending on the results obtained within the loop. Use the following pattern when you write an indeterminate loop in VB .NET that executes at least once (with the test at the bottom):

```
Do
  '0 or more VB .NET statements
Until condition is met
```

Of course, you usually need ways to check for something besides equality. You do so by means of the relational operators, shown in Table 3-10.

Table 3-10. Relational Operators

SYMBOL	CHECKS (TESTS FOR)
< >	Not equal to
<	Less than
<=	Less than or equal to
>	Greater than
>=	Greater than or equal to

For strings, these operators default to testing for Unicode order. This means that "A" comes before "B," but "B" comes before "a" (and a space comes before any typewriter character). The string "aBCD" comes after the string "CDE" because uppercase letters come before lowercase letters.

> **NOTE** *As in VB6, you can make all comparisons in the code attached to a module or form case insensitive by putting the statement* `Option Compare Text` *before any statement (including the one that names the module or form).* `Option Compare Binary` *returns the default behavior of comparing strings by ANSI order.* `Option Compare Text` *uses the order determined by the country character set you specified when you installed Windows.*

You can replace the `Until` keyword with the `While` keyword in a loop. For example:

```
Do
  '0 or more VB .NET statements
Loop Until X <> String.Empty
```

is the same as:

```
Do
  '0 or more VB .NET statements
Loop While X = String.Empty
```

where we are using the constant `String.Empty` instead of the harder-to-read (and more error prone) `""`. To do the test at the top (so the loop may not be executed at all), move the `While` or `Until` keywords to the top. For example:

```
Do While Text1.Text <> String.Empty
   'process the nonempty text
Loop
```

When you have to combine conditions in a loop, use the `Or`, `Not`, and `And` keywords. For example:

```
Do While count < 20 And savings < 1000000
```

> **NOTE** *If you still want to use the old* `While-Wend` *construction, be aware that the* `Wend` *keyword has been replaced with the* `End While` *statement.*

Conditionals—Making Decisions

Conditionals in VB .NET are identical to those in VB6, allowing both single line and multiple line versions:

```
If X < 0 Then Console.WriteLine("Number must be positive!")
```

You can also use the keywords `And`, `Or`, and `Not` in an `If-Then` statement. More often than not, you will want to process multiple statements if a condition is True or False. For this, use the block `If-Then`, which looks like this:

```
If thing to test Then
   Zero or more VB Statements
End If
```

or add one or more `Else` clauses:

```
If thing to test Then
   Zero or more VB statements
Else
   Zero or more VB statements
End If
```

or to have multiple `Else` statements use the `ElseIf`:

```
If thing to test Then
   lots of statements<<Continue as above>>
ElseIf thing to test Then
   lots of statements
ElseIf thing to test Then
   more statements
Else
   lots of statements
End If
```

TIP *The* `If-Then` *gives you a way to write a loop that tests in the middle if you are so inclined: combine the* `If-Then` *with an* `Exit Do` *or* `Exit For` *statement. Whenever VB .NET processes an* `Exit Do` *or* `Exit For`*, it pops you out of the loop and takes you directly to the statement following the keyword* `Loop` *or the keyword* `Next`*, as the case may be.*

Scoping Changes

The scope of variables and methods in VB .NET is a little subtler than in earlier versions of VB, and will be completely covered in Chapters 4 and 5. You can see one of the places where new subtleties have been introduced when you declare a variable inside the body of a loop or in a block in an `If-Then`. If you do this, then that variable is *invisible* to other code outside the block in which it was declared. For example, consider this code, which assumes that only one version of the String variable `Risk` would be created and then tries to use it:

```
If income < 100000 Then
   Dim risk As String = "too much risk"
Else
   Dim risk As String = "love to make a deal"
End If
Console.WriteLine("Your risk level is " & Risk)
```

In fact you get the error message:

```
The name 'risk' is not declared.
```

because the visibility of *both* versions of the `risk` variable ends when the block they are declared in exits! The moral is, do not declare variables inside blocks without good reason.

Short Circuiting

Short circuiting refers to the compiler not evaluating another expression if the first is enough. In this code, for example, if `foo` is false, short-circuit evaluation would imply that `bar` never got evaluated:

```
If foo And bar then …
```

This is the way it was in VB .NET beta 1, but *not* the way it was in earlier versions of VB. After many complaints, Microsoft changed it back so that the older keywords do not short circuit. Instead, they added new keywords, `AndAlso` and `OrElse`, which *do* short circuit:

```
If foo AndAlso bar then …
```

Select Case

As an alternative to multiple `ElseIfs`, VB .NET continues to offer the `Select Case` statement, which gives you a clearer way of selecting on the state of a variable or expression, as long as the value of the expression is either numeric or string. Here is an example:

```
Select Case average
Case Is > 90
    Console.WriteLine("A")
  Case Is > 80
    Console.WriteLine("B")
  Case Is > 70
    Console.WriteLine("C")
  Case Else
    console.WriteLine("You fail")
End Select
```

Users coming from C or Java should note that no break statements are needed. because only one clause in a `Select` statement will be executed. Using commas lets you give a discrete set of variables, and the keyword `To` lets you give a range of values:

```
Select Case yourChoice
  Case 1 To 9
    'ok you get it
  Case -1, 0
     'huh??
End Select
```

The GoTo

The final control structure is, of course, the GoTo. To paraphrase the old joke about split infinitives: Modern programmers may be divided into three groups: those who neither know nor care about when they should use the GoTo, those who do not know but seem to care very much, and those who know when to use it.

Routine use of the GoTo leads to "spaghetti code," meaning code that is hard to read and harder to debug. On the other hand, one can argue that there is one time when using the GoTo actually makes your code cleaner and easier to understand. In VB .NET, this situation could occur when you are deep inside a nested loop and some condition forces you to leave all the loops simultaneously. You cannot use the various forms of the Exit statement, because all that does is get you out of the loop you are currently in.

> **NOTE** *We would argue that you should use exceptions (see Chapter 7) for this situation and not a* GoTo, *but some people prefer the older approach.*

To use a GoTo in VB .NET, you must label a line. Labels must begin with a letter, end with a colon, and start in the first column. You should use as descriptive a label as possible. Here is an example:

```
BadInput:
  'Code we want to process can GoTo here
```

Suppose we are using a nested For loop to input data and want to leave the loop if the user enters **I am done**:

```
Sub Main()
  Dim getData As String
  Dim i, j As Integer
  For i = 1 To 10
    For j = 1 To 100
    Console.Write("Type the data, hit the Enter key between " & _
           "ZZZ to end:  ")
    getData = Console.ReadLine()
    If getData = "ZZZ" Then
      Goto BadInput
    Else
     'Process data
    End If
```

```
    Next j
  Next i
Exit Sub
BadInput:
  Console.WriteLine("Data entry ended at user request")
  Console.ReadLine()
End Sub
```

Notice how using an `Exit For` keyword would be cumbersome here—for example, it would require extra code in order to break completely out of the nested loop. Also notice that the `Exit Sub` statement then prevents us from "falling into" the labeled code.

The Logical Operators on the Bit Level

Beginning in beta 2, the logical operators (`Not`, `And`, `Or`, and so on) go back to the way they were in earlier versions of VB. In beta 2, they are again functions that work on the bit (binary-digit) level. Suppose you are given two integers, `X` and `Y`. `X And Y` make a binary digit 1 only if both binary digits are 1; otherwise, the result is zero. For 32-bit integers, each bit is compared one at a time. For example, if:

```
X = 7 'in decimal= 0111 in binary
Y = 12 'in decimal= 1100 in binary
```

then

```
X And Y = 0100
```

in binary (4 in decimal), because only in the third position are both bits 1. Because `And` gives a 1 only if both digits are 1, using `And` with a number whose binary digit is a single 1 and whose remaining digits are all zero lets you isolate the binary digits of any integer. For example:

(X And 1) = 1: Tells you whether the least significant bit is on.

(X And 2) <> 2: Because 2 in decimal = 10 in binary. This tells you whether the next significant bit is off.

X And 255: Because 255 = 11111111, this gives you the low order byte.

X And 65280 =: Because 65280 = 1111111100000000, this would give you the high order byte.

This process is usually called *masking*.

Arrays

In VB .NET, the name of an array must follow the rules for variable names. For an item in the array, the notation is simply the name of the array followed by a number in parentheses that indicates the position.

Elements in arrays in VB .NET are significantly different than in VB6. The changes are both obvious and not so obvious. The obvious ones are that:

- All array indexes start at 0 (and as we write this, the keyword `To` has vanished—hopefully it will be brought back!).

`Dim stringList(7)` will, starting in beta 2, gives you *eight* elements numbered 0 to 7. Because array indexes are always zero-based in VB .NET, the third entry in this string array is accessed via `stringList(2)`, and the previous entries are `stringList(0)` and `stringList(1)`.

- All arrays in VB .NET are dynamic and can be resized at will using either `ReDim`, which loses the current contents, or `ReDim Preserve`, which keeps them.

For example:

```
Dim x() As Single
ReDim x(20) 'gives 21 slots starting in beta 2
ReDim Preserve x(50) 'keeps the 21 values Intact
```

> **NOTE** `ReDim` *no longer allows an* `As` *clause to change the type of an array, nor can you use* `ReDim` *as a declaration. You must first use* `Dim` *or an equivalent statement before you can use* `ReDim`.

- You can initialize and declare an array at the same time, as in this code:

```
Dim weekend() As String = {Saturday,Sunday}
```

The not-so-obvious changes happen because arrays, like strings, are actually instances of the `Array` class. These subtleties will be covered in Chapter 4, but this does allow you to "dot" an array with very useful methods such as `Sort`, as in this code:

```
Sub Main()
  Dim stuff() As Integer = {9, 7, 5, 4, 2, 1, -37, 6}
  Array.Sort(stuff)
  Dim i As Integer
  For i = 0 To UBound(stuff)
    Console.WriteLine(stuff(i))
  Next
  Console.ReadLine()
End Sub
```

which prints out the array in sorted order using a very fast "QuickSort."

> **NOTE** *VB .NET inherits from the .NET Framework some extraordinarily powerful data structures that give you capabilities way beyond what simple arrays can bring. They make the simple collections of VB5 and later seem trivial by comparison. These structures, such as array lists (a smart array that grows automatically) and dictionaries (keyed access to data), are often preferable to using a simple array. We will cover many of these in Chapters 5 and 6.*

Building VB6-like Arrays with Upper and Lower Bounds

It is not quite correct to say that array indices must start at 0. It is possible to build arrays with upper and lower bounds, but the current syntax and current performance implications make it unlikely that you will ever do that. The following lines of code create an array with bounds 1995 to 2002:

```
Sub Main()
  Dim anArray As Array
  Dim i As Integer
  Dim l(0) As Integer
  Dim lowerBounds(0) As Integer
  l(0) = 7
  lowerBounds(0) = 1995
  'creates an array of objects numbered 1995 - 2002
  anArray = Array.CreateInstance(GetType(System.Int32), l, lowerBounds)
  anArray.SetValue(200000, 1995)
  anArray.SetValue(1000000, 2001)
  Console.WriteLine("The entry in position 1995 is " & _
  (anArray.GetValue(1995).ToString))
```

```
Console.WriteLine("The entry in position 2002 is " & _
(anArray.GetValue(2001).ToString))
Console.ReadLine()
End Sub
```

As you can see you then use the `SetValue (value,entryPosition)` method to add items to the array and the `GetValue(position)` method to retrieve them. However, because arrays created this way this store objects you also need to convert them to the correct type if `Option Strict` is on!

The For-Each Construct

Although you often will use a `For-Next` loop running from 0 to `UBound(arrayName)` to iterate through the elements in an array, you can also use the `For Each` construct, which has syntax like this:

```
For Each variableOfProprType In arrayName
    [statements]
    [Exit For if needed]
    [statements]
Next
```

`For Each` is quite a general construct and will be available whenever the data structure has a way to iterate through its elements. More about this in Chapter 6.

> **NOTE** *Microsoft claims that, unlike VB6, there will be no significant performance penalties in using a* `For Each` *for array access compared to a* `For-Next`*!*

Arrays with More than One Dimension

You can also have arrays with more than one dimension. Suppose you want to store a multiplication table in memory as a table. You could code this as:

```
Dim multTable(11,11) As Integer ' makes a 12x12 array
Dim i As Integer, j As Integer
For i = 0 To 11
  For j = 0 To 11
    multTable(i, j) = (i+1)*(j+1)
  Next j
Next i
```

Although the size of an array can change in VB .NET, the number of dimensions must be fixed.

To make a general multidimensional array, use empty commas. This example shows how to declare a three-dimensional array:

```
Dim salesByDivision( , , ) As Decimal
```

The `ReDim` statement sets or changes the size of each dimension, but the array must always remains the same number of dimensions.

> **NOTE** *You can change only the size of the last dimension in a multidimensional array while preserving the contents with* `Redim Preserve`.

Procedures: User-Defined Functions and Subs

The distinction used to be you used a function when you needed to return a value and a sub if you did not. We recommend keeping to this model, although you can "throw away" the return value of a function and thus make it for all practical purposes into a sub ("C" style functions). Functions and subs are usually lumped into what are called the *members* of the class or module. Within classes (see Chapter 4) they are also sometimes called the *methods* of the class or module.

As with many programming languages, there are two ways to pass a variable argument to a procedure or function: *passing by value* or *passing by reference.* When an argument variable is passed by reference, any changes to the corresponding parameter inside the procedure change the value of the original argument when the procedure finishes. The default in VB .NET is now pass by value as opposed to VB6's pass by reference.

> **CAUTION** *When passed by value, the naïve notion is that the argument variable retains its original value after the procedure terminates, regardless of what was done to the corresponding parameter inside the procedure. Well, sort of. For object variables in VB .NET, the state of the object can change even if you pass it by value. Because VB .NET changes the defaults from earlier versions of VB to passing by value instead of by reference, you might expect any changes you make to the parameters inside the body of the procedure to be discarded, but this may not happen to objects being passed to procedures and functions. Look for more on this subtle source of bugs in Chapter 4.*

Functions

The easiest way to start a function or a sub in the code window is to go someplace inside the module that is not already inside a sub or function and then start typing. The moment you hit Enter after typing the header of the function or sub, the IDE editor obliges with an `End` statement of the correct type. For example, this is the header for a function that takes an integer by value and returns True or False, depending on whether the number passed in is between 1 and 10:

```
Function IsBetween1And10(ByVal num As Integer) As Boolean
```

> **NOTE** *With* `Option Strict` *on, you must supply a type for the return value. (*`Boolean` *in the previous example.)*

Here is an example of a module that uses this simple function to tell you if a number entered at the console is between 1 and 10. Notice how the order of the code is unimportant—the `Sub Main` can occur after the definition of the function that it uses.

```
Module Module1
Function IsBetween1And10(ByVal num As Integer) As Boolean
    If num >= 1 And num <= 10 Then
      Return True
    Else
     Return False
    End If
  End Function
```

```
Sub Main()
     Console.WriteLine(IsBetween1And10(3))
     Console.ReadLine()
End Sub
End Module
```

In VB .NET, parentheses are always required around a nonempty parameter list in any function or sub call, hence this was needed in the `Console.WriteLine` method:

```
IsBetween1And10(3)
```

Notice the use of the `Return` keyword. When you use the `Return` keyword, the function ends[1] and the value following the `Return` keyword is the value of the function. (You must supply a value; returning the equivalent of a "void" is not allowed.) The method used in earlier versions of VB of assigning to the function name is still allowed:

```
Function IsBetween1And10(ByVal num As Integer) As Boolean
    If num >= 1 And num <= 10 Then
      IsBetween1And10 = True
    Else
     IsBetween1And10 = False
    End If
  End Function
```

Using `Return` is a matter of taste; we think using `Return` is a whole lot clearer but the older technique leaves you in the function, which is sometimes convenient.)

The general form of a function definition is as follows:

```
Function FunctionName(argument1, argument2, ...) As Type
  statements
  Return expression 'or FunctionName = Expression
End Function
```

where `argument1` and `argument2` are variables. Function names must follow the same rules as variable names. When you use a function, VB .NET executes the

1. Unless you have a `Finally` clause; see Chapter 7.

statements in the function definition; the value following the `Return` (or the last value assigned to `FunctionName`) is the return value of the function.

> **NOTE** *Although you usually use the return value of a function, VB lets you simply call a function for its side effects with a statement such as* `foo(3)` without an assignment.

You can usually call a function only when you use the same number of arguments as there are parameters in the function definition. The types must be compatible as well, so only widening conversions will be made automatically. For example, these two lines are allowed:

```
Dim bar As Short = 3
Console.WriteLine(IsBetween1And10(bar))
```

because going from Short to Integer is a lossless conversion.

VB .NET lets you to create your own procedures with optional, or a varying number of, arguments. More information on this later in this chapter.

Sub Procedures

A sub does not return anything, so it exists only for its side effects. You call it with its name and, as with functions, parentheses are always required around a non-empty parameter list in any sub call. Here is an example with the key calling line in bold:

```
Option Strict On
Module Module1
Sub ShowBottlesOfBeer(ByVal nbot As Integer)
  Console.WriteLine(nbot & " bottles of beer on the wall")
  Console.WriteLine(nbot & " bottles of beer.")
  Console.WriteLine("if one of those bottles should happen to fall")
  Console.WriteLine(nbot - 1 & " bottles of beer on the wall")
End Sub
```

```
Sub Main()
    Dim I As Integer
    For I = 10 To 1 Step -1
     ShowBottlesOfBeer(I)
    Next
    Console.WriteLine("All beer gone…")
    Console.ReadLine()
End Sub
End Module
```

When using sub calls, the `Call` keyword is optional. The key calling line (in bold) in the preceding example can be rewritten as:

```
Call ShowBottlesOfBeer(I)
```

More generally, a sub procedure must have a header that gives its arguments and either has a `ByVal` or `ByRef` keyword with `ByVal` the default.

```
Sub SubprocedureName(ByVal argument1 As Type, ByVal argument2 As Type, ...)
  statement(s)
End Sub
```

When VB .NET executes statements in this form:

```
SubprocedureName(argument1, argument2,...)
```

or this:

```
Call SubprocedureName (argument1, argument2, ...)
```

it makes a *copy* of the data in the arguments and then executes the code in the body of the procedure (because pass by value is now the default).

Leaving Functions or Procedures Prematurely

You do not have to give every function an explicit value. Sometimes you are forced to exit a function prematurely. Once a `Return` statement is processed, the function ends (except if there is a so called `Finally` clause waiting—see Chapter 7 for more on these).

```
Function BailOut (X As Double) As Double
  If X < 0 Then
   Return 0 'must return something
  Else
.  'stuff
  End If
End Function
```

When you leave a function prematurely, it has the last assigned value or the appropriate default value as its return value. Use `Exit Sub` to leave a `Sub` prematurely.

Using Arrays with Functions and Procedures

VB .NET continues the VB tradition of having an extraordinary facility to use both one- and multidimensional arrays in procedures and functions. There are, however, some subtleties in how pass by value versus pass by reference works, but we will address those in Chapter 4. The key is to use either the `For Each` construct or (more commonly) the `UBound` function, the highest entry in an array. For example, you can easily write this function to find the maximum element in an array:

```
Function FindMax(ByVal a() As Integer) As Integer
  Dim finish As Integer = UBound(a)
  Dim max As Integer = a(0)
  Dim i As Integer
  For i = 0 To finish
    If a(i) > max Then max = a(i)
  Next i
  Return max
End Function
```

In general, `UBound(NameOfArray, I)` gives the lower and upper bound for the I'th dimension. For a list (a one-dimensional array), the I is optional, as in the preceding example.

> **NOTE** *The* `Length` *method built into the array class is an alternative, but this will return the number of elements and not the upper bound (and they are not necessarily the same, for multidimensional arrays).*

Procedures with a Variable or Optional Number of Arguments

You can use subs and functions with optional arguments, but in VB .NET (as opposed to VB6), every optional parameter must specify a default value. This example shows an optional parameter declaration:

```
Sub ProcessAddress(TheName As String, _
 Address As String, City As String, State As String,  _
 ZipCode As String, Optional ZipPlus4 As String = "0000")
```

In this case, the last argument (for a ZipPlus4 code) is optional but defaults to `"0000"`.

> **NOTE** *See Chapter 4 for information on overloading, another way to deal with functions with optional arguments.*

You can also have procedures and functions that accept an arbitrary number of arguments. For this, use the `ParamArray` keyword with an array, as in this example:

```
Function AddThemUp(ByVal ParamArray stuff() As Double) As Double
  Dim total As Double = 0
  Dim number As Double = 0
  Dim I As Integer
  For I = 0 To UBound(stuff)
    total = total + stuff(I)
  Next
Return total
End Function
```

and you can use this function for example in a line like:

```
x = AddThemUp(3, 4, 5, 6)
```

which would give x the value 18.

Named Arguments

Named arguments give you an elegant way of dealing with functions and procedures that have many parameters—especially optional ones. In general, when you call a procedure using named arguments use a := (a colon plus an equal sign) together with the name of the argument, so you do not have to worry about the order of the arguments. (Although the spelling of the argument must match, case is irrelevant.) Named arguments work in every part of VB .NET, unlike earlier versions of VB, in which they sometimes worked and sometimes did not.

You separate named arguments from each other by a comma. If you are careful in selecting parameter names, using named arguments help make your code easier to read. This is especially true if you use lots of optional arguments. For example, consider a header to our `ZipCode` function that looks like this:

```
Sub ProcessAddress(TheName As String, _
 Address As String, City As String, State As String,  _
 ZipCode As String, Optional ZipPlus4 As String = "0000")
```

We call this procedure as follows:

```
ProcessAddress(Address:="The Whitehouse" _
Name :="GeorgeW", _
City :="DC", _
State := String.Empty _
ZipCode := "12345"
```

even though the order of the arguments in the definition of the procedure is different.

Recursion

As with all versions of VB (or any serious programming language), VB .NET supports *recursion*, a method of solving problems by reducing them to simpler problems of a similar type. One common use of recursion is in dealing with the subdirectory structure of a disk (see the I/O chapter).

The general framework for a recursive solution to a problem looks like this:

```
Solve recursively (problem)
  If the problem is trivial then
    do the obvious
  Else
    Simplify the problem to be of the same type--only simpler
    Solve recursively (simpler problem)
  End If
    (Possibly) combine the solution to the simpler problem(s) into a solution
        of the original problem
```

A recursive procedure constantly calls itself, each time in a simpler situation, until it gets to the trivial case, at which point it stops. For the experienced programmer, thinking recursively presents a unique perspective on certain problems, often leading to particularly elegant solutions and, therefore, equally elegant programs. (For example, most fast sorts, such as the QuickSort, built into the .NET `Array` class `Sort` method are recursive.)

As an example, we will look at the greatest common divisor (GCD) of two integers. (For those who have forgotten their high-school mathematics, this is defined as the largest number that divides both of them. It is used when you need to add fractions.) For example:

- GCD(4,6) = 2 (because 2 is the largest number that evenly divides both 4 and 6)
- GCD(12,7) = 1 (because no integer greater than 1 divides both 12 and 7)

Around 2,000 years ago, Euclid gave the following method of computing the GCD of two integers, a and b:

```
If b divides a, then the GCD is b. Otherwise, GCD(a,b) = GCD(b, a mod b)
```

Next recall that the `Mod` function gives the remainder after integer division and is zero precisely when b divides a. Therefore:

```
GCD(126, 12) = GCD(12, 126 Mod 12) = GCD(12, 6) = 6
```

Here is the code for writing and using a recursive GCD function. The line in bold is the recursive call that uses the GCD function itself in a simpler situation:

```
Option Strict On
Module Module1
  Function GCD(ByVal P As Long, ByVal Q As Long) As Long
    If Q Mod P = 0 Then
      Return P
    Else
      Return GCD(Q, P Mod Q)
    End If
  End Function
  Sub Main()
    Console.WriteLine("The GCD of 36 and 99 is " & GCD(36, 99))
    Console.ReadLine()
  End Sub
End Module
```

Here, the pattern is to first take care of the trivial case. If `Q Mod P` does not equal `0`, then you are not in the trivial case; so, the code allows us to call the same GCD function in a simpler case, because using the `Mod` function always leads to smaller numbers. (In this example, there is no need to combine results as there would be in, say, a sorting routine.)

CHAPTER 4

Classes and Objects (with a Short Introduction to Object-Oriented Programming)

THIS CHAPTER, ALONG WITH Chapters 5 and 6, forms the core of this book. The reason is simple: VB .NET is the first fully object-oriented version of VB, and if you are not comfortable with OOP, you will find it extremely hard to take advantage of VB .NET's new powers. Of course, you may be wondering: because VB could create classes and then make objects from these classes since VB4, what is so different about VB .NET that it requires rethinking your programming style? The short answer is "plenty." A more detailed answer will be presented in these next three chapters.

We also think it fair to say, especially in light of our own consulting experience, that many VB programmers did not take full advantage of the OOP features in earlier versions of VB. This was partly because of the clumsy and, to be honest, half-baked implementation of OOP in earlier versions of VB, and partly because programmers did not understand how to use OOP successfully. With the improvements in VB .NET, you no longer have to worry about the former problem. As for the latter, well, that is why we start this chapter with an introduction to the OOP way of thinking. In any case, you cannot write VB .NET code very well without fully using its OOP nature.

This chapter, with Chapters 5 and 6, covers OOP from a practical, VB .NET programmer's point of view, without getting bogged down in OOP theory. We stress practical examples and techniques that a VB .NET programmer can use to solve real problems. And we try not to fall into the seductive trap of discussing everything from an abstract point of view and being needlessly complete. (There are dozens of books out there that teach the theory of OOP if you are interested in this approach.) Still, you need to understand a fair amount of terminology to make sense of OOP, so we will start with a discussion of the key concepts and terms. (If you are experienced with OOP, you might want to skip this discussion.)

After that, we will move on to using existing classes and the objects that you can create from them. For example, we will show you how to use the important `StringBuilder` class, and how to use some of the nifty new collection classes in the .NET Framework, such as hashtables and array lists. We will also discuss some of the subtleties that come with passing objects to functions and procedures. Then we will discuss building your own classes and the objects that you stamp out from them. (Although we introduce you to inheritance and interfaces in this chapter, we only cover these key OOP concepts in detail in Chapter 5.)

> **NOTE** *C# and VB .NET are very similar languages from an OOP point of view, even if they look very different. If you master the techniques we show you in this chapter and in Chapter 5, moving to C# (or Java for that matter) will be easy.*

Introduction to OOP

OOP is a vast extension of the event-driven, control-based model of programming used in early versions of VB. With VB .NET, your entire program will be made up of self-contained objects that interact. These objects are stamped out from factories called *classes*. These objects will:

- Have certain properties and certain operations they can perform.
- Not interact with each other in ways not provided by your code's public interface.
- Only change their current state over time, and only in response to a specific request. (In VB .NET this request is made through a property change or a method call.)

The point is as long as the objects satisfy their specifications as to what they can do (their *public interface)* and thus how they respond to outside stimuli, the user does not have to be interested in how that functionality is implemented. In OOP-speak, you only care about what objects *expose.*

> **NOTE** *VB programmers know all about the value of self-contained packets of code with well-defined functionality (or controls). The reusability of the code packaged into controls helped make VB programmers, on average, far more productive than programmers working with a more traditional (procedural) model.*

Finally, one of the great advantages of .NET is that you can use your favorite language to build classes, and everyone can use them equally well. If you build a control in VB .NET, it can be used in C#, for example, or vice versa. Moreover, because of the magic of the Common Language Runtime, there should not be any significant difference in performance, regardless of the language that you choose.

Classes As (Smart) User-Defined Types

Another way to approach classes is to think of them as an extension of user- defined types where, for example, the data that is stored inside one can be validated before any changes take place. Similarly, a class is able to validate a request to return data before doing so. Finally, imagine a type that has methods to return data in a special form rather than simply spew out the internal representation.

From this point of view, an object is then simply a generalization of a specific (data-filled) user-defined type with functions attached to it for data access and validation. The key point you need to keep in mind is that:

- You are replacing direct access to data by various kinds of function calls that do the work.

For example, in a user-defined type such as this:

```
Employee Info Type
   Name As String
   Social Security Number As String
   Address as String
End Employee Info Type
```

the pseudocode that makes this user-defined type "smart" would hide the actual data and have functions instead to return the values. The pseudocode might look like this:

Employee Info as a CLASS

(hidden) Name As String - instead has functions that validate and return and change name

(hidden)Social Security Number As String - instead has functions that validate and return and change the Social Security number

(hidden) Address as String - instead has functions that validate and return and change the address and also return it in a useful form

End Employee Info as CLASS

> **NOTE** *Although having functions to return the data instead of giving users direct access to the data might seem like a lot of extra effort and might sound more complex, the advantages of having validation and access-control code more than outweigh the extra layer of complexity.*

Of course, as you get more sophisticated in your approach to OOP, objects can and will do more than merely validate or return internal data.

How Should Objects Interact with Other Objects?

One key practice in OOP is making each class (= object factory) responsible for carrying out only a small set of related tasks. You spend less time designing the class and debugging it when your classes are designed to build small objects that perform relatively few tasks, rather than architected with complex internal data along with many properties and methods to manipulate the internal data. If an object needs to do something that is not its responsibility, make a new class whose objects will be optimized for that task instead of adding the code to the first object and thus complicating the original object. If you give the first object access to the second type of object, then the first object can ask the second object to carry out the required task.

If you have used earlier versions of VB, you have already seen such requests between objects. For example, this is exactly what merely calling the methods or setting the properties of a control does. More generally, from the point of view of the user of an object, the request to another object is made by accessing a property or calling a method of the second object. Internally, the second object carries out the task using generalized versions of the function and procedures that you saw the VB .NET versions of in Chapter 3. The point is, the second object can hide the gory details from the world if there is no reason to expose the plumbing.

OOP jargon says it this way:

- Objects should only send messages to other objects.[1]

We cannot stress this enough: an object should never directly manipulate the internal data of another object. All communication between objects should be done via messages (property settings and method calls). Design your objects to handle a specific set of messages with the actual implementation as a black box to the outside world. To sum it up:

- Manipulate the objects in your program only by changing their properties or calling their methods. Use no public (global) variables inside the classes or objects that you create from them.

The Vocabulary of OOP

It is worth repeating that the most important OOP term is class:

- A *class* is a template from which objects are made.

Each object you make from this template is said to be an *instance* of the class. The methods, properties, and events inside your class are called the class's *members*. For example, suppose you were designing a personnel management program for a company. You would certainly have a class called `Employee`; each instance of the `Employee` class would correspond to a specific employee. The members of the `Employee` class would be properties such as `Name` or methods such as `RaiseSalary`.

The Relationships between Classes in Your Programs

Traditional OOP provides three possible relationships between classes:

- Use: dependency
- Containment: "has a"—this is sometimes called *aggregation*
- Inheritance: "is a"

1. Here is the standard joke to check whether you really understand OOP thinking. Question: How many OOP programmers does it take to change a light bulb? Answer: None. A properly OOP-compliant light bulb socket would accept a `ChangeBulb` message.

> **NOTE** *For languages such as VB .NET, C#, and Java, there is a fourth relationship between classes to add to the classic three. We usually call it "supports a"—more precisely, implementing an interface. The idea of implementing an interface is that your class supports certain functionality by making a contract that your class will have certain types of members. Interfaces have existed in VB since VB5, and you will still use them frequently in VB .NET. We will have much more to say about them in Chapter 5.*

Back to the classic three for the moment: the *use* relationship is both the most obvious and the most common, because it is just a fancy way of saying one class depends on another. Whenever an object sends a message to another object, the two obviously depend on each other. For example, an object of the `CheckRegister` class (an actual check register) uses objects of the `DepositSlip` class, because a check register needs to know what has been deposited. But the `DepositSlip` class does not use the `Check` class, because deposit slips have nothing to do with checks. While a class obviously uses another class if it manipulates objects of that class, more generally, a class A uses a class B if:

- A member of class A sends a message to an object of class B.

or

- A member of class A creates or returns objects of class B.

> **TIP** *It is best to minimize the number of classes that use each other. In other words, do not make your classes needlessly or overly intertwined. (In OOP-speak, this is called the loose coupling of classes.) The reason to do this is that if a class A does not use a class B, it does not care about any changes to B. (And this also means that changes to B will not introduce bugs into A!)*

Containment (*aggregation*) means that objects of class A contain objects of class B. For example, a specific `CheckRegister` object could contain `Check` and `DepositSlip` objects.

Containment is used to carry out *delegation*: you can delegate to the internal contained object the tasks that need to be carried out. Aggregation with method delegation was extremely common in earlier versions of VB, because that was how you built controls with VB5 and VB6. (Recall that you made a better textbox by placing a textbox inside a user control form and then running the control interface wizard to write the delegation code for you automatically.)

Aggregation is still common in VB .NET, but inheritance takes its place in many situations. Inheritance is not only one of the three ways classes depend on each other, it is also one of the four sacred buzzwords of OOP. Abstraction, encapsulation, and polymorphism are the other three, and we take them up in the following sections.

Abstraction

Abstraction is a fancy term for building a model of an object in code. In other words, it is the process of taking concrete day-to-day objects and producing a model of the object in code that simulates how the object interacts in the real world. For example, the first object-oriented language was called Simula (`http://java.sun.com/people/jag/SimulaHistory.html`), because it was invented to make simulations easier. Of course, the more modern ideas of virtual reality carry abstraction to an extreme. (Check out the influential book *Mirror Worlds, or the Day Software Puts the Universe in a Shoebox* by David Gelernter for more on this.) Abstraction is necessary because:

- You cannot use OOP successfully if you cannot step back and abstract the key issues from your problem.

Always ask yourself: What properties and methods will I need to mirror in the object's code so that my code will model the situation well enough to solve the problem?

Encapsulation

Encapsulation is the formal term for what we used to call data hiding. It means hide data, but define properties and methods that let people access it. Remember that OOP succeeds *only* if you manipulate data inside objects, only sending requests to the object. The data in an object is stored in its *instance fields*. Other terms you will see for the variables that store the data are *member variables* and *instance variables*. All three terms are used interchangeably, and which you choose is a matter of taste; we usually use instance fields. The current values of these instance fields for a specific object define the object's current state. Keep in mind that you should:

- Never ever give anyone direct access to the instance fields.

As a simple example, we will now return to the design of an object-oriented, personnel management program in which we have a class called `Employee`. The instance fields in an `Employee` class might be variables that hold the:

- Name
- Date hired
- Current salary

Instead of direct access to these instance fields, users of your class would modify properties such as `TheName`, or use methods such as `RaiseSalary`. The `RaiseSalary` method would obviously manipulate a `currentSalary` instance field, but it is possible in a more sophisticated `Employee` class that a method such as `RaiseSalary` might work with more than one instance field. For example, the `RaiseSalary` method might look at a person's sales record and hire date as well as their current salary.

To sum up:

- The behavior (functionality) of encapsulation is a way of describing what an object can do, which in turn corresponds to its members (methods, events, and properties) in VB .NET.

> **CAUTION** *At the risk of repeating ourselves too often, we still cannot stress enough that the key to making encapsulation work is to make sure that the other parts of your programs never directly access the instance fields (variables) in your classes. Programs should interact with these variables through the object's members. Keeping data private is the only way to give an object its black box behavior. Data hiding is critical to both successful reuse and long-term reliability.*

Inheritance

As an example of inheritance, imagine specializing the `Employee` class to get a `Programmer` class, a `Manager` class, and so on. Classes such as `Manager` would inherit from the `Employee` class. The `Employee` class is called the *base* (or *parent*) class, and the `Manager` class is called the *child* class. Child classes are:

- Always more specialized than their base (parent) classes.
- Have at least as many members as their parent classes (although the behavior of an individual member may be very different).

For example (alas), the `RaiseSalary` method of the `Manager` class may give a larger increase than the `RaiseSalary` method of the `Programmer` class for the same amount of time and performance rating. You can also:

- Add new methods to the inherited class that have no counterpart in the base (parent) class.

For example, a `Manager` class might have a `Secretary` property.

Developers have wanted inheritance in VB for a long time and have bemoaned loudly the lack of it. Although this was not much ado about nothing, neither was it as important as people made it out to be. The reason is that inheritance, when you get down to it, is just a way to avoid having to recode common functionality: inheritance is not a mystical process—it is all about simplifying code reuse. In our example, both the `Employee` and `Manager` classes share common behavior, such as having a hire date, a salary, and so on. Why recode a `Salary` property in two places if they use exactly the same code? With true inheritance, almost no code needs to be written in the child class to gain access to the same functionality present in the parent class: the extended class starts out with all the members of its parent. You then pick and choose which methods of the parent class to override by recoding in order to change their behaviors. For example, if managers automatically get an 8 percent raise when ordinary employees get a 4 percent raise, the `RaiseSalary` method in the `Manager` class must override the `RaiseSalary` method in the parent `Employee` class. On the other hand, methods such as `GetName` do not need to change at all, so you do not do any recoding.

> **NOTE** *Because inheritance is really all about code reuse, whenever source code is available, many influential OOP thinkers would argue that you should avoid inheritance in favor of using only interfaces (both of which are supported in VB .NET, of course). This is because of the fragile base class problem, which .NET goes a long way toward solving (more on this in Chapter 5)). Using interfaces in place of classic inheritance is sometimes called* interface inheritance; *classic inheritance involving automatic code reuse is called* implementation inheritance.

We will end this brief introduction to inheritance with a warning: Do not use inheritance where it is not absolutely clear that an "is a" relationship holds. For example, do not have a `Contractor` class that inherits from an `Employee` class to save yourself the trouble of duplicating the code for, say, Social Security or name properties. A good way to keep this vital point in mind is that the Internal Revenue Service (IRS) has also made this point very clear: contractors are not employees, and if you treat them the same way, you will bring yourself no end of grief from the IRS. Similarly, if you use inheritance where the "is a" relationship does not hold, you will also bring your programs a lot of grief. (More on this in Chapter 5.)

Polymorphism

Traditionally, *polymorphism* (from the Greek "many forms") means that inherited objects know what methods they should use, depending on where they are in the inheritance chain. For example, as we noted before, an `Employee` parent class and, therefore, the inherited `Manager` class both have a method for changing the salary of their object instances. However, the `RaiseSalary` method probably works differently for individual `Manager` objects than for plain old `Employee` objects.

The way polymorphism works in the classic situation where a `Manager` class inherits from an `Employee` class is that an `Employee` object would know if it were a plain old employee or really a manager. When it got the word to use the `RaiseSalary` method, then:

- If it were a `Manager` object, it would call the `RaiseSalary` method in the `Manager` class rather than the one in the `Employee` class.
- Otherwise, it would use the usual `RaiseSalary` method.

> **NOTE** *If you are coming from VB5 or VB6, the term polymorphism has been extended to not only cover inheritance-based polymorphism but also interface-based polymorphism, where objects that satisfy an interface know how to use the interface methods rather than some other method with a similar name. If an object satisfies the* `Manager` *interface, it would choose the correct* `RaiseSalary` *method based on how it was used.*

The point is that in both cases the object knows which method to use based on the message it gets. You do not need to know what class an object ultimately belongs to when you send it a message; you just send all `Employee` objects a message and leave the gory details of choosing the right polymorphic method in individual `Employee` objects to the compiler. The importance of this feature *cannot* be overstated.

Here is an example of why this feature is so important: One of us once did some consulting for a vendor of medical testing programs. Every time they introduced a new chemical (called a *reagent* in their jargon) for testing, they had to search through many thousands of lines of code for a bunch of different `Select Case` statements. They then had to add to all of them a case for how the new reagent worked. And if they missed one, well, we would not want to be the person whose blood was being tested using that new reagent. In any case, there was no question that adding code to multiple `Select Case` statements was a maintenance nightmare requiring countless hours of testing and recoding.

With polymorphism, you can write a program that needs to make only one change for this situation. You merely:

- Add a new class corresponding to the new reagent with the correct code for the methods that you need to *override* or *add*.

Why? Because if you write code in your main program that looks like this:

```
For Each reagent in Reagents
   reagent.Method
Next
```

it will work automatically with the new reagent—no more `Select Case` hunting parties.

```
Select Case reagent
   Case iodine
    'work with iodine
  Case benzene
  'work with benzene
'etc etc for a 100 more cases in 100 different places
```

The `For Each` presumably loops through the collection of all possible testing chemicals and, through the magic of polymorphism, the *compiler* will find the right method to call in all the different reagent instances, depending on exactly which class a specific reagent was an instance of. Use polymorphism correctly, and you will never need to search for or those evil `Select Case` (switch) statements that look at an object's type in order to determine what to do.

How to Objectify Your Programs

In the really old days we practiced what we called structured, procedure-oriented programming. We identified what needed to be done and then did one of two things, either:

1. Broke the task to be accomplished into subtasks, and these into smaller subtasks, until the subtasks were simple enough to be implemented directly (in other words, the top-down approach).

or

2. Wrote procedures to solve simple tasks and combine them into more sophisticated procedures, until we had the functionality we wanted (the bottom-up approach).

Most experienced programmers did not do what the professors suggested, of course (which was the top-down approach), and instead used a mixture of the top-down and bottom-up strategies to solve a programming problem.[2]

There are two important differences between OOP and procedure-oriented programming:

1. In OOP, you first isolate the classes. Only then do you look for the methods and properties of the class.

2. You then associate each method or property with the class that is responsible for carrying out the operation.

Which leads to the obvious question: How do you find the classes? A good rule of thumb is that classes are the nouns in your analysis of the problem. In our example, employees are one of the obvious nouns. The methods in your objects correspond to the verbs that describe actions that affect the noun, as in `RaiseSalary` (verb) which affects an `Employee` (noun). The properties are the adjectives that describe the noun. Of course, the noun-verb-adjective correspondence to classes, methods, and properties is only a first step. Only experience can help you decide which nouns, verbs, and adjectives are the important ones.

Here is another example: Suppose you want to design a program to manage your checking account using an object-oriented approach. Some obvious nouns are:

- Account
- Check
- Check register
- Deposit slip

These would lead to classes called `Account`, `Check`, `CheckRegister`, `DepositSlip`, and so on. Next, look for verbs. Accounts need to be *opened* or *closed*. Checks need to be *added* to the register. The check register needs to be *reconciled*. Deposit slips need to be *totaled*. With each verb, such as add, reconcile, and total, you have to identify the one object that has the major responsibility for carrying it out. For example, the deposit slip has the major responsibility for totaling itself up. Thus, `Total` should be a method of the `DepositSlip` class.

At this point, we want to repeat one golden rule of programming that has not changed in the march to OOP: *keep things simple*. Object-oriented programming is much easier when the classes you build are not complex. A class with a simple

2. Sometimes called the "meet in the middle" approach to programming

internal structure and limited relationships (*coupling* is the buzzword) to other classes is much easier to grasp (and hence to code).

Describing relationships between classes is so important in OOP that a whole industry has sprung up to explain how to make diagrams that make class relationships clearer. The most common tool is called the *uniform modeling language* (UML). These diagramming tools are usually part of the computer-assisted software engineering (CASE) tools, such as Microsoft's Visual Modeler, Visio, and Rational Software's Rational Rose. (A version of Visual Modeler is included with some versions of VS .NET.)

A UML-based CASE tool can go from the diagram to actually building the code skeletons for your classes. We recommend the Rational Web site (`www.rational.com/uml`) for general overviews of UML.

> **TIP** *One common low-tech method for finding (and documenting) the classes in your program is to start with a stack of index cards. You brainstorm on individual index cards the various possible classes, using one card for each class. Make sure each index card lists the name of the class, its responsibilities, and the other classes it uses. You can use the back of each card for the instance fields. (Hence the name CRC cards for them: CRC stands for class, responsibility, and collaboration.)*

What about Individual Objects?

Now that you have decided on the classes in your project, you will soon be working with objects that are specific instances of these classes. The key to working with specific objects is to identify the three "what's" of an object:

1. What is the object's *state*?
2. What is the object's *identity*?
3. What is the object's *behavior*?

Objects have information in their instance fields about what they do; you can use special instance fields to store information about the object's history. Together, this information defines what is usually called the object's *state*. An object's state is not fixed forever, but, as we have said before, any change in the state of an object must happen because of a message sent to the object.

The current state of an object does not completely describe it. Despite two objects appearing to be in the same state and thus even looking, feeling, and reacting the same, they are still different objects (as are two arrays with the same data, for example.) Thus, each object also has a distinct identity. The behaviors of an object are what it can do at a given moment and what it can *potentially do* in the future. These are the members of the object, and in VB .NET this corresponds to an object's properties, methods, and events.

These three characteristics obviously influence each other, so inside the class your code needs to take this into account. For example, the behavior an object can exhibit is influenced by its current state: a textbox that is disabled has quite different behavior than one that is enabled, and your code must take this into account when building the class. Or, if a deposit slip has not been totaled, it may send out a caution message before allowing itself to be added to the check register.

Advantages to OOP

At first glance, the OOP approach that leads to classes and their associated methods and properties is much like the structured approach that leads to modules. But the key difference is that:

- Classes are factories for making objects whose states can diverge over time.

Sound too abstract? Sound as though it has nothing to do with VB programming? Well, this is exactly what the Toolbox is! Each control on the Toolbox in earlier versions of VB was a little factory for making objects that are instances of that control's class.

Suppose the Toolbox was not a bunch of little class factories waiting to churn out new textboxes and command buttons in response to your requests. Can you imagine how convoluted your VB code would been if you needed a separate code module for each textbox? After all, the same code module cannot be linked into your code twice, so you would have to do some fairly complicated coding to build a form with two identical textboxes whose states can diverge over time.

Because of the existence of the Toolbox, VB has always been object-based and, since VB4, has had the ability to build certain kinds of objects. However, VB .NET is the first version of VB that lets you build a class (factories) that can churn out *any* kind of object using the full power of OOP—and do it on an equal footing with C++ and C#. Moreover, as far as performance goes, all .NET languages are essentially equally good at turning out classes.

Creating Object Instances in VB .NET

Except for strings and arrays where there is a shorthand for creating objects, you use the `New` keyword every time you create an object in VB .NET, just as you did in earlier versions of VB.

- In OOP-speak, this is called *instantiating* a class.

This term makes sense because, after all, you are making an *instance* of the object.

For example, the .NET Framework comes with a useful `Random` class that has quite a bit more functionality than the `Rnd` function that comes with the VB compatibility layer. You can fill an array of bytes with random numbers from 0 to 255 in one stroke, for example, or get a random positive integer in a specified range. But `Random` is not a function; it is a class with methods that you can call on `Random` object instances. And you can do this *only* after you make an instance of the `Random` class.

So, before you can use the `Random` class's nifty new features, you need to have an instance of the `Random` class. There are various ways to do this, and they all require calling the special `New` method. A longwinded way, but often the clearest, way is to separate the declaration from the call to `New`:

```
Dim aRandomInstance As Random  'a declaration
aRandomInstance = New Random()  'followed by an instantiation
```

However, often you will see code that takes advantage of VB .NET's ability to initialize a variable at declaration:

```
Dim aRandomInstance As New Random  'combine declare and instantiation
```

which is functionally equivalent to the previous, except that it takes advantage of VB .NET's ability to initialize a variable at declaration.

In OOP-speak, the `New` method is called a *constructor* method or a *constructor* for short (because you use it to construct instances of classes).

CAUTION *Users coming from earlier versions of VB should note that:*

- *The* `Set` *keyword is gone (see the section on "Properties" later in this chapter for a side effect of this departure).*
- *There is no functional difference between the two syntaxes for using* `New` *except if an exception occurs (see Chapter 7) when instantiating the object.*

> **CAUTION** *In earlier versions of VB, the shorthand form of object construction had subtle differences from the longer form. These differences occurred because the shorthand form did not actually create the object until it was first used. This inconsistent behavior has been banished—VB .NET no longer allows for the possibility of* implicit creation of objects.

Some people, especially C# and Java programmers, like to code with a third version that looks like a combination of the other two:

```
Dim foo As Random = new Random() 'very C#/Java like
```

This works exactly like the second form of object construction above.

You can also use the `New` method to construct an object in any VB .NET expression in which the result makes sense. For example, the following is perfectly legal VB .NET code (if not particularly easy to understand and hence a style we think to be avoided):

```
Console.WriteLine(New Random().Next())
```

(Of course, because you might see this style in code you have to maintain, it is good to know it is possible. People coming with a C++/Java background often code this way.)

Once you have an instance of the `Random` class, you access its functionality with the familiar dot notation. Given the richness of the various classes in the .NET Framework, IntelliSense will, of course, be there to show you what you can do with instances of a class, as you can see in Figure 4-1.

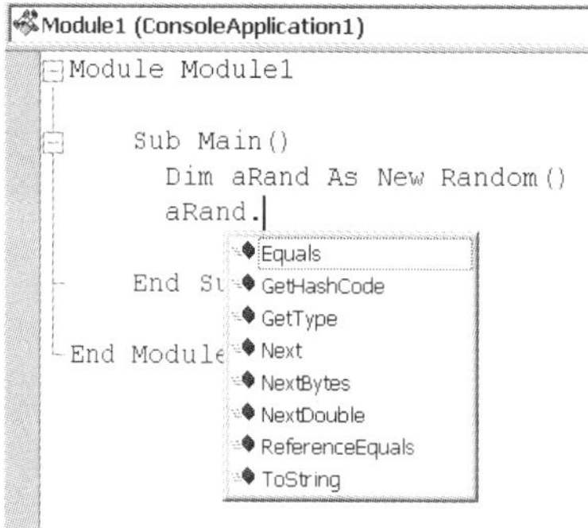

Figure 4-1. IntelliSense on the `Random` *class*

For example, unlike the `Rnd` function from earlier versions of VB, you will not have to convert numbers between 0 and 1 to useful positive integers. Instead, you call the `Next` method, which returns a positive integer. Want a random integer between 1 and 6? Use this code:

```
Dim aRandomInstance As New Random()
Dim die As Integer
die = aRandomInstance.Next(1, 6)
Console.WriteLine(die)
```

> **TIP** *The* `Random` *class is not useful for serious cryptography because the algorithm it uses to generate the next random number is easily broken. The .NET Framework is actually rich enough to include a (slower of course) cryptographically secure random number generator in the* `RandomNumberGenerator` *Class, which is part of the* `System.Security.Cryptography` *namespace. (More on namespaces later in this chapter.)*

A reminder: while you usually must have an object instance to get access to the power built into the class, there is an exception to the rule. The exception is that certain functionality can be built into the class itself. You saw that in Chapter 4 with the `Math` class, where we were able to use `Math.PI` or `Math.Sin()` without using the `New` method. Recall that members that belong to the class and not an instance of the class are called *shared* members. Shared members may be accessed either by using the name of the class or the name of an object variable that is declared to be of the appropriate type. For example, if there is a class called `Bar` which has a shared method called `Foo` you can use either:

```
Bar.Foo()
```

or

```
Dim test As Bar
test.Foo()
```

> **NOTE** *Shared members are called* static *members in some other languages, such as C# and Java. Another term you will see occasionally is* class *member.*

More on Constructors: Parameterized Constructors

On the surface, the `New` constructor method does not seem all that different than it was in earlier versions of VB. Under the hood, however, a lot has changed. The most exciting change is that `New` can now take parameters. As you will shortly see, when you create your own classes, your custom version of `New` replaces the `Initialize` event from earlier versions of VB, which did not support parameters.

For example, the `Random` class has two versions of its constructor available. You can use it without a parameter as we just did. In this case, you get random numbers generated from a random seed based on the system clock. The other version looks like this:

```
Dim aRandomInstance As Random
aRandomInstance = New Random(42)
```

You get a version of the `Random` class that generates repeatable values using 42 as the seed (being able to use the same seed and thus getting the same sequence of random numbers is absolutely necessary for debugging).

Ironically, the adding of parameterized constructors to VB is probably more important to fully implementing OOP than is inheritance. You can work around inheritance (often by aggregation), but it is a lot harder to work around not having parameterized constructors. The point of adding parameterized constructors is to prevent you from inadvertently creating an object in an indeterminate state. This was always a problem in earlier versions of VB, because the `Initialize` event did not take parameters. All you could do was use the convention of adding a routine (often called `Create`) to your class to initialize objects, and it was up to the user of your class to remember to call it. If they did not, then your object may not have been properly conceived and its instance fields would have their default values. This in turn could lead to subtle, hard-to-track-down bugs.

In VB .NET, as in all fully object-oriented languages, the only way to create an object is with a constructor and, as you will see later in this chapter, you can *require* that parameters be used for constructor methods in order to insure that your objects are not created in an indeterminate state.

> **NOTE** *Having multiple versions of a function that differ only in their parameters is called* overloading. *As you will see a little later on in this chapter, VB .NET supports overloading in any function or procedure, not just the special* `New` *constructor method. Overloading also can replace the use of optional parameters.*

Example: The String *Class*

The String class is another good example of a class that comes with multiple constructors. Although you can make a string by the shorthand means of simply surrounding a bunch of characters with double quotes, for more specialized string construction, it is best to change to the constructor approach. For example, one of the constructors makes multiple copies of the same character:

```
Dim str As String = New String(CChar(" "), 37)
```

which gives you a string consisting of 37 spaces. Using this constructor is thus equivalent to using the Space function. (Note that having Option Strict On requires that you convert the string that contains a single space character to an actual character using a conversion function.)

The general version of this constructor is:

```
New(ByVal c As Char, ByVal count As Integer)
```

The other common String constructor is New(ByVal value() As Char), which takes an array of characters and converts it to a string.

> **TIP** *Since a string variable is now an object variable, remember that when you add the "." at the end of any string variable, IntelliSense will help you with a list of the members of the* String *class.*

Example: The StringBuilder *Class*

The next example, a built-in class, is the very useful StringBuilder class that is part of the utility System.Text namespace. (See the next section for more on namespaces.) You should use this class instead of the ordinary String class whenever you need to constantly change a string. The reason is, every time you change a string say by adding a new character to it, VB .NET needs to create a new string and that takes time. With an instance of the StringBuilder class, VB .NET just keeps on adding to the original StringBuilder object.

> **NOTE** *How much more time does this take? We ran a test using some code, which you can see in the sidebar that follows. We found that using a* `StringBuilder` *to build a string of characters was usually hundreds of times faster than using a* `String`. *This ratio could be even larger in practice, because we did not use any of the extra power of the* `StringBuilder` *class to avoid constantly reallocating space. An optimized use of the* `StringBuilder` *class could be even faster. (On the other hand, using an ordinary* `String` *is faster than using a* `StringBuilder` *when you just want to access parts of a string and do not need to change it.)*

When you create an empty `StringBuilder` object with `New`, VB .NET sets aside space for 16 characters and automatically adds space when you add more information to the `StringBuilder`. Think of a `StringBuilder` object as being a very smart array of characters that grows and shrinks as needed, and is thus in a way far closer to what the `String` type did in VB6. The current size is called the *capacity*. The `StringBuilder` class has six constructors that are described in Table 4-1.

Table 4-1. Six Constructors of the `StringBuilder` *Class*

CONSTRUCTOR	DESCRIPTION
`New()`	Parameterless, makes an empty `StringBuilder` object with a starting capacity of 16 characters.
`New(ByVal value As String)`	Constructs a `StringBuilder` object whose initial state is the specified string.
`New(ByVal capacity As Integer)`	Makes an empty instance but sets aside space for a specified number of characters. Can still grow if needed. (This is more efficient then letting the `StringBuilder` object grow itself from scratch if you know beforehand that you will need at least this much space.)
`New(ByVal capacity As Integer, ByVal maxCapacity As Integer)`	Makes an empty `StringBuilder` instance and sets aside space for the specified number of characters beforehand, but allows growth only to the specified maximum. Any attempt to add more than the maximum number of characters results in an exception (see Chapter 7).
`New(ByVal value As String, ByVal capacity As Integer)`	Makes a new `StringBuilder` object from the specified string, starting with the specified capacity.
`New(ByVal value As String, ByVal startIndex As Integer, ByVal length As Integer, ByVal capacity As Integer)`	Constructs a `StringBuilder` object from a substring of a given string with a given starting capacity.

To quickly make a StringBuilder with 25,000 copies of the letter A, for example, you would write:

```
Dim bar As New String("A", 25000)
Dim foo As New System.Text.StringBuilder(Bar)
```

The Chars property allows you to get or set a specific character in a StringBuilder. It is zero based, so, if foo is a StringBuilder instance, then:

```
foo.Chars(1) ="b"
```

replaces the *second* character with a b.

The Length property lets you get or set the current length of the StringBuilder. If you specify a Length less than the current size, VB truncates the StringBuilder object. If you have created a StringBuilder object with a maximum capacity, then you get an exception if the length you specify is greater than the maximum capacity. (See Chapter 7 for more on exceptions.)

The members of the StringBuilder class that you will use most frequently are *very* overloaded. They come in so many versions so that you can, for example, add or remove strings, numbers, characters, or an array of characters equally well. For example, the useful Append method adds characters at the end of the StringBuilder:

```
Dim foo As New System.Text.StringBuilder()
foo = foo.Append("A")
foo.Append("hello") 'adds 5 character
foo.Append(37) 'adds two characters
foo.Append(new Random()) '??
```

As the last line in the example indicates, you can actually append generic *objects* to a StringBuilder. When you do this, VB automatically figures out the string representation of the object (more precisely it calls the ToString method of the object) and adds that string to the StringBuilder. Of course, how useful the string representation of an object is depends on the implementer of the class. In our example code, you get the not very useful string System.Random rather than a random number. (But foo.Append(New Random().Next works fine.)

An Insert method:

```
Insert(ByVal index As Integer, ByVal thing As Object)
```

inserts the specified object or value into the StringBuilder at the specified position.

The `Remove` method, which removes the specified number of characters starting at the specified position, is similar:

```
Remove(ByVal startIndex As Integer, ByVal length As Integer)
```

The `Replace` method is overloaded to allow you do a bunch of neat things:

- `Replace(ByVal oldChar As Char, ByVal newChar As Char)`: Replaces all instances of the old character with the new one
- `Replace(ByVal oldValue As String, ByVal newValue As String)`: Replaces all instances of the old string with the new one

You can also use:

```
Replace(ByVal oldChar As Char, ByVal newChar As Char, ByVal startIndex As Integer, _
ByVal count As Integer)
```

and

```
Replace(oldValue As Stringr, ByVal newValue As String, ByVal startIndex As Integer, _
ByVal count As Integer)
```

to replace all instances of the string or the character in a specified range (the `count` parameter gives you the length of the region).

You call the `ToString` method to convert a `StringBuilder` to a `String` when you do not want to make any more changes to it and only want to look at its parts from that point on.

> **CAUTION** *There is an* `Equals` *method in the* `StringBuilder` *class, but unlike strings, two* `StringBuilder` *objects with the same content are not necessarily equal. (The rationale is that in the .NET Framework, once* `a.Equals(b)` *is true it must always be true, which obviously cannot happen for* `StringBuilder` *objects because they can change.) We recommend not using the* `Equals` *method on* `StringBuilder` *objects.*

Timing Operations—And Just How Much Faster Is a StringBuilder, Anyway?

Although Microsoft does not allow you to publish explicit timings with beta software (for the very good reason they are pretty much meaningless due to the amount of debugging code contained in beta builds), relative timings are often useful and will almost certainly remain relatively true. (It is possible that optimizations in the released version may slightly affect relative timings, but this is much less likely than with absolute timings.)

Timing code in VB .NET is easily done by combining the `Now` method with the `Ticks` method in the `DateTime` class. As you might expect, the `Now` method tells you what time the system clock is reporting. The `Ticks` method returns a Long equal to the number of 100-nanosecond intervals that have elapsed since 12:00 AM on 1/1/0001 (the year 1). (A nanosecond is 10^-9 of a second or 1 billionth of a second in U.S. units.)

Here is the code we used to test how much faster appending to a `StringBuilder` class is than appending to a `String`. (The larger the number of characters you add to the string, the faster a `StringBuilder` will be; with 50,000 characters, we were getting 800+ times improvement!)

```
Option Strict On
Module Module1
  Sub Main()
    Dim i As Integer
    Dim StartTime As New DateTime()
    Dim EndTime As New DateTime()
    StartTime = DateTime.Now()
    Dim theText As New System.Text.StringBuilder()
    For i = 1 To 50000
      theText = theText.Append("A")
    Next
    EndTime = DateTime.Now
    Dim answer1, answer2 As Long
    answer1 = EndTime.Ticks() - StartTime.Ticks() 'number of 100 nanosecond pulses
    StartTime = DateTime.Now()
    Dim aString As String
    For i = 1 To 50000
      aString = aString & "A"
    Next
    EndTime = DateTime.Now
    answer2 = (EndTime.Ticks() - StartTime.Ticks()) 'number of 100 nanosecond pulses
    Console.WriteLine("StringBuilder was " & answer2 / answer1 & " times faster.")
    Console.ReadLine()
  End Sub
End Module
```

Namespaces

The potential for conflicts between method names exists whenever you use other people's code. And even forgetting about these kind of conflicts, you need some way to group thousands of methods in such a way that you have some hope of remembering how they fit together. Thus, there *has* to have a way of organizing information in as rich a framework as is supplied with .NET. In .NET this is done with *namespaces*. (You can create your own namespaces, and we show you how to do so later in this chapter.)

The idea is that, just as every town seems to have its own Main Street, every library of networking code might have its own `Open` method. Namespaces give you a way to distinguish between them. For example, the `System.IO` namespace is where you find methods to handle files and, as you might expect, there is a class called `File` in it for handling files and it has an `Open` method. Its full name is:

```
System.IO.File.Open
```

because the `File` class is part of the `System.IO` namespace and will not conflict with another `File` class that might be part of the `Cornell.Morrison.NiftyClasses` namespace, which could have its own `Open` method.

Imports

Just as we normally do not use a person's full name when referring to people familiar to us, .NET also has a way of avoiding a lot of superfluous verbiage. This is done through the use of the `Imports` statement. With the right `Imports` statement, we can replace all those uses of:

```
System.Text.StringBuilder
```

with just a simple:

```
StringBuilder
```

Note that the `System` class is automatically imported into every solution you build with Visual Studio. This is why you can use:

```
Console.WriteLine()
```

rather than

```
System.Console.WriteLine()
```

You can get or change the list of the namespaces that are automatically imported for a solution by looking at the Imports page in the solution's property pages, as you can see in Figure 4-2:

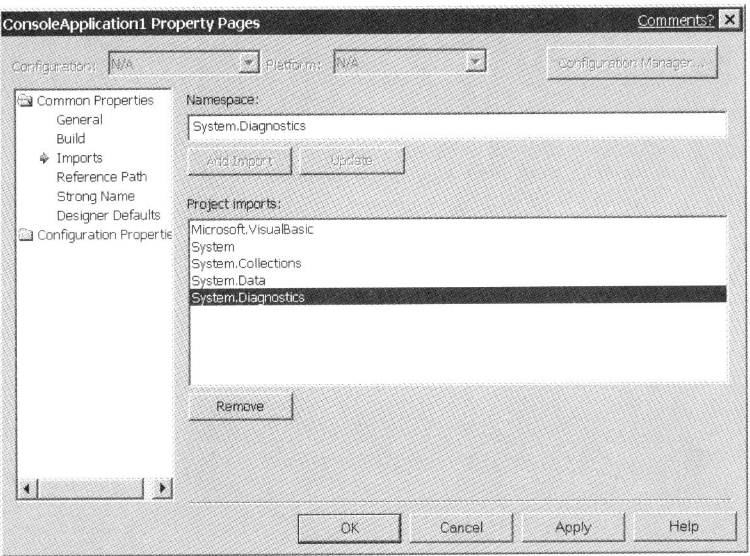

Figure 4-2. The Imports page in the solution's property pages

In the Object Browser, the automatically imported `Microsoft.VisualBasic` namespace contains the functions (such as the financial functions) that were part of Visual Basic and were kept in VB .NET (see Figure 4-3).

If you import the `Microsoft.VisualBasic.Constants`, you can reuse most of the VB constants that you have used before, such as `vbCRLF`. Note that the .NET versions of many of these constants do not use a VB prefix (for example, `CrLf`) and are stored in the `Microsoft.VisualBasic.ControlChars` namespace.

The `Imports` statement goes before any other declarations, such as the ones defining the name of a module, but after any `Option` directives, such as `Option Strict On` or `Option Compare Text`.

> **TIP** *We have to confess that we were amazed to discover that IntelliSense works with the* `Imports` *statement and shows you which namespaces you can import into your project. It does this by looking at what assemblies are referenced in the solution.*

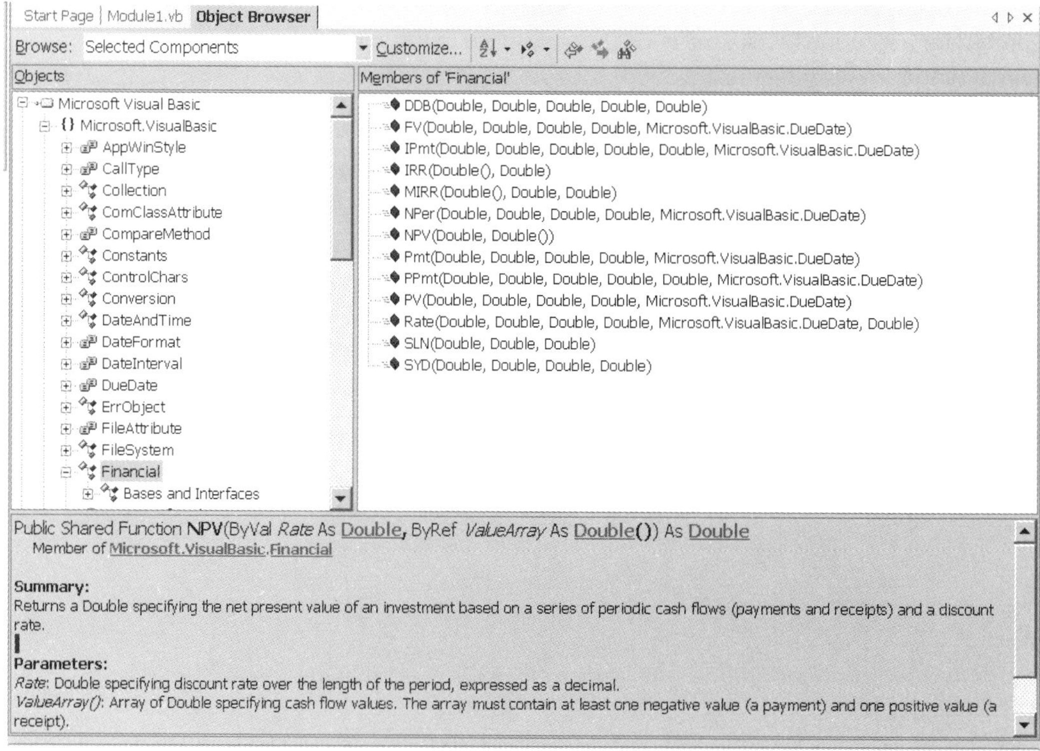

Figure 4-3. The `Microsoft.VisualBasic` *namespace in the Object Browser*

Using `Imports` does not bloat your code, because it does not make all the code in the namespace part of your project—it merely simplifies the typing of the names of members of the classes in the namespace in your code. It does not affect the speed of the resulting program either. Also, you can only import namespaces that are part of a referenced *assembly*, which are what you get by working with the Project|Add Reference dialog box. (See Chapter 13 for more on assemblies.)

Note that if two imported namespaces contain classes with identical names, you have to give the full name of the class, including its namespace, to distinguish them. (VB .NET will not allow you to create two classes with the same name in the same namespace.)

Next, you can use a special version of `Imports` to simplify typing when you have the potential for name conflicts with classes you have already imported. For example, if you really wanted to use the VB6 compatibility layer (not that we recommend it), you have to be aware that it will almost certainly introduce namespace conflicts. You can add a reference to the VB compatibility layer and then use a line like this:

```
Imports VB6Stuff = Microsoft.VisualBasic.Compatibility.VB6
```

and start writing `VB6Stuff` followed by a "." whenever you need a member of the compatibility layer, without having to worry about name conflicts.

You cannot import an individual class to avoid typing the class name for its members. A statement such as:

```
Imports System.IO.DirectoryInfo
```

to simply get at the members of the `DirectoryInfo` class is not allowed.

A DirectoryInfo Example

As an example of using `Imports` in some mildly interesting code, we will use `DirectoryInfo` class in the `System.IO` namespace. As you might expect, `DirectoryInfo` has methods to get subdirectory information inside a directory, print out the full name of a directory, and so on. One of the constructors for this class takes a string that gives the name of the directory you want to analyze. (If you do not give the full path name, it resolves the name relative to the location of the program.) With the correct `Imports` statement, you can replace the longwinded:

```
Dim dirInfo As New System.IO.DirectoryInfo("C:\")
```

with

```
Dim dirInfo As New DirectoryInfo("C:\")
```

which is shorter and easier to understand. The following small program uses recursion and the `DirectoryInfo` class to display a list of all the directories on your hard drive. The key to this code is that the `GetDirectories()` method returns a collection of subdirectories. By using this collection, we can call our function recursively on individual subdirectories.

```
Option Strict On
Imports System.IO
Module Module1

    Sub Main()
       Dim dirInfo As New DirectoryInfo("C:\")
       ListDirectories(dirInfo)
    End Sub

    Sub ListDirectories(ByVal theDirectory As DirectoryInfo)
      Dim tempDir As DirectoryInfo
      Console.WriteLine(theDirectory.FullName())
      For Each tempDir In theDirectory.GetDirectories()
        ListDirectories(tempDir)
      Next
    End Sub
End Module
```

(If you are accustomed to using a cached version of the old `Dir` function to work recursively with a directory structure, you will appreciate how short such a program can be in .NET, with the power of the `DirectoryInfo` method!)

> **CAUTION** *When we were developing this example, we originally named this solution DirectoryInfo without thinking. This had the effect of essentially preventing the* `Imports` *statement from working correctly! The moral of the hour or so we lost in trying to figure out what was wrong is: do not give your solutions the same names as classes in the .NET libraries!*

Help and the (Vast) .NET Framework

The .NET Framework provides hundreds of namespaces with many useful classes inside each of them. The Framework's size and power rivals that of the full Win32 API. It is so complex that to fully describe every piece of it in a single book is impossible. Although we give you a glimpse of many of the Framework's classes in this chapter, you really need to start browsing the .NET documentation as soon as possible. You might start by looking in the .NET Framework Class Library for descriptions of the namespaces that interest you. The help system lists all the classes in each namespace, as you can see in Figure 4-4.

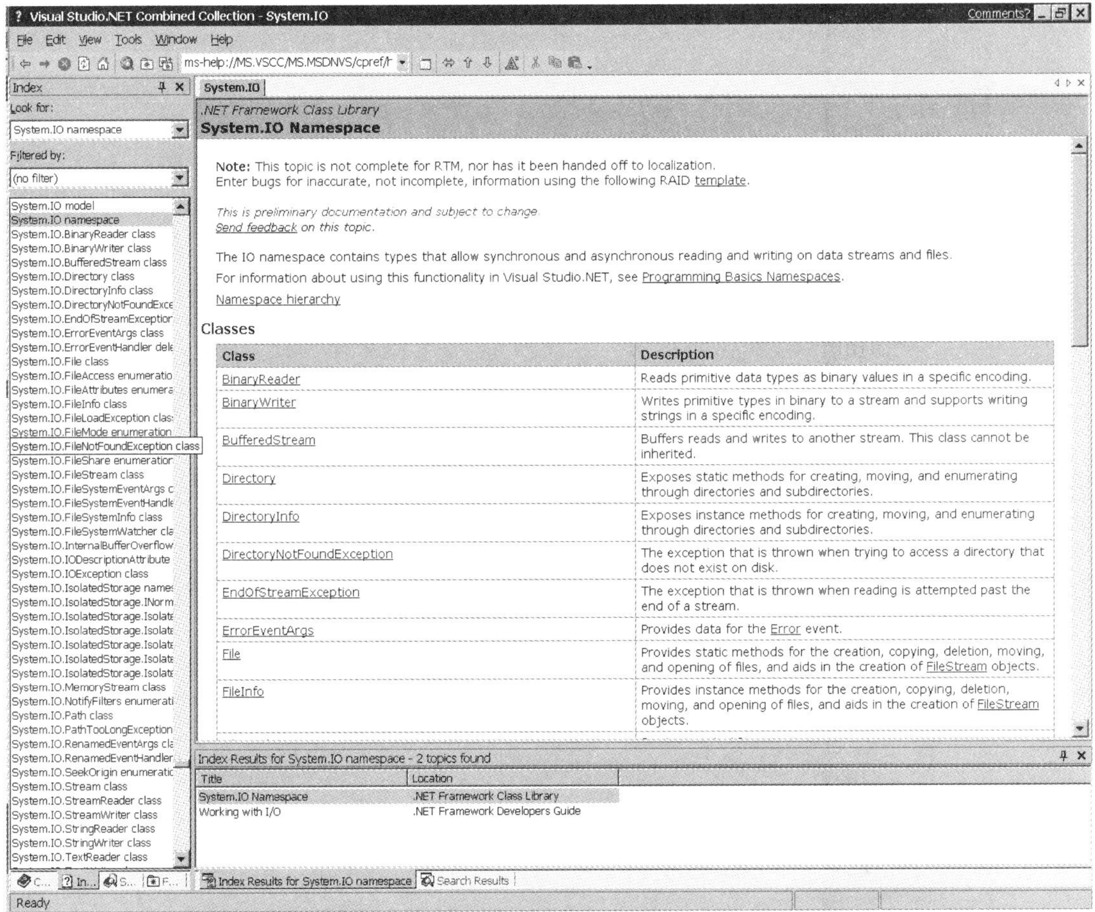

Figure 4-4. System.IO namespace in the Help system

Each class name in the namespace page is a hyperlink to a description of the class. Once you are in the class that interests you, a hyperlink to the members of the class is shown at the bottom of the page that describes the class. Clicking on the hyperlink takes you to a page that lists all the members of class, where the name of each member is itself a hyperlink to a more detailed discussion of that member. Note that the .NET Framework does not treat VB .NET as a second-class citizen—the syntax for all members is given in VB, VC, and C#. Figure 4-5 shows an example of the beta 2 documentation for the members of `DirectoryInfo`.

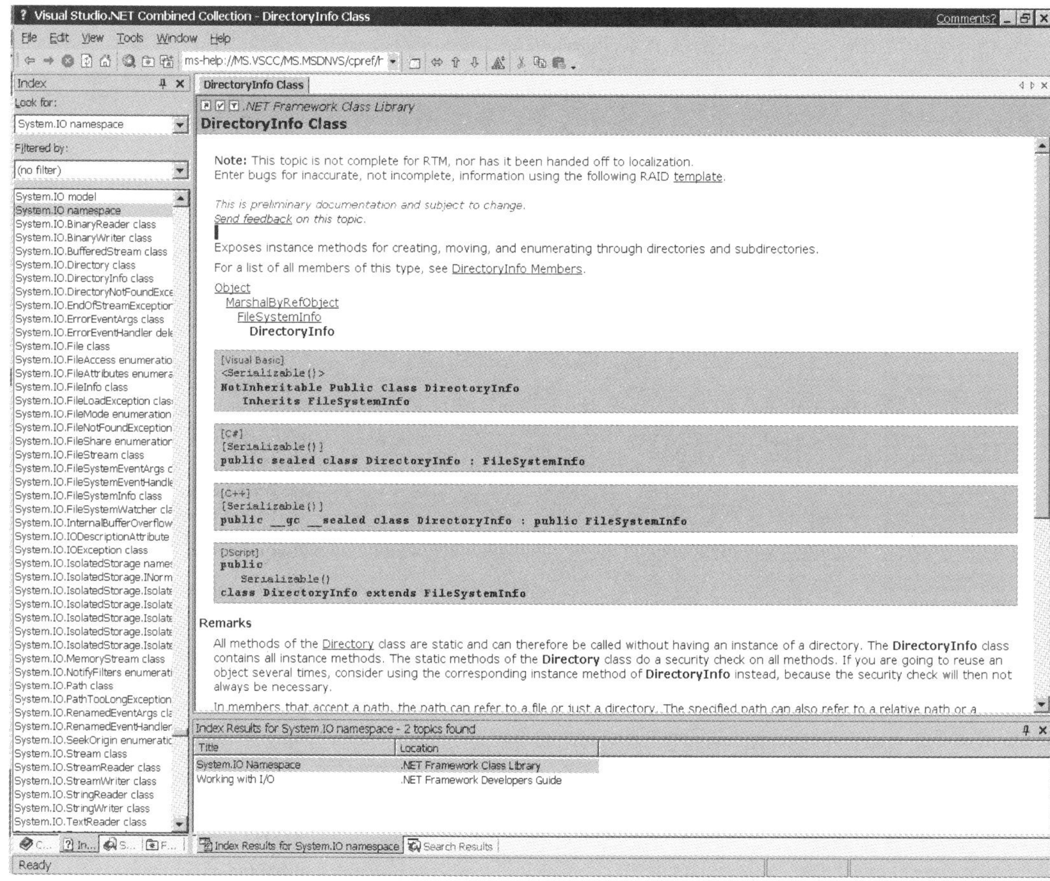

Figure 4-5. The Help system at work for the `DirectoryInfo` *class*

To figure out how to code the previous example, we clicked on the `DirectoryInfo` members link at the bottom of the page and then on `GetDirectories` hyperlink to look at the syntax for this method, shown in Figure 4-6. (We will explain terms in the documentation such as "Private" later in this chapter.)

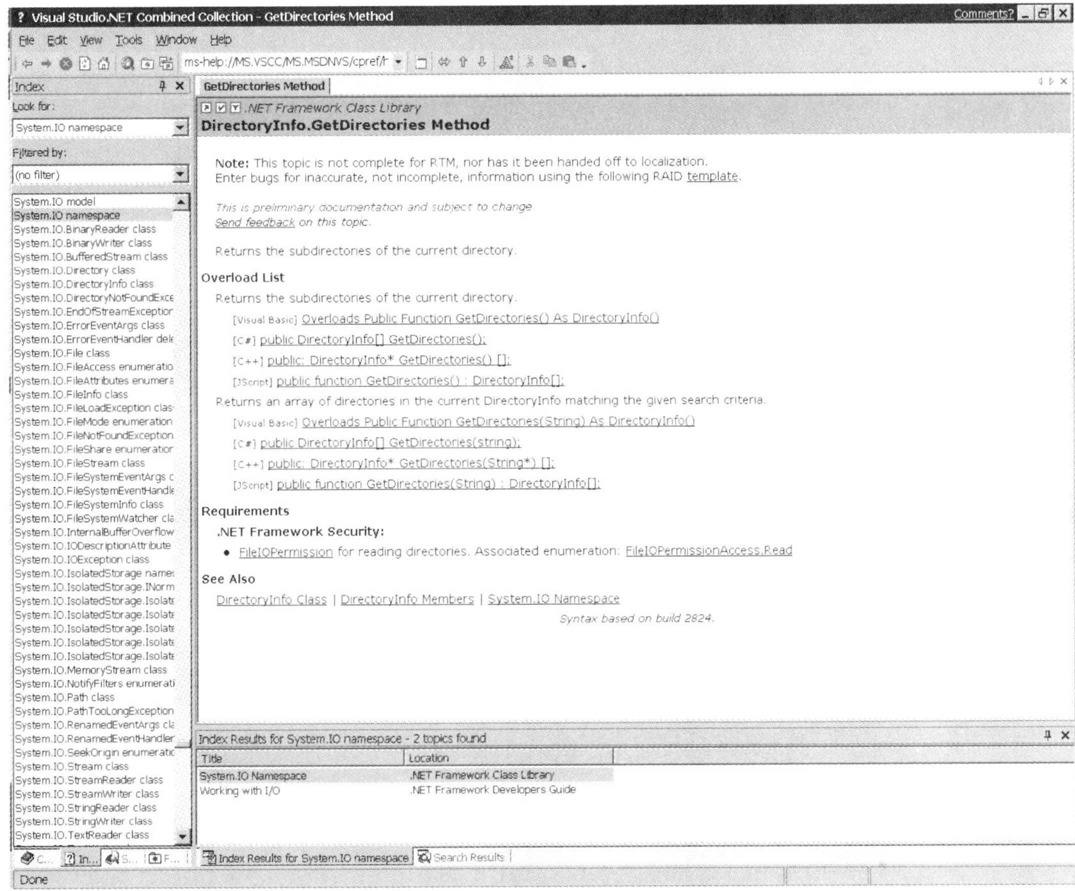

Figure 4-6. The Help system at work for the `GetDirectories` *method*

Example: The Framework Collection Classes

We wanted to whet your appetite for studying the .NET Framework by briefly discussing some of the framework's collection classes. *Collection classes* give you access to the typical data structures that many sophisticated programs need. They are so important that they are automatically imported in every VB .NET solution by default (as part of the `System.Collections` namespace).

Collectively, these classes go way beyond what you had with VB6's primitive `Collection` class. Table 4-2 summarizes the most useful collection classes. The next two sections cover the fundamentals of two of the most useful classes (`ArrayList` and `HashTable`); we will leave the very important `DictionaryBase` class to the next chapter, when we cover inheritance.

Table 4-2. Useful Collection Classes

CLASS NAME	DESCRIPTION
ArrayList	A smart array whose size dynamically increases and shrinks as needed.
BitArray	Useful for individual bit manipulations. (Very popular in benchmarks for things such as primality testing.)
DictionaryBase	The base (parent) class for various kinds of dictionaries. Dictionaries let you store key/value pairs in a way that is usually more useful then the various collection classes. (There is a comparable CollectionBase class, however, for collection classes.) DictionaryBase is similar to a PERL associative array. It can be used only via inheritance (see Chapter 5).
Hashtable	Represents a collection of associated keys and values that are organized based on the hash code of the key.
Queue	For first-in, first-out (FIFO) structures.
Stack	For last-in, first-out (LIFO) structures.

ArrayList

This class implements a *smart array*—an array that automatically grows and shrinks as needed. Although a little slower than ordinary arrays, they make certain coding tasks much, much easier. Also, unlike most arrays, an ArrayList is always potentially heterogeneous. This means a basic ArrayList can always hold items of differing types. (See Chapter 5 for how to make an ArrayList that can hold items of only a single type, and for some of the subtleties that arise because an ArrayList can hold generic objects.)

Using an ArrayList instead of a basic array means that you do not need to constantly use ReDim Preserve in order to build up the data. Just call the Add method and let ArrayList handle the bookkeeping. The class also has quite a few other useful built-in methods. For example, AddRange lets you add all the items in an array to an array list with a single command. You can always copy an array list back to an array when you are finished. This gives you a quick way to merge two arrays, for example. Table 4-3 describes the most important members of the ArrayList class (consult the online Help for a complete list).

Table 4-3. Important Members of `ArrayList` *Class*

MEMBER	DESCRIPTION
`Add`	Adds an object to the end of the `ArrayList`.
`AddRange`	Allows you to add, for example, the contents of another array or array list at the end of the current array list. This and `InsertRange` allow let you to merge arrays quickly via an `ArrayList` helper class.
`BinarySearch`	Implements a binary search to look for a specific element in a sorted `ArrayList` or a portion of it.
`Capacity`	Gets or sets the number of elements that potentially can be stored in the `ArrayList`. Changes when you add items, of course, but changes are made in gulps, or large increments for efficiency reasons.
`Clear`	Removes all elements from the `ArrayList`.
`Contains`	This useful method searches the array list to determines whether an element is in the `ArrayList`.
`CopyTo`	Copies the `ArrayList` or part of it to a one-dimensional array at a specified index in the target.
`Count`	Gives the actual number of elements currently stored.
`GetRange`	Returns another `ArrayList` that is a continuous part of the current `ArrayList`.
`IndexOf`	`ArrayLists`, like arrays, are zero based so this returns the zero-based index of the first occurrence of an item.
`Insert`	Inserts an element into the `ArrayList` at the specified index.
`InsertRange`	Inserts the elements of a collection into the `ArrayList` at the specified index.
`Item`	Gets or sets the element at the specified index. Is the default property of `ArrayList`.
`LastIndexOf`	Returns the (zero-based) index of the last occurrence of an item.
`Length`	Returns the number of items.
`ReadOnly`	Returns a new `ArrayList` that is read-only. (Use `IsReadOnly` to check to see if an array list is read-only.)
`Remove`	Removes the first occurrence of the specified item.
`RemoveAt`	Removes the item at the specified index.
`RemoveRange`	Removes a range of elements.

Table 4-3. Important Members of `ArrayList` *Class (Continued)*

MEMBER	DESCRIPTION
`Repeat`	Returns an `ArrayList` containing a specified number of elements, all of which are the same.
`Reverse`	Reverses the order of the elements in the `ArrayList` or a portion of it.
`SetRange`	Copies the elements of a collection over a range of elements in the `ArrayList`.
`Sort`	Sorts the elements in the `ArrayList` (or a portion of it).
`ToArray`	Overloaded. Copies the elements of the `ArrayList` to a new array.
`TrimToSize`	Use this method after you are finished with the `ArrayList` in order to trim the capacity to the actual number of elements currently stored. (It can grow later, of course.)

One of the more interesting properties of `ArrayList` is the `Item` property, which gives you the item at a specified (zero-based) index. For example:

```
Console.WriteLine(myList.Item(1))
```

`Item` is actually the *default* property of the `ArrayList` class. This means that you do not have to use it explicitly. For example, the above line and this line:

```
Console.WriteLine(myList(1))
```

have the same effect. (See the section in this chapter on Properties for more on how default properties have changed in VB .NET from the way they were in earlier versions of VB.)

The following short program shows you how you can use an `ArrayList` to pick up an indeterminate amount of data and store it without using the `ReDim Preserve` that would be necessary with an ordinary array:

```
Option Strict On
Module Module1
  Sub Main()
    Dim myList As New ArrayList()
    Dim theData As String
    Console.Write("Please enter each item and hit Enter key," _
      & " enter ZZZ when done: ")
    theData = Console.ReadLine()
    Do Until theData = "ZZZ"
      myList.Add(theData)
```

```
      Console.Write("Please enter each item and hit Enter, " _
       & " enter ZZZ when done: ")
      theData = Console.ReadLine()
    Loop
    Console.WriteLine("You entered " & myList.Count() & " ITEMS.")
    Console.ReadLine()
  End Sub
End Module
```

Hashtables

One of the nifty features of arrays and array lists is the ability to go directly to an item given its index. The trouble, of course, is that you have to know the index of an item. *Hashtables* are a data structure that give you this kind of random access to data from a *key*. The idea is, given a hashtable named `theData`, for example:

```
theData("Bill's Address")
```

you get back Bill's address without having to write code for walking through every item in the hashtable. Hashtables are therefore extremely useful when you need quick access to a value by working backwards from a (unique) key. Of course, implementing the code for a hashtable class is nontrivial, but thankfully, it is already written for you as part of the .NET Framework.[3]

> **NOTE** *A* `Dictionary` *is another kind of data structure you use to get at values from keys. Dictionaries are most often implemented as hashtables with some extra code for special purposes such as detection of duplicate values or keys.*

3. The problem is to come up with a good *hashing function* to compute the index of the data from the key as well as dealing with the inevitable problem of two items having the same *hash code* which causes a *collision*. Pretty colorful terminology…

Table 4-4 describes the most useful methods in the `Hashtable` class (as before, you will find the complete list in the on-line help):

Table 4-4. Useful Methods in the `Hashtable` *Class*

NAME	DESCRIPTION
`Add`	Adds the key/value pair to the `Hashtable`.
`Clear`	Removes all the items from the `Hashtable`.
`ContainsKey`	Determines whether the `Hashtable` contains a specific key (case sensitive).
`ContainsValue`	Determines whether the `Hashtable` contains a specific value (case sensitive).
`CopyTo`	Copies the `Hashtable` entries to an array.
`Count`	The number of key/value pairs in the `Hashtable`.
`Item`	Default property. Gets or sets the value associated to with the specified key.
`Keys`	Returns an object you can iterate over (via `For-Each`) to get all the keys in the `Hashtable`.
`Remove`	Removes the value with the specified key from the `Hashtable`.
`Values`	Returns an object you can iterate (via `For-Each`) to get all the keys/values in the `Hashtable`.

CAUTION *The methods in the basic* `Hashtable` *class are case sensitive for string keys and this is not affected by any* `Option Compare Text` *statements in effect. (See Chapter 5 for how to write a case-insensitive hashtable.)*

An example of using the `Hashtable` class is to store the items returned by the `System.Environment` class's nifty `Environment.GetEnvironmentVariables` method. Here is a little program that reports all the environment variables and their values. (You can end the program at any time by closing the console window.) We will explain a couple of subtle points after you have a chance to look at the code.

```
1  Option Strict On
2  Imports System.Environment
3  Module Module1
4    Sub Main()
5      Dim eVariables As Hashtable
6      eVariables = CType(GetEnvironmentVariables(), Hashtable)
7      Console.WriteLine("Press Enter to see the next item")
8      Dim thing As Object
9      For Each thing In eVariables.Keys
10        Console.WriteLine("The environment variable named " _
11        & thing.ToString()& " has value " & eVariables(thing).ToString())
12        Console.ReadLine()
13     Next
14   End Sub
15 End Module
```

First off, Line **6**:

```
eVariables = CType(GetEnvironmentVariables(), Hashtable)
```

takes advantage of the `Imports` statement in order to simplify typing. Next, it uses the `CType` function[4] to convert the return value of the `GetEnvironmentVariables()` method to a hashtable. Lines **8** and **9** use a variable of type `Object` to iterate over the hashtable:

```
Dim thing As Object
For Each thing In eVariables.Keys
```

This is necessary because hashtables, out of the box, store only objects. However, because everything in VB .NET is ultimately an object, you can store environment strings in the `thing` variable. Next, the code iterates over the `Keys` collection to get each key and then uses this key together with the default `Item` property to get the value. Note that line **11** could have also been written:

```
eVariables.Item(thing)
```

Also, line **11** repeatedly uses the `ToString` method, which every class has (see Chapter 5 for more on this important method) to print out a string representation of the key.

4. It is possible this conversion will fail in future versions of .NET.

More on Object Variables

When we use lines of code such as:

```
Dim thing As New Object
Dim aRandomInstance As New Random
```

to declare and instantiate two variables, we create two object variables called `thing` and `aRandomInstance`. The former holds a new instance of `Object` type, and the latter holds an instance of the `Random` class. Note that even with `Option Strict On` (which you always should have set) the following line is acceptable, because everything in VB .NET is ultimately an object:

```
thing = aRandomInstance
```

but this one is not

```
aRandomInstance = thing
```

because not every object is an instance of the `Random` class.

Think of an object variables as (potentially) being a *handle* on an area of memory (although because memory can move around, it will not be a *fixed* area of memory). Object variables are also referred to as *references* or *smart pointers*. In most cases, once you use the equals sign together with `New`, you attach the handle to the area of memory being used for that object. (There are some subtleties involved with what are called *value types*, which we cover later in this chapter.)

> **TIP** *As you will see in the next chapter, every VB .NET type inherits from the* Object *type. This is why you can store anything in VB .NET in a variable declared as an* `Object` *type. You can also use the methods of the* `Object` *class on any object you create in VB .NET. For example, because the* `Object` *class has a* `ToString` *method, every class gives you (depending on the implementer of the class) a more or less useful string representation of the object.* `ToString` *is automatically called in code such as* `Console.WriteLine(foo)`.

Because you have a handle on an area of memory, assignment statements between two object variables give you another handle on the *same* area of memory. It is as if you have a piece of luggage with two handles and thus can lift it up by either handle. Still, if you do not keep in mind that you are grabbing onto the same chunk of memory with two different variable handles, this *will* come back and bite you. More precisely, changes you make to the state of the object using one of the variables that refers to it will also affect the other. In this code, for example:

```
Sub Main()
    Dim A As New ArrayList()
    Dim B As ArrayList
    B = A
    B.Add("foo")
    Console.WriteLine(A.Count)
    Console.ReadLine()
End Sub
```

the `A` array list also contains the string `foo` and so returns a count of 1.

> **NOTE** *If you are familiar with languages that make extensive use of pointers, such as C or Pascal, then you will see that object variables have many of the features of pointers. The key differences are that object variables are automatically dereferenced and arithmetic is not possible on them.*

Because strings and arrays are objects in VB .NET, keep in mind that the variables you used for them are now object variables. As you saw in Chapter 3, this has the useful consequence that you can use the "." to access features built into their associated classes. For example, if `anArray` is a variable storing an array, you can simply use `anArray.Sort()` and it is sorted by an awesomely efficient QuickSort.

> **CAUTION** *Nothing comes without a price, however; there are some hidden gotchas for object variables that are passed into procedures by value, which therefore affect commonplace objects such as arrays. We take this up in the section called "Subtleties of Passing Object Variables by Value," later in this chapter.*

As with earlier versions of VB, you can also use object variables to save typing. For example, this lets you use the shorter `aBox` in code such as this:

```
Dim aBox As System.Windows.Forms.TextBox
aBox = MyForm.TextBox1
```

This shortcut is often combined with the `With` keyword, as in:

```
With aBox
  .AutoSize = False
  .Height = 1000
  .Width = 200
  .Text = "Hello"
End With
```

`Is` *and* `Nothing`

The `Is` operator lets you determine whether two object variables are handles that refer to the same area of memory. For example, the following code gives you `True` twice, because all the object variables after the assignment statement refer to the same area of memory:

```
Dim Object1 As New Object()
Dim Object2 As New Object()
Dim Object3 As New Object()
Object2 = Object1
Object3 = Object2
Console.WriteLine(Object1 Is Object2)
Console.WriteLine(Object1 Is Object3)
```

As in earlier versions of VB, you assign an object variable to `Nothing` in order to remove its "attachment" to an area of memory. When an object variable "is" `Nothing`, there is no object currently assigned to that variable. This is also the initial state of object variables that you declare but have not yet initialized or assigned. You can test to see whether an object variable is `Nothing` using code such as this:

```
If  anObject Is Nothing Then
    ' nothing to work with so assign it
Else
    ' already assigned
End If
```

(See the section on "Garbage Collection and Termination" for more on what assigning object variables to `Nothing` does.)

`TypeName` *and* `TypeOf`

Because variables you declare as `Object` can hold varying things, you obviously need a way of determining the type of object currently stored in an object variable. VB .NET gives you two ways of doing this: the `TypeName` function and the `TypeOf...Is` operator.

The `TypeName` function returns a string that describes the type. For all but basic types, you must first use the `New` operator or `Nothing` is returned. For example, this code displays the sting "Nothing" in a console window:

```
Dim anSBuilder As System.Text.StringBuilder
Console.WriteLine("My type name is " & TypeName(anSBuilder))
```

but this gives the string "StringBuilder" in the console window:

```
Dim anSBuilder As New System.Text.StringBuilder()
Console.WriteLine("My type name is " & TypeName(anSBuilder))
```

Note that `TypeName` does not give the full name of the class, which is why you do not see

```
System.Text.StringBuilder
```

as the result of this call.

If you ask for the `TypeName` of an array that is dimensioned, you get a string followed by empty parentheses. For example:

```
Dim aThing(5) As Integer
Console.WriteLine("My type name is " & TypeName(aThing))
```

returns `Integer()`.

The `TypeName` function is usually the best choice for debugging, but the `TypeOf…Is` operator is usually a better choice in production code, because using it is much faster than doing the string comparison necessary when using `TypeName`. The syntax looks like this:

```
If TypeOf aThing Is System.Text.StringBuilder Then
   ' is a StringBuilder
End If
```

> **CAUTION** *The* `TypeOf...Is` *operator returns True if an object is of a specific type or inherits from this type. So, because everything in .NET inherits from* `Object`*, if you use this operator to determine whether something is an* `Object` *you will always get True, even though it is probably a more sophisticated type than* `Object`*. If you need to find out the exact type of an object variable, use the* `GetType` *method.*

Subtleties of Passing Object Variables by Value

You cannot have programmed in earlier versions of VB (or most any other language) without having a pretty clear idea in your mind about the difference between passing by reference and passing by value into a procedure or function. (Remember that in VB .NET, variables default to passing `ByVal` for every parameter if you do not explicitly use `ByVal`.)

Still, most programmers use the rule of thumb that if you pass by reference, any changes you make inside the procedure live back in the calling code, but if you pass by value, then changes will be forgotten. Unfortunately, when it comes to object variables, what you have always thought or used as a rule of thumb is *no longer unconditionally true.* We strongly suggest you run the following code, which passes an array to a procedure by value. Notice that it *changes* the array in the original code after a "pass by value"!

```
Module Module1
  Sub Main()
    Dim a() As String = {"HELLO", "GOODBYE"}
    Console.WriteLine("Original first item in array is: " & a(0))
    Console.WriteLine("Original second item in array is: " & a(1))
    Yikes(a) 'call sub ByVal!
    Console.WriteLine("After passing by value first item in array now is: " _
    & A(0))
    Console.WriteLine("After passing by value second item in array is: " _
    & A(1))
    Console.ReadLine()
  End Sub
  Sub Yikes(ByVal Foo As String())
    Foo(0) = "GOODBYE"
    Foo(1) = "HELLO"
  End Sub
End Module
```

You should see the ouput shown in Figure 4-7:

```
C:\book to comp\chapter 4\PassByValueProblems\PassByValueProblems\bin\PassByValueProblems.exe
Original first item in array is: HELLO
Original second item in array is: GOODBYE
After passing by value first item in array now is: GOODBYE
After passing by value second item in array is: HELLO
```

Figure 4-7. Output from previous code

The behavior of this program is disconcerting to say the very least: we are passing the array by value and yet changes persist back to the calling code. This would certainly not have happened in earlier versions of VB. Just what is going on here?

The root cause of the strange behavior is that passing by value has always meant that you make a copy of the variable, and when the procedure exits, you lose the copy of the variable. But when you pass an object variable by value to a procedure, you are telling VB .NET to make a copy of a *handle* to an area of memory. And, for the duration of the procedure, you can use that temporary handle to affect that area of memory. At the end of the procedure call, the copy of the original handle is disposed of, but the *changes made to the area of memory persist.*

A good analogy to what goes on when you pass an object variable by value is that you are temporarily attaching a new handle to an old piece of luggage; you can move the luggage via the new handle and even after the new handle is taken off, the luggage is still in its new position.

The one exception to this strange behavior is if the object type is *immutable.* The only common immutable object type you will use on a daily basis is the `String` class. Because immutable means unchangeable, passing by value does what you expect, as the following code demonstrates:

```
Option Strict On
Module Module1
Sub Main()
  Dim A As String = "hello"
  NoProblem(A)
  Console.WriteLine("After passing by value the string is still " & A)
  Console.ReadLine()
End Sub

Sub NoProblem(ByVal Foo As String)
  Foo = "goodbye"
End Sub
End Module
```

NOTE *VB .NET does have what are called value types, such as ordinary numbers, dates, and enumerated types. (You can also build your own value types, as you will see later on in this chapter.) For a value type, passing by value works like traditional passing by value. Only mutable reference types that you pass by value have the unexpected behavior we just showed you.*

Building Your Own Classes

It is now time to start building your own classes. You can choose Project|Add Class, which gives you a way to have the code for the class in a separate class module file, just as in VB6, or you can simply type the code for the class inside a module, such as the startup module that contains the entry point to your console application.

TIP *For testing purposes, we like the idea of tying each class to a* `Sub Main` *that can test it. So, we tend not to put individual classes inside separate class modules but rather place them inside a code module that contains a separate* `Sub Main` *to test them. If you choose to follow us, keep in mind that code defined at the module level is visible even without the module name, wherever the module itself is visible. Thus, these form the equivalent of global variables and functions in VB .NET—and have all the dangers associated with global data.*

VB .NET does not care how many class definitions you put into a file. Class members typically include one or more constructors, properties for finding and affecting the object's state, and methods for actions you want to perform. For example, consider the simplest possible `Employee` class, one that encapsulates only a name and a salary, along with some test code to run it. The class has only two read-only properties to give back the name and salary; it has no methods.

```
Module EmployeeTest1
    Sub Main()
      Dim Tom As New Employee("Tom", 100000)
      Console.WriteLine(Tom.TheName & " salary is " & Tom.Salary)
      Console.ReadLine()
    End Sub
```

```
7     'define the class
8   Public Class Employee
9        Private m_Name As String
10       Private m_Salary As Decimal
11       Public Sub New(ByVal sName As String, ByVal curSalary As Decimal)
12           m_Name = Sname
13           m_Salary = curSalary
14       End Sub
15       Public ReadOnly Property TheName() As String
16           Get
17               Return m_Name
18           End Get
19       End Property
20       Public ReadOnly Property Salary() As Decimal
21           Get
22               Return m_Salary
23           End Get
24       End Property
25  End Class
26 End Module
```

First off, in lines **2–6** we again use a `Sub Main` in a module as the entry point for the compiler. When a `Sub Main` is the startup object (which is the default, but you can also you set in via the Project Properties dialog box), it is responsible for creating the initial object instances. After that, the object created most often goes off and creates other objects in response to messages they receive. This does not happen in this simple program, of course.

The actual object creation is done in line **3,** which is the key line for testing this program. This line constructs a new `Employee` object by passing as parameters into the `New` method the name of the employee and the initial salary. In line **4**, we access two properties, `TheName` and `Salary`, to verify that the employee object was created with the correct initial state.

Lines **8–25** define the `Employee` class. As we said previously, for ease of testing we decided to make this class code part of the original module, although we could have selected Project|Add Class to get a separate file for the class.

Now we will dissect the definition of the class line by line. In line **8**, the keyword `Public` is an *access control attribute* that determines who can create instances of the class. In this case, we are making this class `Public` so, in theory, anyone can use the class once we compile it by adding a reference to the assembly that contains it. (See Chapter 13 for more on assemblies.) To make this class usable only by the code in our project and not by any outside code, we would replace the `Public` access keyword with the `Friend` access keyword.

Lines **9** and **10** define private instance fields in order to maintain the state of the object. As we have said repeatedly, instance variables should always be private. We always use an `m_`or simply an `m` prefix for instance fields in our class and module definitions.

Lines **11–14** define the all-important constructor that we call to create an instance of this class. As is usually the case, the constructor sets the values of the hidden instance fields, depending on the parameters passed into it.

Lines **15–19** and **20–24** define two public read-only properties that let you read the current state of the object. We use the new keyword `Return`, but you can also use the older assignment statement form, using the name of the property:

```
Get
  TheName =  m_Name
End Get
```

Even in this form the syntax for a property procedure is a little different than in VB6: the old `Property Get/Property Set` syntax is gone.

We will now modify the program to change the salary property to be read-write. All we have to do is remove the `ReadOnly` keyword and write:

```
Public Property Salary() As Decimal
    Get
      Return m_Salary
    End Get

    Set(ByVal Value As Decimal)
      m_Salary = Value
    End Set
End Property
```

The key point in this modified code is that you use the reserved word `Value` to pick up the new value of the property. In other words, when you assign to this property using a line like this:

```
Tom.Salary = 125000
```

the value of the `Value` parameter is automatically set to 125000.

> **NOTE** *Although they are unusual, you can use write-only properties as well. Use the keyword* `WriteOnly` *before the name of the property and then use only the* `Set` *part with no* `Get` *part.*

Next, suppose we want to go back to having `Salary` as a read-only property and add a method to raise the salary. A method is simply a function or sub, and we do not need to return a value for this method, so we choose a sub:

```
Public Sub RaiseSalary(ByVal Percent As Decimal)
      m_Salary = (1 + Percent) * m_salary
End Sub
```

Members of a class can be either `Public`, `Private`, or `Friend`. Use the `Private` modifier if that member is a helper member to be used internally only.

> **NOTE** *Interestingly, you can also have private constructors. Under what circumstances would you have a private constructor? Make a constructor private if that particular constructor should be used only within the class.*

> **CAUTION** `Friend` *(accessible only from within the program) apparently is the default access level in VB .NET for classes and their members. As you know, we think leaving the access control modifiers off of your members is a very bad programming practice—especially because the default is not* `Private`.

Instancing and Access Control Attributes

Access control attributes on the class control who can create objects of that type. Roughly speaking, they are the VB .NET equivalent of the `Instancing` property used in VB6, although you often have to use the correct one on the constructors in your class in order to obtain a match to certain VB6 instancing values. Table 4-5 summarizes how the VB6 `Instancing` property matches to an access attribute of the class combined with an access attribute on the constructors of the class.

Table 4-5. Instancing Properties and Access Control Attributes

VB6 INSTANCING	VB .NET VERSION
`Private`	`Private` class
`PublicNotCreatable`	Class is `Public` but declare the constructor as `Friend`
`MultiUse`	Class and constructors should be `Public`
`SingleUse` and `GlobalSingleUse`	No counterparts in VB .NET

Me

Because you are using a class to stamp out object instances, you need a way to refer to the object whose code is being executed. The `Me` reserved word always acts as an object variable that refers to the current instance whose code is running. Use `Me` to be sure that you will be executing code in the current class.

Having said that, we also have to point out that one of the most common, annoying (we think) uses of `Me` is found in code like this:

```
Public Class Point
    Private x As Integer
    Private y As Integer
    Public Sub New(ByVal x As Integer, ByVal y As Integer)
      Me.x = x
      Me.y = y
    End Sub

    ' more code
End Class
```

Here the code uses `Me.x` to distinguish the instance field `x` from the parameter `x` used in the `New` method. We think the `m` prefix convention is a whole lot clearer, but C# uses this kind of code a lot, so you may see it in code you have to maintain.

Overloading Class Members

We can be a little more sophisticated in our approach to the `RaiseSalary` method in our `Employee` class. For example, suppose a raise of up to 10 percent goes through automatically, but anything larger requires a special password. In earlier versions of VB, you would have used an optional parameter to do this. Although you can still do this in VB .NET, your code will be much clearer if you use two different

`RaiseSalary` methods. The idea is to take advantage of VB .NET's support for *overloading* to show that there are two methods involved.

VB .NET makes it pretty easy to indicate that a method is overloaded: you use two methods with the same name and different parameters. However, we strongly recommend using the `Overloads` keyword to tell users of your code that you are deliberately overloading a method. For example, here is code that gives you the two different methods for raising salaries we just described:

```
Public Overloads Sub RaiseSalary(ByVal Percent As Decimal)
  If Percent > 0.1 Then
    'not allowed
    Console.WriteLine("MUST HAVE PASSWORD TO RAISE SALARY MORE THAN 10%!!!!")
  Else
    m_Salary = (1 + Percent) * m_salary
  End If
  End Sub
  Public Overloads Sub RaiseSalary(ByVal Percent As Decimal, _
    ByVal Password As String)
  If Password = "special" Then
    m_Salary = (1 + Percent) * m_Salary
  End If
End Sub
```

> **CAUTION** *You can overload members of a class only based on their parameters; you cannot overload a member based on its return value type or access level.*

Here is the code for our sample `Employee` class that overloads the `RaiseSalary` method, along with some code to test it. (Note that we use a constant for the 10 percent limit instead of a hard-coded "magic number.")

```
Option Strict On
Module Module1
  Sub Main()
    Dim Tom As New Employee("Tom", 100000)
    Console.WriteLine(Tom.TheName & "  has salary " & Tom.Salary)
    Tom.RaiseSalary(0.2D) 'D necessary for decimal
    Console.WriteLine(Tom.TheName & " still has salary " & Tom.Salary)
    Console.WriteLine()
```

```
    Dim Sally As New Employee("Sally", 150000)
    Console.WriteLine(Sally.TheName & " has salary " & Sally.Salary)
    Sally.RaiseSalary(0.2D, "special") 'D necessary for decimal
    Console.WriteLine(Sally.TheName & " has salary " & Sally.Salary)
    Console.WriteLine()
    Console.WriteLine("Please press the Enter key")
    Console.ReadLine()
  End Sub
End Module

Public Class Employee
  Private m_Name As String
  Private m_Salary As Decimal
  Private Const LIMIT As Decimal = 0.1D
  Public Sub New(ByVal theName As String, ByVal curSalary As Decimal)
    m_Name = thename
    m_Salary = curSalary
  End Sub
  ReadOnly Property TheName() As String
    Get
      Return m_Name
    End Get
  End Property
  ReadOnly Property Salary() As Decimal
    Get
      Return m_Salary
    End Get
  End Property
  Public Overloads Sub RaiseSalary(ByVal Percent As Decimal)
    If Percent > LIMIT Then
      'not allowed
      Console.WriteLine("MUST HAVE PASSWORD TO RAISE SALARY MORE THAN LIMIT!!!!")
    Else
      m_Salary = (1 + Percent) * m_salary
    End If
  End Sub
  Public Overloads Sub RaiseSalary(ByVal Percent As Decimal, _
    ByVal Password As String)
    If Password = "special" Then
      m_Salary = (1 + Percent) * m_Salary
    End If
  End Sub
End Class
```

More on Constructors

If you do not supply a constructor to your class, VB .NET automatically supplies one that takes no arguments. This has the effect of initializing all instance fields to their default values. These automatically created constructors are called *default* or *no-arg* (because they have no arguments) constructors. If you create even one constructor of your own, VB .NET will not create a default no-arg constructor for you.

Nothing prevents you from having constructors with different access levels in your class. For example, you can have a `Friend` constructor that is a bit dangerous to use and a `Public` constructor that is safe. Of course, to do this they would have to have a different set of parameters, because it is the parameter list and not the access modifiers that VB .NET users to distinguish among methods.

You can overload constructors, too, but you cannot use the `Overloads` keyword here. For example, here is the beginning of a modified version of the `Employee` class that allows a nickname in an alternative version of the constructor:

```
Public Class Employee
  Private m_Name As String
  Private m_NickName As String
  Private m_Salary As Decimal
  Public Sub New(ByVal sName As String, ByVal curSalary As Decimal)
    m_Name = sName
    m_Salary = curSalary
  End Sub
  Public Sub New(ByVal theName As String, ByVal nickName As String, _
    ByVal curSalary As Decimal)
    m_Name = theName
    m_NickName = nickName
    m_Salary = curSalary
  End Sub
```

The compiler chooses the nickname version only when you give it two string parameters and a salary; otherwise, it picks the first constructor when you give it a single string and a salary.

Overloading constructors leads to code duplication. For example, in the code shown above we have the same assignments to `m_Name` and `m_Salary` in both versions of the constructor. VB .NET lets you use a shorthand in this case: you use `MyClass.New` to call another constructor in the class.[5] For example:

5. As we write this, you can also use the reserved word `Me`, but `MyClass` seems like a better bet.

```
Public Sub New(ByVal sName As String, ByVal curSalary As Decimal)
    m_Name = Sname
    m_Salary = curSalary
  End Sub
  Public Sub New(ByVal sName As String, ByVal nickName As String, _
    ByVal curSalary As Decimal)
    MyClass.New(sName, curSalary)
    m_NickName = nickName
End Sub
```

Note that when you use `MyClass.New` in this way to call another constructor in the class, the order of the constructors inside your code is irrelevant. VB .NET matches up the correct constructor by the parameters you use, not by any ordering.

CAUTION `MyClass` *is a keyword, not a real object. You cannot assign* `MyClass` *to a variable, pass it to a procedure, or use it in with the* `Is` *operator. Instead, use the keyword* `Me`*, which gives you a way to refer to the specific object whose code is being executed.*

More on Properties

One difference between the way properties work in VB6 and VB .NET is that the `Get` and `Set` must have same access level. You are not allowed to have a `Public Get` and a `Private Set` anymore.

TIP *It is easy to work around this by adding a bit of code to effectively make the* `Set` *private, such as by making the property* `Public Read Only` *while having another internal private property that is private for the* `Set`.

Another difference is that in VB6 you could not change a property in a procedure even if you passed it `ByRef`. In VB .NET, you can change properties passed `ByRef`.

The really big change, however, is how default properties work. Earlier versions of VB had the seemingly neat idea of a default property. In practice, this frequently led to really buggy code. For example, what does this next line mean?

```
Me.Text1 = Text2
```

As experienced users of VB learned by tracking down the bugs that lines of code such as this caused, this line would assign the text property of the textbox named `Text1` to the value of the (presumed) variable `Text2`. Not only did default properties cause problems in code, they also required you to use the `Set` keyword to make object assignments, because there had to be a way to distinguish object assignments from property assignments. VB .NET eliminates the problematic uses of default properties and allows them only where they make sense—where parameters are involved. The idea is that if `aTable` is a hashtable, it is nice to be able to write:

```
aTable("theKey")
```

and this is only possible if `Item` is the default property of the `HashTable` class. You add a default property to a class by using the `Default` keyword. You can only do this for a property that takes at least one parameter. If you overload the potential default property, then all the overloaded versions must be marked as `Default`. The most common use of default properties is when your object has a property whose value is returned as an array or other object that can hold multiple values such as a hashtable. For example, suppose you have a class called `Sales` and a property called `InYear` that takes a year and returns a value. The class might look like this:

```
Public Class Sales
    Private m_Sales() As Decimal = {100, 200, 300}
    Default Public Property InYear(ByVal theYear As Integer) As Decimal
      Get
        Return m_Sales(theYear)
      End Get

      Set(ByVal Value As Decimal)
        m_Sales(theYear) = Value
      End Set
    End Property
 'lots more code
End Class
```

Now you can write:

```
Dim ourSales As New Sales()
Console.WriteLine(ourSales(1))
```

instead of:

```
Dim ourSales As New Sales()
Console.WriteLine(ourSales.InYear(1))
```

Or you can use:

```
ourSales (2) = 3000
```

instead of:

```
ourSales.InYear(2) = 3000
```

> **NOTE** *Because* `Set` *is no longer needed, the designers of VB .NET decided to use the* `Set` *keyword in the syntax for property procedures.*

Encapsulation and Properties

If you use public instance fields in VB .NET, they will seem to behave like properties. If you have a public instance field in a class `A` called `evil`, people can say `A.evil` and nobody will notice that you implemented the property as a public variable. And it is true that sometimes it may seem a lot of work to provide both a `Get` and a `Set` instead of simply having a public instance field. But:

- Do not succumb to the temptation. Encapsulation is not to be broken lightly. (Actually, it should never be broken at all!)

However, if you are not careful you can break encapsulation inadvertently in other ways. For example, you will break encapsulation if you do not watch the return values of your properties. How? One way is that, if you have a mutable object variable as an instance field (such as an array), returning it as the value of a property breaks encapsulation because others can change the state of the instance field using the object variable that you returned. Instead, return a *clone* of it (see Chapter 5 for more on cloning objects). In sum:

- Do not return mutable objects that are instance fields as properties.

Scope of Variables

Variables inside a class (such as private instance fields) that are declared outside member functions are visible to all the members of the class. Variables declared in a member function are local to that member function.

CAUTION *Variables defined at the module level are visible to all classes defined in the module and to any code that has access to that module's code.*

Thus, changes you make to these kinds of variables persist. For example:

```
Module Module1
  Dim aGlobal As Integer = 37
    Sub Main()
    Dim anA As New A()
    Dim aB As New B()
    Console.ReadLine()
    End Sub

  Public Class A
    Sub New()
      aGlobal = aGlobal + 17
      Console.WriteLine(aGlobal)
    End Sub
  End Class
  Public Class B
    Sub New()
      Console.WriteLine(aGlobal)
    End Sub
  End Class
End Module
```

Here, the integer variable `aGlobal` is defined at the module level, which means that changes made to `aGlobal` in the `A` class persist in the `B` class. We think using module-level variables is a bad idea—communication between classes should only be carried out by messages!

TIP *In earlier versions of VB, using global variables for shared class data was standard operating procedure. VB .NET no longer requires this somewhat dangerous practice. See the section on shared data in this chapter for more on this.*

Nested Classes

VB .NET programmers will occasionally want to nest class definitions. You do this whenever you want to tightly couple two classes so that the "inner" class essentially belongs to the outer class. *Nested classes* are usually helper classes whose code is not relevant to the user of the outer class. A good rule of thumb is that, if when looking at the outer class you usually have collapsed the code for the inner class, an inner class works well. Of course, whenever you use an inner class, encapsulation is slightly broken—the inner class can refer to private members of the outer class (but not vice versa). If this is by design, then there is really nothing wrong with it, because the inner class is merely a specialized member of the outer class.

> **CAUTION** *VB .NET does not allow you to increase the visibility of a nested class via a member function. For example, a public member of an outer class cannot return an instance of a private or friend nested class.*

Linked Lists: An Example of Nested Classes at Work

Data structures are a common use of nested classes. For example, a linked list is a data structure that is used when you need a chain of links, so that it is easy to find the next link from a given link, but you will always look sequentially starting from a specific link. Linked lists are obvious candidates for coding using nested classes because the code for the class that defines the link objects is irrelevant to the users of the `LinkedList` class, and `Link` objects have no real independent existence apart from the `LinkedList` object that contains them. (A single link of a chain is not a chain…)

Here is some code for a very basic linked list class. We will explain the pieces after you have a chance to look it over. Please note there is one important line in the following code (line 49) that we have bolded; this line shows off a very unexpected feature of object-oriented programming that we will soon explain!

```
1  Option Strict On
2  Module Module1
3    Sub Main()
4      Dim aLinkedList As New LinkedList("first link")
5      Dim aALink As LinkedList.Link
6      aLink = aLinkedList.MakeLink(aLinkedList.GetFirstLink, "second link")
7      aLink = aLinkedList.MakeLink(aLink, "third link")
8      Console.WriteLine(aLinkedList.GetFirstLink.MyData)
9      aLink = aLinkedList.GetNextLink(aLinkedList.GetFirstLink)
```

```
    Console.WriteLine(aLink.MyData)
    Console.WriteLine(aLink.NextLink.MyData)
    Console.ReadLine()
  End Sub
  Public Class LinkedList
    Private m_CurrentLink As Link
    Private m_FirstLink As Link
    Sub New(ByVal theData As String)
      m_CurrentLink = New Link(theData)
      m_FirstLink = m_CurrentLink
    End Sub
    Public Function MakeLink(ByVal currentLink As Link, ByVal _
theData As String) As Link
      m_CurrentLink = New Link(currentLink, theData)
      Return m_CurrentLink
    End Function
    Public ReadOnly Property GetNextLink(ByVal aLink As Link) _
As Link
      Get
        Return aLink.NextLink()
      End Get
    End Property
    Public ReadOnly Property GetCurrentLink() As Link
      Get
        Return m_CurrentLink
      End Get
    End Property
    Public ReadOnly Property GetFirstLink() As Link
      Get
        Return m_FirstLink
      End Get
    End Property

    'nested class for link objects
    Friend Class Link
      Private m_MyData As String
      Private m_NextLink As Link
      Friend Sub New(ByVal myParent As Link, ByVal theData As String)
        m_MyData = theData
        myParent.m_NextLink = Me
      End Sub
      Friend Sub New(ByVal theData As String)
        m_MyData = theData
      End Sub
```

```
54          Friend ReadOnly Property MyData() As String
55            Get
56              Return m_MyData
57            End Get
58          End Property
59          Friend ReadOnly Property NextLink() As Link
60            Get
61              Return m_NextLink
62            End Get
63          End Property
64        End Class
65      End Class
66    End Module
```

In line **4** we create the new linked list. In line **5** we make an object variable of `Link` type. Note that because this class is nested inside the `LinkedList`, we must use the dot notation to specify its "full name" as `LinkedList.Link`. Lines **6–12** are just some code for testing.

Lines **17–20** define the constructor of the `LinkedList` class, which calls the second constructor (lines **51–53**) in the `Link` class. Because these were declared with the `Friend` access modifier, the outer `LinkedList` class has access to it. If we made it `Private`, the outer class could not use it.

Another interesting point is how, in the first constructor of the `Link` class (lines **47–50**), we insure that the newly created link has a reference to the previous chain. We do that using the `Me` keyword in line **49** which we bolded because what is happening here is so important! This line:

```
myParent.m_NextLink = Me
```

may seem impossible, because we are accessing a private instance field of the `myParent` link class. Well, it is obviously not impossible, because this code runs. You *must* keep in mind that:

- An instance of a class always has access to the private instance fields of other objects of the same class.

> **NOTE** *You do not have to use this somewhat subtle feature of classes in VB .NET to write this kind of class. You could instead add a member to the* `Link` *class that allows you to set the next link. Which you choose to do is ultimately a matter of programming style. However, because code that accesses a private member (such as the previous example) can bite you if you are not aware of the possibility, we chose to illustrate the more subtle approach here.*

Shared Data and Shared Members Inside Classes

We will now go back to our `Employee` class. Imagine that you need to assign individual employees consecutive ID numbers. In the old days of VB, you used a global variable for this, which:

- Violated encapsulation
- Made it possible for someone to inadvertently change the ID number

It would have been better if the ID number was incremented only when you created a new employee object.

VB .NET finally adds the ability to do this. The idea is: you have data within a class that is accessible by all instances of the class, but only accessible to the outside world if you allow it (for example, through a property). Of course, you would never make an instance field public….)

These special instance fields are called *shared instance fields* and are ideal for use in situations such as our employee ID number. You also can have shared members, such as properties, functions, and procedures. The downside is that shared members cannot access the nonshared instance fields or nonshared members of the class. In other words, they only access shared information. The reason for this limitation is that shared data exists even before an object is created, so it would not make sense to allow shared members to have access to individual objects.

Here are the key lines in a modified version of our employee class that use shared data to implement an employee ID. Notice that there is a `Private` shared integer variable that:

- Starts out as equal to 1
- Has a read-only property to get back its current value
- Is changed (incremented) only in the constructor of the class

Taken together, this means that you never have an employee #0 and the only way you only can get a new ID number is when you make a new employee object—which is exactly what you want.

```
Public Class Employee
  Private m_Name As String
  Private m_Salary As Decimal
  Private Shared m_EmployeeID As Integer = 1
  Public Sub New(ByVal theName As String, ByVal curSalary As Decimal)
    m_Name = thename
    m_Salary = curSalary
    m_EmployeeID = m_EmployeeID + 1
  End Sub

  ReadOnly Property EmployeeId() As Integer
    Get
      EmployeeId = m_EmployeeID
    End Get
  End Property
End Class
```

Here is the full code for an employee class with a shared instance field that includes a little test routine:

```
Option Strict On
Module Module1
  Sub Main()
    Dim Tom As New Employee("Tom", 100000)
      System.Console.WriteLine(Tom.TheName & " is employee# " & _
    Tom.EmployeeID & " with salary " & Tom.Salary())
    Dim Sally As New Employee("Sally", 150000)
    System.Console.WriteLine(Sally.TheName & " is employee# " & _
      Sally.EmployeeID & " with salary " & Sally.Salary())
    System.Console.WriteLine("Please press the Enter key")
    System.Console.Read()
  End Sub
End Module

Public Class Employee
  Private m_Name As String
  Private m_Salary As Decimal
  Private Shared m_EmployeeID As Integer = 1
  Public Sub New(ByVal theName As String, ByVal curSalary As Decimal)
    m_Name = thename
    m_Salary = curSalary
    m_EmployeeID = m_EmployeeID + 1
  End Sub
```

```
  ReadOnly Property EmployeeId() As Integer
    Get
      EmployeeId = m_EmployeeID
    End Get
  End Property
  ReadOnly Property TheName() As String
    Get
      TheName = m_Name
    End Get
  End Property
  ReadOnly Property Salary() As Decimal
    Get
      Salary = m_Salary
    End Get
  End Property
End Class
```

> **CAUTION** *Do not confuse* shared *data with* static *data. For shared data, there is one copy for all instances of the class, so shared data implicitly has a kind of global scope as far as instances of the class are concerned. Static variables are simply variables whose state is remembered when a member is used again. You can have static data in both shared members and nonshared members of a class.*

Constants in classes are accessed in the same way that shared instance field members are, but they use the `Const` keyword instead of the `Shared` keyword. Constants can be public, of course, without violating encapsulation.

Shared Members

Private shared instance fields together with read-only properties are very useful, but that does not exhaust the uses of the new `Shared` keyword. You can also have shared members that belong to the class. As you have seen in the `Math` class, you can access this kind of shared functionality either with the name of the class or an object variable that refers to an instance of the class. For example, suppose our employee class has a shared member called `CalculateFICA`[6] with code that depends on two public constants:

---

6. FICA is the official name for Social Security. See `http://www.irs.ustreas.gov/tax_edu/faq/faq-kw79.html`

```
Public Const FICA_LIMIT As Integer = 76200
Public Const FICA_PERCENTAGE As Decimal = 0.062D
```

and code for the function like this:

```
Public Shared Function CalculateFICA(ByVal aSalary As Decimal) As Decimal
    If aSalary > FICA_LIMIT Then
      Return FICA_LIMIT * FICA_PERCENTAGE
    Else
      Return aSalary * FICA_PERCENTAGE
    End If
End Function
```

Then you can use the shared member without creating an instance of the `Employee` class using the class name alone. For example:

```
System.Console.WriteLine(Employee.CalculateFICA(100000))
```

Or you could use it with a specific `Employee` instance:

```
System.Console.WriteLine(Tom.CalculateFICA(Tom.GetSalary())
```

You can also have a shared *constructor* by marking a `New` method with the keyword `Shared`. Shared constructors:

- Do not use the `Public` or `Private` keyword.
- Cannot take parameters.
- Can only access or effect shared instance fields. You would normally use a shared constructor only to initialize certain shared data. The code in a shared constructor runs the first time you instantiate an object from this class. The shared constructor runs before any other constructors are called.

The Object Life Cycle

As you have seen, you create an instance of a class by using the `New` operator, which then calls the correct `New` constructor method in the definition of the class (possibly running a shared constructor first if you supplied one). The match with the correct version of `New` inside your class is made by matching up the parameter list. The `New` method corresponds to the old `Class_Initialize` event in earlier versions of VB.

You do not always want to have public constructors in your classes. You can even have a situation where all the constructors are private and the only way to create object instances is through a shared method. In general, make a constructor private if:

- **Only the class itself should have access to it.** For example, there may be one public constructor which calls a private constructor under special conditions, depending on the parameters it was passed.

or:

- **There is no reason to create instances of your class.** For example, a class with only shared members should have only private constructors, because there is no reason to create an object of that type. In this situation, you must supply at least one private constructor or VB .NET will supply a public no-arg constructor for you.

or:

- **Where using a shared method to call the private constructor allows you to validate the creation of the instance.** This is especially useful if the object is costly to create in terms of time and resources and you want to make sure it is created only under special circumstances.

Finally, note that once you create an object using `New`, you cannot use `New` again to change the state of the object. For example:

```
Dim Tom As New Employee("Tom", 100000)
Tom = New Employee("Tom", 125000)
```

actually creates two separate `Employee` objects and the first `Tom` is lost after the second assignment. Whether this fits with what you want to do depends on the specific situation. For example, if you were using a shared `EmployeeID` variable to assign ID numbers, the second line would give a different ID number to the second `Tom` than was originally assigned to him. In any case, you certainly cannot do this:

```
Dim Tom As New Employee("Tom", 100000)
Dim Tom As New Employee("Tom", 125000)
```

If you do, you will see this error message in the Build window:

```
The local variable 'Tom' is defined multiple times in the same method.
```

Object Death

One metaphor for object death in VB .NET is that, in a way, objects do not die a natural death; they sort of fade away over time. More precisely, the big change from earlier versions of VB is that you cannot explicitly reclaim the memory used for an object. The built-in garbage collector will (eventually) notice areas of memory that are no longer referred to and automatically reclaim them. Automatic garbage collection leads to some big changes in programming VB .NET. In particular:

- The garbage collection process should be regarded as totally and completely automatic and totally and completely out of your control.

Although you certainly can force a garbage collection to occur—using the `System.GC.Collect()` method—it simply is not a good .NET programming practice to do so. We recommend that you rely on the automatic garbage collection scheme.

Recall that in earlier versions of VB you had a `Terminate` event inside each class. This event was *guaranteed* to be called when the number of references to it fell to 0. (This process is called *deterministic finalization* in OOP speak.) VB .NET, fortunately or unfortunately, only has *nondeterministic finalization*, which means that you cannot count on the equivalent of a `Terminate` event to run at a specific time. And, in fact, you should not count on anything like a `Terminate` event to run at all!

> **NOTE** *Although some people regard* `Finalize` *as a special method that you can add to your classes as the equivalent of the* `Terminate` *event, this is a false analogy. The* `Finalize` *method merely includes code that you want to run when your object's memory is garbage-collected. However, because you have no control over when this happens, we strongly suggest only using them to repeat code (such as in a* `Dispose` *method that the user of the class should explicitly call. We take up* `Dispose` *methods next.)*

You are probably thinking, "But I used the `Terminate` event all the time for cleanup code, so where do I do my cleanup now?" The answer is a very strong convention in .NET programming:

- If your class has to release resources other than pure memory (such as a database connections, graphics contexts, or file handles or any unmanaged resources), it *must* contain a method called `Dispose` that other code can call.

We will have a lot more to say about `Dispose` methods Chapter 5, when we cover the `IDisposable` interface. For now, we point out that *any* GUI application, even one as simple as the one you saw way back in Chapter 1, is the kind of code that needs a `Dispose` method. This is because graphics programs grab "graphics contexts" that eventually need to be released in order to reclaim those resources. (Graphics contexts are not areas of memory, so the automatic garbage-collection process cannot help you.) This is why the automatically generated code you saw in Chapter 1 included a call to `Dispose`. Nondeterministic finalization is one of the more controversial aspects of .NET, but automatic garbage collection is part of .NET and it would have been impossible for VB .NET to keep its earlier, deterministic method of handling memory and remain .NET-compliant. In any case, the method used in earlier versions of VB (called reference counting) had problems with memory leaks caused by circular references. (This occurs when an object variable `A` points to an object variable `B`, and vice versa as you can see in Figure 4-8.)

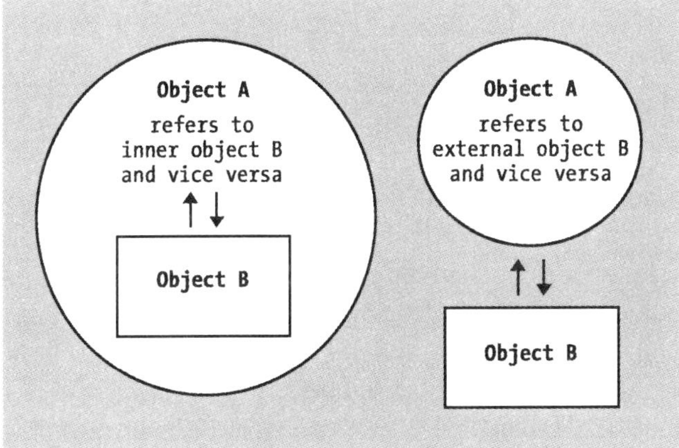

Figure 4-8. Two kinds of circular references

> **NOTE** *Languages such as Java have clearly shown that the advantages you gain from automatic garbage collection are worth the small changes in programming style required to counterbalance the lack of deterministic finalization.*

Value Types

Traditionally, fully object-oriented languages have had a problem with things such as ordinary integers. The problem is that, in a fully object-oriented language, you want everything to be an object. But creating an object requires a bit of time for bookkeeping, such as for creating the area of memory used for the object. Similarly, sending an "add" message is generally going to be slower than using arithmetic operators and so on. (In languages with automatic garbage collection, you also pay a small price for the automatic garbage collection scheme that cleans up after objects.)

The early object-oriented languages went the purist route. Smalltalk, for instance, treated everything as an object. This tended to make these kind of languages slower than languages that maintained the value/object distinction. Because of performance issues, languages such as Java treat numbers differently from objects. The trouble with that approach is that it leads to ugly code, because you have to distinguish code that works with objects from code that works with values. The result is that you need to do things like wrap integer values in an `Integer` object in order to mix and match integers and objects. In Java, for example, to put a bunch of values in the equivalent of an array list, you have to use code that would look something like:

```
anArrayList.Add(Integer(5));
```

where you "wrap" the value 5 into an `Integer` object. This leads to both ugly *and* slower performing code.

The .NET Framework combines the best of both worlds. It gives you the ability to treat integers as ordinary integers when performance is important, and it automatically treats values as objects when this is needed. This is why you can "dot" an ordinary literal value or put it inside a hashtable without any extra work. This magic process is called *automatic boxing* and *unboxing* of value types.

The significance of this to programmers is that, although everything in VB .NET is ultimately an object, not every kind of object variable is a handle to an area of memory and needs to be created with the `New` operator. Of course, nothing comes for free: a programmer has to be alert to the distinction between value types and reference types. One obvious difference is that you do not have to use `New` to create a new instance of a value type. You do not have to (in fact, you cannot) write:

```
Dim a as New Integer(5)
```

The more serious distinction comes when passing variables into procedures by value. As you have seen, when you pass a mutable object by value into a procedure, the procedure *can* change the state of the object. When you pass a value type by value into a procedure, it works in the traditional manner—all changes are discarded when the procedure ends. (This is sometimes called *value semantics* versus *reference semantics*.)

All numeric types in VB .NET are value types, as are types such as dates. As you will see in a moment, you can create your own value types whenever you need lightweight objects for performance reasons or want objects that have value semantics.

TIP *You can find out whether an object has value semantics or reference semantics by passing a variable of that type to the following function:*[7]

```
Function IsValueType(ByVal foo As Object) As Boolean
    If TypeOf (foo) Is System.ValueType Then
      Return True
    Else
      Return False
    End If
End Function
```

For value type objects, the `equals` operator should always return true if the value objects have the same value. The syntax is:

```
a.equals(b)
```

Keep in mind that this generally is not true for reference types. For example, two arrays can have the same values but may not be equal.

In VB .NET you can build two types of value types, *enums* and *structures* (some people call these *structs*, after the term used for them in C#). We take up enums first and then move on to structures, which are true lightweight objects.

Enums

Enums are useful when you want to have a series of named constants. Use an enum type as shorthand for a bunch of related integral values. You create enums using the `Enum-End Enum` pair of keywords together with an access modifier. Enums can contain only integral types such as Integer or Long (they cannot contain Char types). For example, the following code creates a public enum named `BonusStructure`:

```
Public Enum BonusStructure
  None = 0
  FirstLevel = 1
  SecondLevel = 2
End Enum
```

7. We think that you cannot use `TypeOf` directly with value types, as in `If TypeOf (a) Is System.ValueType Then` This is bad, but since it is documented, we suppose it is not a bug.

You can then declare a variable of type `BonusStructure` anywhere:

```
Dim bonusLevel As BonusStructure
```

(As with any value type, you do not need to use the `New` operator with an enum.)

> **NOTE** *If you leave off the explicit values for an enum, .NET starts with zero and increases them by one. Similarly, if you only set the first value, then the other values will come from adding one to the previous value.*

Once you have the enum type in your project, you can write code like this:

```
Bonus = Tom.Sales* bonusLevel.SecondLevel
```

Because values in enum types are implicitly shared, you can also use the name of the `Enum` rather than a variable of that type:

```
Public Function CalculateBonus(ByVal theSales As Decimal) As Decimal
   Return theSales * BonusStructure.SecondLevel
End Function
```

Traditionally, one problem with enums has been the lack of a way to get the string representation of the enum from the value, making debugging difficult. The `Enum` class, which all the enums you create inherit from, has some very useful members that let you get back this kind of information. For example, this code returns the string "FirstLevel" as its value:

```
BonusStructure.GetName(bonusLevel.GetType, 1)
```

and this fragment prints out all the names used in the enum:

```
Dim enumNames As String(), s As String
enumNames = BonusStructure.GetNames(bonusLevel.GetType)
For Each s In enumNames
   System.Console.WriteLine(s)
Next
```

Structure Types

Some people think of VB .NET structures as the equivalent of user-defined types in earlier versions of VB or most other programming languages. VB .NET structures certainly can be used like user-defined types, but you need not limit them to such uses. Code in a structure can have everything a traditional class has, including constructors and public, private, or friend members. The only differences from ordinary class-based objects is that structure-based objects have value semantics. Recall that this means:

- Pass by value cannot change the state of a variable.
- They need not be created using the `New` operator, and therefore always have a default value obtained by taking the default values of their instance fields.
- They have an `Equals` method that returns true if two structs have the same internal data. (You use the `Equals` method in the form `A.Equals(B)`.)

CAUTION *With the current version of VB .NET, you cannot use the "=" sign to test for equality between two instances of a structure type. Use the* `Equals` *method instead.*

Note that by default the `Equals` *method does a so-called shallow compare—more on what this means in the "Cloning" section of Chapter 5. You can redefine the* `Equals` *method in the definition of your Structures if you want your version to have some special behavior.*

Some people overuse structures because they are described as lightweight objects, figuring they will always be more efficient to use than objects coming from ordinary classes. The problem with this approach is that you do not always want two objects to be the same if they have the same state, which is inevitable with structures. In particular, people who use your code *expect* structures (value types) to be analogous to the built-in value types such as integers and doubles.

NOTE *All of the built-in types such as Integer, Long, and so on are implemented in the .NET Framework as structures.*

Building a Structure Type

You declare a structure type by starting with an access modifier and the `Structure` keyword:

```
Public Structure NameOfStructure
'code for the structure

End Structure
```

Every member of a structure must have an access modifier such as `Public` or `Private`. Using the `Dim` statement alone outside of functions and procedures gives that instance variable public access. Here is how a structure to implement complex numbers might start out:

```
Public Structure ComplexNumber
    Private m_real As Double
    Private m_complex As Double
    Public Property real() As Double
      Get
        Return m_real
      End Get
      Set(ByVal Value As Double)
        m_real = Value
      End Set
    End Property
    Public Property complex() As Double
      Get
        Return m_complex
      End Get
      Set(ByVal Value As Double)
        m_complex = Value
      End Set
    End Property
    Public Sub New(ByVal x As Double, ByVal y As Double)
      real = x
      complex = y
    End Sub
```

```
    Public Function Add(ByVal z1 As ComplexNumber) As ComplexNumber
      Dim z As ComplexNumber
      z.real = Me.real + z1.real
      z.complex = Me.complex + z1.complex
      Return z
    End Function
    'much more code
End Structure
```

Notice how we are returning a structure as the value of the `Add` function.

By the way, you cannot initialize an instance field in a structure:

```
Private m_real As Double = 0 'error
```

We confess that one other difference between structures and reference objects is that having public instance fields instead of `Get-Set` properties is not all that uncommon and is not necessarily as poor a programming practice as it is for objects. The reason is that the instance fields are often just values. For example, rewriting the complex numbers structure just shown to have public instance fields called `Real` and `Imaginary` is probably not going to cause problems.

You can build up a structure via a call to `New` or by directly assigning the properties that set the instance fields. You access the values of an item within a structure in the same way you access a property on an object. For example, you could use the complex number structure in code such as this:

```
Sub Main()
    Dim Z1 As New ComplexNumber(2.3, 2.4)
    Dim Z2, Z3 As ComplexNumber
    Z2.real = 1.3
    Z2.complex = 1.4
    Z3 = Z1.Add(Z2)
    Console.WriteLine(Z3.real)
    Console.ReadLine()
End Sub
```

NOTE *The current version of VB .NET does not allow giving operators like "+" new meaning (operator overloading in the jargon). This is why we created an* `Add` *method instead of giving a new definition to "+" when used with complex numbers. VB .NET will eventually allow operator overloading, but as of now, you will need to use C# if you want to use a "+" sign in your complex number package for the addition of two complex numbers.*

You can put any VB .NET object inside a structure type. Structures can contain other structures, enums, or objects such as arrays. For example, this allows you to build a matrix handling package in VB .NET. The code for this kind of structure might start out like this:

```
Public Structure Matrix
    Private TheData( , ) As Double
  'more code
  End Structure
```

Namespaces for Classes You Create

You can place any class, enum, structure, or module in a namespace. Of course, you cannot create an instance of a module—only instances of the classes defined in the module. In the Project Properties dialog box, as shown in Figure 4-9, you see a space for the assembly name and also for the root namespace.

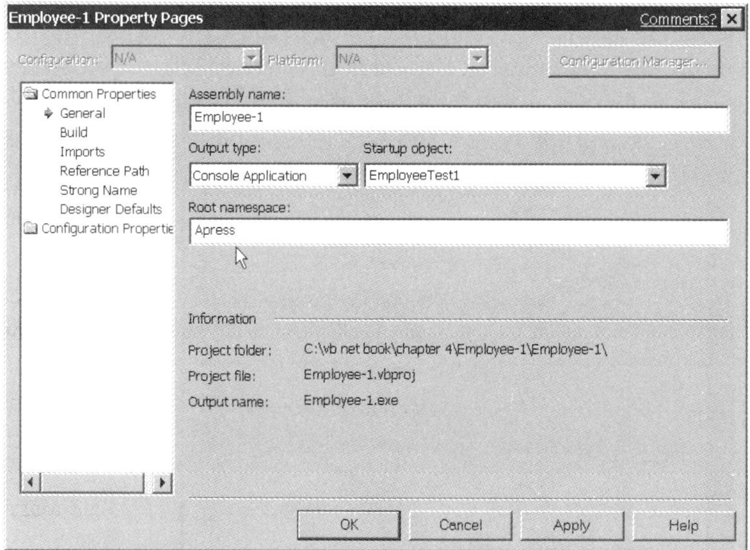

Figure 4-9. Project properties for namespaces

Notice in Figure 4-9 that we made the root namespace *Apress*. We then can give a namespace declaration in our code that uses as many "." as we want, to make clear the hierarchy of our code. For example, we might prefix the definition of a class with:

```
Namespace Cornell.Morrison.VB.NET.CH4
  Module Module1
    Sub Main()
      Console.WriteLine("test code goes here")
    End Sub

    Public Class EmployeeExample1
      'code
    End Class

  End Module
End Namespace
```

Then, our `Employee` class would have the full name:

```
Apress.Cornell.Morrison.VB.NET.CH4.EmployeeExample1
```

> **NOTE** *Unlike Java packages, namespaces in .NET are not tied to any special directory structure. You can have two classes in the same namespace, even though they exist in different files in different directories.*

The Class View Window

Now that you know how to build your own classes, you will want to take better advantage of the Class View window, which lets you examine the members of any classes in your solution in a rather nifty hierarchical tree view. It is great for navigating around the code in your solution: double-clicking on a member in the Class View window takes you directly to the code for that member. To open the Class View window, either press Ctrl+Shift+C or click Class View on the View menu. Figure 4-10 shows the window for one of the versions of our `Employee` class.

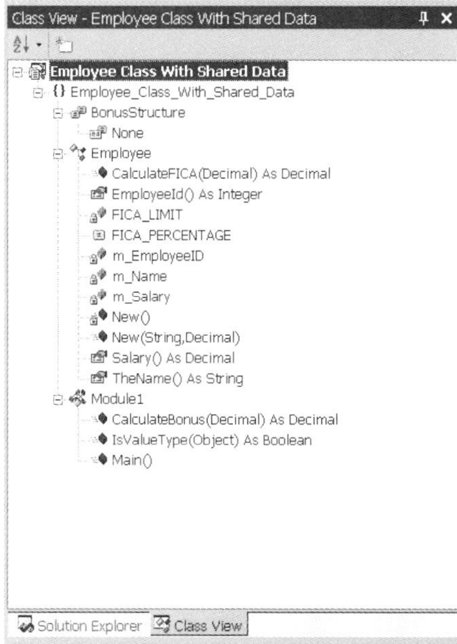

Figure 4-10. Class View window for an `Employee` *class*

You can use the New Folder button to create a new folder, but the most common use of the Class View window is to get a dropdown list with four ways to sort the information presented in the window (click on the first icon, whose tooltip is "Class View Sort By Type"):

- **Sort Alphabetically**: Classes and members are listed alphabetically (a–z).
- **Sort By Type**: Classes and members are listed by type. This lets you see all properties together, for example, such as for base classes, interfaces, methods, and so forth, by the orders listed in the next two bullets.
- **Sort By Access**: Classes and members are listed by their access level.
- **Group By Type**: Classes and members are grouped by type in different tree nodes. For example, all properties are displayed in a node called Properties and all fields are displayed together in a node called Fields.

Debugging Object-Based Programs

The first step in debugging an object-based program is to look at the state of the object variables used in your program to see if their state is different than what you expect. This is why the debugging tools in the VS IDE, such as the Watch and Locals windows, let you drill down into the private instance fields inside your objects. As an example of using these debugging tools, suppose we want to modify our linked list class to be a doubly linked list. This simply means that we have a way of going backward and forward from a given link instead of only going forward. Here is some buggy code for a first attempt at doubly linked list class. We use this code to show you the basic debugging techniques for object-based programs:

```
Option Strict On
Module Module1
  Sub Main()
    Dim aLinkList As New LinkedList("first link")
    Dim aLink As LinkedList.Link
    aLink = aLinkList.MakeLink(aLinkList.GetFirstLink, "second link")
    aLink = aLinkList.MakeLink(aLink, "third link")
    Console.WriteLine(aLinkList.GetFirstLink.MyData)
    aLink = aLinkList.GetNextLink(aLinkList.GetFirstLink)
    Console.WriteLine(aLink.MyData)
    Console.WriteLine(aLink.NextLink.MyData)
    Console.ReadLine()
  End Sub
  Public Class LinkedList
    Private m_CurrentLink As Link
    Private m_FirstLink As Link
    Sub New(ByVal theData As String)
      m_CurrentLink = New Link(theData)
      m_FirstLink = m_CurrentLink
    End Sub
    Public Function MakeLink(ByVal currentLink As Link, ByVal _
 theData As String) As Link
      m_CurrentLink = New Link(currentLink, theData)
      Return m_CurrentLink
    End Function
    Public ReadOnly Property GetNextLink(ByVal aLink As Link) _
 As Link
      Get
        Return aLink.NextLink()
      End Get
    End Property
    Public ReadOnly Property GetCurrentLink() As Link
      Get
        Return m_CurrentLink
      End Get
```

```
      End Property
      Public ReadOnly Property GetFirstLink() As Link
        Get
          Return m_FirstLink
        End Get
      End Property

      'nested class for link objects
      Friend Class Link
        Private m_MyData As String
        Private m_NextLink As Link
        Private m_ParentLink As Link
        Friend Sub New(ByVal myParent As Link, ByVal theData As String)
          m_MyData = theData
          m_ParentLink = Me
          m_NextLink = myParent
        End Sub
        Friend Sub New(ByVal theData As String)
          m_MyData = theData
        End Sub
        Friend ReadOnly Property MyData() As String
          Get
            Return m_MyData
          End Get
        End Property
        Friend ReadOnly Property NextLink() As Link
          Get
            Return m_NextLink
          End Get
        End Property
      End Class
    End Class
End Module
```

The result of this program, shown Figure 4-11, clearly is not what we want.

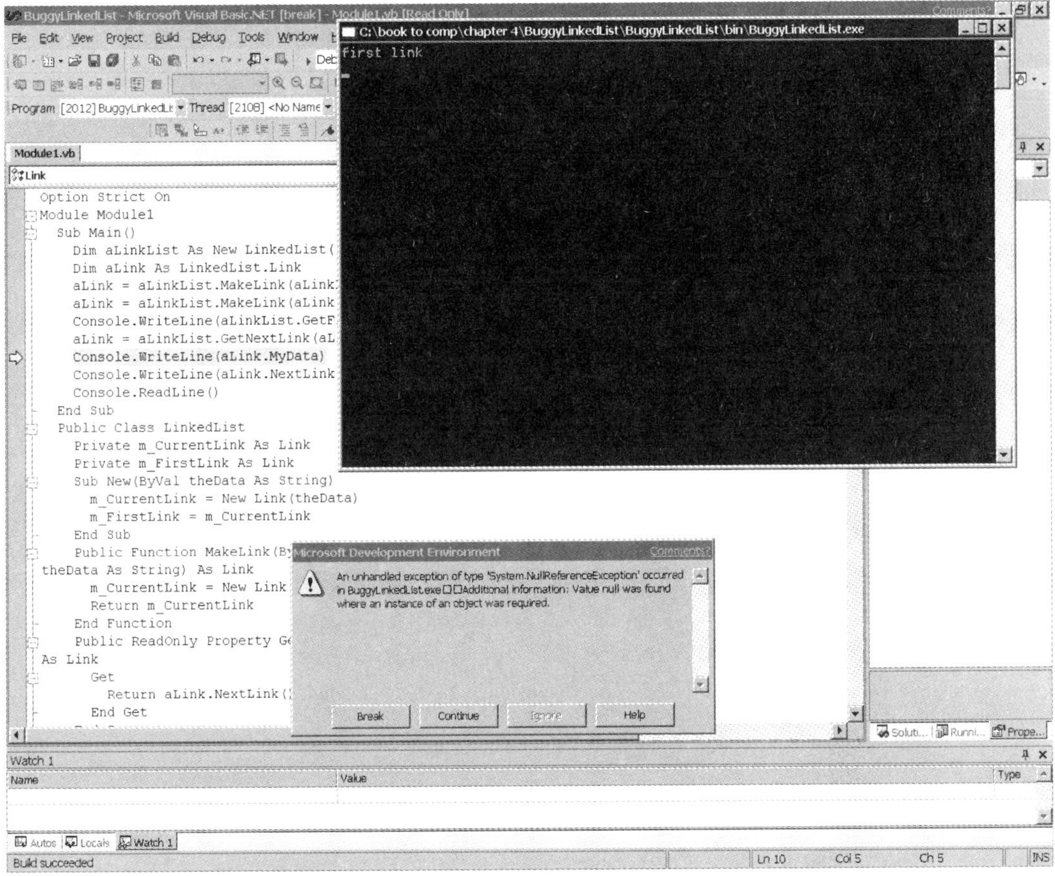

Figure 4-11. The result of a buggy program

When you are faced with this kind of situation, you usually start debugging. Here is one way:

- Click on Break in the dialog box as shown in Figure 4-11.
- Kill the window (the console window in this case), which should bring you back to the IDE.

Now add a breakpoint (F9) at a point where you can start looking at the state of the various objects in the program—in this case, right above the line that caused the exception seems like a good place (line **9** in the preceding listing). Then choose Debug|Start (F5) to run the code up to the breakpoint. Now expand the Locals window and bring it to the foreground. In Figure 4-12, you will see a couple of + signs next to `aLink` and `aLinkedList` that just cry out for clicking.

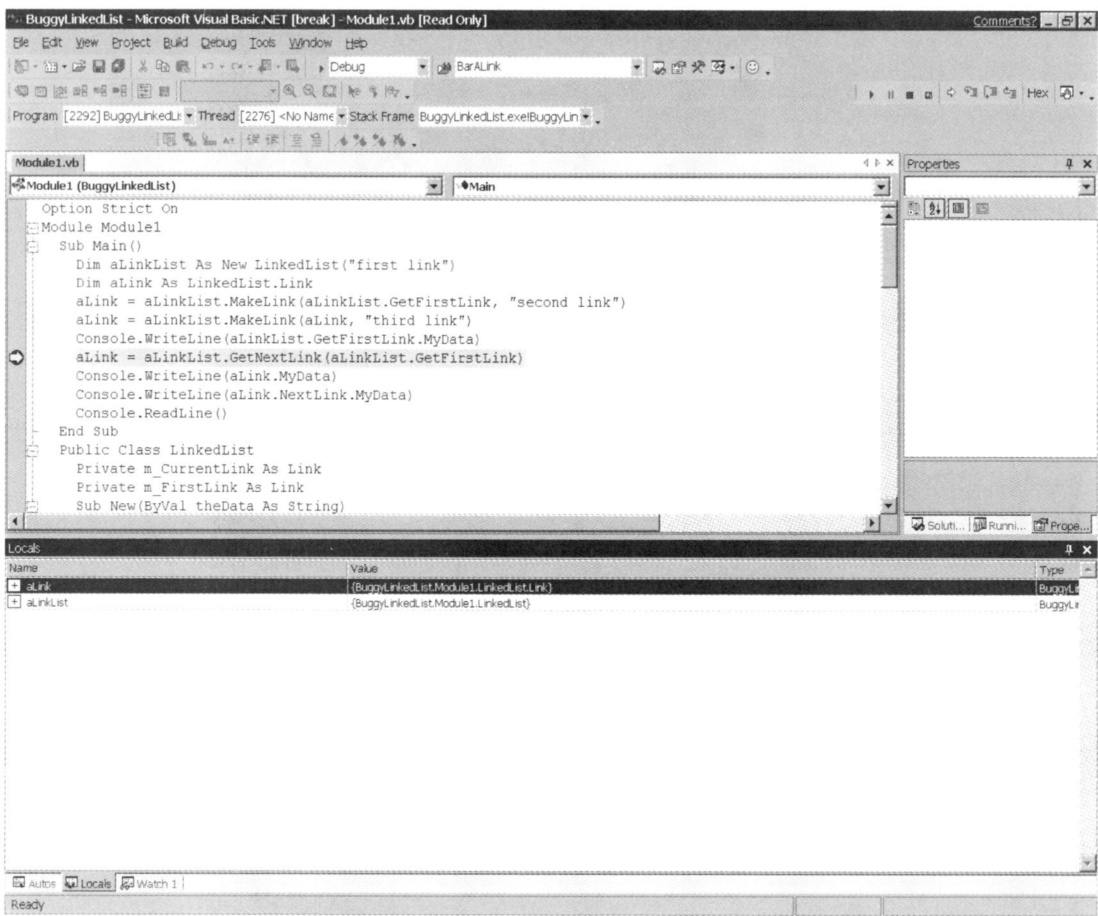

Figure 4-12. First steps in debugging in the Locals window

If you expand the window sufficiently and click a couple of times to reveal the state of the `aLink` variable that represents the third link in the list, you should see what is shown in Figure 4-13.

Because the `aLink` object variable is the third link, it is clear that its parent link should not be `Nothing`. This alerts us to look at the code in our class that assigns to the parent link. If you look at it for a second:

```
Friend Sub New(ByVal myParent As Link, ByVal theData As String)
        m_MyData = theData
        m_ParentLink = Me
        m_NextLink = myParent
End Sub
```

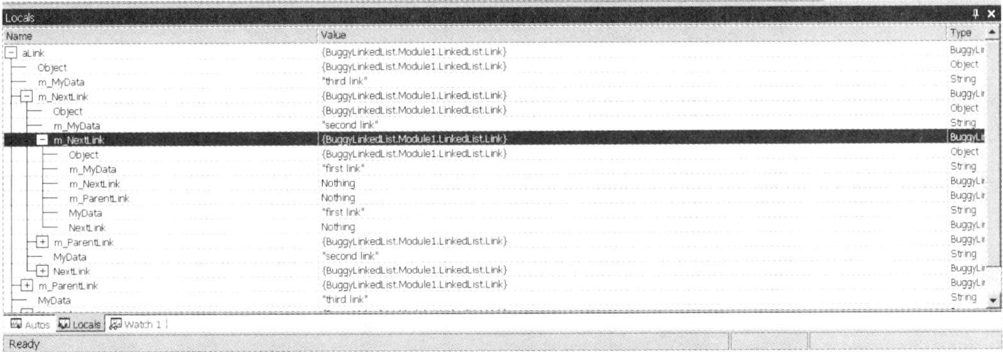

Figure 4-13. The `aLink` *variable*

it should be clear (as is not all that uncommon) that we reversed the assignment statements for the links and forgot to assign the link from the parent to its child. The correct code should be:

```
Friend Sub New(ByVal myParent As Link, ByVal theData As String)
        m_MyData = theData
        m_ParentLink = myParent
        m_ParentLink.m_NextLink = Me
End Sub
```

In addition to the Locals, you can add conditional breakpoints, for example, for when `aLink Is Nothing` or add items via the Add Watch item on the context menu in the code window when a program is in break mode. However, we think it fair to say that, regardless of how you drill down into your objects, being able to see the state of them is key to debugging them!

Summary

This has been a very long chapter! You saw how to use many of the built-in classes in the .NET Framework. But mostly we tried to show you the ins and outs of object creation in VB .NET. There is a lot to this, and it is quite different from the way things were done in earlier versions of VB. For example, you saw how parameterized constructors make object creation much more robust in VB .NET than it was in earlier versions of VB. This chapter contains the core knowledge you need to go further with VB .NET!

CHAPTER 5

Inheritance and Interfaces

IN THE LAST CHAPTER, we briefly introduced you to two of the pillars of object-oriented programming in VB .NET: *implementation inheritance*, which allows for automatic code reuse, and *interface inheritance*, which involves contracting for certain kinds of behavior. In this chapter we cover both of these techniques in depth.

We start by showing you how to do implementation inheritance in VB .NET. Unfortunately, learning only the mechanics for doing implementation inheritance is a very bad idea. This is because, as we said in the last chapter, implementation-style inheritance done carelessly is a disaster in the making. We therefore spend a fair amount of time in this chapter showing you how to avoid these dangers through good design of your inheritance chains.

After covering the mechanics and the design principles behind the use of implementation inheritance, we go on to show you the ins and outs of the `Object` class. This is the class that all .NET objects ultimately inherit from. We finish the discussion of implementation inheritance by showing what .NET does to help solve the *fragile base class* problem that is at the root of many of the implementation inheritance problems in other OOP languages such as Java or C++. (The fragile base class problem is a fancy way of saying that the wrong change to a parent class can cause a disaster in the child classes that inherit from it.)

> **NOTE** *From this point on we will say "inheritance" instead of "implementation inheritance" and "implementing an interface" for writing code that uses interface inheritance. Although the terminology can be confusing at first, most programmers quickly become accustomed to this shorthand.*

After discussing inheritance, we move on to implementing interfaces in VB .NET. We end this chapter by showing you how to use some of the important interfaces in the .NET Framework, such as `IComparable`, `ICloneable`, and `IDisposable`.

> **NOTE** *If you are familiar with how to use interfaces in VB5 or VB6, you will be pleasantly surprised at how much cleaner your code looks when you implement an interface in VB .NET. The syntax is much more sensible than it used to be!*

Inheritance Basics

Although inheritance is hardly the be-all, end-all of OOP, and interfaces are often a better choice, you absolutely should not get the idea that you should avoid using inheritance. Inheritance is a powerful tool that saves you a lot of work *if you use it correctly.* "Correctly" simply means that you should not use inheritance if it is not absolutely clear that the "is a" relationship holds:

- Class `A` should inherit from a class `B` only when it is absolutely clear that, now and forever, you can always use an `A` object in place of a `B` object without getting yourself into trouble.

(As we said in the previous chapter, a good way to remember this rule is to keep in mind the troubles the Internal Revenue Service will cause you if you treat contractors as employees. A `Contractor` class must *not* inherit from an `Employee` class even though your code has to model paying them and having a tax ID in both cases.

You may see this fundamental rule in a more abstract form. This kind of abstraction is necessary when you try to express the rule in a code-oriented way:

- An instance of a child class A that inherits from a parent class B must be usable in every piece of code that would take an instance of its parent type as a parameter.

In other words if you have a function whose header is

```
UseIt(bThing As B)
```

and `aThing` is an instance of the child class `A`, then the following code must make sense:

```
UseIt(aThing)
```

If this seems too abstract, here is a made up (and hopefully humorous) version of where it fails. Suppose you have a class called `Manager` and you want to decide whether a person who manages programmers should inherit from the `Manager` class rather than inherit from the `Programmer` class. Because managers need big hair, as any Dilbert reader knows, you decide you will have a property called `SetHairStyle` in your `Manager` class. Now close your eyes and imagine a typical programmer (say his name is Tom) who is suddenly made a manager of other programmers. What does he look like hairstyle-wise? Can you imagine a call to:

```
tom.SetHairStyle("sharp razor cut')
```

always making sense? Sure, some programmers care about hairstyles but we think it is fair to say that not every programmer does. The moral is a `ManagerOfProgrammers` class should inherit from `Programmer` not `Manager`.

> **NOTE** *Some languages would permit a* `ManagerOfProgrammers` *class to inherit from both a* `Manager` *and a* `Programmer` *class. Though quite logical and appealing in principle, languages that support multiple inheritance (as this ability is called), tend to be incredibly complicated to use in practice. VB .NET uses its ability to implement multiple interfaces to deal with the situations when multiple inheritance would otherwise be needed. As you will soon see, using multiple interfaces it is a much cleaner approach to this kind of situation than classic multiple inheritance.*

Next, you have to be aware that there is no escaping inheritance in your VB .NET programs. Even if you are completely comfortable with the interface style of programming used in VB5 and VB6, and think containment and delegation along with interfaces are the ways to go, you cannot use interfaces exclusively in VB .NET. This is because it is *impossible* to use the .NET Framework without explicitly using inheritance. For example, any .NET GUI application depends on inheritance to work, as do many of the built-in collection classes—even using the `FolderBrowser` object requires inheritance!

> **NOTE** *When you build a GUI application using inheritance, it is often called "visual inheritance" in the marketing literature for VB .NET. This is silly—it is just plain old inheritance for an object that happens to be an instance of the* `Windows.Forms.Form` *class.*

In fact, the way inheritance is used in the .NET Framework is a perfect example of why inheritance should not be completely replaced by interfaces in object-oriented programming. What happened in the .NET Framework may well occur in your own projects:

- When you build frameworks that other programmers will depend on, well-designed, thoroughly debugged base classes can be used over and over again via inheritance as the base on which they build *their* classes.

Getting Started with Inheritance

Let us start by recalling some terminology. The class you inherit from is called the *base* or *parent* class. The class that inherits from it is called the *child* or *derived* class. The child class automatically has all the public functionality of the parent class, but you can modify the behavior of the parent class in the child class. Inheritance is about *specializing* parent class behavior and possible adding *new* behavior as well.

Here is an example of this process at work: suppose you have a company with an enlightened raise policy. Whenever there is an across-the-board raise of, say, 5 percent, programmers automatically get 6 percent (a 20 percent bonus). You are responsible for the design of the employee management system for this company. You decide to make a class called `Programmer` that inherits from `Employee`, and you want to change the behavior of the `RaiseSalary` method in the `Programmer` class to reflect the automatic (and well-deserved!) 20 percent bonus.

To build the code for this Employee⇒Programmer inheritance chain, let us first assume that you have already written the code for a `Public Employee` class that is either part of your solution or is already referenced via Project|References. Assuming this is so, then the code for the `Programmer` class starts out like this (the key line indicating inheritance is in bold):

```
Public Class Programmer
  Inherits Employee

End Class
```

The `Inherits` keyword must be the first nonblank, noncomment line after the name of the child class. (IntelliSense will automatically show you what classes you can inherit from, by the way.) Note that a derived class cannot use the `Public` access modifier if its parent class is marked `Friend` or `Private`. The reason is that the access modifier you use for the derived class cannot be *less* restrictive than the one used for its parent class. But it can be *more* restrictive, so a class marked `Friend` class may inherit from one marked `Public`, for example.

The next step in building a child class is to make sure that you give it the correct kind of constructor. Because the child class must have at least the *same* amount of functionality as its parent class, constructors for child classes usually call the constructor of the parent class to correctly initialize the instance fields of their parent class. This is done using the special keyword `MyBase`, which accesses the parent class (as shown in the following line in bold), passing in the right values for the constructor:

```
Public Sub New(ByVal theName As String, ByVal curSalary As Decimal)
    MyBase.New(Name, curSalary)
End Sub
```

The key line

```
MyBase.New(theName, curSalary)
```

calls the constructor of the base `Employee` class and correctly initializes its instance fields. If you fail to have a call to `MyBase.New` when a parent class requires arguments in its constructor, then VB .NET issues an error message like this:

```
C:\vb net book\chapter 5\Example1\Example1\Module1.vb(55):
'Example1.Programmer', the base class of 'Example1.Employee',
does not have an accessible constructor that can be called with
no arguments. Therefore, the first statement of this constructor
must be a call to a constructor of the base class via 'MyBase.New'
or another constructor of this class via 'MyClass.New' or 'Me.New'.
```

which is about as informative an error message as one could hope to get and clearly reminds you that you must call `MyBase.New` at least once if your parent class does not have a no-argument constructor! After you add the call to `MyBase.New`, things get very interesting: how do you access the instance fields of the parent class? Here is the (we think surprising at first) rule:

- A derived class has *no* privileged access to the instance fields of its parent class.

This rule means that the derived `Programmer` class has *no* privileged access to the *private* instance fields of its parent `Employee` class. For example, suppose you store the salary in the parent class in a private instance field called `m_Salary` and you try to sneak this code into the `Programmer` class's `RaiseSalary` method:

```
Public Sub New(ByVal theName As String, ByVal curSalary As Decimal)
  MyBase.New(theName, curSalary)
  MyBase.m_salary = 1.2 * curSalary
End Sub
```

You would get this error message:

```
'Example1.Employee.m_Salary' is Private, and is not accessible in this context.
```

> **TIP** *A good analogy is that real-life parents should decide what their children can do, not vice versa.*

So what do you do? If you want a child class to have access to specific functionality in the parent class, it is up to the code in the parent class to allow such access. We will show you how to do this in the next section.

Accessing the Parent Class's Functionality

VB .NET comes with a `Protected` access modifier that automatically gives child classes access to the item specified with this modifier. This is true whether the item is a member function or an instance field. You may be tempted to use this modifier to make all instance fields of the parent class `Protected`, to give derived classes a quick and dirty way to gain access to the parent class's instance fields. Do not give in to this temptation. Good design principles dictate that the `Protected` access modifier should be used only for member functions, not for instance fields. Doing anything else violates encapsulation and prevents you from doing validation in the place it belongs—the parent class. You need to rely on the parent class to validate the data. As in real life, "trust but verify" is the default behavior for good parenting!

For example, our original definition of the `Employee` class had members with these signatures:

```
Public ReadOnly Property TheName() As String
Public ReadOnly Property Salary() As Decimal
```

so all classes could access these members. To make them accessible only by derived classes of the parent, change the `Public` access modifier to `Protected`.

You can use these access modifiers (see Table 5-1) for the members of a class in an inheritance chain.

Table 5-1. Access Modifiers for Inheritance

ACCESS MODIFIER	MEANING
`Friend`	Access is limited to code in the current assembly.
`Private`	Only objects of the parent's type have access to these members.
`Protected`	Access is limited to objects of the parent class type and objects of the type of any of its descendents.

Table 5-1. Access Modifiers for Inheritance (Continued)

ACCESS MODIFIER	MEANING
`Protected Friend`	Access is limited to the current assembly *or* types derived from the parent class. (Think of it as the combination of the circle and the square as shown here): 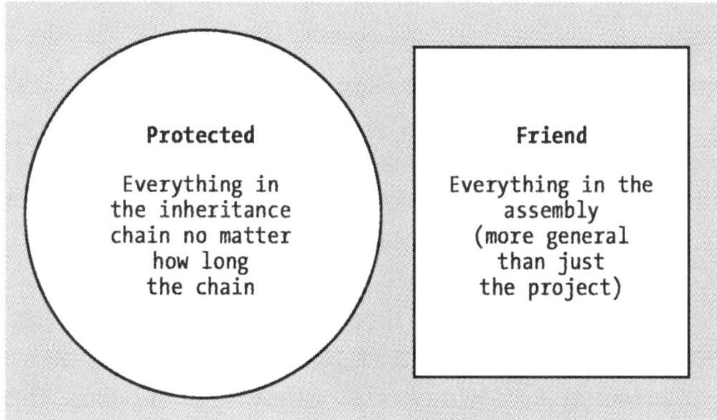
`Public`	All code that can access an object based on this class can access this member.

As we have said, having `Protected` and `Protected Friend` member functions (but not instance fields) is quite common, because they let you prevent outside code from accessing protected members.

However, there is a rather interesting gotcha to using `Protected`. Fortunately, the compiler is quite good about giving you a clear warning you when you fall into this hole. Here is a specific example: suppose you have a class called `GeekFest` which contains a bunch of programmers with a method called `Boast` that wants to access the `Salary` property in the `Programmer` class. (Which means it is accessing the `Salary` property in the parent `Employee` class ultimately). Here is how the code may look:

```
Public Class GeekFest
  Private m_Programmers() As Programmer
  Sub New(ByVal Programmers() As Programmer)
    m_Programmers = Programmers
  End Sub
  Public Function Boast(ByVal aGeek As Programmer) As String
    Return "Hey my salary is " & aGeek.Salary
  End Function
End Class
```

Now suppose the code in your `Employee` class had the read-only `Salary` property marked `Protected` instead of `Public`:

```
Protected ReadOnly Property Salary() As Decimal
  Get
    Return MyClass.m_Salary
  End Get
End Property
```

This results in an error message:

```
C:\vb net book\chapter 5\Example1\Example1\Module1d.vb(19):
'Example1.Module1.Employee.Protected ReadOnly Property Salary() As Decimal'
is Protected, and is not accessible in this context.
```

The point is that even though the `Programmer` class has access to the protected `Salary` property in *its* code, `Programmer` *objects* do not have access to this method when outside the code for the `Programmer` class. To sum up:

- Code can access `Protected` methods of the parent class only when inside objects of the derived class and not from objects of the child type referred to in code outside the derived class.

Overriding Properties and Methods

In our example of inheritance in which programmers automatically get a 6 percent raise when everyone else gets 5 percent, you need to change the behavior of the `RaiseSalary` method to reflect the automatic 20 percent bonus. This is called *overriding a member function.*

> **CAUTION** *You cannot override shared members.*

Unlike many OOP languages, the syntax used in VB .NET makes it clear that you want to override a method in the parent class by a method from the child class. The clarity comes from the two required keywords:

- `Overridable`, which is used in the parent class to indicate that a method can be overridden.

- `Overrides`, which is used in the child class to indicate that you are overriding a method.

> **NOTE** *Of course, the parameters and return types must match. If they do not, you are overloading, not overriding, and no keyword is required.*

To have our basic Employee class override the special method of raising salaries for an eventual Programmer or Manager class, you use code like this (the key lines are in bold):

```
Option Strict On
Public Class Employee
  Private m_Name As String
  Private m_Salary As Decimal

  Private Const LIMIT As Decimal = 0.1D

  Public Sub New(ByVal theName As String, ByVal curSalary As Decimal)
    m_Name = theName
    m_Salary = curSalary
  End Sub

  Public ReadOnly Property TheName() As String
    Get
      Return m_Name
    End Get
  End Property

  Public ReadOnly Property Salary() As Decimal
    Get
      Return MyClass.m_Salary
    End Get
  End Property

  Public Overridable Overloads Sub RaiseSalary(ByVal Percent As Decimal)
    If Percent > LIMIT Then
      'not allowed
      Console.WriteLine("NEED PASSWORD TO RAISE SALARY MORE " & _
  "THAN LIMIT!!!!")
    Else
      m_Salary = (1 + Percent) * m_Salary
    End If
  End Sub
```

```
  Public Overridable Overloads Sub RaiseSalary(ByVal Percent As _
  Decimal, ByVal Password As String)
    If Password = "special" Then
      m_Salary = (1 + Percent) * m_Salary
    End If
  End Sub
End Class
```

As in the previous chapter, we use the optional `Overloads` keyword to make it clear that we have two versions of `RaiseSalary` in this class.

> **NOTE** *We use this* `Employee` *class often in this chapter, so you may want to either type it into Visual Studio or simply download the source code from* `www.apress.com` *if you have not yet done so.*

Now assume that every programmer's salary raise should be treated via a call to the special `RaiseSalary` method. The child `Programmer` class looks like this (again, the key line is bold):

```
Public Class Programmer
  Inherits Employee
  Public Sub New(ByVal theName As String, ByVal curSalary As Decimal)
    MyBase.New(theName, curSalary)
  End Sub

  Public Overloads Overrides Sub RaiseSalary(ByVal Percent As Decimal)
    MyBase.RaiseSalary(1.2D * Percent, "special")
  End Sub
End Class
```

Notice how little code is needed in this child class—most of the functionality remains unchanged, so we simply inherit it!

If you add this code to the `Sub Main`, the correct call to the `RaiseSalary` method (the one with the 20 percent bonus) is made by the compiler for any object that is an instance of the `Programmer` class:

```
Sub Main()
  Dim sally As New Programmer("Sally", 150000D)
  sally.RaiseSalary(0.1D) 'will actually give a 12% raise
  Console.WriteLine(sally.TheName & " salary is now " & sally.Salary())
  Console.ReadLine()
End Sub
```

Sally will get her 20 percent bonus.

To summarize:

- You can override only parent members marked with the `Overridable` keyword.
- If, at any point in the chain you want to stop the possibility of further overriding of a method, mark it with the `NotOverridable` keyword.

VB .NET's `NotInheritable` keyword prevents inheritance from a class (these kinds of classes are sometimes called *sealed* or *final* classes). The main reason to mark an entire class as `NotInheritable` is if the class has such vital behavior that you cannot risk changes to it. Many framework classes such as `String` are marked as `NotInheritable` for this reason. However, you do not have to mark a whole class as `NotInheritable` if all you want to do is place a single member of the class off limits to overriding it: you can mark a member you do not want overridden as `NotOverridable`.

> **NOTE** *Members are not overridable by default (we explain why when we describe the* `Shadows` *keyword later in this chapter). Still, we feel you should use the* `NotOverridable` *keyword to make your intentions clear.*

You may occasionally want to access the parent class version of a method that you have overridden. For example, suppose you want to add an honorific like "Code Guru" to the name of every programmer. `MyBase` lets you access the public `TheName` property of the parent class inside the child class:

```
Public Overrides ReadOnly Property TheName() As String
  Get
    Return "Code Guru " & MyBase.TheName()
  End Get
End Property
```

Note that the `MyBase` keyword does have a few limitations:

- You cannot chain it to move to the "grandparent" if your inheritance chain is that deep; `MyBase.MyBase.MemberFunction` is illegal.
- `MyBase` is a keyword, and unlike `Me`, `MyBase` cannot be used with `Is`, assigned to an object variable, or passed to a procedure.

Similarly, the `MyClass` keyword lets you be sure that even overridden methods get called as defined in the current class whose code is running, rather than as defined in some overridden method in a derived class. The limitations to `MyClass` are similar to that of `MyBase`, as we mentioned in the previous chapter:

- `MyClass` is also a keyword, not a real object. Therefore, as with `MyBase`, `MyClass` cannot be used with `Is`, assigned to an object variable, or passed to a procedure. (Use `Me` to refer to the actual instance.)
- `MyClass` cannot be used to access `Private` members in the class (but `Me` can).

NOTE *We find `MyClass` most useful when we want to indicate that we are modifying the behavior of a class. The trouble we have with using `Me` for `MyClass` is that `Me` really should only mean "the current instance of the object whose code is being run" and using it in any other way confuses the issue for us*

How Can You Promote Someone to Manager?

Suppose you have built a wonderful object-oriented employee management program (with polymorphism working its wonders) and then someone asks you the following simple question: how does your employee management system handle promoting someone to manager?

Interestingly enough answering this kind of question in OOP (that is having a way to change the type of an existing instance in a program that uses OOP) is an extremely complex design issue that rarely gets addressed before the issue becomes a crisis. The problem is that object-oriented programming requires that once an object is created, you cannot change its type.

The only practical solution in the case of our employee management program is to build a method into the `Employee` class that copies the state of the `Employee` to a new `Manager` object and then marks the old `Employee` object as unusable.[1]

1. Interestingly enough this is similar to what the military does. When an enlisted person is promoted to an officer, they actually discharge the enlisted person and then issue a new ID to the newly created officer.

Viewing an Inheritance Chain

The Class View and the Object Browser are useful when your inheritance chain grows in complexity. For example, in Figure 5-1 you can see that the Class View window shows you how the `Programmer` class inherits from the `Employee` class and only overrides the constructor and the `RaiseSalary` method.

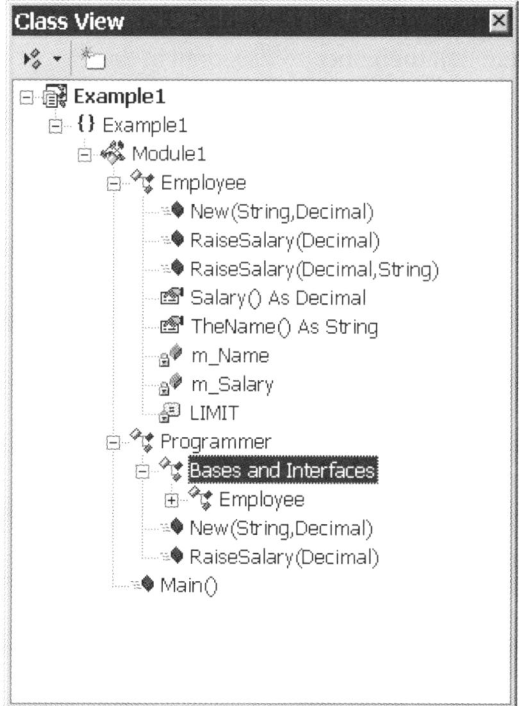

Figure 5-1. Class View in an inheritance chain

> **NOTE** *Unified Modeling Language (UML) tools like Visio or Rational Rose not only show you the relationship between classes in an inheritance chain, they actually create frameworks for the code. Many programmers swear by such CASE (computer-assisted software engineering) tools. Of course some swear at them.*

Rules for Conversions and Accessing Members in Inheritance Chains

You can store a variable of the child class in a variable of the parent class:

```
Dim tom As New Programmer("Tom", 65000)
Dim employeeOfTheMonth As Employee
employeeOfTheMonth = tom
```

If `Option Strict` is on (as it should be), then once `tom` is stored in the `employeeOfTheMonth` variable, you need to use the `CType` function to store `employeeOfTheMonth` in a `Programmer` variable:

```
Dim programmerOnCall As Programmer
programmerOnCall = CType(employeeOfTheMonth, Programmer)
```

since the compiler has no way of knowing this is acceptable beforehand. Of course, storing `tom` in the `programmerOnCall` variable can be done with a simple assignment:

> **CAUTION** *When you access the functionality of the* `tom` *object variable through the* `employeeOfTheMonth Employee` *variable, you do not have access to any of the unique members defined in the* `Programmer` *class. However, as you will see in the next section, you would have access to all the members of the* `Programmer` *class that override members of the* `Employee` *class.*

Polymorphism at Work

One of the main goals of inheritance is to avoid the difficult-to-maintain `Select Case` or `If-Then-Else If` statements by having the compiler and polymorphism do all the work. For instance, this code works with both the `Employee` and `Programmer` class:

```
Sub Main()
  Dim tom As New Employee("Tom", 50000)
  Dim sally As New Programmer("Sally", 150000)
  Dim ourEmployees(1) As Employee
  ourEmployees(0) = tom
  ourEmployees(1) = Sally
  Dim anEmployee As Employee
```

```
  For Each anEmployee In ourEmployees
    anEmployee.RaiseSalary(0.1D)
    Console.WriteLine(anEmployee.TheName & " salary now is " & _
      anEmployee.Salary())
  Next
  Console.ReadLine()
End Sub
```

When you run the code, you see Figure 5-2, which shows that the correct `RaiseSalary` method is called even though we stored both employees and programmers in an array of objects of the `Employee` type.

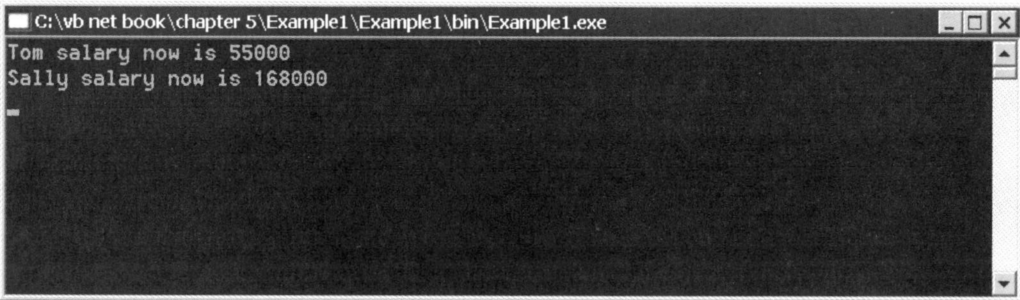

Figure 5-2. Polymorphism at work

> **NOTE** *This is sometimes described by saying that in VB .NET the default is that members of classes are virtual. (Virtual technically means that when the compiler calls a member of an object, it should look at the true type of the object, not just at what sort of container or reference it is used in.)*

In the previous example, what "virtual" means is that even though the references are to `Employee` objects (because everything is stored in an `Employee` array), the compiler looks at the true type of Sally (she is a `Programmer`) in order to call the correct `RaiseSalary` method (the one that gives the better raise).

As you can imagine, the use of virtual methods when storing both parent class objects (employees) and derived class objects (programmers) in a container marked for by the type of the parent—is quite common. However, there are some pitfalls in the simple approach we take to using virtual methods here. To see these pitfalls for yourself, modify the `Programmer` class to include a unique member, so that polymorphism will not be involved. For example, add an instance field and property member as shown here in the lines in bold:

```
Public Class Programmer
  Inherits Employee
  Private m_gadget As String
  Public Sub New(ByVal theName As String, ByVal curSalary As Decimal)
    MyBase.New(theName, curSalary)
  End Sub
  Public Overloads Overrides Sub RaiseSalary(ByVal Percent As Decimal)
    MyBase.RaiseSalary(1.2D * Percent, "special")
  End Sub
  Public Property ComputerGadget() As String
    Get
      Return m_Gadget
    End Get
    Set(ByVal Value As String)
      m_Gadget = Value
    End Set
  End Property
  End Class
```

and then change `Sub Main` by adding the lines in bold:

```
Sub Main()
  Dim tom As New Employee("Tom", 50000)
  Dim sally As New Programmer("Sally", 150000)
  sally.ComputerGadget = "Ipaq"
  Dim ourEmployees(1) As Employee
  ourEmployees(0) = tom
  ourEmployees(1) = sally
  Dim anEmployee As Employee
  For Each anEmployee In ourEmployees
    anEmployee.RaiseSalary(0.1D)
    Console.WriteLine(anEmployee.TheName & " salary now is " _
      & anEmployee.Salary())
  Next
  Console.WriteLine(ourEmployees(1).TheName & " gadget is an " _
    & ourEmployees(1).Gadget)
  Console.ReadLine()
  End Sub
```

The modified code results in this error message:

```
C:\book to comp\chapter 5\VirtualProblems\VirtualProblems\Module1.vb(17):
The name 'Gadget' is not a member of 'VirtualProblems.Employee'.
```

The problem is that although `Sally` is a `Programmer` object and is stored in the `ourEmployees(1)` array element, the compiler has no way of knowing that and thus cannot find the `ComputerGadget` property. What is more, unless you turn `Option Strict` off (which is a dangerous practice, in our opinion), you must explicitly convert this array entry to the `Programmer` type to use these unique members of the `Programmer` class:

```
Console.WriteLine(ourEmployees(1).TheName & " gadget is an " & _
CType(ourEmployees(1), Programmer).ComputerGadget)
```

The process of converting a reference stored in a parent class object variable to a child class object is usually called *down casting*. (Converting from a child class to the parent class is thus called *up casting*) Although it is a common practice, down casting should be avoided whenever possible, because it often requires you to check the type of an object variable via code like this:

```
If TypeOf ourEmployees(1) Is Programmer Then
'
Else If TypeOf ourEmployees(1) Is Employee Then
'
End If
```

which, as you can see, requires bringing back the kind of selection statements that you used polymorphism to banish in the first place! (Up casting, of course, never causes problems because the fundamental rule of inheritance is that child objects can be used any place parent objects are used.)

> **TIP** *It is usually a better programming practice to store* `Programmer` *objects in a container that can hold only programmers, when you want to access programmer functionality. This way you do not have to check to see if you can do the cast via a selection statement like* `If-TypeOf`.

Shadowing

In earlier versions of VB, as in most programming languages, *shadowing* meant that a local variable with the same name as a variable of larger scope hid the variable with larger scope. (This is one reason the convention arose to use `m_` as a prefix for module-level variables and `g_` for global variables. Using a good naming convention helps prevent shadowing bugs.) You can think of overriding an inherited method as a special kind of shadowing. For better or for worse, VB .NET allows another extraordinarily powerful kind of shadowing:

- If you mark a member of a derived class with the `Shadows` keyword (which was introduced in beta 2), it hides any members of the parent class with the same name.

The `Shadows` keyword can even be used to have a sub in the parent class and a function with the *same* name in a child class. For all practical purposes, shadowing makes a totally new member in the derived class with that name, and thus *makes any inherited members with the name being shadowed unavailable in the derived class.* This, in turn, means overriding inherited members that have been shadowed is no longer possible and polymorphism cannot work.

> **CAUTION** *The default in VB .NET is to allow you to shadow members but it will then issue a warning if you do not use the* `Shadows` *keyword. Also, if one member uses the* `Shadows` *or* `Overloads` *keyword, all the members with the same name must use it.*

Shadowing gets tricky and can cause subtle bugs when you want to use polymorphism on a container of, say, `Employee` objects and you have shadowed a member. To see this kind of problem at work, modify the `Programmer` class with the lines in bold:

```
Public Class Programmer
  Inherits Employee
  Private m_gadget As String
  Private m_HowToCallMe As String = "Code guru "
  Public Sub New(ByVal theName As String, ByVal curSalary As Decimal)
    MyBase.New(theName, curSalary)
    m_HowToCallMe = m_HowToCallMe & theName
  End Sub
  Public Overloads Overrides Sub RaiseSalary(ByVal Percent As Decimal)
    MyBase.RaiseSalary(1.2D * Percent, "special")
  End Sub
  Public Shadows ReadOnly Property TheName() As String
    Get
      Return m_HowToCallMe
    End Get
  End Property
End Class
```

Now try this `Sub Main` with the key lines in bold:

```
Sub Main()
  Dim tom As New Employee("Tom", 50000)
  Dim sally As New Programmer("Sally", 150000)
  Console.WriteLine(sally.TheName)
  Dim ourEmployees(1) As Employee
  ourEmployees(0) = tom
  ourEmployees(1) = sally
  Dim anEmployee As Employee
  For Each anEmployee In ourEmployees
    anEmployee.RaiseSalary(0.1D)
    Console.WriteLine(anEmployee.TheName & " salary now is " & _
      anEmployee.Salary())
  Next
  Console.ReadLine()
End Sub
```

Figure 5-3 shows what you will see.

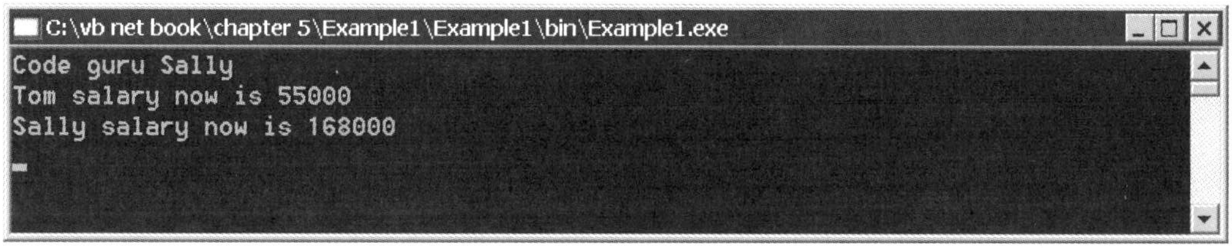

```
C:\vb net book\chapter 5\Example1\Example1\bin\Example1.exe
Code guru Sally
Tom salary now is 55000
Sally salary now is 168000
```

Figure 5-3. Shadowing causes polymorphism to fail.

As you can see, polymorphism has stopped working. The first bold line in the code correctly gives Sally the honorific of "Code Guru" before her name. Unfortunately, the second bold line no longer works polymorphically, so it no longer uses the correct `TheName` method in the `Programmer` derived class. The result is that you do not see the honorific. In other words, if you use the `Shadows` keyword, members of objects get called by the kind of container the object is stored in, not by what their ultimate types are. (You could also say that using the `Shadows` keyword in a derived class makes a member *nonvirtual.*)

Abstract Base Classes

Once you start designing inheritance into your programs, you soon realize that you often can take advantage of a great deal of common functionality. For example, contractors are not employees, but they still have information in common with employees, such as having a name, an address, a tax ID number, and so on. It might make sense to push common code back as far as possible into a base class called `PayableEntity` which has an address and a tax ID number as properties. The process of searching for common functionality that you can put into a common base class, usually called *factoring*, is a useful design practice that lets you take abstraction to its logical conclusion.

However, the factoring process sometimes leads you to a class where some of the methods are not really implementable, even though they clearly are common to all the classes in the inheritance chain. For example, with a class called `PayableEntity` as the common base class for both contractors and employees, you might decide that this foundational class should have a property called `TaxID`. Now, as should be the case, you want to check that the format for the tax ID number is correct, by using code inside a property procedure. Well, here you are faced with a problem: Social Security numbers take a different form from the tax ID used by certain kinds of contractors. This means the verification code for this property cannot be built into the `PayableEntity` base class, but must be in the child classes, because only they can know what form the tax ID must take.

For these kinds of situations, you build an *abstract* base class. This is a class that has at least one member function marked with the `MustOverride` keyword, and the class itself is marked with the `MustInherit` keyword. Here is an example of what an abstract `PayableEntity`, `MustInherit` class looks like:

```
Public MustInherit Class PayableEntity
  Private m_Name As String
  Public Sub New(ByVal itsName As String)
    m_Name = itsName
  End Sub
  ReadOnly Property TheName() As String
    Get
      Return m_Name
    End Get
  End Property
  Public MustOverride Property TaxID() As String
End Class
```

Notice that the member marked with the `MustOverride` keyword consists of just the `Property` statement with no code inside of it. In general, a member marked with the `MustOverride` keyword has only a header and cannot use an `End Property`, `End Sub`, or `End Function` statement. Also notice that we were able to use a concrete implementation of the read-only property `TheName`, which shows abstract classes can combine nonabstract members with abstract members. An `Employee` class that inherits from the abstract `PayableEntity` class might look like this, with the key new lines in bold:

```
Public Class Employee
  Inherits PayableEntity
  Private m_Salary As Decimal
  Private m_TaxID As String
  Private Const LIMIT As Decimal = 0.1D
  Public Sub New(ByVal theName As String, ByVal curSalary As Decimal, _
ByVal TaxID As String)
    MyBase.New(theName)
    m_Salary = curSalary
    m_TaxID = TaxID
  End Sub
  Public Overrides Property TaxID() As String
    Get
      Return m_TaxID
    End Get
    Set(ByVal Value As String)
      If Value.Length <> 11 then
       'need to do something here - see Chapter 7
     Else
        m_TaxID = Value
    End If
    End Set
  End Property
  ReadOnly Property Salary() As Decimal
    Get
      Return MyClass.m_Salary
    End Get
  End Property
  Public Overridable Overloads Sub RaiseSalary(ByVal Percent As Decimal)
    If Percent > LIMIT Then
      'not allowed
      Console.WriteLine("NEED PASSWORD TO RAISE SALARY MORE " & _
  "THAN LIMIT!!!!")
    Else
      m_Salary = (1D + Percent) * m_Salary
    End If
  End Sub
```

```
  Public Overridable Overloads Sub RaiseSalary(ByVal Percent As _
  Decimal, ByVal Password As String)
    If Password = "special" Then
      m_Salary = (1D + Percent) * m_Salary
    End If
  End Sub
End Class
```

The first of the key lines is in the constructor, which now has to call the constructor of the abstract base class in order to set the name properly. The second group of key lines adds the most trivial concrete implementation of the `MustOverRide` `TaxId` property. (Note that this code does not do the needed verification of tax ID numbers here, as you would in a more robust example.)

Here is a `Sub Main` you can use to test this program:

```
Sub Main()
  Dim tom As New Employee("Tom", 50000, "111-11-1234")
  Dim sally As New Programmer("Sally", 150000, "111-11-2234")
  Console.WriteLine(sally.TheName)
  Dim ourEmployees(1) As Employee
  ourEmployees(0) = tom
  ourEmployees(1) = sally
  Dim anEmployee As Employee
  For Each anEmployee In ourEmployees
    anEmployee.RaiseSalary(0.1D)
    Console.WriteLine(anEmployee.TheName & " has tax id " & _
anEmployee.TaxID & ", salary now is " & anEmployee.Salary())
  Next
  Console.ReadLine()
End Sub
```

Finally, you cannot create a `MustInherit` class directly. A line like this:

```
Dim NoGood As New PayableEntity("can't do")
```

gives this error message:

```
Class 'PayableEntity' is not creatable because it contains at least
one member marked as 'MustOverride' that hasn't been overridden.
```

You can, however, assign an object from a derived class to a variable of an abstract base class type or a container for it (which allows polymorphism to work its magic):

```
Dim tom As New Employee("Tom", 50000, "123-45-6789")
Dim whoToPay(13) As PayableEntity
whoToPay(0) = tom
```

> **NOTE** *Although unusual, it is possible to build a* `MustInherit` *class without any* `MustOverride` *members.*

Example: The `CollectionBase` *Class*

The trouble with .NET Framework classes such as `ArrayList` or `HashTable` is that they contain objects, so you always have to use the `CType` function to get back to the correct type after you place something in such a collection. You also run the risk that somebody will put the wrong type of object in the container and the call to `CType` will fail. A *strongly typed collection* is a container that can only hold objects of a single type or its derived types.

A good example of an abstract base class in the .NET Framework is `CollectionBase`, whose derived classes allow you to build strongly typed collections (Before you embark on creating your own collection class inheriting from `CollectionBase`, make sure that the framework does not already contain the class you need, in the `System.Collections.Specialized Namespace`.) Such type-safe collections rely on an abstract base class called `System.Collections.CollectionBase`, and all you have to do is implement concrete `Add` and `Remove` methods and an `Item` property. This is because the `System.Collections.CollectionBase` already has an internal list that holds the data—you need only delegate the other tasks to this internal list.

Here is an example that builds this kind of specialized collection (which assumes the `Employee` class is either referenced or part of this project):

```
Public Class Employees
  Inherits System.Collections.CollectionBase
  ' Restricts to adding only Employee items
  ' delegating to the internal List object's Add method
  Public Sub Add(ByVal aEmployee As Employee)
    List.Add(aEmployee)
  End Sub
```

```
8   Public Sub Remove(ByVal index As Integer)
9     If index > Count - 1 Or index < 0 Then
10      ' outside the range, should throw an exception (Chapter 7)
11      MsgBox("Can't add this item") 'MsgBox as a marker for an exception
12    Else
13      List.RemoveAt(index)
14    End If
15  End Sub
16
17  Default Public ReadOnly Property Item(ByVal index As Integer) As Employee
18    Get
19      Return CType(List.Item(index), Employee)
20    End Get
21  End Property
22  End Class
```

Lines **5–7** implement the abstract `Add` method in the base class by delegating it to the internal `List` object, so that it will accept only `Employee` objects. Lines **8–10** implement the `Remove` method. Here we are delegated to the internal `List` object's `Count` and `Index` properties to make sure we are not at the end or beginning of the list. Finally, lines **17–21** implement the `Item` property. We make this the default property because this is what users expect for a collection. We make it read-only to prevent someone from adding an item except via the `Add` method. It would certainly be acceptable to make it a read-write property, but that would require some extra code to verify that the index you add the item to is acceptable. Assuming you have the basic `Employee` class, here is some code to test this specialized collection with an illegal addition (a string) commented out (but in bold):

```
Sub Main()
  Dim tom As New Employee("Tom", 50000)
  Dim sally As New Employee("Sally", 60000)
  Dim myEmployees As New Employees()
  myEmployees.Add(tom)
  myEmployees.Add(sally)
  ' myEmployees.Add("Tom")
  Dim aEmployee As Employee
  For Each aEmployee In myEmployees
    Console.WriteLine(aEmployee.TheName)
  Next
  Console.ReadLine()
End Sub
```

As an experiment, try uncommenting the `myEmployees.Add("Tom")` line. You will see that the code will not even compile and you end up with this error message:

```
C:\book to comp\chapter 5\EmployeesClass\EmployeesClass\Module1.vb(9):
A value of type 'String' cannot be converted to 'EmployeesClass.Employee'.
```

> **NOTE** *This is a great example of the extra power inheritance gives VB .NET over using delegation in earlier versions of VB. We continue to delegate, of course, to save ourselves work, but we get the* `For-Each` *for free, because we inherit from a class that supports* `For-Each`*!*

Object: The Ultimate Base Class

The .NET Framework (and hence VB .NET) depend on every type inheriting from the common Object type, this is the ultimate ancestor of all classes. (OOP speak often calls such a class the *cosmic base* class.) This includes both reference types (instances of a class) and value types (instance of a struct, enum, dates or numeric types). This means, for example, that any function that takes a parameter of Object type can be passed a parameter of any type (since the fundamental rules of inheritance that we mentioned earlier require that child class variables be usable in any context that parent class variables can be used).

For example, there are a few useful built-in Boolean functions that determine whether the kind of data you are working with take an object variable:

- `IsArray`: Tells you if an object variable is an array
- `IsDate`: Tells you if an object can be interpreted as a date and time value
- `IsNumeric`: Tells you if the object can be interpreted as a number

> **CAUTION** *Developers coming from earlier versions of VB may be tempted to think of the Object type as a glorified Variant data type. Resist this temptation. Variants were just another data type that could store other data types inside themselves; the Object type is the ultimate base class at which all inheritance chains end.*

The `Object` class itself splits up into two streams of descendants: those that inherit from `System.ValueType` (the base class for all value types) and the reference types that descend directly from `Object`. You can determine if a derived type is a value type with code like this:

```
Sub Main()
  Dim a As Integer = 3
  Console.WriteLine("a is a value type is " & IsValueType(a))
  Console.ReadLine()
  End Sub
  Function IsValueType(ByVal thing As Object) As Boolean
  Return (TypeOf (thing) Is System.ValueType)
End Function
```

> **NOTE** *We think this is a design flaw in VB .NET that you cannot use* `TypeOf` *on value type variables without the kludge of creating a function that takes an object. You should be able to pass a value type to* `TypeOf`.

The Most Useful Members of Object

Because every type in VB .NET inherits from `Object`, it is likely that you will often use (or more likely, override) these methods. We cover them in the next few sections.

> **NOTE** *You will often be tempted to override the* `Object` *class's protected* `Finalize` *method. In theory, you override the* `Finalize` *method in your code to create cleanup code that runs when the garbage collector reclaims the memory your object uses. Do not do this in practice. Because you cannot be sure when the* `Finalize` *method will run or in what order it will run, using it for cleanup is chancy at best. Instead, you should implement a* `Dispose` *method as described later on in this chapter in the section on the* `IDisposable` *interface. If you do override the* `Finalize` *method, be aware you must call* `MyBase.Finalize` *inside the* `Finalize` *method, and you should always duplicate any* `Dispose` *code there as well.*

`Equals` *and* `ReferenceEquals`

The `Object` class supplies two versions of `Equals`, one shared and one not. The shared version has this syntax:

```
Overloads Public Shared Function Equals(Object, Object) As Boolean
```

and is used in this form:

```
Equals(a, b)
```

The nonshared version has the syntax:

```
Overloads Overridable Public Function Equals(Object) As Boolean
```

and is used in this form:

```
a.Equals(b)
```

The two versions of the `Equals` method are designed to determine whether two items have the same value, but you should be prepared to overload `Equals` if it makes sense in your class. Keep in mind that because shared members of classes cannot be overridden, you can only override the nonshared version of `Equals`.

For example if you have two ways of representing objects in a value type, you should make sure that `Equals` can handle this (The designers did this for the `String` class as well, although strictly speaking, this is not a value type.)

The `Object` class also provides a shared (and therefore not overridable) version of a method called `ReferenceEquals`. The `ReferenceEquals` method determines whether two items refer to the same object; that is, whether the specified `Object` instances are the same instance. For example, two strings, `a` and `b`, can have `a.Equals(b)` true and `ReferenceEquals(a, b)` false, as this code shows:

```
Sub Main()
  Dim a As String = "hello"
  Dim b As String = "Hello"
  Mid(b, 1, 1) = "h"
  Console.WriteLine("Is a.Equals(b)true? " & a.Equals(b))
  Console.WriteLine("Is ReferenceEquals(a, b) true? " & _
    ReferenceEquals(a, b))
  Console.ReadLine()
End Sub
```

The result is shown in Figure 5-4.

```
C:\vb net book\chapter 5\Equals\Equals\bin\Equals.exe
Is A.Equals(B)true? True
Is ReferenceEquals(A, B) true? False
```

Figure 5-4. The difference between `Equals` *and* `ReferenceEquals`

The ToString *Method*

The `ToString` method returns a string that represents the current object. How successful this representation is to debugging and to the user of the class depends on the implementer of the class. The default implementation of `ToString` returns the fully qualified type name of the object. For example:

```
System.Object
```

or

```
Example1.Programmer
```

You should get into the habit of overriding `ToString` for your own classes where you can give a more meaningful string representation of the class. For example, in our basic `Employee` class contained in the EmployeeTest1 program from Chapter 4, it might be better to override the `ToString` method:

```
Public Overrides Function ToString() As String
  Dim temp As String
  temp = Me.GetType.ToString() & " my name is " & Me.TheName
  Return temp
End Function
```

The result is

```
EmployeeTest1.EmployeeTest1+Employee my name is Tom
```

GetType and Reflection[2]

Every type in the .NET Framework is represented by a `Type` object. The `Type` class is full of mouth-twisting members such as the `GetMembers` method, which lets you get

2. Warning: this section is full of tongue-twisting sentences

at the members of that class by name. The idea is that the `GetType` method in `Object` returns a `Type` object that you can use to query what functionality a type offers you at run time. This extremely useful feature lets you perform *reflection* (which sometimes called *runtime type identification*). In fact, the `Reflection` namespace is so important to the smooth functioning of the .NET Framework that it is automatically imported into every project in the VS IDE.)

To see reflection at work, add a reference to the `System.Windows.Forms` assembly and then run the following program. When you start seeing a prompt (it will take a moment) press Enter and you will eventually see something like Figure 5-5. You can keep on pressing Enter and you will eventually you see all of the members of the `Windows.Forms.Form` class (there are many), which is the basis for GUI applications in .NET.

> **NOTE** *We simply call* `ToString` *in this program, but the online help shows you that a lot more information is encapsulated in* `MemberInfo` *objects.*

```
1  Option Strict On
2  Imports System.Windows.Forms
3  Module Module1
4    Sub Main()
5      Dim aForm As New Windows.Forms.Form()
6      Dim aType As Type
7      aType = aForm.GetType()
8      Dim member As Object
9      Console.WriteLine("This displays the members of the Form class")
10      Console.WriteLine(" Press enter to see the next one.")
11      For Each member In aType.GetMembers
12        Console.ReadLine()
13        Console.Write(member.ToString)
14      Next
15      Console.WriteLine("Press enter to end")
16      Console.ReadLine()
17    End Sub
18  End Module
```

The key lines **6** and **7** let us retrieve a `Type` object that represents a `Windows.Forms.Form` class. Then, because the `GetMembers` method of the `Type` class returns a collection of `MemberInfo` objects that describe the member, we simply iterate through all the members of this class in lines **11–14**.

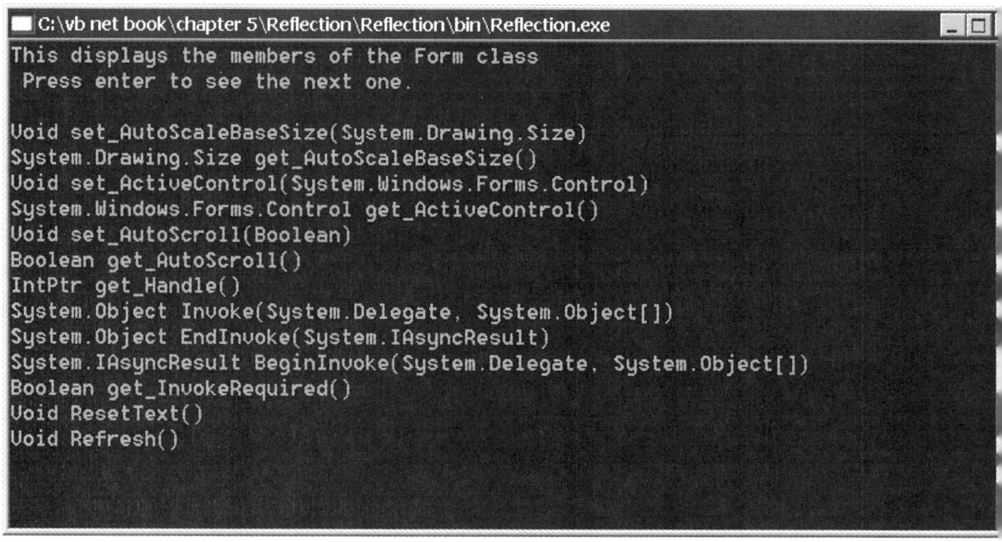

```
C:\vb net book\chapter 5\Reflection\Reflection\bin\Reflection.exe
This displays the members of the Form class
 Press enter to see the next one.

Void set_AutoScaleBaseSize(System.Drawing.Size)
System.Drawing.Size get_AutoScaleBaseSize()
Void set_ActiveControl(System.Windows.Forms.Control)
System.Windows.Forms.Control get_ActiveControl()
Void set_AutoScroll(Boolean)
Boolean get_AutoScroll()
IntPtr get_Handle()
System.Object Invoke(System.Delegate, System.Object[])
System.Object EndInvoke(System.IAsyncResult)
System.IAsyncResult BeginInvoke(System.Delegate, System.Object[])
Boolean get_InvokeRequired()
Void ResetText()
Void Refresh()
```

Figure 5-5. The members of the `Windows.Forms.Form` *class via reflection*

> **TIP** *You can replace this code with an instance of another class to see its members, and you can also get a* `Type` *object by passing the fully qualified name of the class as a string to a version of* `GetType` *that is a shared member of* `Type` *class. Reflection allows for late binding in VB .NET via the* `InvokeMember` *method, which takes a string that identifies the member you want to call (which presumably you discovered by reflection). See the .NET documentation for the* `Type` *class for more on this feature.*

MemberWiseClone

First off, in programming, as in modern science:

- A clone is an identical copy of an object.
- The clone's state can change from the original object's state.

but most important:

- Changes to the clone should not affect the object it was cloned from.

> **CAUTION** *This last point is what makes cloning tricky in any OOP language, and it is why* `MemberWiseClone` *is such a potentially dangerous method. The problem is that objects can have objects inside of them and, if you do not clone the internal objects at the same time as you clone the object that contains them, you end up with objects that are joined at the hip and depend on each other as a result—not what you want in a clone. The problem is that whenever an object has mutable objects as one of its instance fields, the* `MemberWiseClone` *method always gives you just such an ill-formed, half-baked kind of clone, known as a* shallow copy. *The* `MemberWiseClone` *method successfully clones only objects whose instances fields are value types.*

Her is an example of what we mean by this caution. Arrays in VB .NET, unlike in VB6 are objects. Consider this class which has an array as an instance field that we want to try to clone:

```
Public Class EmbeddedObjects
  Private m_Data() As String
  Public Sub New(ByVal anArray() As String)
    m_Data = anArray
  End Sub
  Public Sub DisplayData()
    Dim temp As String
    For Each temp In m_Data
      Console.WriteLine(temp)
    Next
  End Sub
  Public Sub ChangeData(ByVal newData As String)
    m_Data(0) = newData
  End Sub
  Public Function Clone() As EmbeddedObjects
    Return CType(Me.MemberwiseClone, EmbeddedObjects)
  End Function
End Class
```

Now run this `Sub Main`:

```
Sub Main()
  Dim anArray() As String = {"HELLO"}
  Dim a As New EmbeddedObjects(anArray)
  Console.WriteLine("Am going to display the data in object a now!")
  a.DisplayData()
  Dim b As EmbeddedObjects
  b = a.Clone()
```

```
    Dim newData As String = "GOODBYE"
    b.ChangeData(newData)
    Console.WriteLine("Am going to display the data in object b now!")
    b.DisplayData()
    Console.WriteLine("Am going to re-display the data in a" & _
    " after making a change to object b!!!")
    a.DisplayData()
    Console.ReadLine()
  End Sub
```

The result is pretty dramatic, as you can see in Figure 5-6: the change to the "clone" affected the original object!

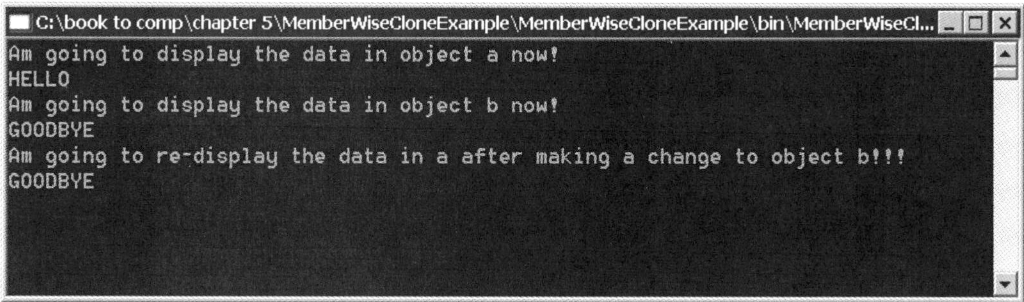

Figure 5-6. Why `MemberWiseClone` *generally will not work*

What is going on in this example? Why does `MemberWiseClone` fail? Why do changes to object `b` affect object `a`? The reason is that in lines **2** and **4** of the `EmbeddedObject` class, we used an *array* as an instance field that is set in the constructor. Arrays are mutable objects and, as you saw in Chapter 3, this means the contents of an array can be changed even when passed `ByVal`. We changed the state of the internal array in lines **12–14** of the `EmbeddedObjects` class. Because the object and its "clone" are joined by the reference to the `m_Data` array, these changes persist when we changed the clone, as you just saw.

You will see how to fix this example in the section on `ICloneable` later in this chapter. For now, we merely point out that a true clone (sometimes called a *deep copy*) creates clones of all the instance fields of the object, and continues doing it recursively if necessary. For example, if a class has an object instance field that in turn has another object instance field, the cloning process must go two layers down.

> **TIP** *There are some clever ways to do cloning that depend on serialization. See Chapter 9 for more on these tricks.*

Finally, as a way of dealing with its potential problems, the designers of the .NET Framework made MemberWiseClone a protected member of Object. This means, as you saw earlier, that only the derived class itself can call MemberWiseClone. Code from outside the derived class cannot call this dangerous method in order to clone an object. Also note that MemberWiseClone returns an Object, which is why we had to use the CType function in line **16** of the EmbeddedObjects class.

The Fragile Base Class Problem: Versioning

The versioning problem occurred all too often in programming for earlier versions of Windows, usually in the form of DLL hell—you used a version of a DLL and a new version came along that broke your code. Why did it break your code? The reasons were as obvious as someone inadvertently removing a function you depended on in the second version, or as subtle as changing the return type of a function. In any case all the sources of DLL hell amount to variations on a theme: someone changes the public interface of code you depend on, your program is no longer able to use the newer DLL in place of the older one, and the older one is overwritten. Whenever you used inheritance in most other OOP languages, you greatly increased the risk of your code breaking because of versioning issues. You had to depend on all of the public and protected members of classes higher up in the food chain not changing in a way that would break your code. This situation is called the *fragile base class problem*: because inheritance often seems to make our programs resemble a house of cards, and any disturbance to the bottom layer (the base class) causes the whole house to fall down. The best way to see this problem in action is to work with some code. Start by coding the following PayableEntity class into a separate class library and then compile it into an assembly called PayableEntityExample (you can also of course download the code from www.apress.com) by choosing Build. (Recall you create a named assembly by right-clicking on the name of the project in the Solution Explorer and adjusting the options in the dialog box that pops up after you choose Properties.) If you are not using our source code tree then please note the directory in which you built the project.

```
Public MustInherit Class PayableEntity
  Private m_Name As String
  Public Sub New(ByVal theName As String)
    m_Name = theName
  End Sub
```

```
  Public ReadOnly Property TheName() As String
    Get
      Return m_Name
    End Get
  End Property
  Public MustOverride Property TaxID() As String
End Class
```

Close the solution after you have built this DLL.

Now suppose you decide to add a way of getting an address into an `Employee` class that depends on the `PayableEntity` base class, remembering that we are only going to use the class in its *compiled* form. To do this you will need to add a reference to the assembly that contains this project by going into the `\bin` subdirectory where you built the `PayableEntityExample` DLL. The code for our `Employee` class might look like the following; note the line in bold where we inherit from the abstract class defined in the `PayableEntityExample` assembly:

```
Public Class Employee
  'since the namespace is PayableEntityExample, the full name of the class
  'is PayableEntityExample.PayableEntity!
  Inherits PayableEntityExample.Employee
  Private m_Name As String
  Private m_Salary As Decimal
  Private m_Address As String
  Private m_TaxID As String
  Private Const LIMIT As Decimal = 0.1D
  Public Sub New(ByVal theName As String, ByVal curSalary As Decimal,_
 ByVal TaxID As String)
    MyBase.New(theName)
    m_Name = theName
    m_Salary = curSalary
    m_TaxID = TaxID
  End Sub
  Public Property Address() As String
    Get
      Return m_Address
    End Get
    Set(ByVal Value As String)
      m_Address = Value
    End Set
  End Property
```

```
  Public ReadOnly Property Salary() As Decimal
    Get
      Return m_Salary
    End Get
  End Property
  Public Overrides Property TaxID() As String
    Get
      Return m_TaxID
    End Get
    Set(ByVal Value As String)
      If Value.Length <> 11 Then
        'need to do something here - see Chapter 7
      Else
        m_TaxID = Value
      End If
    End Set
  End Property
End Class
```

The `Sub Main` might look like this:

```
Sub Main()
  Dim tom As New Employee("Tom", 50000)
  tom.Address = "901 Grayson"
  Console.Write(tom.TheName & " lives at " & tom.Address)
  Console.ReadLine()
  End Sub
```

and the result, as you expect, would be like Figure 5-7.

Figure 5-7. A simple program with no versioning yet

You compile this into Versioning1.exe and everyone is happy!

Now, let us imagine the `PayableEntity` class is actually supplied by a third party. The brilliant designers of the `PayableEntity` class are not sitting on their laurels, so they decide to do what they actually should have done in the first place: they add an address *object* to their class, then recompile and send you the new DLL. Although they might not send you the source code, we give it to you here. Notice the change to the constructor (in bold):

```
Imports Microsoft.VisualBasic.ControlChars
Public Class PayableEntity
  Private m_Name As String
  Private m_Address As Address
  Public Sub New(ByVal theName As String, ByVal theAddress As Address)
    m_Name = theName
    m_Address = theAddress
  End Sub
  Public ReadOnly Property TheName() As String
    Get
      Return m_Name
    End Get
  End Property
  Public ReadOnly Property TheAddress()
    Get
      Return m_Address.DisplayAddress
    End Get
  End Property
End Class
Public Class Address
  Private m_Address As String
  Private m_City As String
  Private m_State As String
  Private m_Zip As String
  Public Sub New(ByVal theAddress As String, ByVal theCity As String, _
  ByVal theState As String, ByVal theZip As String)
    m_Address = theAddress
    m_City = theCity
    m_State = theState
    m_Zip = theZip
  End Sub
  Public Function DisplayAddress() As String
      Return m_Address & CrLf & m_City & ", " & m_State _
      & crLF & m_Zip
  End Function
End Class
```

This is, of course, an example of truly lousy programming at work. The developers who coded this managed to lose the original constructor in the process of "improving" the original version, something that should never be done. Still, horrors like this did happen and, in the olden days, you probably would have the old DLL installed on a user's hard disk, usually in Windows/System. Then the new DLL would come along, overwrite the previous version, and your previously happily running Versioning1 program would break. (And since the constructor for the parent class changed, you were truly toast.)

Granted, designers of base classes should not do this, but we all know they did. Try this under .NET, however, and something wonderful happens: your old program continues to run just fine, because it uses the original PayableEntity DLL which is automatically stored in the `\bin` directory of the Versioning1 solution.

> **CAUTION** *Ultimately, the .NET Framework solves the versioning problem by making sure your class knows which version of a DLL it depends on and refuses to run if the correct version is not present. This process is successful because of the magic of assemblies (see Chapter 13). However, you can still circumvent the help .NET's versioning scheme gives you by copying the new DLL to the location of the older DLL under the scenario we just sketched.*

.NET's versioning scheme allows the vendor of a .NET component to add new members to the next version of their base class (even though the practice should not be encouraged). Vendors can do this even if the new member happens to have the same name as a member that *you* inadvertently added to a child class that depended on their base class. The old executable created from the derived class continues to work, because it will not use the new DLL.

Actually, this is not quite true: it does run fine—until you reopen the source code for the Versioning1 code in VS .NET, reference the *new* PayableEntityExample DLL and try to rebuild the Versioning1 code. At that point, you will see an like error message like this:

```
C:\book to comp\chapter 5\Versioning1\Versioning1\Module1.vb(21):
No argument specified or non-optional parameter 'theAddress' of
'Public Sub New(theName As String, theAddress
As PayableEntityExample.Address)'.
```

The point is once you load up the old source code for the derived class and *reference the new DLL*, you will not be able to recompile the code until you fix the incompatibility that the vendor of the parent class stuck you with.

Before we end this section, we want to make sure that you are not thinking that eliminating a constructor in favor of a different constructor is a pretty drastic mistake. Does .NET versioning protect you from more subtle problems? The answer is yes.

Consider the most common, if subtle, source of versioning problems when you use inheritance: a `Derived` class depends on a `Parent` base class. You introduce a `ParseIt` method in the `Derived` class (as in the following code where we merely add carriage return/line feed combinations in the parts of the string we want to display):

```
Imports Microsoft.VisualBasic.ControlChars
Module Module1
  Sub Main()
    Dim myDerived As New Derived()
    myDerived.DisplayIt()
    Console.ReadLine()
  End Sub
End Module
Public Class Parent
  Public Const MY_STRING As String = "this is a test"
  Public Overridable Sub DisplayIt()
    Console.WriteLine(MY_STRING)
  End Sub
End Class
Public Class Derived
  Inherits Parent
  Public Overrides Sub DisplayIt()
    Console.WriteLine(ParseIt(MyBase.MY_STRING))
  End Sub
  Public Function ParseIt(ByVal aString As String)
    Dim tokens() As String
'actually split defaults to splitting on spaces
    tokens = aString.Split(Chr(32))
    Dim temp As String
    'rejoin them into one string adding a CR/LF betweeen the words
    temp = Join(tokens, CrLf)
    Return temp
  End Function
End Class
End Module
```

You will see Figure 5-8.

Now imagine you are supplied the `Parent` class in compiled form instead of in source form. And, when you are shipped Version 2 of the `Parent` class, it comes with its own version of `ParseIt` that it uses extensively in *its* code. Because functions in VB .NET are virtual, polymorphism dictates that calls to `DisplayIt` when an object

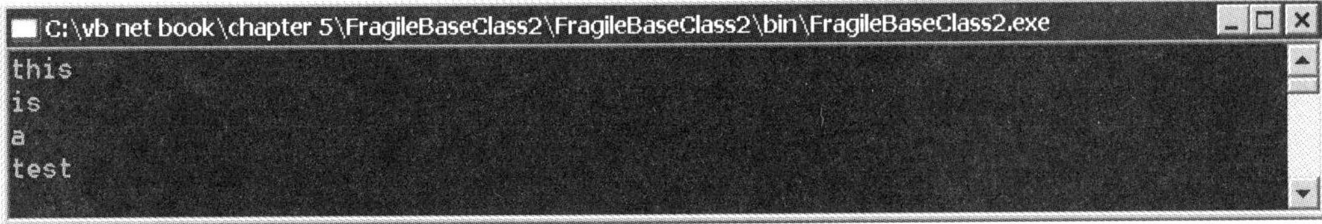

Figure 5-8. A simple parsing program at work

of type `Derived` is stored in an object variable of type `Parent`, will always use the `ParseIt` method of the `Derived` class and not the `ParseIt` method in the parent class. However, we now have a potential, if very subtle, versioning problem. In this scenario, the code in the `Parent` class that uses *its* version of `ParseIt` function does not know how the `Derived` class implemented `ParseIt`. Using the derived class version of `ParseIt`, as polymorphism requires, could break what is needed for the parent class's functioning.

VB .NET versioning works wonders here, too: the code in the compiled base class `Parent` continues to use its version of `ParseIt` under *all* circumstances, even though polymorphism would require it to use the wrong version when `Derived` objects are stored in `Parent` type variables. And, just as we mentioned for the previous example, when you open up the code for `Derived` in Visual Studio, the compiler will tell you that you must either add the `Override` or the `Shadows` keyword to the `ParseIt` member of your child class to eliminate the confusion.

Overview of Interfaces

We hope we have convinced you that inheritance has its place in VB .NET, but you need to also master interfaces to take full advantage of VB .NET's OOP features. We take this powerful feature up in the next few sections.

First off, think of *implementing* an interface as making a binding contract with any class that uses your class. Interface-style programming is the foundation of what is called *object composition* or *black box reuse* in OOP theory. Interfaces, of course, were also at the heart of COM programming, and how OOP was done in earlier versions of VB.) With interfaces, you rely on the class you depend on to expose certain functionality defined by the signature of the header of the member, now and forever. Unlike inheritance, there are no dependencies involved with interfaces—each implementation of an interface can stand on its own.

> **NOTE** *In the world of OOP theory, maxims such as "favor object composition over inheritance" (that is, use interfaces not inheritance) are common. With .NET's solution to the versioning problem, this is much less of a problem. You should feel free to use inheritance where it makes sense: where the "is-a" relationship holds.*

When you implement an interface, you:

- Assert that your code will have methods with certain signatures
- Have code (possibly even empty code) with *those signatures* inside the class

The actual implementation of these members can vary and, as we just said, they can even do nothing. All you do is make a promise to have certain code with certain signatures. This simple promise has a lot of nice consequences. Some of the best ones are:

- It lets a smart compiler replace calls into your code with a fast table lookup and a jump.
- From the programmer's point of view, it lets developers call code in your classes by signature, without fear that the member does not exist.
- The binding contract also lets a compiler use polymorphism just as well as inheritance chains do.

NOTE *Polymorphism works because, when you call a method that is implemented as part of an interface, the .NET compiler finds out at compile time (early binding is the technical term) what code to call based on the signature specified and the type of the class.*

Compare this to what happens if:

- You do not make a contract that you will support a method with a specified signature by implementing an interface.
- You are not in an inheritance chain in which VB .NET can find a method with the right signature.

Here is what happens: if `Option Strict` is on, your code will not even compile. Even if `Option Strict` is off because your code has not promised that it will support the method, the .NET compiler is smart enough not to go looking for what may or may not be there at compile time. It therefore cannot put the equivalent of a function call into compiled code where you call into a class. This means at compile time, the compiler generates a lot more code, which has the effect of politely asking the object at run time if it supports the method with the signature you specified and would it mind running the method if it does. This kind of code has two features that make it *much slower* and *much more error prone*:

1. It needs error-trapping code, in case you were wrong.

2. Because the compiler cannot know at compile time where to jump to find the method inside the memory that the object occupies, it has to rely on more indirect methods to send it the location of the member at run time.

This whole process is called *late binding*, and not only is it significantly slower than early binding, it is not even allowed (except via reflection) when you have `Option Strict` on (as you always should).

Mechanics of Implementing an Interface

Many programming shops (Microsoft, for example) subscribe to the notion of a lead programmer or lead tester on a team. Suppose you want to extend your employee management program to allow for the idea of a Lead Programmer or Lead Tester with certain special properties such as having a morale fund to cheer up people when they have been working too hard.

In building this possibility into an Employee Management system program, you cannot use inheritance in VB .NET, because the `Programmer` class and the `Tester` class already inherit from the `Employee` class and only single inheritance is allowed in .NET. This is a perfect example of where an interface comes to your rescue.

> **NOTE** *The convention in .NET is to use a capital "I" in front of the interface name, so we call our example interface* `ILead`.

The first step is to define the interface. Unlike VB6, in which an interface was merely a class, VB .NET has an `Interface` keyword. For example, let us suppose leads have to rate team members and they get to spend the morale fund. The interface definition would look like this:

```
Public Interface ILead
  Sub SpendMoraleFund(ByVal amount As Decimal)
  Function Rate(ByVal aPerson As Employee) As String
  Property MyTeam() As Employee()
  Property MoraleFund() As Decimal
End Interface
```

Notice that there are no access modifiers such as `Public` or `Private` in an interface definition; the only valid modifiers for `Sub`, `Function`, or `Property` statements are `Overloads` and `Default`. Defining an interface is thus pretty easy. Any class implementing our `ILead` interface makes a contract to have:

- A sub that takes a decimal as a parameter
- A function that takes an `Employee` object and returns a string
- A read-write property that returns an array of `Employee` objects
- A read-write property that returns a decimal

And, as you will soon see, the names of members in the implementing methods do not matter—the key point is that they have the promised signature.

To implement an interface in a class, the first step is to make sure the interface is referenced or already part of the solution. Next, you include the `Implements` keyword in the line following the class name and any `Inherits` statement. For example:

```
Public Class LeadProgrammer
  Inherits Programmer
  Implements ILead
End Class
```

At this point, you will see that the keyword `ILead` is underscored by a blue squiggly line indicating a problem. This is because the compiler is insisting that you fulfill your contract, even if only by using empty methods.

How do you do this? Unlike earlier versions of VB, which used a specific form of the signature to indicate a member implemented an interface, VB .NET indicates this directly, as you can see in the bold second line in this code:

```
Public Function Rate(ByVal aPerson As Employee) As String _
Implements ILead.Rate
End Functio
```

Although it is certainly common to match up the names of the interface member and the member that implements it, it is not necessary. For example, this is perfectly acceptable:

```
Public Property OurMoraleFund() As Decimal Implements ILead.MoraleFund
  Get
    Return m_MoraleFund
  End Get
```

```
  Set(ByVal Value As Decimal)
    m_MoraleFund = Value
  End Set
End Property
```

The key point is that the parameter and return types match the signature used for that part of the interface. You can use any legal attributes on that kind of method—`Overloads`, `Overrides`, `Overridable`, `Public`, `Private`, `Protected`, `Friend`, `Protected Friend`, `MustOverride`, `Default`, and `Static` modifiers—and still fulfill the contract. The `Shared` attribute is the only one you cannot use, because interface methods must be instance members, not class members.

If you use a `Private` member of a class to implement an interface member, then the only way to get at that member is through a variable of that interface's type. Otherwise, unlike earlier versions of VB, you can always access interface members through an object of the class type. You no longer have to assign it to a variable of the interfaces type. For example:

```
Dim tom As New LeadProgrammer("Tom", 65000)
tom.SpendMoraleFund(500)
```

To go the other way, however, you must use `CType`:

```
Dim tom As New LeadProgrammer("Tom", 65000)
Dim aLead As ILead, aName As String
aLead = tom
aName = Ctype(aLead, Programmer).TheName ' OK
```

but a line like this is not possible:

```
aName = tom.TheName 'NOT ALLOWED
```

In general, here are the rules for converting between an object type and an interface it implements:

- You can always assign a variable declared to be of the class type to the variable declared to be of any interface type that the class implements.

In particular, if a method takes as a parameter a variable of an interface type, you can pass into it a variable of any type that implements the interface. (This rule is analogous to the fundamental inheritance rule that derived types can always be used in place of their parent types.) However:

- You must use `CType` to go from a variable of the interface type to a variable of a type that implements the interface.

To determine if an object implements an interface, use `TypeOf` with `Is`. For example:

```
Dim tom As New LeadProgrammer("tom", 50000)
Console.WriteLine((TypeOf (tom) Is ILead))
```

returns `True`.

> **NOTE** *You can even write a single method that implements multiple methods defined in a single interface, as follows:*
>
> ```
> Public Sub itsOK Implements Interface1.M1, Interface1.M2, Interface1.M3
> ```

Here is the full version of our `LeadProgrammer` class. Of course, we have not done much in the implementation of the interface members, but this code gives you an idea of what you can do:

```
Public Class LeadProgrammer
  Inherits Programmer
  Implements ILead
  Private m_MoraleFund As Decimal
  Private m_MyTeam As Employee()
  Public Function Rate(ByVal aPerson As Employee) As String _
  Implements ILead.Rate
    Return aPerson.TheName & " rating to be done"
  End Function
  Public Property MyTeam() As Employee() _
  Implements ILead.MyTeam
    Get
      Return m_MyTeam
    End Get
    Set(ByVal Value As Employee())
      m_MyTeam = Value
    End Set
  End Property
  Public Sub SpendMoraleFund(ByVal amount As Decimal) _
  Implements ILead.SpendMoraleFund
    'spend some money
    Console.WriteLine("Spent " & amount.ToString())
  End Sub
```

```
  Public Property OurMoraleFund() As Decimal Implements ILead.MoraleFund
    Get
      Return m_MoraleFund
    End Get
    Set(ByVal Value As Decimal)
      m_MoraleFund = Value
    End Set
  End Property
  Public Sub New(ByVal theName As String, ByVal curSalary As Decimal)
    MyBase.New(theName, curSalary)
  End Sub
End Class
```

Advanced Use of Interfaces

You can also have one interface inherit from another. An interface definition such as this is allowed, where you merely add one more member to the interface. For example, suppose in our employee management system lead programmers have the authority to upgrade the hardware for members of their team. This would be modeled in code via a method like:

```
Public Interface ILeadProgrammer
Inherits ILead
  Public Function UpGradeHardware(aPerson As Programmer)
End Interface
```

After you do this, implementing `ILeadProgrammer` requires fulfilling the contract for both `ILead` and `ILeadProgrammer`.

Unlike classes, which can only derive from one parent class, an interface may derive from multiple interfaces:

```
Public Interface ILeadProgrammer
Inherits ILead, Inherits ICodeGuru
  Public Function UpGradeHardware(aPerson As Programmer)
End Interface
```

CAUTION *Because you can inherit an interface from multiple interfaces, an interface can be required to implement two identically named methods which only differ in the interface they are part of; for example, if both the* `ILead` *and* `ICodeGuru` *interfaces have methods called* `SpendMoraleFund`*. When this happens, you lose the ability to see either one of the identically named methods via a variable of a type that implements this kind of interface.*

```
Dim tom As New LeadProgrammer("Tom", 65000)
tom.SpendMoraleFund(500)
```

you need to explicitly identify the interface using this kind of code:

```
Dim tom As New LeadProgrammer("Tom", 65000)
Dim aCodeGuru As CodeGuru
aCodeGuru = tom
aCodeGuru.SpendMoraleFund(500)
```

When to Use Interfaces, When to Use Inheritance?

Although an interface seems a lot like an abstract class, this analogy can be more trouble than it is worth to follow. An abstract class can have many concrete members, but an interface can have none. You should create abstract base classes only after a thoughtful process of factoring common behavior out to the most primitive ancestor possible, and for no other reason.

An interface exists outside an inheritance chain—that is its virtue. You lose the ability to automatically reuse code, but you gain the flexibility of choosing your own implementation of the contract. Use an interface when you want to indicate that certain behavior is required, but you are willing to leave the actual implementation of the behavior to the implementing class. In .NET, structures cannot inherit from anything except `Object`, but they can implement interfaces. Interfaces are the *only* choice available to you in .NET when two classes have some common behavior but there is no ancestor they are both examples of.

Important Interfaces in the .NET Framework

We obviously cannot cover all the interfaces in the .NET Framework in these few pages, but we want to mention a few of the most important ones. Two are in some sense marker interfaces, because you implement them to advertise that your classes have a certain type of functionality that many classes may want to exhibit. These marker interfaces are:

- `ICloneable`: Indicates a `Clone` method that provides a deep copy
- `IDisposable`: Tells the user that your class consumes resources that the garbage collectors will not be able to reclaim

We cover the basic interfaces for building special purpose collections later in this chapter. For those who remember how hard it was to implement a `For-Each` in VB6, you are in for a real treat!

ICloneable

As you saw in the `MemberWiseClone` section, cloning an object that contains internal objects is tricky. .NET's designers decided to let you indicate that you are providing this feature through a marker interface called `ICloneable`, which contains one member `Clone`:

```
Public Interface ICloneable
  Function Clone() As Object
End Interface
```

Implement this interface (and hence the `Clone` method) if you want to offer users of your class the opportunity to clone instances of that class. It is then up to you to decide if using `MemberWiseClone` is enough when you actually implement the `Clone` method in your class. As we said previously, `MemberWiseClone` is enough if the instance fields are value types or immutable types like String. For example, in our `Employee` class, using `MemberWiseClone` would work to clone the `Employee` class because all instance fields are either strings or value types. Hence we can implement `ICloneable` as in the following code:

```
Public Class Employee Implements ICloneable
  Public Function Clone() As Object _
  Implements ICloneable.Clone
    Return CType(Me.MemberwiseClone, Employee)
  End Function
'more code
'
End Class
```

With classes like the `EmbeddedObjects` class you saw earlier, you have more work in front of you in order to implement a `Clone` method. (Though Chapter 9 gives you a technique that makes the task fairly easy in most cases.) In the case of the `EmbeddedObjects` class, you only need to add a method to clone the internal array instead of simply copying it.

How can you do this? Well, because the `Array` class implements `ICloneable`, it must come with a method to clone an array. This actually makes our task pretty easy. Here is how a version of `EmbeddedObjects` that implements `ICloneable` could work (the key lines for the `Clone` method are in bold):

```
Public Class EmbeddedObjects
  Implements ICloneable
  Private m_Data() As String
  Public Sub New(ByVal anArray() As String)
    m_Data = anArray
  End Sub
  Public Function Clone() As Object _
  Implements ICloneable.Clone
    Dim temp() As String
    temp = m_Data.Clone 'clone the array
    Return New EmbeddedObjects(temp)
  End Function
  Public Sub DisplayData()
    Dim temp As String
    For Each temp In m_Data
      Console.WriteLine(temp)
    Next
  End Sub
  Public Sub ChangeData(ByVal newData As String)
    m_Data(0) = newData
  End Sub
End Class
```

TIP *You can see a list of the framework classes that implement* `ICloneable` *(and hence have a* `Clone` *method) by looking at the online help for the* `ICloneable` *interface.*

IDisposable

We have mentioned that you should not rely on the `Finalize` method to clean up after resources that the automatic garbage collector cannot know about. The convention in .NET programming is to implement the `IDisposable` interface instead, because it has a single member `Dispose`, which should contain the code to reclaim resources.

```
Public Interface IDisposable
  Sub Dispose()
End Interface
```

The rule is:

- If your class uses a class that implements `IDisposable` you must call the `Dispose` method:

For example, as you will see in the Chapter 8, every GUI application depends on a base class called `Component`, because you need to reclaim the graphics context that all components use:

```
Public Class Component
  Inherits MarshalByRefObject
  Implements IComponent, IDisposable
```

> **TIP** *The online help for the* `IDisposable` *interface includes a list of the framework classes that implement* `IDisposable` *(and hence have a* `Dispose` *method that you must call).*

Collections

Collections are a fancy term for containers that hold methods and give you different ways to add, remove, or access them. These methods can be as simple as retrieving an item by its index, as in arrays, or as sophisticated as the keyed retrieval in the `Hashtable` class you saw in the previous chapter. The .NET Framework contains quite a few of these useful collection classes and, as you have seen, you can easily extend them via inheritance to build your own type-safe collection. However, the most sophisticated use of the built-in collection classes requires knowledge of the interfaces they implement. We show you some of the common collection interfaces in the next few sections.

For Each *and* IEnumerable

In VB6, getting a class to allow a `For Each` was completely unintuitive and, we think, required a terrible kludge (as we pointed out way back in Chapter 1). In VB .NET, you have two ways of allowing `For Each` to work with a collection class. You have already seen the first method: if you inherit from a class that allows `For Each`, then you get it for free. We did this with the `Employees` class that inherited from the `System.Collections.CollectionBase` class.

The second method requires you to implement the `IEnumerable` interface but gives you the most flexibility. Here is the definition of this interface:

```
Public Interface IEnumerable
  Function GetEnumerator() As IEnumerator
End Interface
```

Any time you have a class that implements `IEnumerable`, it uses the `GetEnumerator` method to return an `IEnumerator` object that will let you iterate over the class. The `IEnumerator` interface is the one that has methods to move to the next item, so its definition is:

```
Public Interface IEnumerator
  ReadOnly Property Current As Object
  Function MoveNext() As Boolean
  Sub Reset()
End Interface
```

The idea is a `For Each` allows only read-only, forward movement, so the `IEnumerator` interface abstracts this idea by having methods for moving forward but no methods for changing the data. As a convenience, it also includes a required method to go back to the start of the collection. `IEnumerator` is commonly implemented via containment: you place a container class inside the collection and delegate to that class the fulfillment of the three interface methods (the one from `IEnumerable` and the two from `IEnumerator`).

Here is an example of an enumerable `Employees` collection built from scratch. It is obviously more complicated than merely inheriting from `System.Collections.CollectionBase`, but you get much more flexibility. For example, you can replace the simple array of employees with a custom sorted array.

```
Public Class Employees
  Implements IEnumerable, IEnumerator
  Private m_Employees() As Employee
  Private m_Index As Integer = -1
  Private m_Count As Integer = 0
```

```
6    Public Function GetEnumerator() As IEnumerator _
7    Implements IEnumerable.GetEnumerator
8      Return Me
9    End Function
10    Public ReadOnly Property Current() As Object _
11  Implements IEnumerator.Current
12      Get
13        Return m_Employees(m_Index)
14      End Get
15    End Property
16    Public Function MoveNext() As Boolean _
17    Implements IEnumerator.MoveNext
18      If m_Index < m_Count Then
19        m_Index += 1
20        Return True
21      Else
22        Return False
23      End If
24    End Function
25    Public Sub Reset() Implements IEnumerator.Reset
26      m_Index = 0
27    End Sub
28    Public Sub New(ByVal theEmployees() As Employee)
29      If theEmployees Is Nothing Then
30        MsgBox("No items in the collection")
31        'should throw an exception see Chapter 7
32        'Throw New ApplicationException()
33      Else
34        m_Count = theEmployees.Length - 1
35        m_Employees = theEmployees
36      End If
37    End Sub
38    End Class
```

Line **2** shows that the class is going to implement the two key interfaces itself. To do this, we must implement a function that returns an `IEnumerator` object. As lines **6–9** indicate, we simply return `Me`—the current object. But to do this, our class must implement the members of `IEnumerable`, which we do in lines **10–27**.

> **NOTE** *There is one subtle programming issue in the preceding code that has nothing to do with interfaces but rather with the code we used in this class. In line **4**, we initialize the* `m_Index` *variable to –1, which gives us access to the 0'th member of the array. (As an experiment, change this to 0 and you will see that you always lose the first entry in the array).*

Here is some example code to try, assuming you also have the `Public Employee` class as part of this solution:

```
Sub Main()
  Dim tom As New Employee("Tom", 50000)
  Dim sally As New Employee("Sally", 60000)
  Dim joe As New Employee("Joe", 10000)
  Dim theEmployees(1) As Employee
  theEmployees(0) = tom
  theEmployees(1) = sally
  Dim myEmployees As New Employees(theEmployees)
  Dim aEmployee As Employee
  For Each aEmployee In myEmployees
    Console.WriteLine(aEmployee.TheName)
  Next
  Console.ReadLine()
End Sub
```

ICollection

The `ICollection` interface inherits from `IEnumerable` and adds three read-only properties and one new method. `ICollection`, which is rarely implemented alone, forms a base for the `IList` and `IDictionary` interfaces, which we cover next. Table 5-2 lists the members of this interface.

Table 5-2. Members of the `ICollection` *Interface*

MEMBER	DESCRIPTION
`Count` property	Returns the number of objects in the collection.
`IsSynchronized` property	Used with threading (see Chapter 12). This property returns `True` if access to the collection is synchronized for multithreaded access.
`SyncRoot` property	Also used with threading (see Chapter 12). This property returns an object that lets you synchronize access to the collection.
`CopyTo` method	Provides a way to copy elements from the collection into an array, starting at the array position specified.

> **NOTE** *The* `System.Collections.CollectionBase` *class implements* `ICollection`.

IList

The `IList` interface gives you access to members of a collection by index. Of course, since this interface inherits from `IEnumerable`, you do not lose the ability to use `For Each`. The inheritance chain for `IList` looks like this:

- IEnumerable⇒Collection⇒IList

The `IList` interface is pretty sophisticated—it has three properties and seven methods (see Table 5-3). Of course, as always, you can give empty implementations of some of these methods if they do not make sense for your class.

Table 5-3. Members of the `IList` *Interface*

MEMBER	DESCRIPTION
`IsFixedSize` property	Implement this Boolean property to tell users of your class that the list has a fixed size.
`IsReadOnly` property	Implement this Boolean property to tell users of your class that the list is read-only.
`Item` property	This read-write property lets you get or set the item at the specified index.
`Add( ByVal value As Object) As Integer` method	Adds an item to the list at the current index. Should return the index where the item was added.
`Clear` method	Removes all items from the list.
`Contains(ByVal value As Object) As Boolean` method	Can be tricky to implement efficiently, because it is designed to determine if the list contains a specific value. Returns True if the item was found and False otherwise.
`IndexOf(ByVal value As Object) As Integer` method	Also needs to be implemented efficiently, since it returns the index of the specified item.
`Insert(ByVal index As Integer, ByVal value As Object)` method	Inserts an item into the list at the specified position.

Table 5-3. Members of the `IList` *Interface (Continued)*

MEMBER	DESCRIPTION
`Remove(ByVal value As Object)` method	Removes the first occurrence of the specific object from the list.
`RemoveAt(ByVal index As Integer)` method	Removes the item at the specified index.

> **NOTE** *The* `System.Collections.CollectionBase` *class implements* `IList`.

IDictionary

The `IDictionary` interface represents a collection that you access via keys as you do the hashtables we covered in the previous chapter. In fact, hashtables implement `IDictionary`, `ICollection`, `IEnumerable`, and `ICloneable`, among other interfaces!

Although `IDictionary` inherits from `IEnumerable`, you can use `MoveNext` to move to the next item—objects that implement `IDictionary` are usually not iterated through item by item. Because you use them only where keyed access is needed, the `IDictionary` interface depends on an `IDictionaryEnumerator` interface that extends `IEnumerator` and adds three new properties:

- `Entry`, which returns a `When` implemented by a class, gets both the key and the value of the current dictionary entry
- `Key`, which returns the current key
- `Value`, which returns a reference to the current value

> **TIP** *The .NET Framework comes with a* `DictionaryBase` *class that you can inherit from to get at the functionality of the* `IDictionary` *interface.*

The members of the `IDictionary` interface are shown in Table 5-4.

Table 5-4. Members of `IDictionary`

INTERFACE MEMBER	DESCRIPTION
`IsFixedSize` property	Boolean property, indicates that a list has a fixed size
`IsReadOnly` property	Boolean property, indicates that a list is read-only
`Item` property	A read-write property that lets you get or set the item at the specified index
`Keys` property	Returns an object that implements `ICollection`, which contains the keys of the `IDictionary`
`Values` property	Returns an object that implements `ICollection`, which contains the values in the `IDictionary`
`Add(ByVal key As Object, ByVal value As Object)` method	Lets you add an item to the list using the specified key (which must be unique)
`Clear` method	Removes all items in the dictionary
`Contains(ByVal key As Object) As Boolean` method	Looks for an item with the specified key
`GetEnumerator` method	Returns an `IDictionaryEnumerator` object that allows you to work with keys and values
`Remove(ByVal key As Object)` method	Removes the object that has the specified key

CAUTION *Because dictionaries require unique keys, you must determine whether a key has already been used. The* `Keys` *property returns an object that implements* `ICollection`*, which lets you use the* `Contain` *method in the* `ICollection` *interface to determine whether a key is unique.*

IComparable

Suppose you needed to sort a collection of employee objects by salary. It would certainly be convenient if you could add this ability directly to the `Employee` class, so you could sort arrays or an array list of employees as easily as you sort arrays or array lists of strings. It turns out that the `Sort` method of `Array` and `ArrayList` sort by the order specified in an interface called `IComparable`. (For string arrays, the `IComparable` interface sorts by ASCII order). This interface has one member, `CompareTo`:

```
Function CompareTo(ByVal obj As Object) As Integer
```

whose return value is:

- Less than zero, if this instance is less than the given object
- Zero, if this instance is equal to the given object
- Greater than zero, if this instance is greater than the given object

Here is a version of the `Employee` class that implements `IEnumerable` and `IComparable` and orders the array by salary with the largest salary first:

```
Public Class Employee
  Implements IComparable
  Private m_Name As String
  Private m_Salary As Decimal
  Private Const LIMIT As Decimal = 0.1D
  Public Sub New(ByVal theName As String, ByVal curSalary As Decimal)
    m_Name = theName
    m_Salary = curSalary
  End Sub
  Public Function CompareTo(ByVal anEmployee As Object) As Integer _
  Implements IComparable.CompareTo
    If CType(anEmployee, Employee).Salary < Me.Salary Then
      Return -1
    ElseIf CType(anEmployee, Employee).Salary = Me.Salary Then
      Return 0
    ElseIf CType(anEmployee, Employee).Salary > Me.Salary Then
      Return 1
    End If
  End Function
  Public ReadOnly Property TheName() As String
    Get
      Return m_Name
    End Get
  End Property
```

```
  Public ReadOnly Property Salary() As Decimal
    Get
      Return MyClass.m_Salary
    End Get
  End Property
  Public Overridable Overloads Sub RaiseSalary(ByVal Percent As Decimal)
    If Percent > LIMIT Then
      'not allowed
      Console.WriteLine("NEED PASSWORD TO RAISE SALARY MORE " & _
      "THAN LIMIT!!!!")
    Else
      m_Salary = (1 + Percent) * m_Salary
    End If
  End Sub
  Public Overridable Overloads Sub RaiseSalary(ByVal Percent As Decimal, _
    ByVal Password As String)
    If Password = "special" Then
      m_Salary = (1 + Percent) * m_Salary
    End If
  End Sub
End Class
```

To exercise this class, use this code (the key line is in bold):

```
Sub Main()
  Dim tom As New Employee("Tom", 50000)
  Dim sally As New Employee("Sally", 60000)
  Dim joe As New Employee("Joe", 20000)
  Dim gary As New Employee("Gary", 1)
  Dim theEmployees() As Employee = _
  {tom, sally, joe, gary}
  Array.Sort(theEmployees) 'will use the CompareTo order!
  Dim aEmployee As Employee
  For Each aEmployee In theEmployees
    Console.WriteLine(aEmployee.TheName & " has yearly salary $" _
    & FormatNumber(aEmployee.Salary))
  Next
  Console.ReadLine()
End Sub
```

The result is shown in Figure 5-9.

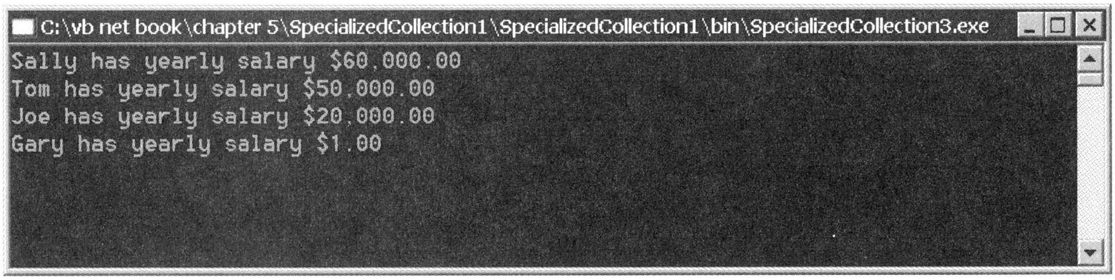

```
C:\vb net book\chapter 5\SpecializedCollection1\SpecializedCollection1\bin\SpecializedCollection3.exe
Sally has yearly salary $60,000.00
Tom has yearly salary $50,000.00
Joe has yearly salary $20,000.00
Gary has yearly salary $1.00
```

Figure 5-9. Doing a special purpose sort using `IComparable`

The `IComparer` *Interface*

The .NET Framework makes it possible to sort by multiple orders. For example, to order our array of employees by salary and then by name, you implement the `IComparer` interface, which also has a single `CompareTo` method. The trick here is that you use one of the overloaded versions of `Array.Sort` (or `ArrayList.Sort`), whose signature looks like this:

```
Public Shared Sub Sort(ByVal array As Array, ByVal comparer As IComparer)
```

Normally you create a separate class that implements `IComparer` and pass an instance of it to the `Sort` method. Following is an example of the kind of class we mean. Notice in the bold lines how we pass the employee names as strings to the `String` class's `Compare` method:

```
Public Class SortByName
  Implements IComparer
  Public Function CompareTo(ByVal firstEmp As Object, ByVal _
  secondEmp As Object) As Integer Implements IComparer.Compare
    Dim temp1 As Employee = CType(firstEmp, Employee)
    Dim temp2 As Employee = CType(secondEmp, Employee)
    Return String.Compare(temp1.TheName, temp2.TheName)
  End Function
End Class
```

With this class, the `Sub Main` might look like this (the key new lines are in bold):

```
Sub Main()
  Dim tom As New Employee("Tom", 50000)
  Dim sally As New Employee("Sally", 60000)
  Dim sam As New Employee("Sam", 60000)
  Dim ted As New Employee("Ted", 50000)
```

```
    Dim theEmployees() As Employee = _
    {tom, sally, sam, ted}
    Array.Sort(theEmployees)
    Dim SortingByName As SortByName = New SortByName()
    Array.Sort(theEmployees, SortingByName)
    Dim aEmployee As Employee
     For Each aEmployee In theEmployees
       Console.WriteLine(aEmployee.TheName & " has yearly salary $" _
      & FormatNumber(aEmployee.Salary))
    Next
    Console.ReadLine()
End Sub
```

The result is shown in Figure 5-10.

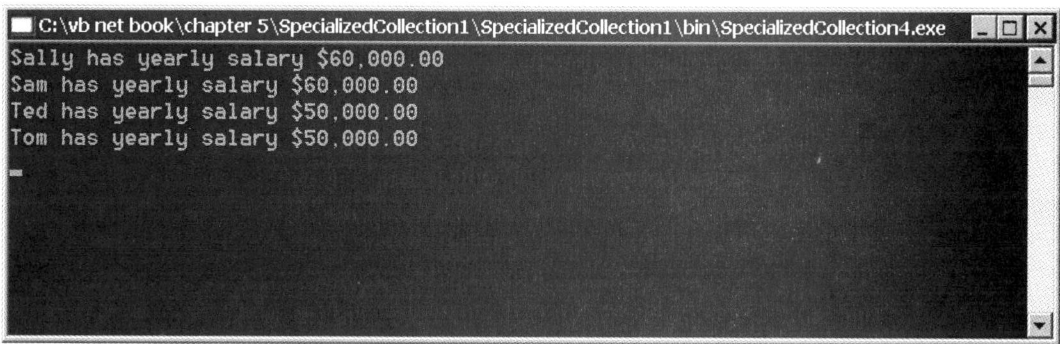

Figure 5-10. The result of using `IComparer` *to sort by mutiple conditions*

> **TIP** *You can implement as many classes that implement* `IComparer` *as you need and then use them sequentially to sort items by as many orderings within orderings as you want!*

CHAPTER 6

Event Handling and Delegates

PREVIOUS VERSIONS OF VISUAL BASIC clearly demonstrated the advantages to an event-driven, object-based programming model for improving programmer productivity. You dragged controls onto a form and they responded to certain events. You wrote code in event procedures such as `Button1_Click` to give a reasonable response to somebody clicking on a button named Button1.

As efficient as the model used in earlier versions of VB was, it was somewhat inflexible. For example, it was difficult to add new events and practically impossible to make a single event handler that handled multiple events. VB .NET combines the best of both worlds. In most situations, you can use a syntax that is very close to the syntax of earlier versions of VB, and VB .NET connects much of the needed plumbing for you. When you need more power, VB .NET gives you that, too.

In this chapter we start with the version of event handling that is similar (although significantly more powerful) to earlier versions of VB. Later in the chapter we show you how to use the new concept of a delegate to fully harness the event-handling power of the .NET platform, as well as how to use delegates for more general purposes, such as callbacks.

Event Handling from an OOP Point of View

Since object-oriented programming is all about sending messages to happily cooperating objects, events have to fit into this framework. In one way, events fall into this model nicely: an object that is the source of the event can, naturally enough, send out a message that says, "Hey, this event happened."

Still, one obvious problem is deciding which objects to send the message to. It would be impractical to send out notifications for every event that happened to *every* object currently instantiated in the program: most objects could not care less and performance would slow to a crawl.

Instead, VB .NET tries to limit the number of interested listeners by using a "subscribe/publish" model. In this model, the event listener objects register (that is, *subscribe* to) event source objects if they are interested in an event that the event source can generate (*publish*). More than one event listener can sign up for notifications from a single source. Only registered event listener objects will receive messages that an event has occurred from the source.

However, this can get tricky. What sort of message should an event listener get from the event source? How should this message be sent? What should it do? Objects send messages to other objects by calling one or more of its members. Ultimately, the same thing happens with an event notification, but there are more hoops to jump through.

The basic idea is that when an event happens, the event source calls predetermined member functions in the various listener objects. The special member function of the listener that will get called is registered by the event source at the same time it registers the listener object. This is called a *callback* notification scheme, because the event source *calls back* a method in the event listener whose address it knows. Figure 6-1 gives a picture of what happens with a callback from an event source (the boss) whose job performance action will trigger the notifications to the event listener objects. (We explain how all this can happen in VB .NET in the last half of this chapter.)

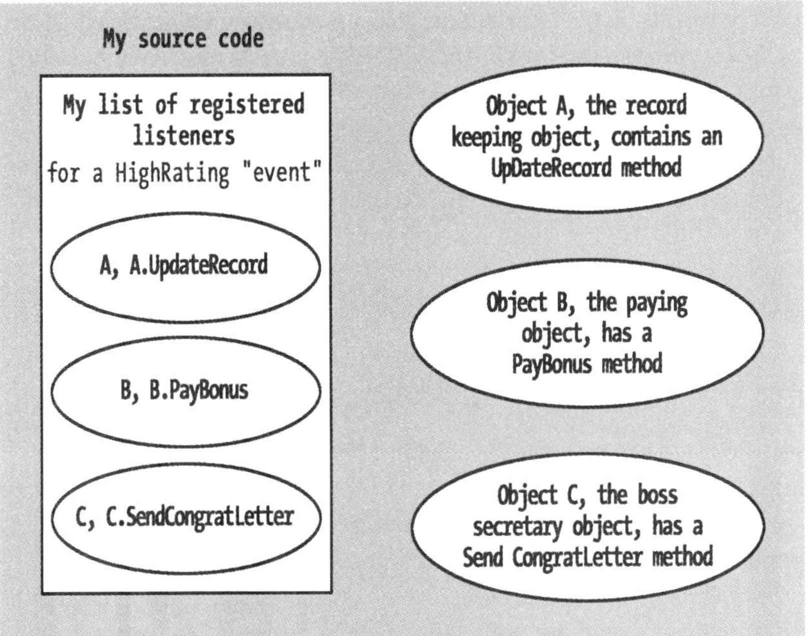

Figure 6-1. A callback notification scheme

> **NOTE** *The methods in the listener object must have a predetermined form (for example, a specific signature) for this registration process to be successful. This is why some languages, such as Java, use interfaces for callback mechanisms—it is the promise of having a method of the correct signature that is all-important.*

What Goes into the Functions Called by Events?

Although you can certainly define your own form for the members of the listener objects to be called back by an event source, there is a pretty strong convention in .NET that the member function in the listener class that gets called back has a special signature with two parameters:

- An object variable that refers to the event source
- An "event" object variable that inherits from the class `System.EventArgs` which encapsulates information about the event. (The idea is that different child classes of `System.EventArgs` will provide different properties, useful for the particular event handler.)

You saw this at work in Chapter 1. When we added a button to a form, the click event procedure in the form looked like this:

```
Private Sub Button1_Click(ByVal sender As System.Object, _
   ByVal e As System.EventArgs) Handles Button1.Click
End Sub
```

Two things happen here:

- The `sender` object variable gives a reference to the object (button) that was clicked. This means the click event procedure has a reference to the source of the event in its code.
- The object variable `e` encapsulates an event object that (potentially) contains the details of the event.

Traditionally, VB did not identify the sender (source) of an event in an event procedure because it was always going to be the object itself. (Control arrays were the sole exception to this, where the index parameter was used to isolate the exact element in the control array that was the event source.) The point of having the `sender` object variable in our generalized VB .NET event procedures becomes pretty obvious when you want to have a single procedure handle multiple events, all coming from different objects. For example, if you use the built-in `ToString` method for all objects in a line of code like this inside the event procedure just shown:

```
MsgBox(sender.ToString)
```

you will see this:

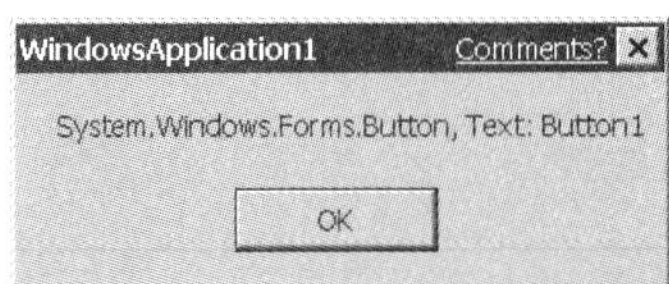

which clearly shows which object was the event source.

The event object variable `e` is not interesting in this situation because it does not provide much useful information for this event. Still, with the right event object variable, this can be very useful. For example, `MouseEventArgs` object variables let you find out where the mouse button was clicked. In general, you should build your own event classes by inheriting from the `System.EventArgs` class, which encapsulates all sorts of useful information about the event. (You see how to do this in a moment.)

Next, notice a new keyword `Handles` was used in the definition of this event procedure. This keyword is used, naturally enough, to specify which event the procedure is handling. It is true that in this case the `Handles` keyword seems unnecessary, but its existence gives you a lot of flexibility down the road. The idea is that event handlers no longer need to have specific names, just required signatures. This makes it possible, for example, for a single event handler to handle multiple events, by supplying multiple `Handles` clauses at the end of the procedure declaration. This new approach gives you a far more flexible mechanism than was possible with the control arrays used in earlier versions of VB. (Control arrays are gone in VB .NET.)

For example, while the IDE may generate an event procedure with a standard name, this is not necessary in VB .NET. As long as your Sub has the right parameters and you use the `Handles` keyword, you can use the code to handle an event. In this code, for example:

```
Private Sub MyClickProcedure(ByVal sender As System.Object, _
    ByVal e As System.EventArgs) Handles Button1.Click
```

`MyClickProcedure` *can* handle the `Button1.Click` event, since `MyClickProcedure` has the right parameters. It *does* handle the event because of the `Handles` keyword!

The key point to notice is how VB .NET explicitly uses the `Handles` keyword to say which events an event handler is handling.

As another example, if you modify the preceding code line to be:

```
Private Sub MyClickProcedure(ByVal sender As System.Object, _
    ByVal e As System.EventArgs) Handles Button1.Click, Button2.Click, _
    mnuTHing.Click
```

then the same code would act as an event procedure for two different buttons. In other words, it handles clicks of two different buttons *and* a menu item! This flexibility was impossible in VB6 because earlier versions of VB called event handlers based on the name of a control. In sum, we hope you are convinced that the `Handles` keyword gives you far more flexibility than control arrays ever could.

Basic Event Raising

Let us return to our simple `Employee` class and walk through the steps needed to define and raise an event. Suppose we want to raise an event if someone without the password tries to raise the salary of an employee by more than 10 percent. The code from Chapter 4 for this method is:

```
Public Overloads Sub RaiseSalary(ByVal percent As Decimal)
    If percent > LIMIT Then
      'not allowed
      Console.WriteLine("MUST HAVE PASSWORD TO RAISE SALARY MORE THAN LIMIT!!!!" )
    Else
      m_Salary = (1 + percent) * m_salary
    End If
  End Sub
```

We need to replace the line in bold, which writes information to the console, with code that raises the event. This is done in stages. In the simplest case, we first declare a *public* variable in the class with the `Event` keyword along with name of the event and its parameters. For example, we can follow the VB6 model quite closely by writing:

```
Public Event SalarySecurityEvent(message as String)
```

which declares a public event that takes a string as a parameter.

NOTE *Events are usually declared as* `Public`*, never have return values, and can take any type of parameters except param arrays.*

Once you have declared the event variable, use a line like this to raise the event (there is still some plumbing left to tie in order to have anything actually happen):

```
RaiseEvent SalarySecurityEvent("MUST HAVE PASSWORD TO RAISE " & _
" Salary MORE THAN LIMIT!!!!" )
```

However, you should not use a string as the only parameter for any event. We much prefer to follow the .NET paradigm of sending the object source *and* encapsulating the event information in an event object as the parameters in any event. As a first attempt, we would write the declaration

```
Public Event SalarySecurityEvent(ByVal who As Employee, _
    ByVal e As system.EventArgs)
```

and then use the `RaiseEvent` keyword:

```
RaiseEvent SalarySecurityEvent(Me, New System.EventArgs())
```

Note how the signature for this event tells the eventual listener who the source is (in this case, which employee's salary was being improperly raised) by using the `Me` keyword. What it does not do yet is take advantage of the possibility of encapsulating information in the event variable `e`. We will soon derive a class from `System.EventArgs` that encapsulates the string in an event object with the warning message and the salary raise that was attempted.

TIP *Although events are usually public, they do not have to be. An event can be declared with any access modifier. You can have private events in a class for events that interest only objects in the class, or protected events for objects in the inheritance chain. You can even have shared events that belong, like all shared members, to the class as a whole and not to an individual instance of the class. (Shared methods can raise only shared events, for example.)*

Hooking Up the Listener Objects to Event Source Objects

We now have all the code in the event source class to start spewing out event notifications, but we do not yet have any interested listeners. A class can tell VB .NET that it is interested in events that another class can generate in various ways. The easiest way to code this in VB .NET is actually done in much the same way as it was done in VB6: just declare a module-level variable (or a class-level variable if you are inside a class) of that class's type using the `WithEvents` keyword. For example, if you put this line in a class outside of any member:

```
Private WithEvents anEmployee As Employee
```

objects of that class become a potential listener to the events that the `Employee` class can trigger. Note that:

- You must explicitly declare the class of the event, `As Object` declarations are not allowed.
- This declaration must be made at the module or class level, without the use of `New`.

After you add this code, you can use the `anEmployee` object variable whenever you are interested in the `SalarySecurityEvent`. In fact, as shown in Figure 6-2, the IDE will automatically add an event handler using the A_B naming convention whenever you declare an object variable using the `WithEvents` keyword. To get the automatically generated framework for the event, you merely choose it from the procedure dropdown listbox, as we did in Figure 6-2.

Putting It All Together

Let us put all the steps together. First, start with a new console solution and add the following code to the first (startup) module:

```
Module Module1
  Private WithEvents anEmployee As EmployeeWithEvents
  Sub Main()
    Dim tom As New EmployeeWithEvents("Tom", 100000)
    anEmployee = tom
    Console.WriteLine(tom.TheName & "  has salary " & tom.Salary)
    anEmployee.RaiseSalary(0.2D) 'D necessary for decimal
    Console.WriteLine(tom.TheName & " still has salary " & tom.Salary)
    Console.WriteLine("Please press the Enter key")
    Console.ReadLine()
  End Sub
End Module
```

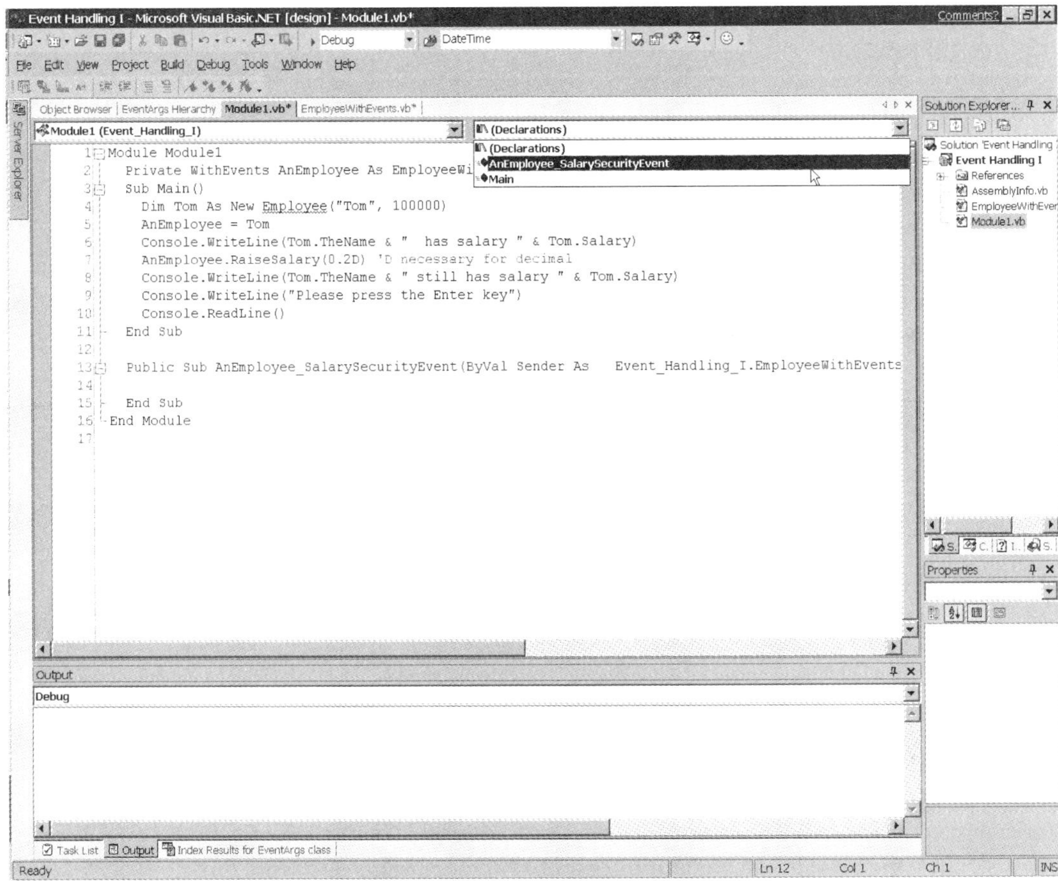

Figure 6-2. The automatically generated code for an event handler

Now choose the `anEmployee_SalarySecurityEvent` from the dropdown listbox. The automatically generated code looks like this (we put it on multiple lines for typographical reasons and bolded the key `Handles` clause):

```
Public Sub anEmployee_SalarySecurityEvent(ByVal Sender As _
   Event_Handling_I.EmployeeWithEvents, ByVal e As System.EventArgs) _
   Handles anEmployee.SalarySecurityEvent

End Sub
End Module
```

Notice how VB .NET automatically adds the underscores between the name of the `WithEvents` variable (`anEmployee`) and the name of the event (`SalarySecurityEvent`), so it looks much like an event procedure did in VB6.

Next, notice how the sender object is identified with its full name (`namespace.classname`). The extra underscores in the namespace are there because spaces are not allowed in the names of namespaces, so VB .NET automatically changes the solution name "Event Handling 1" into a root namespace of `EventHandling_1`, as shown in Figure 6-3. Finally, the `Handles` keyword tells the runtime what event this particular code is handling.

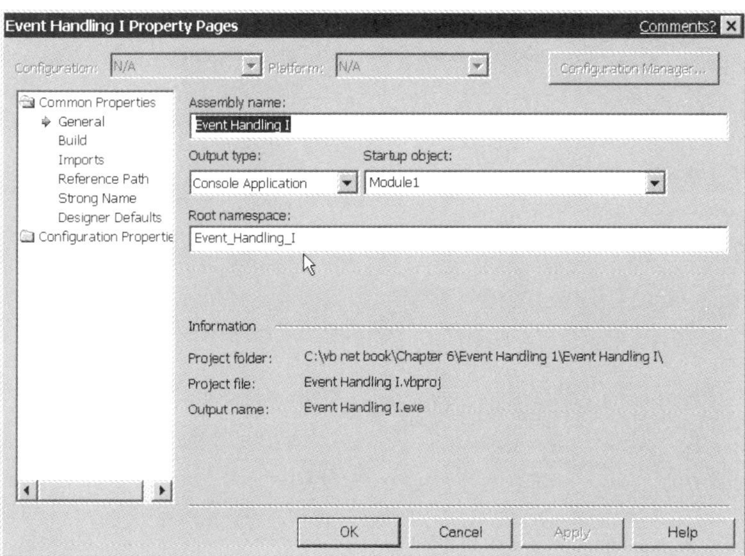

Figure 6-3. Properties for an event handling solution

To make this example more interesting and to test the code, let us add a statement to this event procedure that pops up a message box rather than writes to the console window:

```
Public Sub anEmployee_SalarySecurityEvent(ByVal Sender As _
   Event_Handling_I.EmployeeWithEvents, ByVal e As System.EventArgs) _
   Handles anEmployee.SalarySecurityEvent
      MsgBox(Sender.TheName & " had an improper salary raise attempted!")
End Sub
```

Now we have written the code for the event listener, we need to add the code in the event source. The two changes needed from the employee class from Chapter 4 are in bold in the following code:

```
Public Class EmployeeWithEvents
  Private m_Name As String
  Private m_Salary As Decimal
  Private Const LIMIT As Decimal = 0.1D
  Public Event SalarySecurityEvent(ByVal Sender As EmployeeWithEvents, _
     ByVal e As EventArgs)
  Public Sub New(ByVal aName As String, ByVal curSalary As Decimal)
    m_Name = aName
    m_Salary = curSalary
  End Sub
  ReadOnly Property TheName() As String
    Get
      Return m_Name
    End Get
  End Property
  ReadOnly Property Salary() As Decimal
    Get
      Return m_Salary
    End Get
  End Property
  Public Overloads Sub RaiseSalary(ByVal Percent As Decimal)
    If Percent > LIMIT Then
      'not allowed
      RaiseEvent SalarySecurityEvent(Me, New System.EventArgs())
    Else
      m_Salary = (1 + Percent) * m_Salary
    End If
  End Sub
  Public Overloads Sub RaiseSalary(ByVal Percent As Decimal, _
    ByVal Password As String)
    If Password = "special" Then
      m_Salary = (1 + Percent) * m_Salary
    End If
  End Sub
End Class
```

The first line in bold declares the event, the second actually raises the event when there is an attempt to improperly raise an employee's salary.

If you run this example, you see something like Figure 6-4. The moment you click on OK to make the message box go away, you will see the line that says Tom still has his original salary.

> **TIP** `WithEvent` *variables consume resources. Be sure to set any* `WithEvent` *variable to* `Nothing` *when it is no longer needed.*

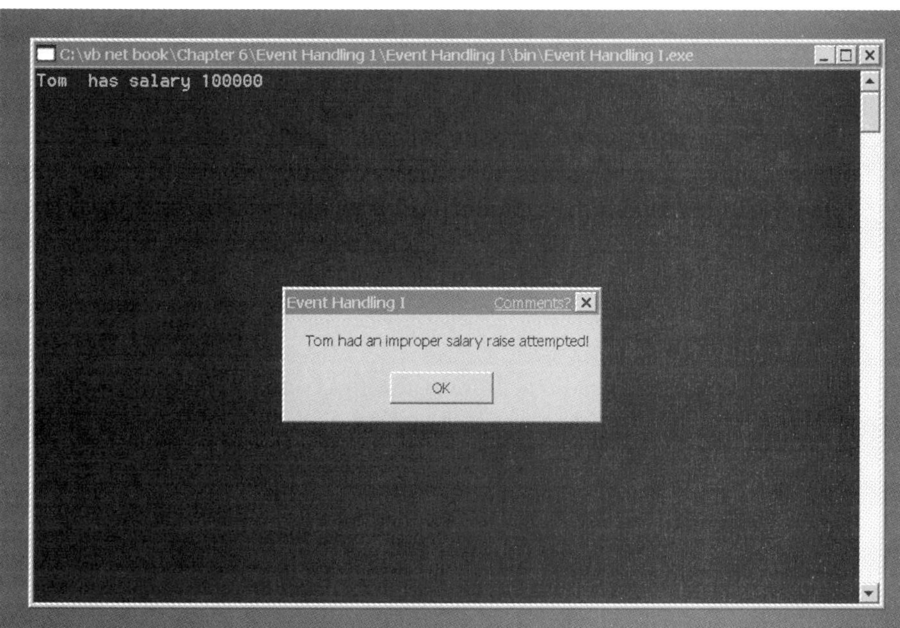

Figure 6-4. Custom event triggered message box

Building Your Own Event Classes

In the preceding example, we simply used a new `System.EventArgs` class. This is a relatively limited class because its constructor takes no arguments. A more professional way to proceed is to code a new event class that extends this generic class. For example, we might add a read-only property that tells us what raise was attempted and a property for a message. Here is an example of the kind of class you can build (the solution in the download is called `CustomEventArgExample`). Notice how the constructor encapsulates the percent raise attempted and a message. We add two read-only properties to get back this information:

```
Public Class ImproperSalaryRaiseEvent
  Inherits System.EventArgs
  Private m_Message As String
  Private m_theRaise As Decimal
  Sub New(ByVal theRaise As Decimal, ByVal theReason As String)
    MyBase.New()
    m_Message = theReason
    m_theRaise = theRaise
  End Sub
  ReadOnly Property Message() As String
    Get
      Return m_Message
    End Get
  End Property
  ReadOnly Property theRaise() As Decimal
    Get
      Return m_theRaise
    End Get
  End Property
End Class
```

After we add this class to our solution, the only changes from the previous employee class are in the declaration of the event:

```
Public Event SalarySecurityEvent(ByVal Sender As _
     CustomEventArgExample.EmployeeWithEvents, _
     ByVal e As ImproperSalaryRaiseEvent)
```

which now takes an `ImproperSalaryRaiseEvent` variable as the second argument. Next we need to change the code that raises the actual event (in bold):

```
Public Overloads Sub RaiseSalary(ByVal Percent As Decimal)
    If Percent > LIMIT Then
      'not allowed
      RaiseEvent SalarySecurityEvent(Me, _
      New ImproperSalaryRaiseEvent(Percent, "INCORRECT PASSWORD!"))
    Else
      m_Salary = (1 + Percent) * m_Salary
    End If
End Sub
```

Once we build the class, we need to modify the calling code as follows (changes in bold):

```
Module Module1
  Private WithEvents anEmployee As EmployeeWithEventsII
  Sub Main()
    Dim tom As New EmployeeWithEventsII("Tom", 100000)
    anEmployee = tom
    Console.WriteLine(tom.TheName & "  has salary " & tom.Salary)
    anEmployee.RaiseSalary(0.2D) 'D necessary for decimal
    Console.WriteLine(tom.TheName & " still has salary " & tom.Salary)
    Console.WriteLine("Please press the Enter key")
    Console.ReadLine()
  End Sub
Public Sub anEmployee_SalarySecurityEvent(ByVal Sender _
      As CustomEventArgExample.EmployeeWithEvents, _
      ByVal e As CustomEventArgExample.ImproperSalaryRaiseEvent) _
      Handles anEmployee.SalarySecurityEvent
    MsgBox(Sender.TheName & " had an improper salary raise of " & _
    FormatPercent(e.theRaise) & " with INCORRECT PASSWORD!")
  End Sub
End Module
```

Here is the result where, as you can see, we can retrieve the percentage raise that was attempted:

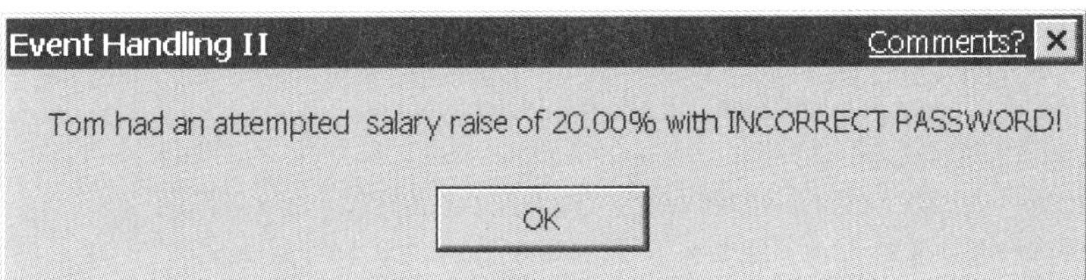

Dynamic Event Handling

The trouble with the `WithEvents` syntax is that it is inflexible. You cannot dynamically add and remove event handling with code—it is essentially all hardwired into your program. However, there is another way to dynamically handle events in VB .NET that is much more flexible. The idea is that you can specify which procedure in the listening class should be called when the event is triggered. (You can also remove them dynamically once they have been added.)

Of course, to add an event handler you not only have to register the class that is listening, but also the method that should be called back in the listener when the event happens. To do this, you use the AddHandler keyword, which takes two parameters:

- The name of the event in the source class
- The address of the method (event procedure) in the listener class that is triggered by the event (so that it can be called back)

The AddHandler code is added to the code in the listener class, not the source class, so the name of the event is usually EventSourceClassName.EventName. The address of the method to be called back is defined through the AddressOf operator. You pass AddressOf the name of the method in an object of the listener class that should be triggered by the event. For example, if we want to have the tom object get a dynamic event handler, we would write:

```
AddHandler tom.SalarySecurityEvent, AddressOf anEmployee_SalarySecurityEvent
```

which would make our test code listen to the SalarySecurityEvent in the tom object and, if it is triggered, call the anEmployee_SalarySecurityEvent code in the current module. (Of course, the anEmployee_SalarySecurityEvent code must have the right signature!)

Here is how it all looks, with the key lines in bold for a solution named AddHandlerExample1:

```
Module Module1
  Private WithEvents anEmployee As EmployeeWithEvents
  Sub Main()
    Dim tom As New EmployeeWithEvents("Tom", 100000)
    Console.WriteLine(tom.TheName & "  has salary " & tom.Salary)
    AddHandler tom.SalarySecurityEvent, _
    AddressOf anEmployee_SalarySecurityEvent
    tom.RaiseSalary(0.2D) 'D necessary for decimal
    Console.WriteLine(tom.TheName & " still has salary " & tom.Salary)
    Console.WriteLine("Please press the Enter key")
    Console.ReadLine()
  End Sub
  Public Sub anEmployee_SalarySecurityEvent(ByVal Sender _
      As AddHandlerExample1.EmployeeWithEvents, _
      ByVal e As AddHandlerExample1.ImproperSalaryRaiseEvent) _
      Handles anEmployee.SalarySecurityEvent
    MsgBox(Sender.TheName & " had an improper salary raise of " & _
    FormatPercent(e.theRaise) & " with INCORRECT PASSWORD!")
  End Sub
End Module
```

The flexibility of AddHandler is amazing. For example, we can add event handling in response to the type name:

```
If TypeName(tom) = "Manager" Then
    AddHandler tom.SalarySecurityEvent, AddressOf _
anEmployee_SalarySecurityEvent e
End If
```

Or we can assign the same event-handling code to several different events that could occur in multiple classes. This lets VB .NET perform centralized event handling with custom dispatch event handlers, a first for VB. For example, the following code listing triggers different events, depending on the command line parameters passed to it. The key lines are

```
Case "first"
  AddHandler m_EventGenerator.TestEvent, _
AddressOf m_EventGenerator_TestEvent1
```

The lines add a specific event handler in response to the command-line argument, the string first.

We make this program work using the useful GetCommandLineArgs method in the System.Environment class, which, as you saw in Chapter 3 , returns an array of the command-line arguments. The first entry in this array is the name of the executable; because arrays are zero-based, we want to use System.Environment.GetCommandLineArgs(1) to get at the first argument but we need to make sure there is a command line first, which we do by looking at the length of the System.Environment.GetCommandLineArgs array. To test this program, you will want to go to the Configuration Properties page on the Project Properties dialog box and set some sample command arguments.

Here is the listing:

```
Option Strict On
Module Module1
  Private m_EventGenerator As EventGenerator
  Sub Main()
    m_EventGenerator = New EventGenerator()
    Dim commandLines() As String = System.Environment.GetCommandLineArgs
    If commandLines.Length = 1 Then
      MsgBox("No command argument, program ending!")
      Environment.Exit(-1)
```

```
      Else
        Dim theCommand As String = commandLines(1)
        Console.WriteLine("The command line option is " & theCommand)
        'check the command line parameter and set the
        'handler accordingly
        Select Case theCommand
          Case "first"
            AddHandler m_EventGenerator.TestEvent, _
      AddressOf m_EventGenerator_TestEvent1
          Case "second"
            AddHandler m_EventGenerator.TestEvent, _
      AddressOf m_EventGenerator_TestEvent2
          Case Else
            AddHandler m_EventGenerator.TestEvent, _
      AddressOf m_EventGenerator_TestEventDefault
        End Select
        'fire the events
        m_EventGenerator.TriggerEvents()
      End If
      Console.WriteLine("Press enter to end.")
      Console.ReadLine()
    End Sub
    'default event handler for non-empty command line
    Public Sub m_EventGenerator_TestEventDefault( _
  ByVal sender As Object, ByVal evt As EventArgs)
      System.Console.WriteLine("Default choice " & _
  m_EventGenerator.GetDescription())
    End Sub
    'event handler #2 for string "first"
    Public Sub m_EventGenerator_TestEvent1( _
  ByVal sender As Object, ByVal evt As EventArgs)
      System.Console.WriteLine("1st choice " & _
  m_EventGenerator.GetDescription())
    End Sub
    'event handler #3 for string "second"
    Public Sub m_EventGenerator_TestEvent2( _
  ByVal sender As Object, ByVal evt As EventArgs)
      System.Console.WriteLine("2nd choice " & _
  m_EventGenerator.GetDescription())
    End Sub
  End Module
```

```
Public Class EventGenerator
  'the one and only event in our class
  Public Event TestEvent(ByVal sender As Object, _
ByVal evt As EventArgs)

  'could allow a default constructor instead
  Public Sub New()
    'no constructor code
  End Sub

  Public Function GetDescription() As String
    Return "EventGenerator class"
  End Function
  'will be called to trigger demo events
  Public Sub TriggerEvents()
    Dim e As System.EventArgs = New System.EventArgs()
    RaiseEvent TestEvent(Me, e)
  End Sub
End Class
```

Cleaning Up Event Handling Code

To remove a dynamically added event handler that was added with `AddHandler`, use `RemoveHandler`, which must take exactly the same arguments as the corresponding `AddHandler` did. Generally speaking, a good place to remove dynamically added handlers is in a `Dispose` method. For this reason we recommend that any class that dynamically adds events implement `IDisposable` to remind users of your class that they will need to call `Dispose`.

Handling Events in an Inheritance Chain

At any time child classes can raise public or protected events in their parent class using the `MyBase` keyword to identify the event. They also automatically inherit any public or protected event-handling code in their parents. Occasionally, however, you may want a child class to override the method used to handle public or protected events in the parent class. You can do this by using the `Handles MyBase` statement. For example:

```
Public Class ParentClass
  Public Event ParentEvent(ByVal aThing As Object, ByVal E As System.EventArgs)
  ' code goes here
End Class
'here's how the child class would work
Public Class ChildClass
  Inherits ParentClass
  Sub EventHandler(ByVal x As Integer) Handles MyBase.ParentEvent
    ' code to handle events from parent class goes here
  End Sub
End Class
```

Delegates

Whenever you set up a callback mechanism, you will need to do a lot of work under the hood to register the functions that are going to be called back. The remainder of this chapter shows you what is going on *and* how to control the under-the-hood behavior to achieve maximum power.

First, callbacks (and so, events) in VB .NET ultimately depend on a special kind of .NET object called a delegate. A *delegate* is an instance of the `System.Delegate` class. The simplest kind of delegate encapsulates an object and the address of a specified function or procedure in that object. Because this kind of delegate encapsulates an object and a method in that object, it is perfect for callback schemes like the ones needed in event handling. Why? Well, if you want to register a listener with an event source, and then to feed the event source a delegate that contains a reference to the listener object and the method inside of it, you want to call back when the event happens. Since the source has this nifty delegate inside of it that encapsulates this information, it can use the delegate to call back the right member in the listener object.

> **NOTE** *More generally, delegates encapsulate shared methods of a class without needing a specific object instance, or they encapsulate multiple objects and multiple procedures on those objects in a multicast delegate.*

Still, before we move on to discussing how delegates work, we want to point out that, while the .NET platform uses delegates for handling events, in most cases you will never need to use them for event handling in VB .NET. Most of the time, `AddHandler` gives you everything you need for flexible event handling in VB .NET. (Of course, delegates have other uses that you will soon see.)

> **NOTE** *Traditionally, calling a function by its address depended on the language supporting function pointers. Function pointers are inherently dangerous, as the sidebar that follows explains. Delegates add a safety net to the idea of traditional function pointers whose value can not be overestimated.*

Function Pointers in VB6 and Their Associated Problems

API calls often require the address of a function to call back. This is why VB6 had an `AddressOf` operator. In VB6, you could pass the address of a function to any API call that expected the address of a parameterless function that returned a Long. But what happened if you passed the address of a function whose parameter list was different than the one expected? The problem was that the receiving function trusted you to send the address of the right kind of function, and if you did not, you likely had a general protection fault (GPF) or perhaps even a blue screen of death.

This shows the weakness of arbitrary function pointers: there is no way to determine whether they point to the right type of function. Delegates are really a form of type-safe function pointers. They follow a trust-but-verify model, with automatic verification of the signature by the compiler—a much safer proposition.

Building Up a Delegate

Let us start by creating the simplest kind of delegate, one that encapsulates an object and a "pointer" to a simple string sub of that object. As you will soon see, the syntax for creating delegates is a bit more convoluted than the one used for creating a simple object. First, we need a class that holds a function with a specific signature. Here is the simplest class we can think of that satisfies this requirement:

```
Class ClassForStringSubDelegate
  'live with the default constructor
  Public Sub TestSub(ByVal aString As String)
    Console.WriteLine(aString & aString)
  End Sub
End Class
```

To build up a delegate that will let us "invoke" this sub indirectly via a callback, we need to tell the compiler that we will be using a single string delegate. The first step in this scenario is done outside `Sub Main` with the following line:

```
Public Delegate Sub StringSubDelegate(ByVal aString As String)
```

Note that this does not declare the delegate, it *defines* it. With this line we tell the compiler to create a new class called `StringSubDelegate` that inherits from `System.Delegate`. The VB .NET compiler does this automatically for you.[1]

Now, inside the `Sub Main` we create an instance of this delegate. You do this by passing in the address of a member function with the right signature. VB .NET then infers the object for you from the name of the member. This is done using the `AddressOf` operator in a line that looks like this:

```
aDelegate = AddressOf test.TestSub
```

VB .NET then automatically figures out the object involved is `test`. You can use the `New` keyword as well, although this is rare since the first form implicitly calls `New`:

```
aDelegate = New StringSubDelegate(AddressOf test.TestSub)
```

Once you have created a delegate, you can use the `Invoke` method in the `Delegate` class to call the member you encapsulated as in the following code:

```
Sub Main()
    Dim test As New ClassForStringSubDelegate()
    Dim aDelegate As StringSubDelegate
    aDelegate = AddressOf test.TestSub
    aDelegate.Invoke("Hello")
    Console.ReadLine()
  End Sub
```

which is certainly a convoluted way to display the string "HelloHello" in a console window!

> **TIP** *Actually, you do not need to use* `Invoke`, *you can just use the delegate as a proxy for the member. VB .NET accepts* `aDelegate("Hello")` *which is a much niftier syntax.*

1. If you look at the resulting IL code with ILDASM, you will see clearly that this is what is happening.

Anyway, there is method to this madness. Suppose you wanted to make this class better and display a message box instead of the line in the console window. You can do that by making the following changes (in bold):

```
Module Module1
  Public Delegate Sub StringSubDelegate(ByVal aString As String)
  Sub Main()
  Dim test As New ClassForStringSubDelegate()
  Dim aDelegate As StringSubDelegate
  aDelegate = AddressOf test.TestMsgBox
  aDelegate("Hello")
  Console.ReadLine()
  End Sub

  Class ClassForStringSubDelegate
  'live with the default constructor
  Public Sub TestSub(ByVal aString As String)
    Console.WriteLine(aString & aString)
  End Sub

  Public Sub TestMsgBox(ByVal aString As String)
    MsgBox(aString & aString)
  End Sub
  End Class
End Module
```

Because a delegate cares only about the signature of the method you are encapsulating inside of it, it is easy to make it refer to another method. Need to have a version that prints to the Debug window rather than the console or a message box? Just make a few changes in the delegate and add the function to the class that the delegate encapsulates.

The key point is that delegates let you invoke the method you want at *run* time. Thus, delegates combined with either an explicit or implicit use of the `Invoke` method potentially go far beyond what you can do with the VB6 `CallByName` method.

A More Realistic Example: Special Sorting

The preceding examples were a little unrealistic and fell more into the toy code scenario. In this section, we show you how you can use callbacks via delegates to do custom sorting routines, one of the most common uses of callback functions. The idea is that, for any given sort method, you may want to use different kinds of comparisons at different times. For example, if an array contains a bunch of names like these:

- "Mike Iem", "Dave Mendlen", "Alan Carter", "Tony Goodhew", "Ari Bixhorn", "Susan Warren"

calling the built in `Sort` method of the array class will only sort on first names. But what if you want to sort on last names?

> **NOTE** *You saw one approach to solving this problem in the Chapter 5: write a custom implementation of the* `IComparer` *interface and pass that to* `Sort`. *Using a delegate to do a callback is a little more elegant and potentially a lot more flexible since, for example, it allows you to define your own sorting routines that may work better for a specific situation than the built-in one.*

To build an array class that can sort on list names, you build a class with multiple `Compare` methods and then use a delegate to give the sorting routine access to the right `Compare` method in the class via a callback. This allows you to change the sorting dynamically at run time, for example.

The first step is to define a class that will do the sorting. To avoid getting bogged down into details of how various sorting algorithms work, we will use a simple "ripple" sort that works like this:

1. Start with the first entry.
2. Look at the remaining entries one by one. Whenever you find a smaller entry, swap it with the first entry.
3. Now start with the second entry and look at the remaining entries.
4. Continue until all items are worked through.

This is the basic code for a ripple sort:

```
For i = bottom To (top - bottom)
  For j = i + 1 To top
    If Stuff(j)< Stuff(i)) Then
      temp = Stuff(i)
      Stuff(i) = Stuff(j)
      Stuff(j) = temp
    End If
  Next j
Next I
```

To implement this via callback routines, we need to set up a SpecialSort class that will contain a delegate to use for the callback. Our SpecialSort class looks like this:

```
1  Public Class SpecialSort
2   'define the delegate
3   Public Delegate Function SpecialCompareCallback(ByVal firstString _
    As String, ByVal secondString As String) As Boolean
4   'define the sub to be called by the delegate
5   Public Shared Sub MySort(ByVal Stuff As String(), _
    ByVal MyCompare As SpecialCompareCallback)
6      Dim i, j As Integer
7      Dim temp As String
8      Dim bottom As Integer = Stuff.GetLowerBound(0)
9      Dim top As Integer = Stuff.GetUpperBound(0)
10      For i = bottom To (top - bottom)
11        For j = i + 1 To top
12          If MyCompare(Stuff(j), Stuff(i)) Then
13            temp = Stuff(i)
14            Stuff(i) = Stuff(j)
15            Stuff(j) = temp
16          End If
17        Next j
18      Next i
19    End Sub
20  End Class
```

Line **3** sets up the class for the function delegate that will be used by this class to learn what special sort order it should use. You can use this delegate to encapsulate any function that takes two strings and returns a Boolean, as any self-respecting compare function should do.

Line **5**, on the other hand, creates a shared (class) member that uses a variable of this delegate type as one of its parameters. This means that in the key line **12**:

```
If MyCompare(Stuff(j), Stuff(i)) Then
```

we can call back to another class in order find out which comparison function encapsulated by the delegate named MyCompare to use. For example, if we build the following class we could use this scheme to use *either* of its Compare methods. (Notice how the various Compare methods are shared members, so we do not even need to make an instance of these classes to access them.)

```
Public Class MyCustomCompare
  Public Shared Function TheBasicCompare(ByVal firstString As String, _
  ByVal secondString As String) As Boolean
    Return (firstString <= secondString)
  End Function
  Public Shared Function TheSpecialCompare(ByVal firstString As String, _
  ByVal secondString As String) As Boolean
    Dim tokens1, tokens2 As String()
    tokens1 = firstString.Split(Chr(32))
    tokens2 = secondString.Split(Chr(32))
    Return (tokens1(1) <= tokens2(1)) ' compare on last name!
  End Function
End Class
```

This class has two shared functions that we will soon use to create the actual delegates. The first function, `TheBasicCompare`, simply asks if one string comes before another. The more interesting function is `TheSpecialCompare`, which for a first name, last name combination stored in a single string, uses the neat `Split` function to compare the last names.

The only remaining step is to create instances of the `SpecialSort` class and instances of the appropriate delegates. That is done in `Sub Main` as follows (the key lines are bold—we will explain them after you have had a chance to look at the code):

```
Module Module1
  Sub Main()
    Dim test() As String = {"Mike Iem", "Dave Mendlen", "Alan Carter", _
    "Tony Goodhew", "Ari Bixhorn", "Susan Warren"}
 'declare the callback variable: ClasaName.DelegateName
   Dim MyCallBack As SpecialSort.SpecialCompareCallback
    MyCallBack = AddressOf MyCustomCompare.TheBasicCompare
    SpecialSort.MySort(test, MyCallBack)
   Console.WriteLine("Here is a basic sort by FIRST name")
     Dim temp As String
     For Each temp In test
       Console.WriteLine(temp)
     Next
    'send a different compare routine
     MyCallBack = AddressOf MyCustomCompare.TheSpecialCompare
     SpecialSort.MySort(test, MyCallBack)
      Console.WriteLine()
     Console.WriteLine("Here is a sort by LAST name")
     For Each temp In test
       Console.WriteLine(temp)
     Next
```

```
22        Console.ReadLine()
23      End Sub
24    End Module
```

In line **6** we declare the callback that we intend to eventually create. To actually make one, we pass it the address of a function with the right signature. This is done in lines **7** and **15**. Because the functions with the right signature are shared, we do not need an instance of the `MyCustomCompare` class to do this. Once we have the delegate, lines **8** and **16** call the correct sorting routine in the `SpecialSort` class. Since `MySort` is being passed a delegate, it can call back into the `MyCustomCompare` class to find out how to compare the items.

Multicast Delegates

In the preceding sections, we encapsulated the address of a single function or procedure inside a delegate. You often want to encapsulate multiple sub procedures inside a delegate. (It does not make a whole lot of sense to encapsulate multiple functions inside a delegate—what would the return value be?) This type of delegate is called a *multicast delegate* and is implemented by having a delegate that can hold multiple delegates of the same type. When you have a multicast delegate you can call all the encapsulated procedures with a single `Invoke` method, and they are called in the order in which their delegates were combined in the multicast delegate.

To create a multicast delegate, you combine at least two delegates of the same type and assign the result to a variable of that same delegate type. You do this with the static `Combine` method in the `System.Delegate` class, which returns another delegate.

Assuming that `firstDel` and `secDel` are both instances of `MyMultiCastDelegate`, then the following code combines `firstDel` and `secDel` into a multicast delegate stored in `firstDel`:

```
firstDel = System.Delegate.Combine(firstDel, secDel)
```

The following simple application passes the address of multiple functions to a multicast delegate:

```
1  Option Strict On
2  Module Module1
3    Sub Main()
4      Console.WriteLine("Calling delegate function...")
5      RegisterDelegate(AddressOf CallBackHandler1)
6      RegisterDelegate(AddressOf CallBackHandler2)
7      CallDelegates()
8      Console.WriteLine( _
9    "Finished calling delegate function...")
10     Console.ReadLine()
11   End Sub
12   Public Sub CallBackHandler1(ByVal lngVal As RETURN_VALUES)
13     Console.WriteLine("Callback 1 returned " & lngVal)
14   End Sub
15   Public Sub CallBackHandler2(ByVal lngVal As RETURN_VALUES)
16     Console.WriteLine("Callback 2 returned " & lngVal)
17   End Sub
18 End Module

19 Module Module2
20   Public Delegate Sub CallBackFunc(ByVal lngVal As RETURN_VALUES)
21   Private m_cbFunc As CallBackFunc
22   Public Enum RETURN_VALUES
23     VALUE_SUCCESS
24     VALUE_FAILURE
25   End Enum
26   Public Sub RegisterDelegate(ByRef cbFunc As CallBackFunc)
27     m_cbFunc = CType(System.Delegate.Combine( _
28 m_cbFunc, cbFunc), CallBackFunc)
29   End Sub
30   Public Sub CallDelegates()
31     Dim lngCounter As Long = 0
32     'call back the callers through their delegate
33     'and return success
34     m_cbFunc(RETURN_VALUES.VALUE_SUCCESS)
35   End Sub
36 End Module
```

In Lines **5** and **6** we call the procedure in Module2 (lines **26–28**) that actually builds up the multicast delegate. This sub can do this because we pass the delegate into it by reference and not by value. Notice how we convert the type of the `Combine` method to the type of our delegate in line **27**. Lines **30–35** do the actual calling of the functions in the multicast delegate. We pass all of the registered function the enum value RETURN_VALUES.VALUE_SUCCESS. If you run the program and you will see this:

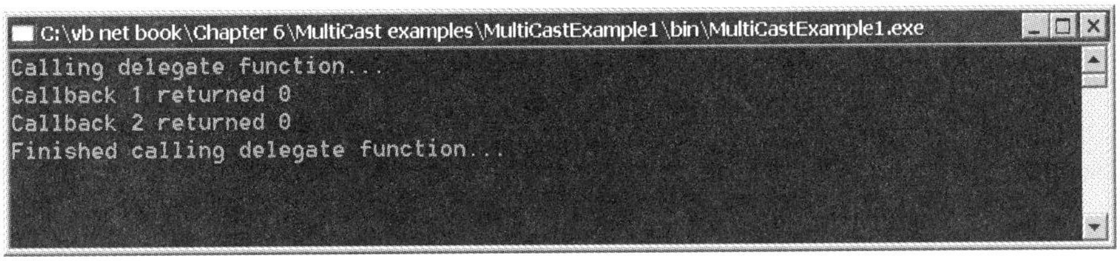

```
C:\vb net book\Chapter 6\MultiCast examples\MultiCastExample1\bin\MultiCastExample1.exe
Calling delegate function...
Callback 1 returned 0
Callback 2 returned 0
Finished calling delegate function...
```

Multicast Delegates as Class Members

The trouble with the preceding example is that all of the modules had access to all of the functions in all of the other modules. This is not a very good design—it is better to expose a delegate as a public member of a class rather than as a public object. This lets you do the same kind of validation before creating it as you do for any member. Here is a modification of the previous design, where the lines in bold let us do some (trivial) validation before adding the new delegate to the multicast delegate:

```
Option Strict On
Public Class DelegateServer
  Public Delegate Sub ClientCallback(ByVal lngVal As Long)
  Private m_Clients As ClientCallback
  'allow default constructor so no Public Sub New()
  Public Sub RegisterDelegate(ByVal aDelegate As _
  ClientCallback, ByVal doIt As Boolean)
    'would normally have serious validation code here
    'register the callback only if True is passe as second parameter
    If doIt Then
      m_Clients = CType(System.Delegate.Combine(m_Clients, aDelegate), _
      ClientCallback)
    End If
  End Sub
  Public Sub CallClients(ByVal lngVal As Long)
    m_Clients(lngVal)
  End Sub
End Class
```

```
Module Module1
  Sub Main()
    Dim delsrv As New DelegateServer()
    delsrv.RegisterDelegate(AddressOf DelegateCallbackHandler1, True)

    'won't be called because of False as second parameter!
    delsrv.RegisterDelegate(AddressOf DelegateCallbackHandler2, False)
    'trigger the server to call acceptable clients
    delsrv.CallClients(125)
    Console.WriteLine("Press enter to end.")
    Console.ReadLine()
  End Sub
  Public Sub DelegateCallbackHandler1(ByVal lngVal As Long)
    System.Console.WriteLine("DelegateCallbackHandler1 called")
  End Sub
  Public Sub DelegateCallbackHandler2(ByVal lngVal As Long)
    System.Console.WriteLine("DelegateCallbackHandler2 called")
  End Sub
End Module
```

Delegates and Events

So far we have shown you how to use delegates for everything but event handling. But how delegates hook up with events in VB .NET is actually pretty simple. The idea is that whenever you use the shorthand for event handling described in the first half of this chapter, VB .NET implicitly defines a delegate class to handle the event. The `AddressOf` statement implicitly creates an instance of a delegate for that event handler. For example, the following two lines of code are equivalent:

```
AddHandler Button1.Click, AddressOf Me.Button1_Click
AddHandler Button1.Click, New EventHandler(AddressOf Button1_Click)
```

where `EventHandler` is the name of the implicitly defined delegate. In fact, every event corresponds to a delegate of the following form:

```
Public Delegate Event (sender As Object, evt As EventArgs)
```

When you call `RaiseEvent`, you are merely calling `Invoke` on a delegate that was automatically generated for you.

CHAPTER 7

Error Handling the VB .NET Way: Living with Exceptions

UP TO NOW, WE HAVE PRETENDED that bad things do not happen to our programs. But bad things happen to good programs all the time: a network connection may be down or the printer may run out of paper, for instance. It is not your fault as the programmer when this happens, but you also cannot blame the user if your program crashes because the network goes down! At the very least, your program must *not* end abruptly when these kinds of things happen. Your program must:

- Log or somehow notify the user of the problem.
- Let the user save his or her work if appropriate.
- Let the user gracefully exit the program if necessary.

This is not always easy. The code to open a network connection is usually not attached to the objects whose state you need to maintain. You often need some way to transfer control as well as to inform other objects what happened so they can deal with the situation.

> **NOTE** *Bad things also happen to bad programs. If you do not validate data before you use it, you may find yourself dividing by zero or stuffing too much data into a container that cannot hold that much stuff. Your job as a programmer is to make sure your program does not do this. Whatever form of error handling you choose, it is not supposed to be a substitute for validating data before using it!*

In any case, good programmers know they live in a world where exceptional behavior often does not seem all that exceptional. This chapter will bring you into the real world.

The idea is that VB .NET finally supports *structured exception handling* (or simply, exception handling) for dealing with common errors. In this chapter, we not only show you the syntax used to add exception handling to a VB .NET application, but we show you the benefits of using it for error handling. For example, with exception handling, even the more or less socially acceptable use of the `GoTo` we showed you back in Chapter 3 is no longer necessary. But because power always comes at a cost, we also alert you to the gotchas that you will encounter when using exception handling.

> **NOTE** *For readers coming from earlier versions of VB, using the older* `On Error` *syntax is still possible. We think, however, that it would be almost foolish to continue using it for new programs. We feel strongly that is has taken far too long for VB to lose an archaic way of treating errors that goes back to the early days of computing! (You also cannot mix the two methods in the same procedure.)*

Error Checking vs. Exception Handling

Traditional error checking (such as that used in earlier versions of VB or in traditional COM or Windows programming) is done by checking the return value of a given function and reacting based on that value. This usually involves the equivalent of a giant switch statement that checks the value returned by the function. And, of course, this return value tends to be random: a 1 is good sometimes and bad other times; a 0 can mean success or just as often failure. Or, as is the case in the VB6 example code given here, the value returned seems truly random:

```
Select Case ErrorNumber
    Case 57
      MsgBox "Your printer may be off-line."
    Case 68
      MsgBox "Is there a printer available?"
   'more cases...
    Case Else
      'eeks
End Select
```

Now, this kind of code gets the job done, but it is hard to read and even harder to maintain. We think it is also fair to say that there is a lot of room for programmer error in this scheme. For instance, suppose that you had made a mistake with one of the error values or, as is all too common, you forgot to check all the possible return values of the error function. Beyond this, it is a pain to write the same error-checking code every time you use a Windows API function in your code. Although there are times you will have to check the return value of a function regardless of what type of error handling scheme you are using, you do not want to do it everywhere. For example, one key benefit is efficiency: exception handling code costs you less time in writing, less time in maintenance, and often less time in executing!

First Steps in Exception Handling

Before we start writing the code that shows you some exception handlers at work, here are some things to keep in mind. First, when you use structured exception handling, you are providing an alternative path for your code that will be executed *automatically* when something bad happens. More precisely, you can create in any VB .NET code an alternate path for code execution when the code cannot complete its work in the normal path. Also, when you enable exception handling, VB .NET automatically creates an object that encapsulates the error information.

Once an exception is triggered, the built-in exception handling mechanism begins its search for a handler that can deal with that particular object (error condition). It is important to keep in mind that what we are describing is not a bunch of `GoTo`s that make for spaghetti code—it is more like the service road that runs parallel to the main highway with various exits. Next, keep in mind that, in a way, this service road is the dream of all drivers that are stuck in traffic. It is a smart service road—if something goes wrong, you will automatically be shunted to the exception handling code sequence. (Well, you will be if you wrote the code for the exception handler.) Once you are on the service road, the code in the exception handler can deal with the problem using *exception handlers* or, optionally, let it bubble up through the call chain.

The actual mechanism for doing this in VB .NET is called a `Try-Catch` block. Here is an example: Suppose you build a console application called `ProcessFile`. The user is supposed to use this application from the command line by typing something like:

```
ProcessFile nameoFile
```

where the argument on the command line is the name of the file. As users are prone to do, the user can do one of many annoying things to your nice program, such as:

- Forget to give you a filename
- Give you the name of a nonexistent file
- Ask you to work with a file that is locked for this operation

We have to write our code in a way that takes into account all the possible ways the user of our program can go wrong. Here is an example of the simple `Try-Catch` block in a VB .NET application that could be part of the `ProcessFile` application:

```
Module Exception1
  Sub Main()
  Dim args() As String
    Try
      args = Environment.GetCommandLineArgs()
      ProcessFile(args(1))
    Catch
      Console.WriteLine("ERROR")
    End Try
  Console.WriteLine("Press enter to end")
  Console.ReadLine()
  End Sub

  Sub ProcessFile(ByVal fileName As String)
    'process file code goes here
    Console.WriteLine("Am processing " & fName)
  End Sub
End Module
```

The code in the `Try` section of the `Try-Catch` block is assumed to be "good" code—in this case, a call to `ProcessFile`. (The reason the call to `Environment.GetCommandLineArgs()`in the exception handler is it can also throw an exception if your code is running on a box that does not support command line arguments.)

The code in the `Catch` section of the `Try-Catch` block is there because, well, users are users and do not always follow directions. In this code snippet, if the user forgets to enter a filename, then the code would try to reference the name of the file, which would trigger an `IndexOutOfRangeException`, because the array would not have an entry in the cited position. Triggering this exception causes the code flow to move down the alternate pathway (the `Catch` block), which in this case simply prints out `ERROR` in the console window.

> **NOTE** *As with most VB .NET control flow constructs such as* `For` *and* `Do`*, there is a way to exit from a* `Try` *block on demand. With a* `Try` *block, put an* `Exit Try` *inside of any* `Try` *block to exit from it immediately. We think using* `Exit Try` *is generally a poor programming practice.*

Analyzing the Exception

The next step is to catch the exception and to analyze it. This is done by modifying the `Catch` line to read something like:

```
Catch  excep As Exception
```

(You can use any variable here, of course, because it is being declared in the `Catch` clause.) Now, the exception object referenced by `excep` contains a lot of information. For example, change the code in the `Catch` clause to read:

```
Catch excep As Exception
  Console.WriteLine(excep)
```

to take advantage of the built-in `ToString` method of the exception object `excep` and you will see something like:

```
System.IndexOutOfRangeException: An exception of type_
System.IndexOutOfRangeException was thrown.
at Exception_1.Exception1.Main() in C:\Documents and_
Settings\x20\My Documents\Visual Studio
        Projects\ConsoleApplication14\Exception1.vb:line 6
```

This message shows there was an error in accessing the array element at line 6. (Not that we recommend printing this information out—unless you want to scare the user—but it is very useful for debugging.)

Finally, while reading this code we hope you are thinking ahead. Suppose the user supplies a filename but the `ProcessFile` method cannot process it. What then? Is there a way to differentiate between exceptions? As you will see shortly, you can make the `Catch` clause more sophisticated to check for different kinds of exceptions. You can even have a `Catch` clause `Throw` an exception object back to the code that called it that encapsulates what went wrong in its cleanup work.

Multiple Catch Clauses

The .NET runtime allows multiple `Catch` clauses. Each clause can trap for a specific exceptions, using objects that inherit from the base `Exception` class to identify the particular errors. For example, consider the following code:

```
Sub Main()
  Dim args(), argument As String
  Try
      args = Environment.GetCommandLineArgs()
     ProcessFile(args(1))
  Catch indexProblem As IndexOutOfRangeException
    Console.WriteLine("ERROR - No file name supplied")
  Catch ioProblem As System.IO.IOException
    Console.WriteLine("ERROR - can't process file named " & args(1))
  Catch except AS Exception
    'other exception
  End Try
  Console.WriteLine("Press enter to end")
  Console.ReadLine()
End Sub
```

In this case, the exception handler looks inside the `Try-Catch` block, attempting to match all of the `Catch` blocks *sequentially* to find a match. If the user leaves out the filename, it will match the first clause. Presumably it will match the second clause if the `ProcessFile` call cannot process the file. (More on why this happens in a moment.) If not, the last `Catch` clause will catch any other kind of exception.

> **CAUTION** *Once a* `Catch` *clause that matches the exception is found, VB processes the code in that* `Catch` *block but will not process any other* `Catch` *block.*

Note that a match that is a `Catch` clause is an exception that is either is of the same type or of a type that *inherits* from that type. For example, the `FileNotFoundException` class inherits from `IOException`, so you should not write code that looks like this:

```
Try
  ProcessFile(args(1))
Catch indexProblem As IndexOutOfRangeException
  Console.WriteLine("ERROR - No file name supplied")
Catch ioProblem As System.IO.IOException
  Console.WriteLine("ERROR - can't process file named " & args(1))
Catch fileNotfound As System.IO.FileNotFoundException
End Try
```

because the more general `FileNotFoundException` clause will be headed off by the clause that caught its parent I/O exception.

> **CAUTION** *This means a clause that says*
>
> `Catch e As Exception`
>
> *kills all the remaining* `Catch` *clauses. Using this clause as the first* `Catch` *block will cause you no end of grief. (Using* `Catch` *without specifying an exception is the equivalent of a* `Catch e As Exception` *clause, by the way.) Also note that if you use* `Catch e As Exception` *and do not put any code in the block, it will act much like the very dangerous* `On Error Resume Next` *from earlier versions of VB.*

In spite of the dangers of a `Catch e As Exception` line of code, a good rule of thumb is to actually have a general `Catch e As Exception` clause as the final `Catch` clause in any `Try` block—especially during the development process. This allows you to better isolate errors. We suggest printing out a stack trace to the console or a log file if all else fails. You can do this using the `StackTrace` method in the generic `Exception` class. For example:

```
Try
  ProcessFile(args(0))
Catch indexProblem As IndexOutOfRangeException
  Console.WriteLine("ERROR - No file name supplied")
Catch fnf As System.IO.FileNotFoundException
  Console.WriteLine("ERROR - FILE NOT FOUND")
Catch ioProblem As System.IO.IOException
  Console.WriteLine("ERROR - can't process file named " & args(1))
Catch e As Exception
  Console.WriteLine("Please inform the writer of this program of this message")
  Console.Write(e.StackTrace)
End Try
```

What happens if there is no `Catch` block that corresponds to the specific type of exception that is thrown, and if there is also no `Catch e As Exception` clause in the code you are trying? Well, when this happens, the exception bubbles up to any `Try` clauses that surrounds the code of an inner `Try` clause. And if there is no outer `Try` block with a matching `Catch` clause, then the exception bubbles up to the calling method and looks for an exception handler there. This is presumably what would happen in the `ProcessFile` method in the code you saw earlier—the `ProcessFile` method would pass on any unhandled exceptions (in the form of an `Exception` *object*) to `Sub Main`.

> **CAUTION** *If no `Try` clause in the method catches the exception, execution processes to any `Finally` clauses, and then jumps immediately out of the method. This explains why you should think of exception handling as an awfully powerful (but smart) `GoTo`. It is smart because it will be able to perform cleanup code automatically through use of `Finally` clauses.*

In general, if your code does not handle an exception even when you go all the way up to the code in the entry point for the application, then .NET displays a generic message with a description of the exception and a stack trace of all the methods in the call stack when the exception occurred.

> **TIP** *VB .NET allows you to add a `When` clause to a `Catch` clause to further specify its applicability. The syntax looks like this:*
>
> ```
> Catch badNameException When theName = String.Empty
> ```

Throwing Exceptions

We said that the `ProcessFile` method would simply propagate the exception back to the code in `Sub Main` that called it. This code, in the `Main` procedure, in turn is inside a `Try` block, so the exception handling we wrote should handle it. But this is actually a little bit naïve and perhaps even becomes dangerous when you write classes that will be reused by other people. (And even if it is not dangerous, people who use your code will not be happy with you if you propagate exceptions willy-nilly without attempting to handle them.)

A better tactic is to do what you can locally to try to clean up the mess and then use the keyword `Throw` to send an exception object back to the calling code. For example, you saw in Chapter 4 how VB .NET no longer has deterministic finalization. Thus, if you create an object that has a `Dispose` method, you should dispose of it before throwing an exception. Ditto if you open a file or grab a graphic context. This snippet is the paradigm for this kind of code:

```
Try
  'code that created a local object that has a Dispose method
  ' more code that might throw exceptions
Catch(e As Exception)
  localObject.dispose()
  Throw e;
End Try
```

The point is that, if you do not call the `Dispose` method of your local object, whatever it grabbed will *never* be disposed of. This is because if you only have a reference to an object locally, other code will not have access to its `Dispose` method! On the other hand, whatever caused the exception did *not* go away and it is quite likely that the calling code needs to know that there was a problem, such as in processing the file. The way you do this is to send it an exception object using the `Throw` statement as you can see in the last bold line.

Actually, if you really want to be a good citizen, do not just (re)throw a generic exception as in the preceding code. Instead, make your code as useful as it can be to the calling code by adding information to the exception object you are throwing back. You can do this in three ways:

1. Add a descriptive string to the current exception and rethrow it with the new string added, and hope this helps.

2. Throw a built-in exception that inherits from the given exception that describes the situation better.

3. Create a new exception class that inherits from the given exception class that describes what happened better than any built-in exception class.

Ideally, these are in ascending order of usefulness, with number 3 being what you should always do. In practice, most people use all three methods based on their judgment of what will happen if they do not send every possible piece of information up the call stack.

As an example of how to perform these various tasks, imagine a situation where you are reading a bunch of key/value pairs back from some data source and the last key does not have a corresponding value. Because you assumed that every key has a value and tried to read its associated value, you are presented with an unexpected I/O exception. (See Chapter 9 for how to write code that reads information back from a file.)

Now you want to tell the caller of the code what has happened. You can add a string to an exception by using this version of the constructor in the `Exception` class:

```
Public Sub New(ByVal message As String)
```

For example, here is how you add a new string to the `IOException` that informs the caller that a value is missing for the last key and then throw it:

```
Dim excep as New IOException("Missing value for last key")
Throw excep
```

The code that calls your code is presented with the exception you throw; it can look at the value returned by the `Message` method in the `Exception` class to see what happened.

> **NOTE** *Actually, in the real world it is more likely that you would get an* `EndOfStreamException`, *which inherits from* `IOException`. *But more on streams in Chapter 9.*

The second situation is trivial to implement because of the cardinal rule of inheritance: any subclass must be usable wherever its parent class is. All you have to do is throw an instance of the child class exception that works better.

The final situation requires a bit more work because you have to build a class that extends an existing exception class. For example, suppose we want to build an exception class that inherits from `System.IO.IOException`. The only change is that we add a read-only property that returns the last key for the lost value:

```
Public Class LastValueLostException
   Inherits System.IO.IOException
  Private mKey As String
  Public Sub New(ByVal theKey As String)
    MyBase.New("No value found for last key")
    mKey = theKey
  End Sub
  Public ReadOnly Property LastKey() As String
    Get
      Return mKey
    End Get
  End Property
End Class
```

Note that the name of the newly created `Exception` class ends with the word `Exception`. This is a standard naming convention that we strongly suggest you follow. Someone who is presented with a `LastValueLostException` can use the read-only `LastKey` property that is set in the constructor of this new exception type to find the key that was not paired with a value. We made sure the `Message` method in the parent `Exception` gave the correct information by adding this line:

```
MyBase.New("No value found for last key")
```

which calls the correct constructor in the parent class (ultimately this constructor is in the parent `Exception` class).

You may notice that we do not override any other methods, such as the generic `ToString` method, which comes from `Exception`. Exception objects should always print out the standard message, if and when required.

How would somebody use our class? If the last key was "oops," then this line:

```
Throw New LastValueLostException("oops")
```

would do exactly that.

Exceptions in the Food Chain

We created a new exception class that inherited from `IOException`, because this was clearly the kind of problem we were having. Suppose, however, that you have a more generic situation where there is no obvious class to inherit from except `Exception` itself. Well, not quite—you always have a better choice. We strongly suggest not inheriting from `Exception` itself, but rather using a subclass of `Exception` called `ApplicationException`.

The reason is that the .NET Framework distinguishes between exceptions that arise because of problems caused by the runtime (such as running out of memory or stack space) and those caused by your application. It is the latter exceptions that are supposed to inherit from `ApplicationException`, and therefore this is the class you should inherit from when you create a generic exception in your program.

> **CAUTION** *Be aware that* `IOException`*, like most built-in non-generic exceptions, also splits off from* `Exception` *and not* `ApplicationException`.

The runtime tries to help you by going a little further. It actually splits the exception hierarchy into two as shown in Figure 7-1.

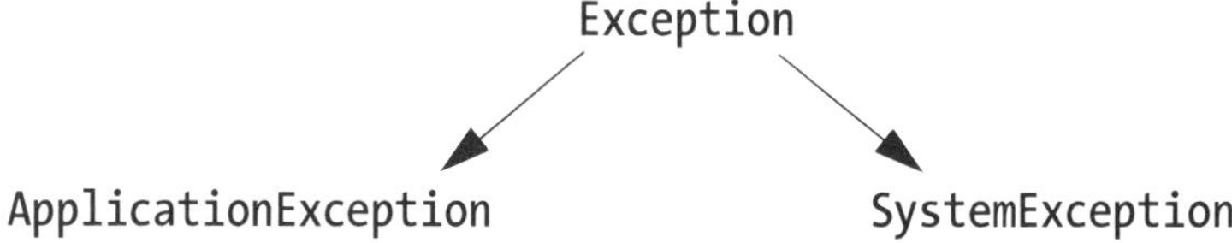

Figure 7-1. The exception hierarchy split into two

The Exception, ApplicationException, and SystemException classes have identical functionality—the existence of the three classes is a convenience that makes the exceptions your programs may cause easier to understand. Here is a summary of the most important members of these classes (which are also important for built-in classes such as IOException that inherit from Exception).

Eliminating the GoTo Using Exceptions

By combining exception handling with building your own exception classes, you can finally eliminate all uses of the GoTo. For example, in the code in Chapter 3 we showed that one possible socially acceptable use of the GoTo was to get out of a deeply nested loop when something bad happened in an inner loop. We would more likely just wrap the whole loop in a Try-Catch block as follows:

```
Sub Main()
  Dim getData As String
  Dim i, j As Integer
  Dim e As System.IO.IOException
  Try
    For i = 1 To 10
      For j = 1 To 100
      Console.Write("Type the data, hit the Enter key between " & _
             "ZZZ to end:  ")
      getData = Console.ReadLine()
      If getData = "ZZZ" Then
        e = New System.IO.IOException("Data entry ended at user request")
        Throw e
      Else
       'Process data
      End If
      Next j
    Next i
  Catch
    Console.WriteLine(e.Message)
    Console.ReadLine()
  End Try
End Sub
```

CAUTION *Do not change the preceding code by eliminating the first line in bold in favor of the following line, which replaces the second line in bold:*

```
Dim e As New System.IO.IOException("Data entry ended at user request")
```

Because of the block visibility rules in VB .NET, the `Catch` *clause would not be able to see the exception object.*

And Finally...Finally Blocks

When you use a `Try-Catch` block, there is often some cleanup code that must be processed in the normal *and* in the exceptional condition. Files should be closed in both cases; for example, `Dispose` methods need to be called, and so on. Even in the simple example that started this chapter, we should have the `ReadLine` code (which keeps the console window up while it waits for the user to press Enter).

You can assure that certain code executes no matter what happens by adding a `Finally` clause as in the bolded code in the following modification of our first example.

```
Sub Main()
  Dim args(), argument As String
  args = Environment.GetCommandLineArgs()
  Try
    ProcessFile(args(1))
  Catch
    Console.WriteLine("ERROR")
  Finally
    Console.WriteLine("Press enter to end")
    Console.ReadLine()
  End Try
End Sub
```

Now the code in bold will always be executed. (And so the DOS window will stay around long enough for the user to see what happened.)

CAUTION *Keep in mind that the code in a* `Finally` *clause will execute before any exceptions get propagated to the calling code and also before a function returns.*

Some Tips for Using Exceptions

Exceptions are cool and people new to them have a natural tendency to overuse them. After all, why go to the trouble to parse what the user enters when setting up an exception for the user's error is so easy? Resist this temptation. Exception handling will make your programs run much slower if misused. Here are four tips on using exceptions—they all come down to variations on the rule that exceptions are supposed to be exceptional:

1. Exceptions indicate an exceptional condition; do not use them as you would a return code for a function. (We have seen code that throws a "SUCCESS_EXCEPTION" every time a function call *does not* fail!)

2. Exception handling is not supposed to replace testing for the obvious. You do not, for example, use exceptions to test for end of file (EOF) conditions.

3. Do not micromanage exceptions by wrapping every possible statement in a `Try-Catch` block. It is usually better to wrap the whole action in a single `Try` statement than to have multiple `Try` statements.

4. Do not squelch exceptions by writing code like

   ```
   Catch e as Exception
   ```

   without a very good reason. This is the equivalent of blindly using `On Error Resume Next` in older VB code and doing so is bad for the same reasons. If an exception happens, handle it or propagate it.

5. Which leads to one final tip—what we like to call the good fellowship rule:

   If you do not handle an exception condition completely and need to rethrow an exception to the calling code, add enough information (or create an new exception class) so that the code you are communicating with knows exactly what happened and what you did to (try to) fix it.

CHAPTER 8
Windows Forms, Drawing, and Printing

EVERYTHING YOU HEAR ABOUT .NET development in the magazines or online seems to focus on features such as Web Services, using the browser as the delivery platform, ASP .NET, and other Web-based topics. The many, many improvements made to client-side Windows GUI development under .NET using the Visual Studio IDE are barely mentioned. This may sound strange to say of a Microsoft product, but GUI development in Visual Studio is under-hyped; there are, in fact, many improvements that VB programmers have long awaited!

Although we agree that using the browser as a delivery platform is clearly becoming more and more important, we also feel pretty strongly that the traditional Windows-based client is not going away. In this chapter, we hope to counterbalance this general trend by showing you the fundamentals of the programming needed to build GUIs in VB .NET.

> **NOTE** *We say the "programming needed" because, unlike earlier versions of VB, the Visual Studio IDE works by writing code for you—and you must understand the code it generates in order to take full advantage of the Windows client-side features in .NET.*

We will not spend a lot of time on how to use the RAD (Rapid Application Development) features of the IDE,[1] or the properties, methods, and events for the various controls in the Toolbox—doing this justice would take a book at least as long as this one. Instead, by concentrating on the programming issues involved, we hope to show you how GUI development in .NET works. At that point, you can look at the documentation as needed or wait for a complete book on GUI development to learn more.

After discussing how to program with forms and controls, we take up the basics of graphics programming in VB .NET, which is quite a bit different than it was

1. But yes, you still can paint the user interface, and the many new properties such as `Anchor` and `Dock` do make the design task using the IDE that much easier.

in earlier versions of VB. (For example, the familiar primitives such as `Circle` and `Line` are gone.) We then look at printing in .NET. Interestingly enough, printing in .NET is really just a special case of drawing. Although you have far more power than was available in earlier versions of VB, the familiar `Printer` object is gone and a bit more work is needed to get at the improved functionality.

First, Some History

Earlier versions of VB depended on the Ruby Forms engine. It was a version of Alan Cooper's Ruby prototype tool that, when married to a version of QuickBasic, became VB1.[2] This meant that GUI development in earlier versions of VB was dependent on an engine whose actions were almost totally hidden from the programmer. Forms magically appeared because they were the startup forms, and controls ended up on forms mostly because of your actions at design time.[3]

The process of creating a window and controls on a form by hand that could respond to events in C or C++ was painful at best, so VB was a definite improvement. The downside to everything happening "auto-magically" was that the Ruby Forms engine was pretty inflexible. You could not extend it very easily, and you had to live with some quirks in its design. How you could use VB forms and controls was limited, unless you wanted to make heavy use of API calls to write really ugly subclassing code that intercepted normal Windows messages.[4] Even things as simple as making a listbox that could be quickly searched required using an API call; the common task of adding items to a listbox was made difficult because the `Items` property of a listbox was read-only and you could not do anything about it. (Fortunately, these tasks are trivial in VB .NET.[5])

Furthermore, many programmers were confused about what a VB form really was—was it a class or an instance of a class? The answer is that forms were both, sort of. The result was very confusing code such as this:

```
Form1.Show 'I'm an instance
Dim newForm As New Form1 'nope, now I am a class
newForm.Show
```

Programmers prefer a consistent model of programming and, from an OOP point of view, the forms engine in earlier versions of VB often seemed like a hodgepodge of hacks. All this has changed in .NET. In .NET, forms are just

---

2. See `www.cooper.com/alan/father_of_vb.html`.
3. It is true that VB6 gave you a way to add controls at run time, but it was not used very much, in part because the event hookup mechanism for these controls was so clumsy.
4. Third-party controls such as Desaware's SpyWorks helped with the subclassing process, but it still was not much fun.
5. For example, to quickly populate a listbox, assign a collection to the box's `DataSource` property.

instances of the `Windows.Forms.Form` class, and you use inheritance to specialize behavior for forms or controls in exactly the same way as you use inheritance for any other class in the .NET Framework. For example, a specialized form would start out like this:

```
Public Class MyForm
Inherits System.Windows.Forms.Form
```

and then you could add new functionality by either overriding members of the parent `Form` class or by adding new members, just as you would for any class (see Chapter 5).

Controls in earlier versions of VB were not even true classes, so the following kind of code was not allowed:

```
Dim myButton As New CommandButton
```

This perfect example of an "is-a" relationship that cries out for inheritance, could not use it to build, say, a better command button based on the built-in command button.

Instead, when building custom controls was finally possible beginning with VB5, control creation depended on containment, delegation, and one of the most convoluted wizards ever invented. (Not to mention that controls you built in VB5 and 6 were not exactly like the controls you built with other languages such as C++ or Delphi.)

In .NET, controls and forms are classes. For example, as you will see a little later on in this chapter, you can create a specialized textbox in VB .NET by building a class that starts out like this:

```
Public Class PositiveIntegerTextBox
  Inherits System.Windows.Forms.TextBox
```

and then you override or add methods just you do in any inheritance chain. (And this control works exactly like a control built with C# or managed C++.)

To be blunt, GUIs in earlier versions of VB depended on a rickety, half-baked, not truly object-oriented structure. That structure needed to be overhauled in order to unify the programming model in a truly OOP-based version of VB—which is exactly what you have in .NET with the new `Windows.Forms` namespace—and VB .NET can take full advantage of this.

Form Designer Basics

For VB6 programmers, adjusting to how the VS .NET IDE handles forms and controls is pretty simple. You have a couple of new (and very cool) tools that we briefly describe later, but the basic idea of how to work with the Toolbox has not changed very much. (See the sections in this chapter on the Menu Editor and on how to change the tab order, for our two favorite additions.)

For those who have never used an older version of the VB IDE, here is what you need to do to add a control to the Form window:

1. Double-click on a control or drag it from the Toolbox to the form in the default size.

2. Position it by clicking inside it and then dragging it to the correct location.

3. Resize it by dragging one of the small square sizing boxes that the cursor points to, as shown in Figure 8-1. (You can still use Shift+ and Arrow key for more precise resizing, if need be.)

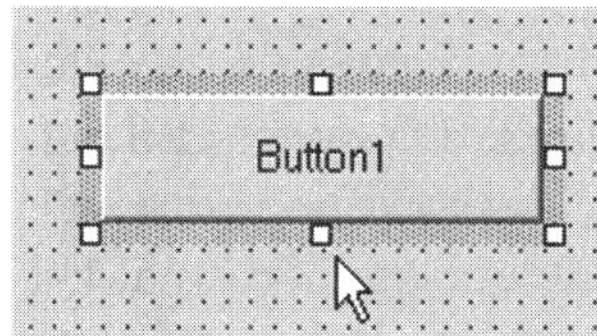

Figure 8-1. Sizing handles on a control

You can also add controls to a form by following these steps:

1. In the Toolbox, click on the control you want to add to your form.

2. Move the cursor to the form. (Unlike earlier versions of VB, the cursor now gives you a clue about which control you are working with.)

3. Click where you want to position the top left corner of the control and then drag to the lower right corner position. (You can then use Shift+ an Arrow key to resize the control as needed.)

For controls without a user interface, such as timers, simply double-click on them. They end up in a tray beneath the form, thus reducing clutter.

> **NOTE** *The key point to always keep in mind about designing a form in the IDE is that the IDE will write (a lot) of code for you. Unlike earlier versions of VB, everything you do in the Form designer or in the Properties window corresponds to automatically generated code that you can see (and change) if needed.*

You can use the Format menu to reposition and resize controls once they are on the form. Of course, many of the items on the Format menu, such as the ones on the Align submenu, make sense only for a group of controls. One way to select a group of controls is to click the first control in the group and then hold down the Control key while clicking the other members you want in the group. At this point they will all show sizing handles but only one control will have dark sizing handles as shown in Figure 8-2 on the button control.

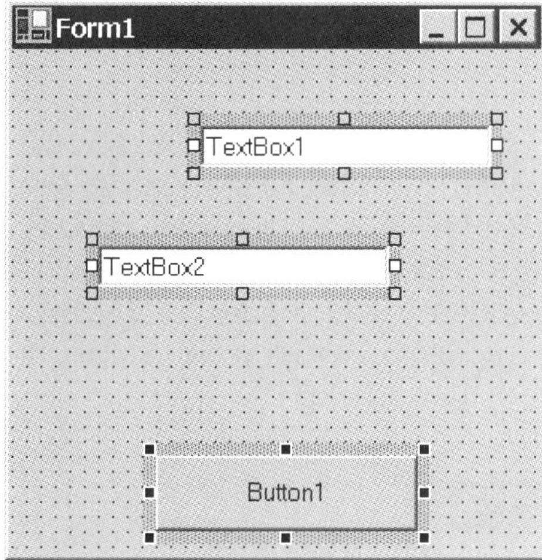

Figure 8-2. Controls as a group

The control with the dark sizing handles acts as the reference for relevant Format menu commands, such as Format|Make Same Size|Width. All controls in a group resize proportionally, regardless of which control is the reference control.

TIP *To change the reference control for a group, simply click on the control you want to be the new reference while the group is selected.*

Once you are happy with the position of a group of controls, use Format|Lock Controls to keep them from accidentally moving. Unlike with earlier versions of VB, locking controls works on a group basis and any additional controls you add to the form are not locked.

> **NOTE** *If you need to work with a group of controls as a unit (a set of radio buttons, for example), put them inside a* `GroupBox` *control instead of a* `Frame` *control. The improved Panel control now lets you use scrollbars that also allow you to group controls. Interestingly enough, you can now drag existing controls into a* `GroupBox` *control or a Panel control.*

Keeping Things in Proportion: The Anchor *and* Dock *Properties*

In earlier versions of VB, you had users who could sometimes resize a form, thus ruining the careful positioning of the controls you made at design time. To solve this problem, you either had to roll your own resize code or invest in a resizing control. With `Windows.Forms`, most resizing code is no longer necessary because two *very* useful properties have been added to every visible control: `Anchor` and `Dock`.

You set the `Anchor` property in the Properties window via a small designer that looks like Figure 8-3.

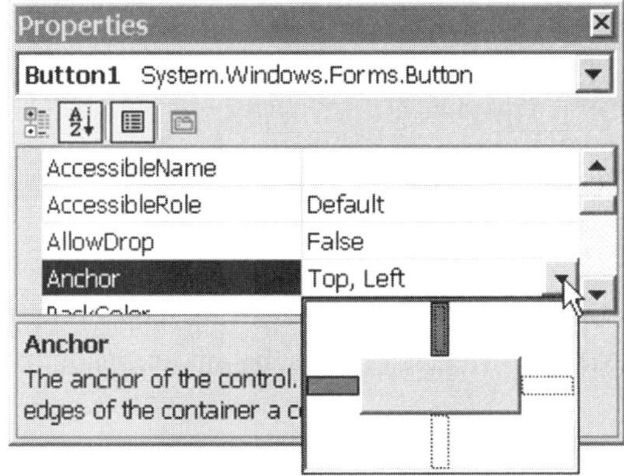

Figure 8-3. The Anchor designer

The `Anchor` property lets you anchor a control to one or more of the edges of the form. Once you anchor a control to an edge of its container, the distance between the control and that edge remains the same, no matter how the container is resized. If you anchor a control to the opposite edges of its container, it is automatically resized when the container is resized. Here is an example of the code generated by setting the `Anchor` property. This code anchors the button to the left and right sides:

```
Me.Button1.Anchor = (System.Windows.Forms.AnchorStyles.Left _
Or System.Windows.Forms.AnchorStyles.Right)
```

The Dock property is a far more flexible version of the older Align property that it replaces. When you dock a control to an edge of the form, it stays flush with that edge no matter how the container is resized. You set the Dock property in the Docking designer, as shown in Figure 8-4.

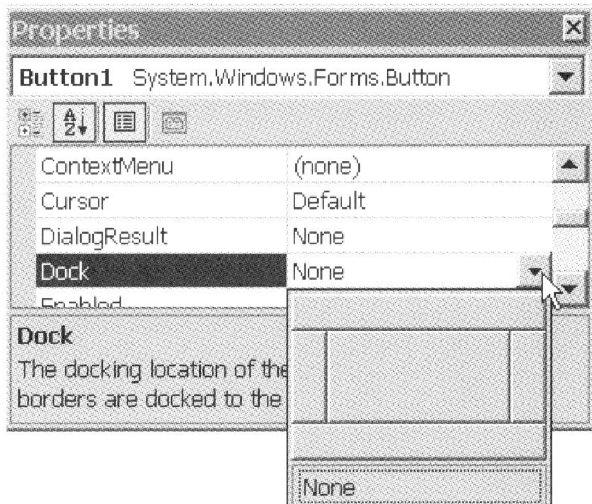

Figure 8-4. The Docking designer

Clicking the middle position in this designer sets the property to the value Fill, which fills the container with the control, if this is possible, and then keeps it that way no matter how the control is resized. (Filling the container is not possible for some controls, such as single-line textboxes, which always stay a specific height dictated by the font they are using.) Setting the Dock property generates code like this:

```
Me.Button1.Dock = System.Windows.Forms.DockStyle.Bottom
```

If you dock multiple controls to the same edge, the first docks to the edge of the container and the others dock as close as possible to the edge without covering the previous one, as you can see in Figure 8-5.

Because docking and anchoring work relative to the container, you can first anchor or dock group boxes or panels to the form and then anchor or dock controls inside these containers. This lets you avoid, in most cases, the need to roll your own resize code. For example, the beginnings of the proverbial calculator shown in Figure 8-6 were created by first docking three group boxes to the left side, and then docking the three command buttons to the bottom of the first group box.

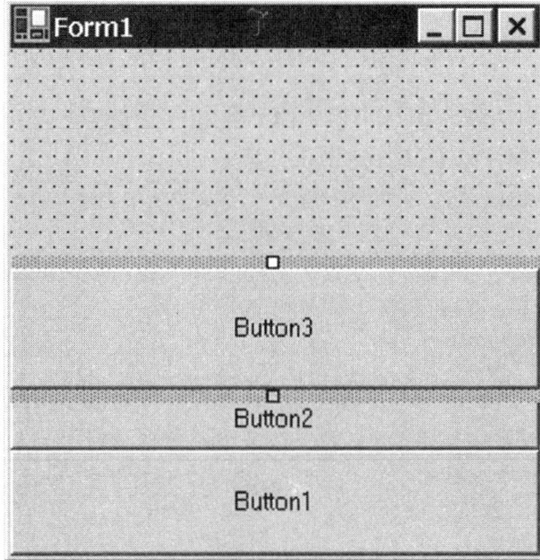

Figure 8-5. Docking at work

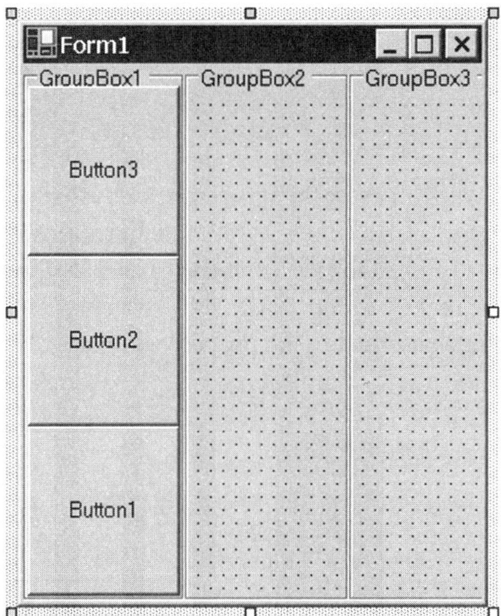

Figure 8-6. Start of a calculator

The Tab Order Menu

Changing the tab order in earlier versions of VB was frustrating, and using an add-in was the only way to ease the pain. In VB .NET, the Tab Order option on the View menu option makes it easy. All you have to do is type the number that you want for the tab order of a control in the little box that attaches to the control when you choose View|Tab Order, as you can see in Figure 8-7. Controls inside container controls have a tab order using a ".". For example, if a group box has tab order number 3, then the controls inside of it have numbers such as 3.0, 3.1, and the like. (To turn off the Tab Order mode, click on the menu item again.)

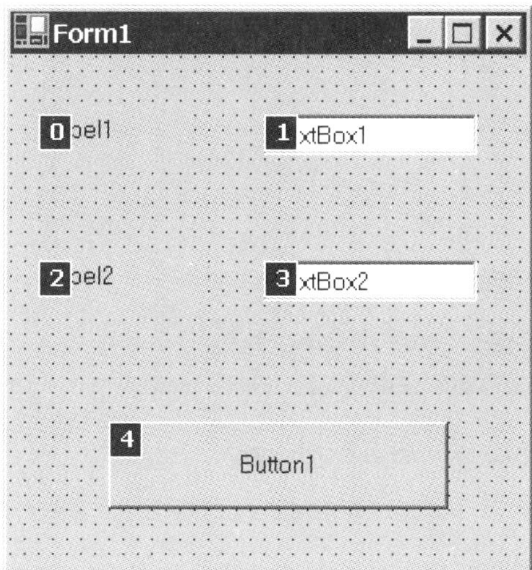

Figure 8 -7. Using the Tab Order menu item

Returning to a Simple Program

In Chapter 1, we showed you the somewhat complicated code automatically generated by the IDE for a simple Windows application that responds to a button click. We also promised you that you would eventually be able to understand how this code works. We now return to that code. (See Chapter 1 for the steps you need to follow to build this application.)

First, we need to point out that when you build a Windows Form application, the VS .NET IDE automatically adds references to two assemblies, as you can see in the Object Browser for our example (see Figure 8-8). The two assemblies are `System.Drawing` and `System.Windows.Forms`. The `System.Drawing` assembly is a single namespace that contains the classes needed for sizing and positioning a form and its controls. You also use it when drawing or placing images on a form. The `System.Windows.Forms` assembly is also a single namespace and contains the classes for all the controls as well as the `Windows.Forms.Form` class for form instances.

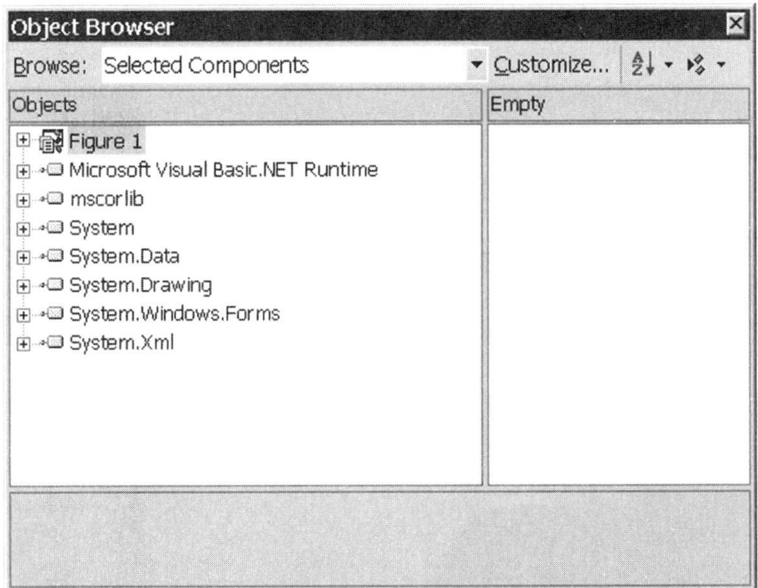

Figure 8-8. The Object Browser for a simple Windows application

```
Public Class Form1
    Inherits System.Windows.Forms.Form

#Region " Windows Form designer generated code "

    Public Sub New()
        MyBase.New()

        'This call is required by the Windows Form designer.
         InitializeComponent()

         'Add any initialization after the InitializeComponent() call

     End Sub

```

```
    'Form overrides dispose to clean up the component list.
    Protected Overloads Overrides Sub Dispose(ByVal disposing As Boolean)
        If disposing Then
            If Not (components Is Nothing) Then
                components.Dispose()
            End If
        End If
        MyBase.Dispose(disposing)
    End Sub
  Friend WithEvents Button1 As System.Windows.Forms.Button

    'Required by the Windows Form designer
    Private components As System.ComponentModel.Container

    'NOTE: The following procedure is required by the Windows Form designer
    'It can be modified using the Windows Form designer.
    'Do not modify it using the code editor.
    <System.Diagnostics.DebuggerStepThrough()> Private Sub _
     InitializeComponent()
    Me.Button1 = New System.Windows.Forms.Button()
    Me.SuspendLayout()
    '
    'Button1
    '
    Me.Button1.Anchor = ((System.Windows.Forms.AnchorStyles.Bottom Or _
System.Windows.Forms.AnchorStyles.Left) Or _
System.Windows.Forms.AnchorStyles.Right)
    Me.Button1.Location = New System.Drawing.Point(46, 216)
    Me.Button1.Name = "Button1"
    Me.Button1.Size = New System.Drawing.Size(200, 48)
    Me.Button1.TabIndex = 0
    Me.Button1.Text = "Click me!"
    '
    'Form1
    '
    Me.AutoScaleBaseSize = New System.Drawing.Size(6, 15)
    Me.ClientSize = New System.Drawing.Size(292, 268)
    Me.Controls.AddRange(New System.Windows.Forms.Control() {Me.Button1})
    Me.Name = "Form1"
    Me.Text = "First Windows Application"
    Me.ResumeLayout(False)

  End Sub

```

```
57 #End Region
58
59   Private Sub Button1_Click(ByVal sender As System.Object, ByVal e As _
System.EventArgs) Handles Button1.Click
60     MsgBox("Thanks for clicking!")
61   End Sub
62 End Class
```

Lines **1** and **2** show that this is a `Public` class that inherits from the `Form` class in the `System.Windows.Forms` namespace. The `#` in line **4** marks the beginning of the region for automatically generated code. It is important to keep in mind that every time you use the Properties window or drag controls around in the designer you are generating code. And in VB .NET, you can actually look at the automatically generated code and change it once you become more experienced.

Lines **6** and **7** mark the beginning of this class's constructor. As is usually the case, we need to call the base class's constructor in the first line of an inherited constructor. (See the section in this chapter on "The Inheritance Chain in the `System.Windows.Forms` Namespace" for more about the inheritance chain used here.)

Line **10** shows a call to the `InitializeComponent` method, which can be found in lines **33–55**. The automatically generated `InitializeComponent` method takes all the design decisions and Properties window settings that you made and translates them into code. For example, the button you added is declared in line **25**, later instantiated in line **34**, and then finally added to the `Form` object via code (line **50**). Also notice how, in lines **44** and **52**, the code sets the `Text` property of both the button and the form according to what you did with the Properties window.

> **NOTE** *The* `Text` *property replaces the* `Caption` *property (used in earlier versions of VB) for all controls.*

Lines **40** and **42** use members of the `System.Drawing` namespace to position and size the button, and lines **48–49** do the same for the form. Pixels (!) are the new default graphic unit—twips are gone.

> **NOTE** *Although older properties such as* `Left`, `Top`, `Width`, *and* `Height` *still work, you can now use structs as the values of the* `Location` *and* `Size` *properties. The* `Location` *property sets or returns a* `Point` *struct that encapsulates the position of a point. Similarly, the* `Size` *property uses a* `System.Drawing.Size` *struct to encapsulate a height and a width. Because both struct classes are merely encapsulations of two integer values, they have properties to set the individual parts, such as the* `Width` *property for a* `Size` *object or the* `Y` *property for a* `Point` *struct.*

Lines **17–24** implement the version of a `Dispose` method needed by a Windows Form application. The exact format for this method is a little different than the simple `Dispose` method you saw in Chapter 5; this `Dispose` method actually disposes of all the resources used by all the controls on the form, as well as the ones used by the form itself.

Line **25** uses the shorthand you have already seen to specify that this button is to be a source of events (see Chapter 6). Lines **59–61** actually hook up the click event procedure using the `Handles` keyword. All automatically generated control or form events in .NET have a syntax such as the one you see in line **59**:

```
Sub ObjectName_eventname(ByVal sender As Object, Byval e As EventArgs) _
Handles ObjectName.eventname
```

`Sender`, in this case, is a reference to the control that raised the event. The `EventArgs` parameter is the object that encapsulates the data about the event. (Event procedures that send additional information such as the `KeyPress` event or `MouseDown` event use an object that inherits from `EventArgs`, such as `KeyEventArgs` or `MouseEventArgs`, to encapsulate the extra information.)

NOTE *You can also start a Windows Form application from the* `Sub Main` *that is the entry point for your application. In this case, you need to make a call to the* `Application.Run` *method with the form name as in the following code:*

```
Public Sub Main()
  Dim myForm As New Form1()
  Application.Run(myForm)
End Sub
```

(There is an implicit call to `Application.Run` *whenever you use a form as the startup object. Interestingly enough, this call is required in C# but not in VB .NET.)*

NOTE *We have to confess we are betraying our heritage as longtime VB programmers with the call to* `MsgBox` *in line* ***60***. *The* `Windows.Forms` *namespace comes with a* `MessageBox` *class that is actually more capable than using the* `MsgBox` *statement, but in this one case, old habits die hard. We suggest you look at the documentation for this class to see if you want to start using it instead of the* `MsgBox` *statement.*

More Form Properties

Although we do not have space to discuss all of the Form class's properties, we do want to point out some of the main differences between the way things worked in earlier versions of VB and the way they work in VB .NET. One dramatic change is in the way fonts work. Instead of the older Font properties such as FontBold, you use the Font class in System.Drawing, whose most common constructor looks like this:

```
Sub New(ByVal family As FontFamily, ByVal emSize As Single, _
ByVal style As FontStyle)
```

(*Font families* are familiar to Word users: They are groups of individual fonts, such as Times New Roman, Courier New, or Arial, in different point sizes and often with bold or other attributes.)

For example, because the Or statement combines bit values, this code assigns the MyFont variable to an Arial font in 12 point bold italic:

```
myFont = New System.Drawing.Font("Arial", 12, _
FontStyle.Bold Or FontStyle.Italic)
```

and then modifies the Button1_Click event procedure so that clicking on the button changes the font:

```
Private Sub Button1_Click(ByVal sender As System.Object, _
ByVal e As System.EventArgs) Handles Button1.Click
  Dim myFont As System.Drawing.Font
  myFont = New System.Drawing.Font("Arial", 12, _
  FontStyle.Bold Or FontStyle.Italic)
  Me.Font = myFont
End Sub
```

Figure 8-9 shows the button with the new font.

> **CAUTION** *When you make font assignments to a form's* Font *property, the new font is automatically used by the* Text *property of all the controls it contains. The exception is that if you have specified a font for an individual control, this overrides the inherited font.*

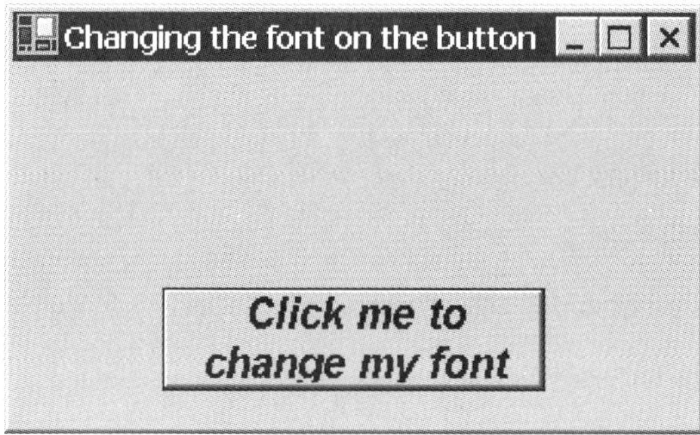

Figure 8-9. A button with text reset to bold and italic

In addition to the `Anchor` and `Dock` properties, you use the new `MinimumSize` and `MaximumSize` properties to specify how small or large a user can make your form. The properties take `Size` objects. This code, for example, would prevent the form from being made smaller than the size of the button:

```
Me.MinimumSize = New Size(Button1.Size)
```

Because the `MinimumSize` property actually controls changes to the form's `Size` property, this *includes* the title bar. The result is that, with a line of code such as we have just shown you, you would not see much of the button with this value for the minimum size. Your are better off using something like this:

```
Me.MinimumSize = New Size(Button1.Size.Width*2, Button1.Size.Height*2)
```

> **TIP** *For setting the* `MaximumSize` *property, you may want to use the* `System.Windows.Forms.Screen` *class, which lets you get at the screens used by the user (multiple monitors are supported). This class is also useful when setting the* `DesktopBounds` *and* `DesktopLocation` *properties.*

The new `ClientSize` property lets you get at the usable area of a form (the area minus the border and title bar). The useful `Bounds` property takes or returns a `Rectangle` structure that encapsulates a form's width and height, and the location of its upper left corner.

> **TIP** *The* `Rectangle` *structure class in* `System.Drawing` *has some very useful members: it is worth checking out the documentation for this helpful utility structure. We often find ourselves using a lot the* `Inflate` *member, which lets you quickly create a larger rectangle from a smaller one.*

Many form properties, methods, and events have changed from their VB6 counterparts. The most important changes are shown in Table 8-1.

Table 8-1. Changes to VB6 Form Properties, Methods, and Events

OLD FORM ELEMENT	NEW FORM ELEMENT
`Activate` and `Deactivate` events	Renamed `Activated` and `Deactivated`
`Container` property	Renamed `Parent`
`DblClick` event	Renamed `DoubleClick`
`hWnd` property	Renamed `Handle`
`MouseCursor` property	Renamed `Cursor` and now returns an instance of the `Cursor` class
`Parent` property	Replaced by the `FindForm` method
`Picture` property	Replaced by the `BackgroundImage` property
`SetFocus` method	Renamed `Focus`
`Startup` property	Replaced by the `StartPosition` property
`ToolTip` property	Replaced by the ToolTip control which can be associated to any control via that control's `ToolTip` property
`Unload` command	Gone, replaced with the `Close` method
`Unload` event	Replaced by the `Closing` event (there is also a new `Closed` event that fires after the form has closed)
`ZOrder` method	Replaced by the `BringToFront` and `SendToBack` methods

Menu Controls and the New Visual Studio Menu Editor

Although we do not have much space in this book to cover form design issues, we cannot resist taking the time to cover the new "in-place" menu editor. VB programmers have long been waiting for something like this. Yet as nifty and user friendly as the new menu editor is, you must understand the code generated by the IDE in order to take full advantage of it.

Building a menu with the Menu Editor is simple. You start by dragging a `MainMenu` control from the Toolbox onto your form, after which you will see the beginnings of a menu appear on the form, as shown in Figure 8-10.

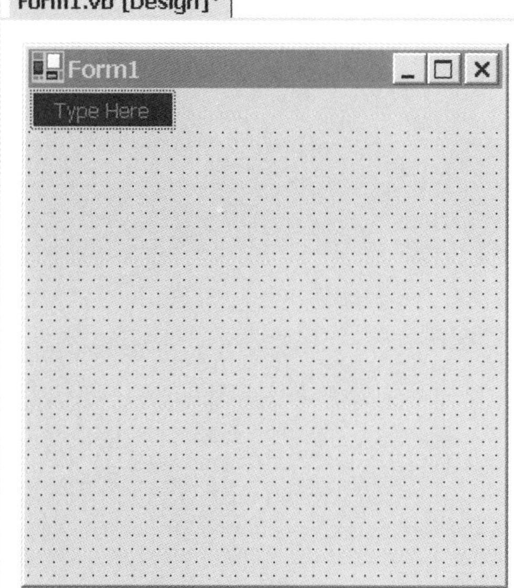

Figure 8-10. Start of building a menu with the new Menu Editor

Now start typing the captions for the menu items. At any given stage you can type in a location and the menu item appears, along with ways to move across or down (see Figure 8-11). To modify a menu item you have already created, simply click on it (you can modify existing menus by clicking on the `MainMenu` control in the component tray below the form). You cut and paste menu items to change their order (even on the main menu bar). As in earlier versions of VB, you insert an ampersand (&) before the letter you want to be a shortcut key. Figure 8-11 shows both a shortcut key and a separator bar.

Before jumping into the code behind Figure 8-11, you need to know that an instance of the `System.Windows.Forms.MainMenu` class encapsulates the entire menu of the form. A `MainMenu` object acts as a container for `MenuItem` instances. To allow submenus, `MenuItem` instances have a `MenuItems` property that holds other `MenuItems` as a collection called, naturally enough, an instance of the `Menu.MenuItemCollection` class.

As far as the code behind Figure 8-11, this starts with the declarations for the menu items. As you can see, we changed the names of the menu items to things such as `mnuFile` instead of the default of `MenuItem1`:

```
Friend WithEvents MainMenu1 As System.Windows.Forms.MainMenu
Friend WithEvents mnuFile As System.Windows.Forms.MenuItem
Friend WithEvents mnuEdit As System.Windows.Forms.MenuItem
Friend WithEvents mnuHelp As System.Windows.Forms.MenuItem
Friend WithEvents mnuOpen As System.Windows.Forms.MenuItem
Friend WithEvents mnuSave As System.Windows.Forms.MenuItem
Friend WithEvents mnuExit As System.Windows.Forms.MenuItem
```

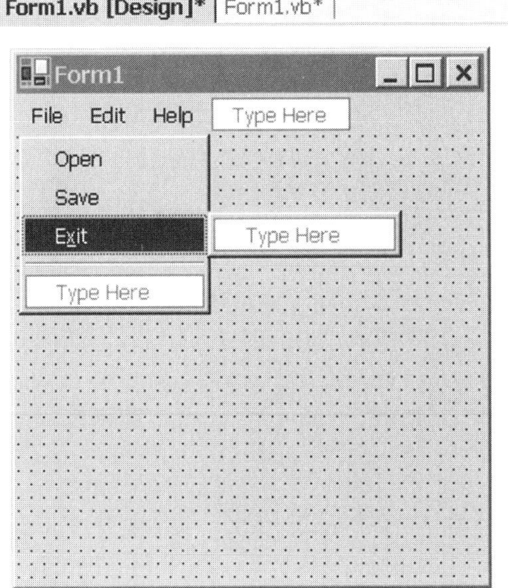

Figure 8-11. Creating a menu with Visual Studio's new Menu Editor

> **TIP** *A quick way to set the* `Name` *property of menu items is to right click on a menu item and choose Edit Names (use the context menu to turn this feature off when you are finished with it).*

The IDE adds code like this to `InitializeComponent` in order to create the main menu instance:

```
Me.MainMenu1 = New System.Windows.Forms.MainMenu()
```

This kind of code gets added to `InitializeComponent` to create the individual menu items:

```
Me.mnuFile = New System.Windows.Forms.MenuItem()
Me.mnuNew = New System.Windows.Forms.MenuItem()
Me.mnuOpen = New System.Windows.Forms.MenuItem()
```

Notice how the top-level File menu is also represented by a `MenuItem` instance. Individual menu items are added to the `MainMenu` instance via a call to the `AddRange` method of the `MenuItems` class with code like this, which uses the `AddRange` method to add three menu items at once:

```
Me.MainMenu1.MenuItems.AddRange(New Sys8tem.Windows.Forms.MenuItem() _
{Me.mnuFile, Me.mnuEdit, Me.mnuHelp})
```

Because individual menu item instances also have a `MenuItems` property, the automatically generated code looks similar to add items to the various menus, for example:

```
Me.mnuFile.MenuItems.AddRange(New System.Windows.Forms.MenuItem() _
 {Me.mnuNew, Me.mnuOpen, Me.mnuExit, Me.mnuSep})
```

The IDE performs the final step of hooking up the click events. The code it generates looks like this:

```
Private Sub mnuExit_Click(ByVal sender As System.Object, _
ByVal e As System.EventArgs) Handles mnuExit.Click
```

Context Menus

In earlier versions of VB, context menus were a bit cumbersome to build. In .NET, a context menu is simply an instance of the `ContextMenu` class that you can edit in place. You assign a control or form a context menu simply by setting the `ContextMenu` property of the control or form. The standard Windows convention is that context menus pop up in response to a right (non-primary for lefties) mouse click, which is handled automatically for you through the magic of inheritance in .NET. (There is no need to code any behavior in the a `MouseDown` event.) Context menu functionality is part of the `Control` class that both forms and controls inherit from.

When you drag a `ContextMenu` control to a form, the IDE generates code much like it did for main menu items:

```
Friend WithEvents ContextMenu1 As System.Windows.Forms.ContextMenu
```

and

```
Me.ContextMenu1 = New System.Windows.Forms.ContextMenu()
```

and the `AddRange` method is called here:

```
Me.ContextMenu1.MenuItems.AddRange(New System.Windows.Forms.MenuItem()
{Me.MenuItem1})
```

You can also use the useful Edit Names feature for context menus by right-clicking, in order to quickly assign a value to the `Name` property to context menu items as well.

> **TIP** *Because both main menus and context menus are driven by executing code, you have a way to generate a menus from scratch at run time!*

MDI Forms

In earlier versions of VB, Multiple Document Interface (MDI) applications required you to decide which form was the MDI parent form at design time. In .NET, you need only set the `IsMdiContainer` property of the form to `True`. You create the child forms at design time or at run time via code, and then set their `MdiParent` properties to reference a form whose `IsMdiContainer` property is `True`. This lets you do something that was essentially impossible in earlier versions of VB: change a MDI parent/child relationship at run time. It also allows an application to contain multiple MDI parent forms, which you also could not do in VB6.

For example, if you modify a `Form1_Load` to this:

```
Private Sub Form1_Load(ByVal sender As System.Object, _
ByVal e As System.EventArgs) _
Handles MyBase.Load
  Me.Text = "I'm an MDI Parent"
  Me.IsMdiContainer = True
  Dim MyChild As New System.Windows.Forms.Form()
  MyChild.MdiParent = Me
  MyChild.Show()
  MyChild.Text = "MDI Child"
End Sub
```

you will see something like Figure 8-12.

Figure 8-12. The simplest MDI example

Of course, this is a pretty sad excuse for an MDI application. MDI applications usually have a Windows menu that allows the user to tile or cascade the open child windows or to make any child window active. The Windows menu belongs to the parent menu, and the code to create it can be as simple as this:

```
Public Sub InitializeMenu()
  Dim mnuWindow As New MenuItem("&Window")
  MainMenu1.MenuItems.Add(mnuWindow)
  mnuWindow.MenuItems.Add(New MenuItem _
  ("&Cascade", AddressOf WindowCascade_Clicked))
  mnuWindow.MenuItems.Add(New MenuItem _
  ("Tile &Horizontal", AddressOf WindowTileHoriz_Clicked))
  mnuWindow.MenuItems.Add(New MenuItem _
  ("Tile &Vertical", AddressOf WindowTileVert_Clicked))
  mnuWindow.MdiList = True
End Sub

Protected Sub WindowCascade_Clicked(ByVal Sender As Object, _
  ByVal e As System.EventArgs)
  Me.LayoutMdi(MdiLayout.Cascade)
End Sub

Protected Sub WindowTileHoriz_Clicked(ByVal Sender As Object, _
  ByVal e As System.EventArgs)
  Me.LayoutMdi(MdiLayout.TileHorizontal)
End Sub

Protected Sub WindowTileVert_Clicked(ByVal Sender As Object, _
  ByVal e As System.EventArgs)
  Me.LayoutMdi(MdiLayout.TileVertical)
End Sub
```

If you call `InitializeMenu` in the `Form Load` of the previous example, you get a window similar to the one shown in Figure 8-13.

To send a notification to a parent form when the user activates a child window, you register an event handling method for the `MdiChildActivate` event. You determine which child window is active by using the `ActiveMdiChild` property of the `Form` class. For example, this code adds a handler that will eventually update a `StatusBar` control on the parent form with the caption of the child window:

```
AddHandler Me.MdiChildActivate, AddressOf Me.MdiChildActivated
```

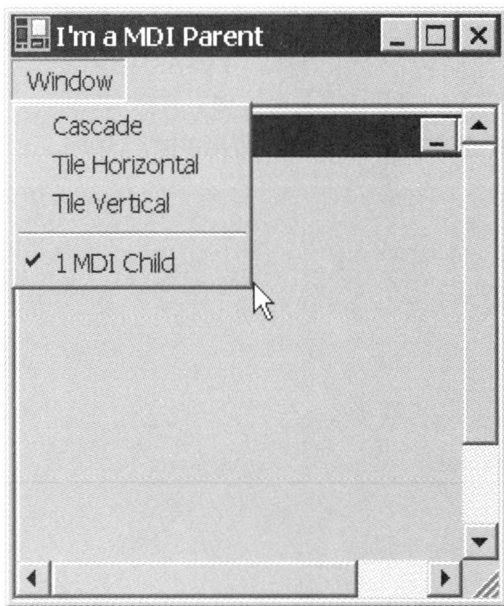

Figure 8-13. A typical Windows menu for an MDI application

You then use code like this:

```
Protected Sub MdiChildActivated(sender As object, e As System.EventArgs)
  If (Me.ActiveMdiChild <> Nothing) Then
    statusBar1.Text = Me.ActiveMdiChild.Text
  End If
End Sub
```

Dialog Forms and Dialog Boxes

The .NET Framework comes with a rich supply of dialog boxes that are located toward the bottom of the Toolbox (see Figure 8-14). These dialog boxes have various properties that control what the user sees. For example, the two file dialog boxes have a `Filter` property. We show you the basics of using these useful controls in this section, and we strongly recommend that you look at the .NET online help to see a list of these properties.

> **NOTE** *We show you how to use the printing dialog boxes in the "Printing" section later in this chapter.*

OpenFileDialog
SaveFileDialog
FontDialog
ColorDialog
PrintDialog
PrintPreviewDialog
PrintPreviewControl

Figure 8-14. The dialog box controls on the Toolbox

Regardless of which dialog box you use, they all inherit from an abstract `CommonDialog` class. The most important member of this class is `ShowDialog`, which uses polymorphism to determine which box to show. `ShowDialog` is actually a function whose return value lets you determine if the user clicked on the Cancel or OK button. (There is no longer a need to trap errors to determine if this quite normal user activity happens!) The `ShowDialog` method syntax is:

```
Public Function ShowDialog() As DialogResult
```

where you check the return value to see if it equals `DialogResult.OK` or `DialogResult.Cancel`.

ColorDialog

The code to use a ColorDialog typically grabs the value of the `Color` property and assigns it the `ForeColor` or `BackColor` property of the control or form. For example, here is a little procedure that allows you to change the background color of the form by clicking on the command button.

```
Private Sub btnColor_Click(ByVal sender As System.Object, _
  ByVal e As System.EventArgs) Handles btnColor.Click
  Dim myDialog As New ColorDialog()
  Dim Temp As Color = btnColor.BackColor
  If myDialog.ShowDialog() = DialogResult.OK Then
    Me.BackColor = myDialog.Color
    btnColor.BackColor = Temp
  End If
 End Sub
```

When you run this code the usual color dialog box pops up, and you can choose which color you want.

FontDialog

The FontDialog box should be pretty familiar to anyone who has used a Windows-based word processor. The key point to remember is that its `Font` property returns a `Font` object that you assign to a control or form's `Font` property. Here is some example code that assumes you have a textbox named `TextBox1` on your form, along with a button that uses the default name of `Button1`:

```
Private Sub Button1_Click_1(ByVal sender As System.Object, _
ByVal e As System.EventArgs) Handles Button1.Click
    Dim myDialog As New FontDialog()
    If myDialog.ShowDialog() = DialogResult.OK Then
      TextBox1.Font = myDialog.Font
    End If
End Sub
```

(Notice how the size of a single line textbox adjusts to fit the new font.)

FileDialog

The `FileDialog` class is an abstract class that has two concrete subclasses:

- `OpenFileDialog`
- `SaveFileDialog`

As an example of using these dialog boxes, the `RichTextbox` in .NET, like its counterpart in earlier versions of VB, has `LoadFile` and `SaveFile` methods to quickly open or save a file. To make this example more realistic, we want to set the `Filter` property of the file dialog box to be either `.txt` or `.rtf` using the line in bold in the following code. Also notice how the `LoadFile` method requires you to specify if the file is a text file (you can load RTF files without specifying the second parameter):

```
Private Sub mnuOpen_Click(ByVal sender As System.Object, _
ByVal e As System.EventArgs) Handles mnuOpen.Click
  Dim myDialog As New OpenFileDialog()
  myDialog.Filter = "text (*.txt), RTF (*.rtf)|*.txt;*rtf"
```

```
  If myDialog.ShowDialog = DialogResult.OK Then
    'can't load text files without specifying them as second parameter
    Dim Temp As String = myDialog.FileName.ToUpper
    If Temp.EndsWith("TXT") Then
      RichTextBox1.LoadFile(myDialog.FileName, RichTextBoxStreamType.PlainText)
    Else
      RichTextBox1.LoadFile(myDialog.FileName, RichTextBoxStreamType.RichText)
    End If
  End If
End Sub
```

Rolling Your Own Dialog Box

To roll your own dialog box, use an invisible form where you have:

- Set the ControlBox, MinimizeBox, and MaximizeBox properties to False and the ModalProperty to True.
- Used the form's ShowDialog method to show it as a modal dialog box. (If you also set the TopMost property of the form to be True, it will be on top of every window. You no longer have to use the SetWindowPos API function)

However, default buttons work in a different way than they did in VB6: the Default and Cancel properties are gone, so you assign a button control to the form's AcceptButton and CancelButton properties, as in this code:

```
Me.AcceptButton = btnOK
Me.CancelButton = btnCancel
```

Finally, once you use the ShowDialog method, you can then use the DialogResult property associated with the button you clicked to find out which button you clicked. (Clicking any button that has its DialogResult property set automatically closes its containing form.)

Adding Controls at Run Time

Prior to VB6, the only way to add controls at run time was via a control array. With VB6 came a better way to dynamic add a control, but there were still some problems with hooking up event handling for the controls you added. In VB .NET, the whole process has been overhauled. For example, start up a new Windows application and add this code to it (we explain it after you have a chance to run it):

```
1  Private Sub Form1_Load(ByVal sender As System.Object, ByVal e As _
2     System.EventArgs) Handles MyBase.Load
3    Dim newButton As New System.Windows.Forms.Button()
4    'set properties of newButton for example
5    With newButton
6      .Visible = True
7      .Size = New Size(100, 100)
8      .Text = "I'm a new button"
9      'more properties would usually be set
10    End With
11    Me.Controls.Add(newButton)
12    AddHandler newButton.Click, AddressOf Me.newButton_Click
13    End Sub
14    Public Sub newButton_Click(ByVal sender As _
15     System.Object, ByVal e As System.EventArgs)
16     MsgBox("You clicked on my new button")
17  End Sub
```

Line **3** creates the new button and lines **5–10** use the convenient `With` shorthand to add a bunch of properties to the `newButton` object. Note that it is only with line **11** that the new button is actually added to the form. Line **12** is another example of the wonderful flexibility of event handling in .NET: we are making the code contained in lines **14–17** the event handler for the button. The result of this code looks like Figure 8-15.

Figure 8-15. A new button added at run time

Form Inheritance: AKA Visual Inheritance

First, the much-hyped term *visual inheritance* used in the VB .NET marketing literature is definitely marketing speak—it simply refers to using a form you create as the basis for an inheritance chain. This is indeed a nice feature, but once you have inheritance, it is exactly what you expect to have. The idea is you inherit from the `Windows.Forms.Form` class and any custom properties, methods, and events you add, you get for free.[6]

For example, suppose you set up a splash screen for your company and want individual departments to be able to add things to it. To create this base form:

1. Choose File|New|Project.
2. Choose the Windows Application type and in the Name field type **SplashScreenBase** and click OK.

Now say you want to keep on using the Form designer while changing the type to be a class library instead of a standard Windows application so you can compile it into a DLL rather than an EXE. Here is a trick to do this efficiently:

1. Right-click on SplashScreenBase in the Solution Explorer and choose Properties.
2. Change the Output Type dropdown listbox from Windows Application to Class Library and then click OK.
3. Design the form the way you want, adding whatever controls, custom properties, methods, and events you want.
4. Compile the code.

Once you have the DLL, you can use this class in your code like any other class by adding a reference to it. If you choose Project|Add Inherited Form, you can have the IDE add the code necessary for this by working through some dialog boxes. However, we think the process of working through a bunch of dialog boxes is a bit silly, because all you have to do *after* adding the reference to the form's DLL is change the first line in a Windows application to something like this:

```
Public Class Form1
Inherits SplashScreenBase.Form1
```

---

6. Personally, we think this is a perfect example of how silly some marketing is to people in the know. Managers may be impressed with the term "visual inheritance," but programmers are likely to take it with a grain of salt.

and let the magic of inheritance do its work! (And what makes this method so nice is that the designer will sync up with your inherited form as well.)

Building Custom Controls through Control Inheritance

The use of inheritance in implementing "visual inheritance" for forms also works for building controls. For example, to make a textbox that accepts only positive integers, start out with:

```
Public Class PositiveIntegerTextBox
  Inherits System.Windows.Forms.TextBox
```

Now you need only add the code to make this box work the way you want. In the rest of this section, we show you how you might start building such a `PositiveIntegerTextBox` with its own custom properties, events, and methods.

> **NOTE** *To reduce the amount of coding for this example, we will not deal with all the issues involved in a full-featured version of a positive integer textbox. In particular, we will not cover licensing or security issues at all—you will find coverage of these issues in a more advanced book on custom control creation in .NET.*

To follow along with us, start up a new Class Library and add a reference to the `Windows.Forms.dll` assembly.

> **NOTE** *The reason we start with a Class Library rather than a User Control project is because a User Control works best for a control built from scratch or for controls that depend on many different controls working together (such as the controls you built in VB6). If you want to build a control that contains multiple controls, choose Windows Controls Library in the New Project dialog box, which gives you a container that you can use to build a complicated control via containment.*

Overriding an Event

The first feature we add to our custom control is the ability to override an existing event in the base class. For example, you would override the `OnChange` event in order to prevent a user from entering anything that is not an integer in the box. Here is the code to allow only positive integers to be entered or pasted:

```
1  Public Class PositiveIntegerTextBox
2    Inherits System.Windows.Forms.TextBox
3    Protected Overrides Sub OnTextChanged(ByVal e As EventArgs)
4    MyBase.OnTextChanged(e)
5      If Not (IsNumeric(Me.Text)) Then
6        Me.Text = String.Empty
7       Else
8        Dim temp As Decimal
9        temp = CType(Me.Text, Decimal)
10        If temp - Math.Round(temp, 0) <> 0 Then
11          Me.Text = String.Empty
12        End If
13      End If
14    End Sub
15  End Class
```

Lines **1** and **2** *specialize* an ordinary textbox. Because specialization via inheritance keeps everything you do not explicitly change intact, you do not have to use a wizard (as in VB6) to handle the unchanged properties, such as for color. Code such as line **4**, which sends the change event up to the parent, is usually necessary when overriding an event. Having a line such as this is necessary because you usually do not override all the behavior that the event triggers, and you need to make sure that the behaviors you do not override in the inheritance chain can handle the event correctly. Lines **5–6** make sure a user does not enter lines like "32Skiddoo. Lines **9–12** take care of the case where a user enters something like "32.3"; the code uses the built-in `Round` function to make sure the number is equal to its rounded version. (We admit killing the previous text the user enters is rather cruel—in a more sophisticated example you should cache the previous text so that you can restore it; that way users will not lose everything they typed because of a single mistake.)

At this point, you can compile the code into a DLL and have a perfectly good control. To see this after you compile it, you can start up a new Windows application and then add this control to the Toolbox:

1. Choose Tools|Customize Toolbox (Ctrl+T).
2. Choose the .NET Framework Components tab.
3. Click on Browse and then select the DLL for the control you want to use (it will be in the `\bin` subdirectory where you stored the code for the custom control).

The custom control is added to the .NET Framework Components tab (see Figure 8-16).

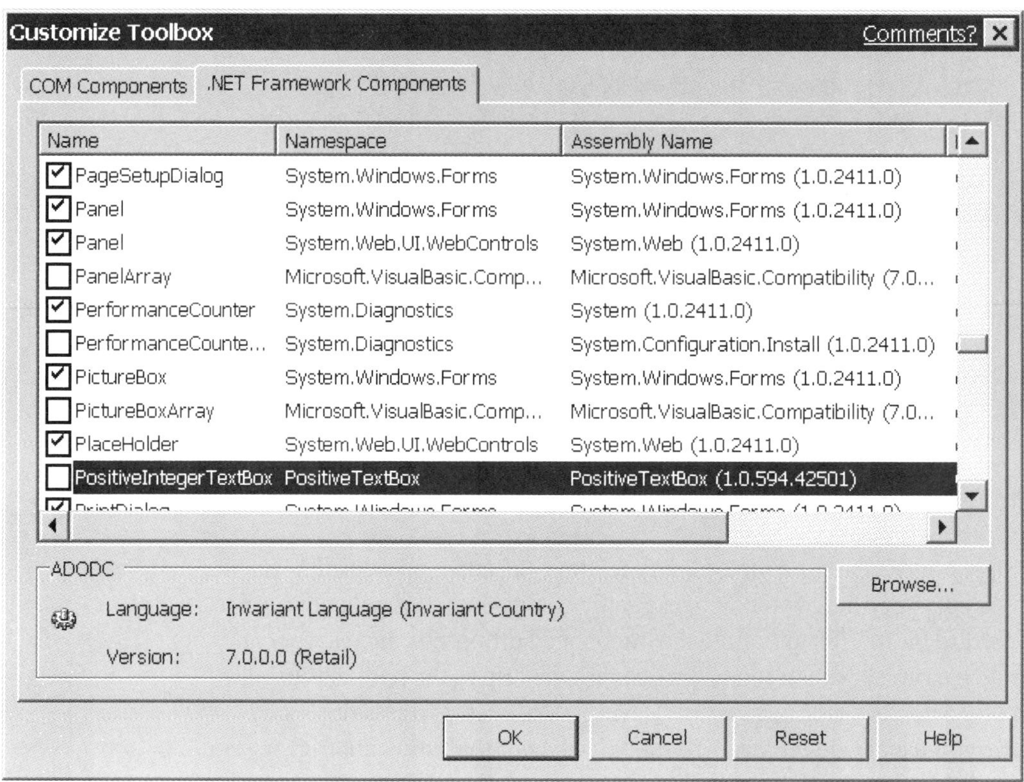

Figure 8-16. A custom control on the Components tab

The custom control then appears at the bottom of the Toolbox, as you can see in Figure 8-17. Double-click on this control and the control appears on your form. Notice that even this very simple control has the full set of textbox properties, as well as the design time behavior you would expect of a textbox. All of this behavior is automatically inherited from the ordinary textbox class (`Windows.Forms.TextBox` class), with no work on your part.

> **CAUTION** *Once you add a custom control to the Toolbox, it stays there even for other new projects. To remove it from the Toolbox, right-click on it and choose Delete.*

Figure 8-17. Adding a custom control to the Toolbox

Adding a Custom Event

As you might expect, adding a custom event to a control is no different than adding an event to a class (see Chapter 6 for a refresher). Suppose, for example, we wanted to raise a BadDataEntered event if the user entered something that was not a positive integer. The new code for the class is in bold:

```
Public Class PositiveIntegerTextBox
  Inherits System.Windows.Forms.TextBox
  Public Event BadDataEntered(ByVal Sender As Object, _
  ByVal e As EventArgs)
  Protected Overrides Sub OnTextChanged(ByVal e As EventArgs)
  MyBase.OnTextChanged(e)
  If Not (IsNumeric(Me.Text)) Then
    Me.Text = String.Empty
    RaiseEvent BadDataEntered(Me, New System.EventArgs())
  Else
    Dim temp As Decimal
    temp = CType(Me.Text, Decimal)
    If temp - Math.Round(temp, 0) <> 0 Then
      Me.Text = String.Empty
      RaiseEvent BadDataEntered(Me, New System.EventArgs())
    End If
  End If
  End Sub
End Class
```

Next, one of the niftier features of VB controls that goes back to older versions of VB is the idea of a *default event*. These are the events that you get automatically when you double-click on an instance of the control in the Form designer. You use an attribute to indicate what the default event is. Attributes are instances of the System.Attribute class; the DefaultEvent attribute we need is part of System.ComponentModel. Attributes are surrounded by angle brackets and the DefaultEvent attribute takes the name of the event in quotes. To make the BadDataEntered event the default event for this control, modify the beginning of the class to read as follows:

```
Imports System.ComponentModel
<DefaultEvent("BadDataEntered")> Public Class _
PositiveIntegerTextBox
Inherits System.Windows.Forms.TextBox
```

Adding a Custom Property

Suppose you want to add MinValue and MaxValue properties to your class. The code to do this is relatively straightforward. You start out with instance fields set to 1 and the maximum value for a Long, respectively. You then make sure that the minimum value cannot be set to less than 1 and that the maximum value cannot be less than the minimum value:

```
Private m_Min As Long = 1
Private m_Max As Long = Long.MaxValue
Public Property MinValue() As Long
  Get
    Return m_Min
  End Get
  Set(ByVal Value As Long)
    m_Min = Math.Max(1, Value)
  End Set
End Property
Public Property MaxValue() As Long
  Get
    Return m_Max
  End Get
  Set(ByVal Value As Long)
    m_Max = Math.Min(m_Min, Value)
  End Set
End Property
```

If you add this code to the control and compile it, you get the custom property but you will not be able to see it in the Properties window. To see it, add the `Browsable` attribute to the name of the property:

```
<Browsable(True)> Public Property MinValue
```

If you do this for both the `MinValue` and the `MaxValue` properties and look at the Properties window, you will see something like Figure 8-18.

As you can see, our custom property is definitely browsable, and both the `MaxValue` and `MinValue` properties are shown with the initial values we gave them. Better yet, if you try to change them in a way that the code forbids, such as making `MinValue` less than 1, you will see that this change is rejected in the Properties window.

Use `<Browsable(False)>` to keep a property from appearing in the Properties window. You can do this for new properties or ones that you are overriding. For example, this code hides the ordinary `Text` property of our custom textbox from the Properties window:

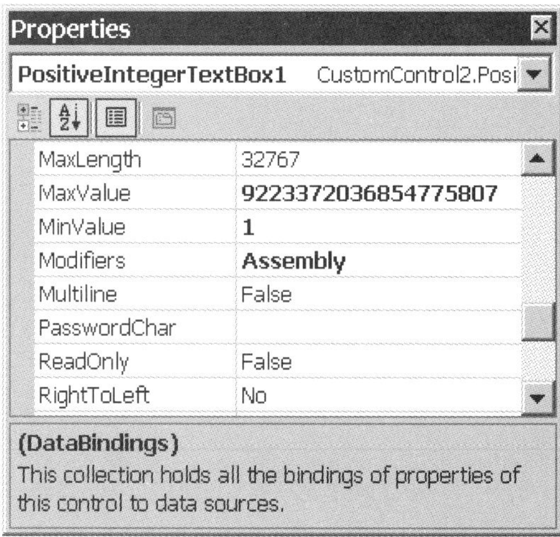

Figure 8-18. Adding a browsable minimum and maximum value property

```
<Browsable(False)> Public Overrides Property Text() As String
  Get
    Return MyBase.Text
  End Get
  Set(ByVal Value As String)
    MyBase.Text = Value
  End Set
End Property
```

As you can see in Figure 8-19, the `Text` property no longer shows up in the Properties window.

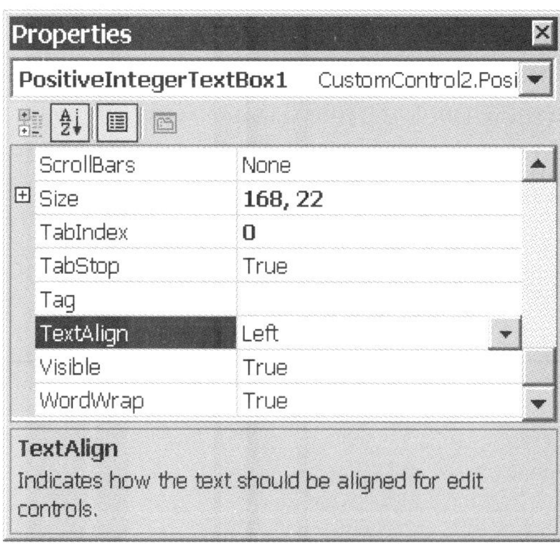

Figure 8-19. Text property does not show up if `<Browsable(False)>` *is set*

The Inheritance Chains in the `System.Windows.Forms` Namespace

Now that you have seen the basics of how to use the `Windows.Form` namespace, we want to return again to the inheritance chain described in Figure 8-20.

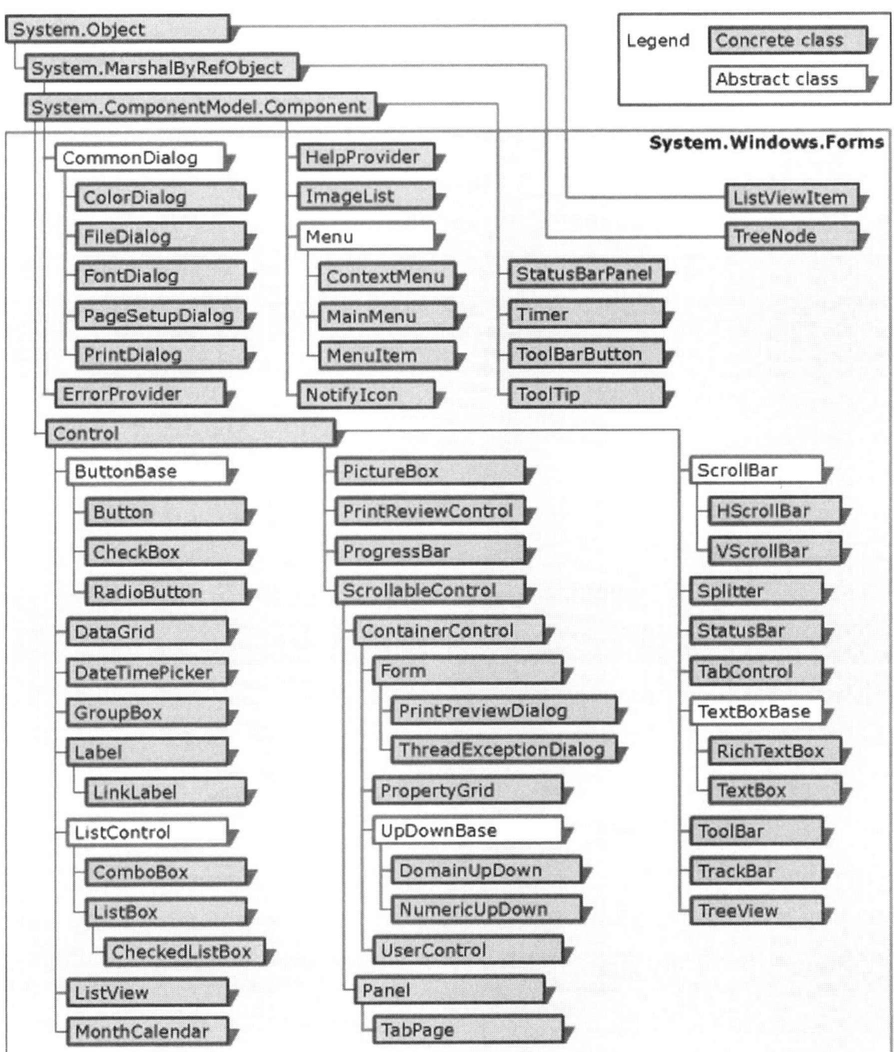

Figure 8-20. The Windows Forms component hierarchy

This is about as complicated a tree as one can imagine, but we want to concentrate on introducing you to its most important branch:

System.ComponentModel.Component

➥Control

In Figure 8-20, notice that both forms and controls inherit from the `Control` class, resulting in chains like these:

↪ScrollableControl

↪ContainerControl

↪Form

but also:

Control

↪TextBoxBase

↪RichTextBox

↪TextBox

and:

Control

↪ButtonBase

↪Button

↪CheckBox

↪RadioButton

The `Control` class is both the largest in terms of member functions (more than 300) and functionality. Both forms and controls inherit the `Control` class members.

NOTE *We hope we have given you a pretty good start in this chapter, but to truly master the* `Windows.Forms` *namespace you need to carefully study the online help for these classes and consider buying a more specialized book.*

The `Component` class is the base class for all components in the `System.Windows.Forms` namespace. It contains the members needed to deal with containment (such as a control inside a form or MDI children inside an MDI parent). These members are usually implementations of members in the `IComponent` interface. Because `Component` also contains the code for cleaning up the resources involved in visual development, this class implements `IDisposable`.

As the base class for controls *and* forms, the `Control` class handles most user interaction, including keyboard and mouse events. It also defines the color, position, and size of the form or control.

We show you how to handle the basic control class functionality, such as the key events, in the next section. First, however, we move further down the inheritance tree to forms. Because forms inherit from `ScrollableControl`, they have a cool feature that anyone who has tried to implement a scrolling form in VB6 will appreciate:

- Forms scroll if the controls they contain exceed the current boundaries of the form.

Look at Figure 8-21, which shows a form that would let you scroll through a *big* picture (ours was 5MB zipped) of the basic Mandelbrot Set fractal that all Apress cover art ultimately comes from. (For an introduction to the Mandelbrot Set, see `www.olympus.net/personal/dewey/mandelbrot.html`.)

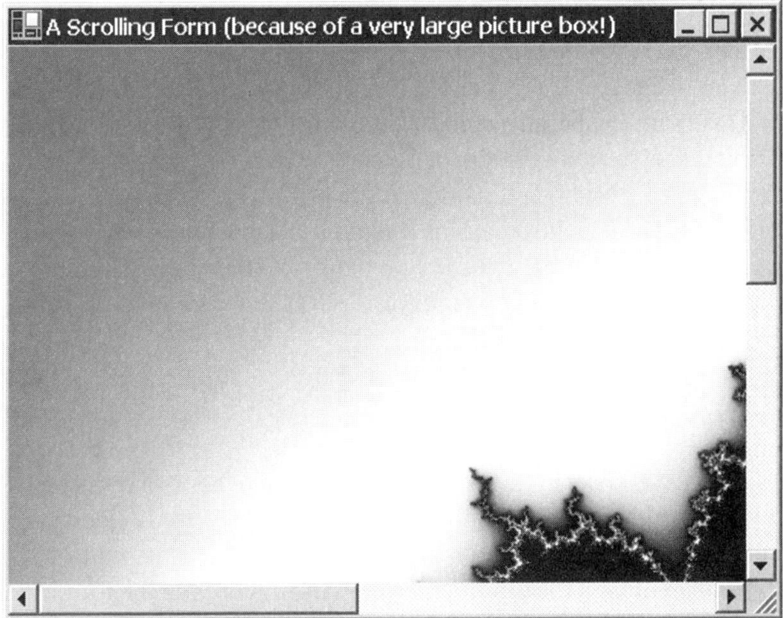

Figure 8-21. The basic Mandelbrot set in a scrollable form

To see the scrollable form feature at work with any large picture:

1. Add a picture box to a form and set its `SizeMode` property to `AutoSize`.

2. Next, find a *big* bitmap image.

3. Modify this code accordingly:

```
1  Private Sub Form1_Load(ByVal sender As System.Object, _
ByVal e As System.EventArgs) Handles MyBase.Load
2    Me.AutoScroll = True
3    Me.VScroll = True
4    Me.HScroll = True
5    Dim aBigBox As Rectangle = Rectangle.Inflate _
6    (Me.ClientRectangle, 6, 6)
7    PictureBox1.Bounds = aBigBox
8     'assumes this bitmap is in \bin below the solution's directory
9    PictureBox1.Image = Image.FromFile("Mandelbrot Set.bmp")
10 End Sub
```

The key line is line **2**, which sets the `AutoScroll` property that originates in `ScrollableControl` to `True`, without which the process cannot even get started. You use combinations of lines such as **3** and **4** to determine which scrollbars will appear. Line **5** uses a utility shared method in `System.Drawing.Rectangle` to create a rectangle object that is six times the size of the client area of the form, and line **7** then changes the picture box to that size by assigning the large rectangle to the `Bounds` property that all controls share. Line **9** assumes, as the comment says, that the bitmap is in the solution's `\bin` directory—a more realistic program would replace this by a call to the OpenFile dialog box.

Basic Control Class Functionality

With more than 300 members in the `Control` class, we cannot hope to cover all or even most of the functionality of this important class. You really need to look a the online documentation.[7] Still, the important key and validation events work in a manner subtly different than the same named ones did in VB6, and there are a couple of hidden pitfalls you need to watch out for.

Key Events

The three key events are triggered for the same reasons as their counterparts in earlier versions of VB:

7. By the way, the Windows Forms package automatically recognizes a mouse scroll wheel and uses it to scroll forward through a form or control where this makes sense. Thus, you do not have to use the new `Control.MouseWheel` event in most cases.

- `KeyPress`: Occurs when a key is pressed while the control has focus
- `KeyDown`: Triggered when a key is pressed down while the control has focus
- `KeyUp`: Triggered when the key is released while the control has focus

As in VB6, the `KeyDown` event is triggered before the `KeyPress` event, which in turn precedes `KeyUp`. The `KeyPress` event uses a `KeyPressEventArgs` object that encapsulates the pressed key as the value of the `KeyChar` property of the event object. For example, this code pops up a message box if the user enters a nondigit:

```
Private Sub TextBox1_KeyPress(ByVal sender As Object, _
ByVal e As System.Windows.Forms.KeyPressEventArgs) _
Handles TextBox1.KeyPress
  If e.KeyChar < "0" Or e.KeyChar > "9" Then
    MsgBox("only digits allowed")
  End If
End Sub
```

The `KeyDown` and `KeyUp` events, as in VB6, let you check for use of modifying keys, such as Ctrl or Alt. They use a `KeyEventArgs` object that is slightly richer in functionality than the `KeyPressEventArgs` class used by the `KeyPress` event. The `KeyEventArgs` object has a property called `KeyData` that uses the `Key` enumeration to tell you everything you want to know about combinations of keys plus modifying keys a user presses. You use the `Modifiers` and `Shift` properties to determine whether a chord is pressed (two modifiers, as in Alt+Shift+another key). This code detects pressing the Alt key for example:

```
If e.Modifiers = Keys.Alt Then
```

> **TIP** *If you do not need to worry about things such as the difference between the left and right Shift key, you can use the simpler* `Control`, `Shift`, *and* `Alt` *properties of the* `KeyEventArgs` *class.*

Unfortunately,[8] you cannot reset the `KeyChar or KeyData` properties like you could in VB6, because they are now read-only. However, you can still "eat" the character the user typed—and thus prevent it from appearing in the control—by

8. We think this is a design flaw that hopefully will be fixed.

setting the `Handled` property of the various key event objects to `True`. For example, change the `MsgBox` statement to:

```
If e.KeyChar < "0" Or e.KeyChar > "9" Then
  e.Handled = True ' handle the char = make it go away in the textbox
End If
```

and the user will not see the incorrect character inside the box.

Validating Events

.NET gives you two validate events instead of one: `Validating` and `Validated`. `Validating` is triggered *before* the control loses the focus. For example, to make sure that there is something in a textbox, use:

```
Public Sub TextBox1_Validating(ByVal sender As Object, _
ByVal e As System.ComponentModel.CancelEventArgs) _
Handles TextBox1.Validating
  ' cancel the focus shift if the textbox is empty
  If TextBox1.Text.Trim = String.Empty Then e.Cancel = True
End Sub
```

where the code that sets `e.Cancel = True` prevents the shift of focus away from the textbox if there is nothing in the box.

The `Validated` event, on the other hand, fires after the focus has shifted away from the control, but before other controls get the focus. Thus, you can use `Validated` to update the state of the other controls on the form.

> **CAUTION** *If you set the* `CausesValidation` *property of a control to* `False`, *the* `Validating` *and* `Validated` *events will not be triggered.*

Graphics: Using GDI+

Graphics programming in the .NET Framework is totally different than in earlier versions of VB. The familiar commands (some of which originated in QuickBasic) are gone. The key global change is that there is *no* counterpart to the `AutoRedraw` property, which you set to be `True` in earlier versions of VB to avoid having to write code in the `Paint` event to add persistence to graphics.

Programming graphics in VB .NET is based on drawing onto a graphics *context*, much as you did under the Windows GDI system. (Think of a graphics context as being like a artist's canvas that you can draw on.) Interestingly enough, the new system is called GDI+, even though the way you work with it is not all that similar to working with GDI.

> **CAUTION** *Programmers who know GDI well are in for a shock when working with GDI+, because drawing in .NET is completely stateless. This is a fancy way of saying that every drawing command must specify how it draws. The graphics contexts you paint on have no memory of what you did to them. For example, if you use a black brush in line 1 of your code and want to paint with a black brush again in line 2, you must tell the graphics system you are still using a black brush. It will not remember that in the previous line you were using the same brush.*

The GDI+ classes are in the `System.Drawing`, `System.Drawing.Drawing2D`, `System.Drawing.Imaging`, and `System.Drawing.Text` namespaces.[9] The namespaces are contained in the `System.Drawing.DLL` assembly and are automatically referenced when you choose Windows Application in the New Project dialog box.

You do most drawing in GDI+ by overriding the `Paint` procedure[10] of the form or control. This serves the same purpose it did in earlier versions of VB: it makes what you draw persist, even if the form is covered or minimized. Here is the signature of this important procedure for a form:

```
Protected Overrides Sub OnPaint(ByVal e As PaintEventArgs)
```

Next, you get a GDI+ drawing surface, which is represented by an instance of the `Graphics` class. The `Paint` procedure of the `Form` class encapsulates one of these drawing surfaces as the value of `e.Graphics`.

---

9. These are amazingly rich namespaces and we can only touch on them here. They deserve a book on their own and, if you are willing to put the energy into learning enough about them to write a book, please contact `gary_cornell@apress` about writing one! For now, we recommend the comprehensive chapter in Andrew Troelsen's book *VB .NET and the .NET Platform* (Apress, 2002. ISBN: 1-893115-26-7) for more on GDI+.

10. This is not an event, although it eventually calls the `OnPaint` event in the `Form` base class.

> **CAUTION** *Although every form or control (such as picture box) that you can draw on lets you get at its graphics context by a call to* `ControlName.CreateGraphics()`, *be very careful about doing this when you are not in the* `Paint` *procedure. There are subtle hazards in drawing on the graphics context you get from using* `e.Graphics` *in the* `Paint` *procedure, and in writing code that calls* `CreateGraphics`. *We encountered this in an early version of the program to show all fonts that you will see shortly.*

Simple Drawing

We now look at a very simple drawing example. This code displays a bitmap named `sample.bmp` (which is assumed to be in the `\bin` directory of this solution) in the upper left corner of the form:

```
Protected Overrides Sub OnPaint(ByVal e As PaintEventArgs)
  MyBase.OnPaint(e)
  Dim g As Graphics
  g = e.Graphics()
  g.DrawImage(New Bitmap("sample.bmp"), 0, 0)
  g.Dispose()
End Sub
```

Note the call to `Dispose` in the line in bold. Because the garbage collector does not reclaim graphics contexts, you should make a habit of doing it yourself at the end of the `Paint` procedure.

- This is worth repeating: if there is a `Dispose` method, you should call it when your are done with the object.

The next step might be to draw lines, boxes, and other figures. The first step for this kind of drawing is to get a `Pen` object, which is an instance of the `System.Drawing.Pen` class. The syntax for the most common `Pen` constructor is

```
Public Sub New(Color, Single)
```

where the first parameter defines the `Color` (a member of the `System.DrawingColor` enumeration) and the second parameter defines the width of the pen. (Other constructors let you use different kinds of brushes to fill the interior of the object.) To draw a rectangle, for example, you define the rectangle and then call `g.DrawRectangle`. This code draws the rectangle shown in Figure 8-22.

```
Protected Overrides Sub OnPaint(ByVal e As PaintEventArgs)
  MyBase.OnPaint(e)
  Dim g As Graphics
  g = e.Graphics()
  Dim myPen As New Pen(Color.Purple, 6)
  Dim aRectangle As New Rectangle(Me.ClientRectangle.Width \ 4, _
  Me.ClientRectangle.Height \ 4, Me.ClientRectangle.Height \ 2, _
  Me.ClientRectangle.Width \ 2)
  g.DrawRectangle(myPen, aRectangle)
  g.Dispose()
End Sub
```

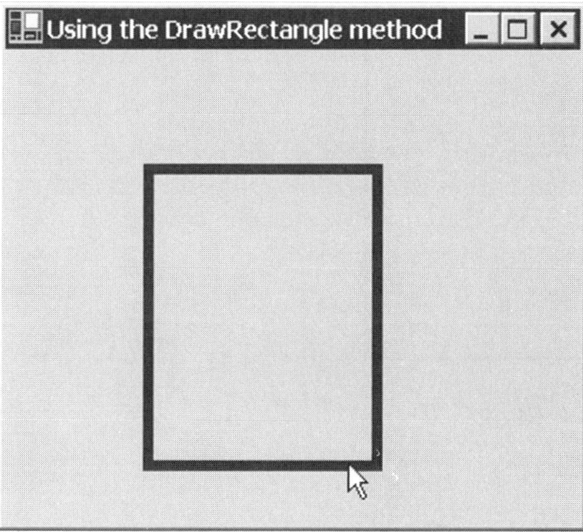

Figure 8-22. The result of using `DrawRectangle`*: a (purple) rectangle with a boundary 6 pixels wide*

Drawing Text

A graphics object's `DrawString` method lets you display text (in jargon you say you *render* text), usually by passing a font object, color, brush, and location to the `DrawString` method. For example, somewhat in keeping with the tradition of all modern programming books, the following code displays the text "Hello World" by using the form's current font and a purple brush on a white background as shown in Figure 8-23.

```
Protected Overrides Sub OnPaint(ByVal e As System.Windows.Forms.PaintEventArgs)
  MyBase.OnPaint(e)
  Dim g As Graphics = e.Graphics
  Dim theColor As Color = Color.Purple
  Dim theFont As New Font("Arial", 22, FontStyle.Bold Or FontStyle.Italic)
  Me.BackColor = Color.White
  g.DrawString("Hello World!", theFont, New SolidBrush(theColor), 0, 0)
  g.Dispose()
End Sub
```

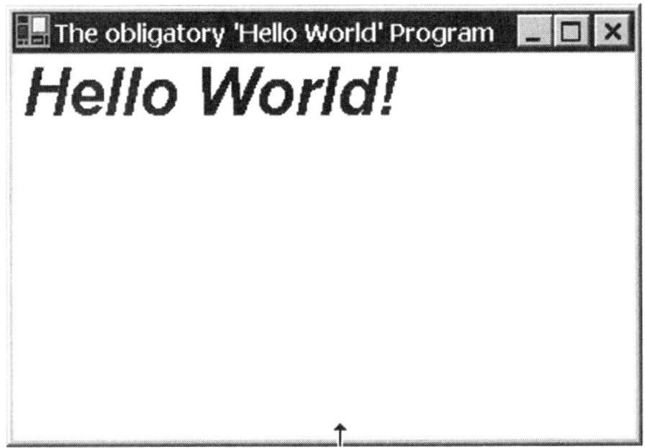

Figure 8-23. Rendering "Hello World" using GDI+

> **NOTE** *GDI+ provides full Unicode support, making it possible to render text in any language.*

An Example: Show All Fonts

To show you how to display text, we created a program that renders all of a system's fonts in a picture box, with the fonts displayed by name in that font. (Along the way, we came across a gotcha that we explain at the end of this section.) The program includes both a custom control and a scrolling form, as shown in Figure 8-24.

You get at the system fonts by using a call to the `InstalledFontCollection()` method in `System.Drawing.Text`. This returns a `System.Drawing.Text.FontCollection` object. The individual objects in a `FontCollection` object contain not fonts but *font families* such as Arial or Courier. You select individual fonts from the family. However, some fonts do not have regular versions, because all the fonts in that family

Figure 8-24. All installed fonts rendered in a scrolling form

are bold, italic, narrow, light, or some other variation. Thus, you need lines of code like this:

```
For Each aFontFamily In TheFonts.Families
  If aFontFamily.IsStyleAvailable(FontStyle.Regular) Then
```

We decided to write the code in the form of a special-purpose picture box that you add to a form with the appropriate code to turn on the scrollbars in the form load, like this:

```
Private Sub Form1_Load(ByVal sender As System.Object, _
ByVal e As System.EventArgs) Handles MyBase.Load
  Me.VScroll = True
  Me.HScroll = True
  Me.AutoScroll = True
  FontPictureBox1.Left = 0
  FontPictureBox1.Top = 0
End Sub
```

Here is the code for the special purpose picture box:

```
1  Public Class FontPictureBox
2    Inherits System.Windows.Forms.PictureBox
3    Protected Overrides Sub OnPaint(ByVal pe As _
     System.Windows.Forms.PaintEventArgs)
4      'always call Mybase.OnPaint!
5      MyBase.OnPaint(pe)
6    DisplayFonts(pe.Graphics)
7  End Sub
8    Private Sub DisplayFonts(ByVal g As Graphics)
9    'THIS DOESN'T WORK: Dim g As Graphics = Me.CreateGraphics()
10    Dim aFontFamily As FontFamily
11    Dim curx, curY As Single
12    Dim TheFonts As System.Drawing.Text.FontCollection
13    Dim tempFont As Font
14    Dim spacing As Integer = 2 '2 pixels apart
15    TheFonts = New System.Drawing.Text.InstalledFontCollection()
16    For Each aFontFamily In TheFonts.Families
17      Me.Height += 2
18      If aFontFamily.IsStyleAvailable(FontStyle.Regular) Then
19        tempFont = New Font(aFontFamily, 14, FontStyle.Regular)
20      ElseIf aFontFamily.IsStyleAvailable(FontStyle.Bold) Then
21        tempFont = New Font(aFontFamily, 14, FontStyle.Bold)
22      ElseIf aFontFamily.IsStyleAvailable(FontStyle.Italic) Then
23        tempFont = New Font(aFontFamily, 14, FontStyle.Italic)
24      End If
25      g.DrawString("This is displayed in " & aFontFamily.Name, _
26       tempFont, Brushes.Black, curx, curY)
27      Dim theSize As SizeF = g.MeasureString("This text is displayed in " _
28      & aFontFamily.Name, tempFont)
29      curY = curY + theSize.Height + spacing
30      Me.Height = Me.Height + CInt(theSize.Height) + spacing
31      Me.Width = Math.Max(CInt(theSize.Width), Me.Width)
32    Next
33    End Sub
34  End Class
```

Note in Line **6** that we send the current graphics context to the helper `DisplayFonts` routine contained in lines **9–33**, rather than create a new graphics context via a call to `Me.CreateGraphics()`. We originally had this helper procedure grab its own graphics context using the commented out line instead of using the one that came from the `PaintEventArgs` object, by passing in the value of `pe.Graphics`, as you see in line **6**. This did not work for reasons that are, as far as we know, undocumented.[11] (We left in the original call on line **9** as a comment so that you can uncomment it out to see the problem we ran into!)

To space the text out two pixels apart, we need to know the height at which a string displays. We do this in lines **27** and **28**, using the very useful `MeasureString` function:

```
Public Function MeasureString(String, Font) As SizeF
```

where the `SizeF` object returned is a version of the `Size` structure that uses singles rather than integers. Because `SizeF` encapsulates two singles, we use the `CInt` function in lines **30** and **31**. Also notice in line **30** that we increase the height of the picture box, and in line **31** we make sure that the width of the picture box is always large enough for any of the strings by using the `Max` method in the `Math` class.

Printing

Printing in .NET can be tricky, but the power you get is worth the extra hassles. In this section, we explain the steps needed to print a single page, using mostly automatically generated code, and then show you how to print multiple pages. We also show you how to roll your own printing code by using a delegate. We start by printing an image in a picture box via a button click.

> **NOTE** *To avoid certain limitations in GDI+, we assume that this image was set via the* `Image` *property, not by drawing it directly onto the picture box.*

Printing ultimately works by displaying information on a graphics context, but instead of attaching the context to the screen, the graphics object comes from a printer or a print preview window.

Whether you print to a printer or use .NET's Print Preview feature, the first step is to get a `PrintDocument` object, which is an instance of the `System.Drawing.Printing.PrintDocument` class. You can get such an instance by either:

- Using the `PrintDocument` control on the Toolbox and relying on automatically generated code, or using the `New` operator in the form like this:

  ```
  Dim aPrintDocument As New PrintDocument()
  ```

- Setting the value of the `Document` property of an instance of the `PrintDialog` class to an object you declare as the `PrintDocument` type.

11. We offer a free glow-in-the-dark Apress T-shirt to the first person who can explain why calling `CreateGraphics` in the `DisplayFonts` routine does not work and using the original graphics context does!

To use the Toolbox, you add the invisible `PrintDocument` control to a form and get this declaration:

```
Friend WithEvents PrintDocument1 As _
System.Drawing.Printing.PrintDocument
```

You get this line in the `InitializeComponent` procedure, which creates the instance:

```
Me.PrintDocument1 = New System.Drawing.Printing.PrintDocument()
```

That the `PrintDocument` object was declared `WithEvents` is the key to using automatically generated code for printing. The point is that, when you call the `Print` method on an instance of the `PrintDocument` class, .NET triggers at least *three* events:

- `BeginPrint`
- `PrintPage` (can be triggered multiple times if there are multiple pages to print)
- `EndPrint`

At the very least, you need to write code in the `PrintPage` event to do the actual printing.

> **TIP** *You can write code in the other two events if needed, but the* `PrintPage` *event is the one that does the actual printing. You usually use the other two events for any preliminaries or after-the-fact reporting.*

The `PrintPage` event has a `PagePrintEventArgs` object as its second parameter. This is a very rich object that encapsulates (among other things):

- A graphics object as the value of its `Graphics` property. This is what you draw on, and in turn is what the printer will print.
- A `PageSettings` object that encapsulates instructions for how the page should be printed. This object's properties include landscape mode (or not), printer resolution, margins, and so on.

In this simple example, a button click calls the `Print` method of the `PrintDocument` class:

```
Private Sub Button1_Click(ByVal sender As System.Object, _
ByVal e As System.EventArgs) Handles Button1.Click
  PrintDocument1.Print()
End Sub
```

The `Print` method then calls the `PrintPage` event, so you have to put the code in the `PrintDocument1_PrintPage` event, which does the actual printing. If you use the designer to generate this event, you also get the automatic hookup for the event via the correct `Handles` clause:

```
1  Private Sub PrintDocument1_PrintPage(ByVal sender As System.Object, _
   ByVal e As System.Drawing.Printing.PrintPageEventArgs) _
   Handles PrintDocument1.PrintPage
2    Dim g As Graphics
3    g = e.Graphics
4    g.DrawImage(PictureBox1.Image, 0, 0)
5    g.Dispose()
6    e.HasMorePages = False
7  End Sub
```

When you run this code, you see the image printed on the default printer (see the following section for how to change printers). Although our example code is relatively simple, each line in is important enough to warrant an explanation. Line **1** hooks up the event to a procedure with the correct signature without you having to explicitly use a delegate (see Chapter 6). Line **3** gets a graphics object that encapsulates a drawing surface on the current printer. Line **4** draws the image, starting in the upper left corner, but draws it on the printer, which is where the graphics context lies. Using the call to `Dispose` in line **5** is a good practice because, as you saw earlier, graphics contexts are not reclaimed by the garbage collector. Line **6** tells the `PrintPage` event that there are no more pages to print.

Printing Multiple Pages

The trick to printing multiple pages is that when the `HasMorePages` property of the `PrintPageEventArgs` object is set to be `True` in the procedure that handles the `PrintPage` event, the `PrintDocument` object knows there are more pages to print and automatically re-raises the `PagePrint` event.

The problems you may encounter in printing multiple pages have little to do with printing. They are the same problems you encounter in any complicated form of drawing to a graphics object: you must keep track of *everything*. For example, suppose you want to write a small program to print the contents of a textbox or text file. The pseudo code is simple:

- Read a line from the box or file.
- Is it too wide for a line? If so, break it up into pieces.
- Can you fit all these lines on the current page?
- If so, print them using `DrawString` at the current location; if not, print as many as you can, then start a new page and print the remaining lines there.
- Repeat the process until there are no more lines in the box or file.

But the code that determines if you can fit a new line on a page has nothing to do with printing, and everything to do with beating on the various metrics you get from the width and height of the text line. These in turn depend on both the font family and the size of the font you use. Fortunately, you can safely rely on methods such as `MeasureString`, which use the metrics associated with the current graphics context.

More on the `PrintPageEventArgs` *Class*

A `PrintPageEventArgs` object has two read-only properties that tell you about the boundaries of the page. Both use hundredths of an inch as units:

- `PageBounds`: Gets the rectangular area of the entire page
- `MarginBounds`: Gets the rectangular area inside the margins

The `PrintPageEventArgs` object's `PageSettings` property gives you a `PageSettings` object that gives you more options. Table 8-2 lists the key `PageSettings` object properties (most printers let you read these properties, but some will not let you set them).

Table 8-2. `PageSettings` *Object Properties*

PROPERTY	PURPOSE
`Bounds`	Gets the bounds of the page. Takes into account whether the user has chosen Landscape. Read-only.
`Color`	A read-write Boolean property that indicates whether to print the page in color.
`Landscape`	A read-write Boolean property that indicates page orientation
`Margins`	Gets or sets page margins. Default is 1 inch.
`PaperSize`	Gets or sets the paper size.
`PaperSource`	Gets or sets the paper source (for example, a printer's single-sheet feeder, if it has one.
`PrinterResolution`	Gets or sets the printer resolution. Some printers allow custom resolutions, others allow only a choice between Draft and High.
`PrinterSettings`	Gets or sets printer settings associated with a page.

For example, because most printers can print to within ½ inch of the boundary, you can use this code to set the margins:

```
e.PageSettings.Margins = New System.Drawing.Printing.Margins(50, 50, 50, 50)
```

and this to print starting at the new margin bounds:

```
Dim g As Graphics
g = e.Graphics
g.DrawImage(PictureBox1.Image, e.MarginBounds.Left, e.MarginBounds.Top)
```

Using a Print Dialog Control

You will also need to users select the printer and make other changes. The `PrintDialog` control lets you do so. The code might look like this:

```
Private Sub Button1_Click(ByVal sender As System.Object, _
ByVal e As System.EventArgs) Handles Button1.Click
  Dim PrintDialog1 As New PrintDialog()
  'needed because PrintDialog needs a PrinterSettings object to display
  PrintDialog1.Document = PrintDocument1
  If PrintDialog1.ShowDialog() = DialogResult.OK Then
    PrintDocument1.Print()
  End If
End Sub
```

The line in bold tells the PrintDialog instance that the document associated to it should be the PrintDocument1 instance (assuming that this object has already been created). This line is necessary, because a PrintDialog control needs certain print settings (in the form of a PrintSettings object) *before* it can be displayed. The easiest way to give it this information is by assigning a PrintDocument object to its Document property.

Rolling Your Own Printing Code

Although using the Toolbox and automatically generated code is sufficient in most cases, you may occasionally need to roll your own code when you need to allow for specialized printing. The trick is to write a procedure that has the following signature:

```
Private Sub ProcedureToDoThePrinting(ByVal Sender As Object, _
ByVal e As System.Drawing.Printing.PrintPageEventArgs)
```

You then connect this procedure to the PrintPage event of the PrintDocument class via a delegate. For example, to call the PrintDocument object, aPrintDocument, and the aPrintDocument_PrintPage procedure just shown, use a handler like this:

```
AddHandler aPrintDocument.PrintPage, _
 AddressOf Me.aPrintDocument_PrintPage
```

This code shows how you could code a Print item on a menu:

```
Private Sub mnuPrint_Click(ByVal sender As System.Object, _
ByVal e As System.EventArgs) Handles mnuPrint.Click
  Dim aPrintDocument As New PrintDocument()
  AddHandler aPrintDocument.PrintPage, _
  AddressOf Me.aPrintDocument_PrintPage
  aPrintDocument.Print()
End Sub
```

Print Preview

Although printing a basic document is somewhat more painful now than it was in VB6, implementing a print preview function in VB .NET is easy. You merely set the document property of a PrintPreviewDialog control instance to the PrintDocument object. For example, this code is almost identical to the code you saw earlier, but gives you print preview functionality, as you can see in Figure 8-25.

```
Private Sub btnPreview_Click(ByVal sender As System.Object, _
ByVal e As System.EventArgs) Handles btnPreview.Click
  Dim PrintPreviewDialog1 As New PrintPreviewDialog()
  PrintPreviewDialog1.Document = PrintDocument1
  If PrintPreviewDialog1.ShowDialog() = DialogResult.OK Then
    PrintDocument1.Print()
  End If
End Sub
```

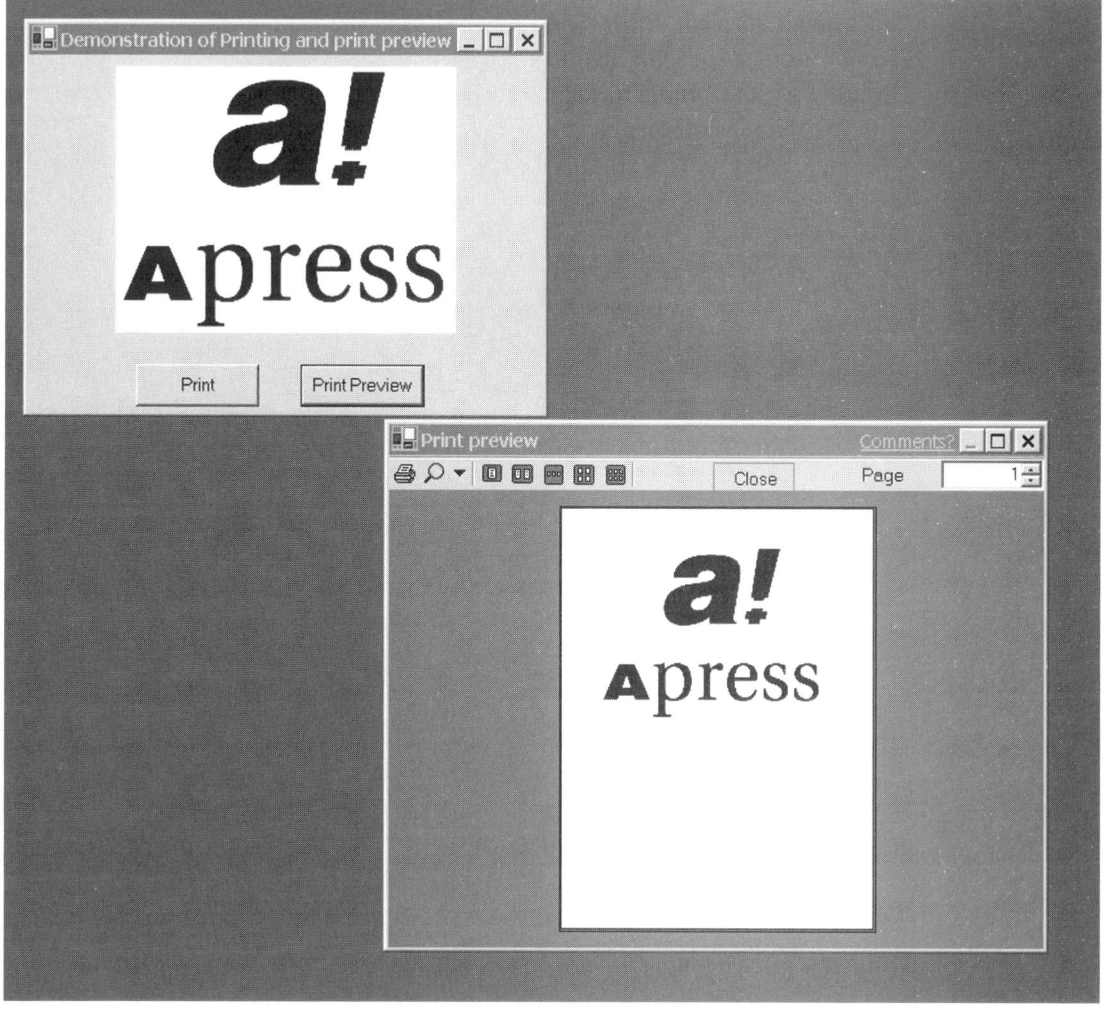

Figure 8-25. Demonstration of print preview

CHAPTER 9

Input/Output

EARLIER VERSIONS OF VISUAL BASIC had different methods of dealing with data, depending on the data source. For example, you had to program in a fundamentally different way for information coming from a disk file than for information coming over the Internet. No more: the .NET Framework is designed from the ground up to handle data in a consistent way, no matter what the source.

The key to this is the notion of a *stream*. The word stream comes from the phrase *stream of bytes*, which, when you get down to it, is what you have manipulated in your computer programs all along. After all, everything a computer deals with—numbers, text, or graphics—can be reduced to a stream of bytes. So it should come as no surprise that the designers of the .NET Framework did what we described as good "OOP think" in Chapter 5: they came up with an abstract class that contains common operations for working with data. This makes the process of input/output programming in VB .NET simpler and the resemblances between what are ultimately similar programs more obvious. In sum, an abstract `Stream` class that is marked as `MustInherit` is the perfect base on which to build an object-oriented approach to input and output.

To work with streams from the keyboard, memory, files, or a network connection, .NET programmers use classes that accommodate these different sources of information. However, before you can deal with most kind of streams, you also need to know how to deal with the user's local storage. We therefore begin this chapter by showing you how to handle files and directories and then move on to cleaning up the whole .NET stream zoo: file streams, network streams, and object streams that allow you to store objects to disks, and other avenues to data.

We wrap up this chapter with an example of using the nifty new server-side RAD (Rapid Application Development) features of VB .NET to write a file system monitor. This program waits for changes in a directory, such as files being added or deleted, and then runs code for various file change events that get triggered in response to the directory having changed. This kind of program was hard to write in earlier versions of VB, because you needed to use the Windows API in a rather a sophisticated matter. And while we obviously cannot cover many of the server-side RAD features of VB .NET in this book, we hope this example will whet your appetite to go further with this extremely useful new feature of VB .NET.

> **NOTE** *While we hope we give you a firm foundation in this chapter, we cannot completely cover all of .NET input/output in this chapter. It is quite possible to write a whole book on this important topic—and another one on server-side RAD!*

Directories and Files

VB .NET provides two types of classes that deal with directories and two that deal with files.

- `Directory` and `DirectoryInfo` classes
- `File` and `FileInfo` classes

The `Directory` and `File` classes use shared methods to access their functionality. Because methods in the `Directory` or `File` classes are shared, you do not have to use the `New` operator to get at the functionality of these classes. This certainly makes them more efficient if you are not repeatedly accessing a specific file or directory. They are less efficient, however, if you have to repeatedly access a single file or directory. The `DirectoryInfo` and `FileInfo` classes use member functions, so they require object instances to access their members.

Another difference between these pairs is that while `Directory` and `File` both inherit directly from `Object`, `DirectoryInfo` and `FileInfo` inherit from a common abstract (`MustInherit`) class called `FileSystemInfo` that contains common members like `LastAccessTime` or `FullName`.

Perhaps the most important difference is that `DirectoryInfo` and `FileInfo` are much better choices whenever you have to use the results recursively, as in the example in Chapter 4. This is because the members of the `Directory` and `File` classes tend to return strings that identify the directories or files, while the members of the `DirectoryInfo` and `FileInfo` classes usually return instances of themselves, which, as you saw in Chapter 4, is exactly what you need to make a recursive process easy to program.

> **NOTE** *There is a more subtle difference between the pairs: they have a different security profile. Although we obviously cannot cover the security aspects of .NET programming in any substantial way in this book, you do need to be aware that the* `Directory` *and* `File` *classes check for permission for your code to access or modify the file or directory each time you use them, whereas* `DirectoryInfo` *and* `FileInfo` *check only once, when an object instance is created. This makes the latter classes a lot more efficient for multiple uses of the same file or directory.*

Keep in mind that, because you are accessing data that may or may not exist, you often have to wrap the code that accesses files or directory in a `Try-Catch` block. However, the same rules hold: you should not catch an exception if you can do a simple test instead. Thus, for example, you would not normally catch a `DirectoryNotFoundException`, because you can simply use the `Exists` method to check that the directory exists first. The following list shows the most common exceptions you will encounter when working with I/O. They all extend the base class `IOException`.

```
IOException
➥ DirectoryNotFoundException
➥ EndOfStreamException
➥ FileLoadException
➥ FileNotFoundException
```

The Path Class

Before we discuss handling directories and files, we will briefly survey the `Path` class, whose shared members give you a convenient way to handle path names.[1] These methods are useful because network path names are quite a bit more complicated to parse than local path names. (And even parsing local path names is not much fun). Table 9-1 lists the most useful members of this class.

Table 9-1. Key Members of the `Path` *Class*

MEMBER	DESCRIPTION
`DirectorySeparatorChar`	Gives the platform-specific directory separator character
`InvalidPathChars`	Provides an array that lists invalid characters in a path
`PathSeparator`	Provides the platform-specific directory separator character
`VolumeSeparatorChar`	Provides the platform-specific volume separator character

1. Interestingly enough, the VB .NET documentation for this class also mentions handling things in a cross-platform manner. For example, it notes the difference between a "\" and the "/" used as the directory separator in Unix systems (such as the BSD systems that Microsoft has announced CLR support for).

Table 9-1. Key Members of the `Path` *Class (Continued)*

MEMBER	DESCRIPTION
`ChangeExtension(ByVal path As String, ByVal extension As String)`	Changes a filename extension and returns the new name
`GetDirectoryName(ByVal path As String)`	Returns the directory path of a file
`GetExtension(ByVal path As String)`	Returns the extension
`GetFileName(ByVal path As String)`	Returns the name and extension for the specified file path
`GetFileNameWithoutExtension (ByVal path As String)`	Gets a filename without its extension
`GetFullPath(ByVal path As String)`	Expands the specified path to a fully qualified path and returns this as a string
`GetPathRoot(ByVal path As String)`	Returns the root of the specified path
`GetTempFileName(ByVal path As String)`	Returns a unique temporary filename and creates a zero-byte file by that name on disk
`GetTempPath(ByVal path As String)`	Returns the path of the current system's temporary folder

The Directory Class

Most of the members of the `Directory` class return strings that identify directories. Because all of its members are shared, you do not need to create instances of this class in order to use the functionality. For example:

```
System.IO.Directory.GetCurrentDirectory()
```

returns a string that identifies the current directory. `GetDirectories(pathString)` returns an array of strings that identify the subdirectories of a directory that you identify by the `pathString` parameter. The path string is either interpreted as a path relative to the current application's directory or as a Universal Naming Convention (UNC) description of a path. This example program lists the current directory and all its subdirectories:

```
Imports System.IO
Module Module1

  Sub Main()
    Dim curDir, nextDir As String
    Try
      curDir = Directory.GetCurrentDirectory()
      Console.WriteLine(curDir)
      For Each nextDir In Directory.GetDirectories(curDir)
        Console.WriteLine(nextDir)
      Next
    Catch ioe As IOException
      Console.WriteLine("eeeks - i/o problems!" & ioe.message)
    Catch e As Exception
     Console.Write(e.stacktrace)
    Finally
      Console.ReadLine()
    End Try
  End Sub
End Module
```

If you want to do anything more than list the directories, you are better off using the `DirectoryInfo` class, as you saw in Chapter 4, and which we cover in more depth shortly.

In addition to passing a string to `GetDirectories` that identifies the directory, you can also pass a DOS-style wildcard pattern to `GetDirectories`.[2] Table 9-2 lists the most important members of the `Directory` class, all of which take their parameters by value (using the `ByVal` keyword).

Table 9-2. Key Members of the `Directory` *Class*

MEMBER	DESCRIPTION
`CreateDirectory(ByVal pathName As String)`	Creates a specified directory and returns a `DirectoryInfo` object for the new directory. Any new directories required to create this directory will also be created.
`Delete(ByVal pathName As String)`	Deletes an empty directory and its contents. To delete a nonempty directory *including all subdirectories and files,* use `Delete(PathName As String, True)`.
`Exists(ByVal pathName As String)`	Returns a Boolean value indicating whether the directory exists.

2. Use a ? to match a single character and a * to match multiple characters.

Table 9-2. Key Members of the `Directory` *Class (Continued)*

MEMBER	DESCRIPTION
`GetCreationTime(ByVal pathName As String)`	Returns a date object that encapsulates the creation date and time of the directory.
`GetCurrentDirectory`	Returns a string that identifies the current directory.
`GetDirectories(ByVal pathName As String)`	Returns an array of strings that identify subdirectories. Can accept a second string parameter for a pattern to use.
`GetDirectoryRoot(ByVal pathName As String)`	Returns a string that identifies the root portion of the specified path.
`GetFiles(ByVal pathName As String)`	Returns an array of strings that identify the files in the directory. Can accept a second string parameter for a pattern to use.
`GetLastAccessTime(ByVal pathName As String)`	Returns a date object that encapsulates the last access time of the directory.
`GetLastWriteTime(ByVal pathName As String)`	Returns a date object that encapsulates the last time the directory was written to.
`GetLogicalDrives`	Returns an array of strings for the drives in the current computer in the form "`<drive letter>:\`", i.e., `C:\`.
`GetParent(ByVal pathName As String)`	Returns a string that identifies the parent directory of the specified path.
`Move(ByVal sourceDirName As String, ByVal destDirName As String)`	Moves a directory and its contents to the new path *on the same drive.*
`SetCurrentDirectory(ByVal pathName As String)`	Sets the current directory.

The `File` *Class*

As with the `Directory` class, the `File` class consists of shared members that usually take a path name. You can use its methods to copy, delete, or move files. Table 9-3 lists the most common methods in the `File` class. Again note that all parameters are passed by value. (We have left out the methods of the `File` class that are used for working with streams, because we cover these methods later.)

Table 9-3. Common `File` *Class Methods*

MEMBER	DESCRIPTION
`Copy(ByVal sourceFileName As String, ByVal destFileName As String)`	Copies the file from the source path to the destination path. Overloaded to add a third Boolean `overWrite` parameter that you set to be `True` if you want it to overwrite an existing file
`Delete(ByVal path As String)`	Deletes the specified file. Interestingly enough, does not throw an exception if the file does not exist (see the `Exists` method)
`Exists(ByVal path As String)`	Returns a `Boolean` value that indicates whether the file exists on the fully qualified path
`GetAttributes(ByVal path As String)`	Returns a member of the `FileAttributes` enum that describes whether the file is archive, system, etc. (See the section later on the various I/O enums for more on how to work with this return value)
`GetCreationTime(ByVal path As String)`	Returns a date object that shows when the specified file was created
`GetLastAccessTime(ByVal path As String)`	Returns a date object that shows when the specified file was last accessed
`GetLastWriteTime(ByVal path As String)`	Returns a date object that shows when the specified file was last written to
`Move(ByVal sourceFileName As String, ByVal destFileName As String)`	Lets you move a file from one path to another—even across drives—and rename the file if the `destFileName` parameter so indicates.
`SetAttributes(ByVal path As String, ByVal fileAttributes As FileAttributes)`	Sets the attributes of the file as specified

The File Attribute Enums

Because you often need to work with the various attributes of files and directories, such as `System` or `Archive`, the .NET Framework comes with a convenient `FileAttribute` enum class to help you. (It probably should have been called the `FileDirectoryAttribute` enum class since it applies to directories as well.)

The values in this enum need to be combined with masking techniques in order to avoid subtle and not-so-subtle bugs. For example *do not use this:*

```
If File.GetAttributes("c:\foo.txt") = FileAttributes.ReadOnly Then...
```

because it does not take into account other attributes that may be set. *Use this instead*:

```
If File.GetAttributes("c:\foo.txt") And FileAttributes.ReadOnly _
    = FileAttributes.ReadOnly Then...
```

Use the `Or` operator if you need to combine attributes. For example, this line:

```
File.SetAttributes("c:\foo.txt", _
    Not (FileAttributes.Archive) Or FileAttributes.Hidden)
```

sets the attributes of `C:\foo.txt` so that the archive bit is not set but the file is hidden. These are the most important members of this enum class.

- `Archive`
- `Compressed`
- `Directory`
- `Encrypted`
- `Hidden`
- `Normal` (has no attributes set)
- `ReadOnly`
- `System`

The `DirectoryInfo` and `FileInfo` Classes

Unlike the `Directory` or `File` classes, the `DirectoryInfo` and `FileInfo` classes encapsulate a (potential) directory or file: you need to construct them before using them. We say "potential" because you can create a `DirectoryInfo` or `FileInfo` object associated with a path even if the file or directory corresponding to the path does not yet exist. You then can invoke the `Create` method to create the corresponding file or directory.

You typically create an instance of these classes by passing a path name into the appropriate constructor. For example:

```
Dim myDirectory As DirectoryInfo
myDirectory = New DirectoryInfo("C:\Test Directory")
```

Use a "." to indicate the current directory:

```
Dim currentDir As New DirectoryInfo(".")
```

Once you have a `DirectoryInfo` object, you can get information from it, such as the creation time:

```
MsgBox(myDirectory.CreationTime)
```

As we mentioned earlier, one of the nicest things about these classes is that the various members return objects of the requested type, not strings. For example, the line in bold in the following program gets a bunch of `FileInfo` objects that we can access again recursively if necessary:

```
Imports System.IO
Module Module1
  Sub Main()
    Dim myDirectory As DirectoryInfo
    Try
      myDirectory = New DirectoryInfo("C:\Test Directory")
      Dim aFile As FileInfo
      For Each aFile In myDirectory.GetFiles
        Console.WriteLine("The filenamed " & aFile.FullName & _
        " has length " & aFile.Length)
      Next
    Catch e As Exception
      MsgBox("eeks  - an exception " & e.StackTrace)
    Finally
      Console.WriteLine("Press enter to end")
      Console.ReadLine()
    End Try
  End Sub
End Module
```

Working Recursively through a Directory Tree

What makes the previous setup nice is that you can easily build it into a general framework to work recursively through a directory tree. The easiest way to do this, as explained Chapter 4, is to use a helper procedure called `WorkWithDirectory`. This procedure in turn calls another procedure to work with the files in a given directory. One framework for this recursive process looks like this:

```
Option Strict On
Imports System.IO
Module Module1
  Sub Main()
    Dim nameOfDirectory As String = "C:\"
    Dim myDirectory As DirectoryInfo
    myDirectory = New DirectoryInfo(nameOfDirectory)
    WorkWithDirectory(myDirectory)
  End Sub
  Public Sub WorkWithDirectory(ByVal aDir As DirectoryInfo)
    Dim nextDir As DirectoryInfo
    WorkWithFilesInDir(aDir)
    For Each nextDir In aDir.GetDirectories
      WorkWithDirectory(nextDir)
    Next
  End Sub
  Public Sub WorkWithFilesInDir(ByVal aDir As DirectoryInfo)
    Dim aFile As FileInfo
    For Each aFile In aDir.GetFiles()
      'do what you want with the file
      'here we simply list the full path name
      Console.WriteLine(aFile.FullName)
    Next
  End Sub
End Module
```

As a more realistic example, the following code would activate the form in Figure 9-1, which shows all hidden files inside a given directory in a listbox and then proceeds recursively through the rest of the directory tree. We change the cursor (.NET speak for the mouse pointer) to an hourglass to remind the user that program is working. (As always, you can download the full source code for this example from `www.apress.com`.)

> **NOTE** *This program really needs to be rewritten using threads, to keep the form responsive—see the next chapter for how to do this. (It is true that you can use a call to* `DoEvents()` *inside the code that updates the listbox, but threads are a more professional way to go.)*

```
Private Sub Button1_Click(ByVal sender As System.Object, _
  ByVal e As System.EventArgs) Handles Button1.Click
    'change the cursor to an hourglass
    Me.Cursor = Cursors.WaitCursor
    ListBox1.Items.Clear()
    WorkWithDirectory(New DirectoryInfo(TextBox1.Text))
    Me.Cursor = Cursors.Default
End Sub
Public Sub WorkWithDirectory(ByVal aDir As DirectoryInfo)
    Dim nextDir As DirectoryInfo
    Try
      WorkWithFilesInDir(aDir)
      For Each nextDir In aDir.GetDirectories
        WorkWithDirectory(nextDir)
      Next
    Catch e As Exception
      MsgBox(e.message & vbCrLf & e.StackTrace)
    End Try
End Sub
Public Sub WorkWithFilesInDir(ByVal aDir As DirectoryInfo)
    Dim aFile As FileInfo
    For Each aFile In aDir.GetFiles()
      If aFile.Attributes And FileAttributes.Hidden = FileAttributes.Hidden Then
        ListBox1.Items.Add("FOUND hidden filenamed " & aFile.FullName)
      End If
    Next
End Sub
```

CAUTION *For more sophisticated manipulations, you will not only want to use multiple threads, you will want to wrap the code in the* `WorkWithFilesInDir` *routine in a* `Try-Catch` *block.*

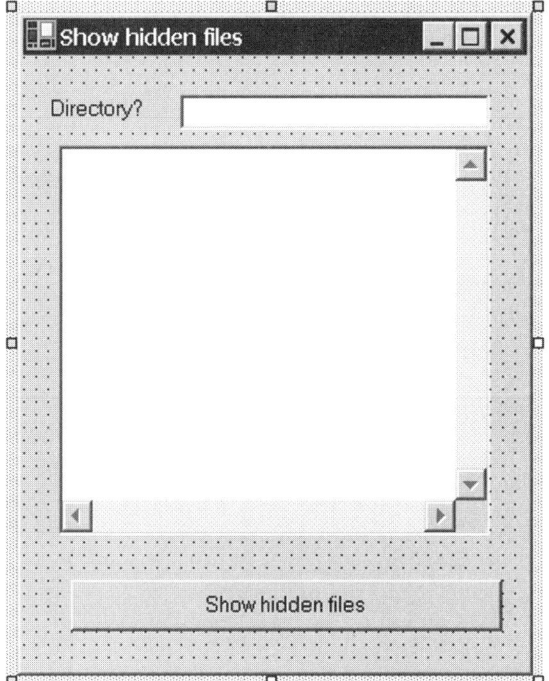

Figure 9-1. Form for a recursive directory search

The Most Useful Members of the FileSystemInfo, FileInfo, *and* DirectoryInfo *Classes*

The `FileSystemInfo` class is the base for both the `DirectoryInfo` and the `FileInfo` classes, and so it contains much of the common functionality you would expect. As an example of the virtues of having an abstract base class, the existence of the `FileSystemInfo` class allows the `DirectoryInfo` class to have a method `GetFileSystemInfos`, which returns an array of `FileSystemInfo` objects that represent both the files and the subdirectories in the given directory.

Table 9-4 lists the most useful methods of the `FileSystemInfo` base class.

Table 9-4. FileSystemInfo Base Class Methods

MEMBER	DESCRIPTION
`Attributes` property	Gets or sets the attributes of the object.
`CreationTime` property	Gets or sets the creation time of the object.
`Exists` property	Boolean value that indicates whether the file or directory exists.
`Extension` property	The file extension.
`FullName` property	The full path of the directory or file.
`LastAccessTime` property	Gets or sets the date/time the object was last accessed.
`LastWriteTime` property	Gets or sets the time when the object was last written to.
`Name` property	For files, this is the name of the file. For directories, it gets the name of the last directory in the directory tree hierarchy if this is possible. Otherwise, it gives you the fully qualified name.
`Delete`	Deletes the object.
`Refresh`	Refreshes the state of the object.

> **NOTE** *While the idea of having an abstract base class with common functionality is the right one, we think the execution was a little bit flawed. The* `Length` *property is in the* `FileInfo` *class but not in the* `FileSystemInfo` *class, which means that there is no convenient way to get at the size of a directory tree including subdirectories without using a different object—more precisely, the* `Size` *method in the* `Folder` *object contained in the* `FileSystemObject` *model, which was introduced in VBScript and requires a reference to the COM-based Microsoft scripting library.*

Tables 9-5 and 9-6 list the most useful methods of the `DirectoryInfo` class and the methods of the `FileInfo` class that do not deal with streams since we are covering streams a little later on in this chapter.

Table 9-5. Key `DirectoryInfo` *Class Methods*

MEMBER	DESCRIPTION
`Exists` property	Boolean value that indicates whether the directory exists
`Name` property	The name

Table 9-5. Key `DirectoryInfo` Class Methods (Continued)

MEMBER	DESCRIPTION
`Parent` property	Returns a `DirectoryInfo` object that represents the parent directory (or `Nothing` at the root directory).
`Root` property	Returns a `DirectoryInfo` object that represents the root directory of the current directory.
`Create`	Creates a directory corresponding to the path specified in the `DirectoryInfo` constructor.
`CreateSubdirectory(ByVal path As String)`	Creates a subdirectory on the specified path needed. Returns a DirectoryInfo object that represents the subdirectory created.
`Delete`	Deletes an empty directory represented by the DirectoryInfo object. Use an option Boolean parameter = to True to recursively delete nonempty directories and all subdirectories.
`GetDirectories`	Returns an array of DirectoryInfo objects for the subdirectories of the current directory.
`GetFiles`	Returns an array of `FileInfo` objects for files in the current directory.
`GetFileSystemInfos`	A nice example of an abstract class at work: gets an array of `FileSystemInfo` objects representing all the files and subdirectories in the current directory objects.
`MoveTo(ByVal destDirName As String)`	Moves a `DirectoryInfo` and its recursive contents to a new path.

Table 9-6. `FileInfo` Class Members That Do Not Return Streams

MEMBER	DESCRIPTION
`Directory` property	Returns a `DirectoryInfo` object that represents the parent directory.
`DirectoryName` property	Returns the file's full path as a string.
`Exists` property	Boolean indicating whether the file exists.
`Length` property	Gets the size of the current file.
`CopyTo(ByVal destFileName As String)`	Copies an existing file to a new file and returns a FileInfo object representing the new file. Optionally takes a Boolean parameter to indicate if you want to overwrite an existing file.

Table 9-6. `FileInfo` *Class Members That Do Not Return Streams (Continued)*

MEMBER	DESCRIPTION
`Create`	Creates a file corresponding to the path used to construct the `FileInfo` object and returns a `FileSystem` object corresponding to this new file.
`Delete`	Deletes the file corresponding to the `FileInfo` object.
`MoveTo(ByVal destFileName As String)`	Moves the file to a new location giving it the specified name.

Streams

As we said in the introduction, the `System.IO.Stream` class is designed to abstract the most primitive operations for working with streams of bytes. The idea then is that each concrete implementation of the `Stream` class must provide the following implementations:

1. **A `Read` method for reading from the stream.** This can be as primitive an operation as reading one byte at a time, or the derived class can give you more sophisticated methods that read data in much larger chunks.

2. **A `Write` method for writing to streams.** Again this can be as primitive an operation as writing one byte at a time, or the derived class can give you more sophisticated methods that read data in much larger chunks.

Some stream classes may do more: an implementation of the `Stream` class may give you a way to move through the stream other than from the first to the last byte, for example, such as moving backward or directly to a specified location within the stream. This is possible for file streams but makes no sense (and hence is impossible) for a stream derived from a network connection. You can even use the `CanSeek` property to ask a stream whether it can be accessed nonsequentially! If the property is `True`, then the derived class provides implementations of a `Seek` and `SetLength` methods and `Position` and `Length` properties.

> **TIP** *There is a convenient* `SeekOrigin` *enum that contains three values:* `Begin`, `Current`, *and* `End` *that you use with implementations of the* `Seek` *method.*

Table 9-7 lists the most useful methods in the abstract `Stream` class that should retain the same functionality in any derived class.

Table 9-7. Key Methods in the `Stream` *Class*

MEMBER	DESCRIPTION
`CanRead` property	Boolean value that indicates whether the stream supports reading.
`CanSeek` property	Boolean value that indicates whether the stream supports nonsequential access ("seeking").
`CanWrite` property	Boolean value that indicates whether the stream supports writing.
`Length` property	Gets the length of the stream in bytes.
`Position` property	A Long that gets or sets (if allowed) the position within the current stream.
`Close`	Closes the stream and releases any resources such as operating system file handles used by the current stream.
`Flush`	Clears and writes data in all buffers used by this stream.
`Read(ByVal buffer() As Byte, ByVal offset As Integer, ByVal count As Integer)`	Reads the specified number of bytes from the current position plus the offset specified. Returns the number of bytes successfully read (usually with `count`).
`ReadByte`	Reads a single byte (oddly, in the form of an Integer) from the current position in the stream, or -1 if at the end of the stream.
`Write(ByVal buffer() As Byte, ByVal offset As Integer, ByVal count As Integer)`	Writes the specified number of bytes from the current position plus the offset specified.
`WriteByte(ByVal value As Byte)`	Writes a byte to the current position in the stream.

> **TIP** *All* `Stream` *classes support a* `Close` *method that releases any operating-system resources such as file handles or network connections it grabbed. This means that closing the stream in a* `Try-Catch-Finally` *block is a good programming practice for pretty much any program that works with a stream. Note that you cannot use* `Close` *in a* `Finally` *clause, since you can call* `Close` *only on a stream where the construction call succeeded and the stream actually exists. The prototype code to do the check before the call to* `Close` *in the* `Finally` *clause looks like this:*
>
> ```
> Finally
>   If Not (myFileStream Is Nothing) Then myFileStream.Close()
> End Try
> ```
>
> *You also might also want to consider implementing* `IDisposable` *in your file handling classes and having the* `Dispose` *method close any open streams.*

The main classes derived from `Stream` are shown in Table 9-8..

Table 9-8. Key Classes Derived from `Stream`

CLASS	DESCRIPTION
`FileStream`	Supports random access to files.
`MemoryStream`	Encapsulates an area of memory (useful for buffers).
`NetworkStream`	Data received as a `Stream` over a network connection. In the `System.Net.Sockets` namespace.
`CryptoStream`	Lets you encrypt and decrypt data. In the `System.Security.Cryptography` namespace.
`BufferedStream`	Essentially a layer you can wrap around a stream that adds a cache for buffering to a stream that originally lacked it. You can also specify the buffer size. For example, file streams automatically buffers input but network streams do not, and you may occasionally want to wrap a buffered stream around a network stream using the layering techniques we demonstrate later in this chapter.

NOTE *The .NET Framework comes with classes designed for working with XML that work like* `Stream` *classes. The XML namespaces in .NET are quite large and sophisticated, and might be the subject of a book of their own.*

Writing to Files: File Streams

First, look at the following line of code, which is a prototype for code that works with a file stream:

```
Dim myFileStream As New FileStream("MyFile.txt", _
FileMode.OpenOrCreate, FileAccess.Write)
```

As you can see, this version of the `FileStream` constructor takes a filename (assumed to be relative to the current directory unless a full path name is given) and two parameters that come from enums called `FileMode` and `FileAccess`, respectively. Thus, the version of the `FileStream` constructor in the example either creates a file named "MyFile.txt" in the current directory or opens the file if it already exists. In either case we will be able to write to it. The other common versions of the `FileStream` constructor are:

- `Sub New(String, FileMode)`: Makes a `FileStream` object with the specified path and mode
- `Sub New(String, FileMode, FileAccess, FileShare)`: Makes a `FileStream` object with the specified path, creation mode, and read-write and sharing permission

The permissible `FileAccess` modes are, `Read`, `Write`, and `ReadWrite`. Table 9-9 summarizes the important `FileMode` enums. Note that you need to have the right kind of file access privileges in order to use certain file modes.

Table 9-9. The `FileMode` Enum Members

MEMBER	DESCRIPTION
`Append`	Opens the file if it exists (creates one if is does not) and moves to the end of the file for future writes. Must be used `FileAccess.Write`.
`Create`	Creates a new file. Caution: overwrites an existing file.
`CreateNew`	Creates a new file, but unlike `Create`, throws an `IOException` if the file already exists.
`Open`	Opens an existing file. Throws an `IOException` if the file does not exist. Specifies that the operating system should open an existing file. This requires `FileIOPermissionAccess.Read`.
`OpenOrCreate`	Opens or creates a file.
`Truncate`	Opens an existing file but deletes the contents.

NOTE *The following methods of the* `File` *and* `FileInfo` *classes also return* `FileStream` *objects:* `File.Create`, `File.Open`, `File.OpenRead`, `File.OpenWrite`, `FileInfo.Create`, `FileInfo.Open`, `FileInfo.OpenRead`.

Unfortunately, although file streams do support random access through the `Seek` method, the basic `FileStream` class is totally byte oriented, so you cannot do much more than write a byte or an array of bytes to it using the `WriteByte` or `Write` methods. For example, this code results in the file shown in Figure 9-2:

```
Option Strict On
Imports System.IO
Module Module1
Sub Main()
    Dim i As Integer
    Dim theBytes(255) As Byte
    For i = 0 To 255
      theBytes(i) = CByte(i)
    Next
    Dim myFileStream As FileStream
```

```
      Try
        myFileStream = New FileStream("C:\foo", _
          FileMode.OpenOrCreate, FileAccess.Write)
        myFileStream.Write(theBytes, 0, 256)
      Finally
        If Not (myFileStream Is Nothing) Then myFileStream.Close()
      End Try
      DisplayAFile("C:\foo")
    End Sub
  End Module
```

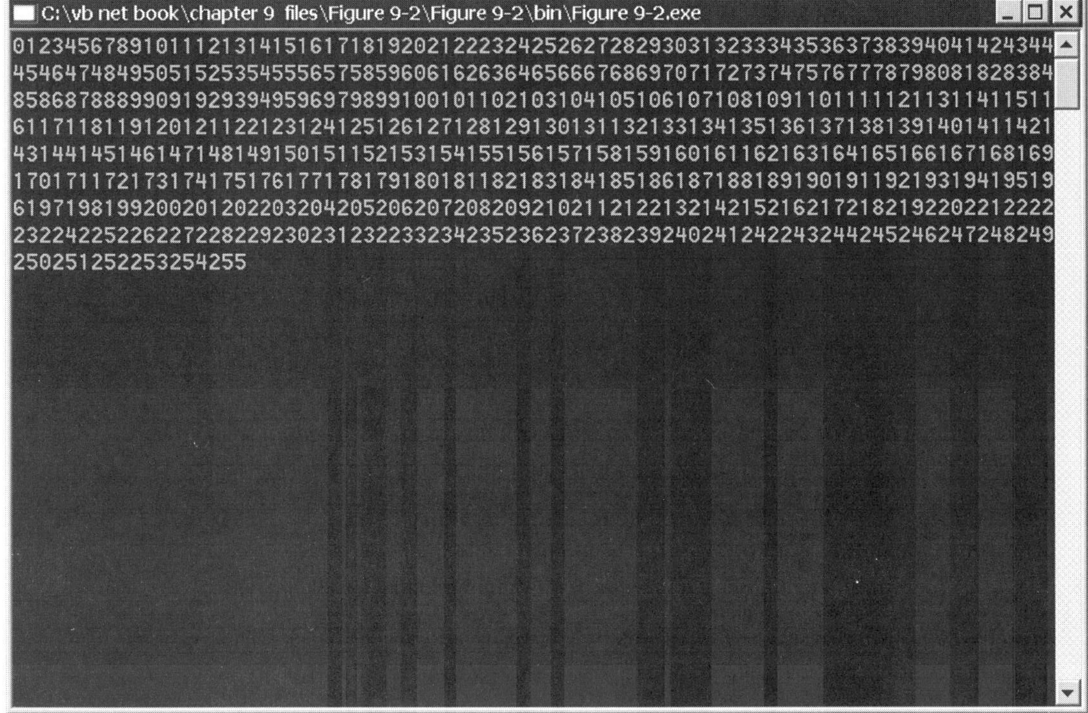

Figure 9-2. Binary data written to a file

At this point, you can read back the data using the `Read` method and use the `Seek` method as needed to move at random within the file. However, as will always be the case for raw file streams, you are responsible for converting the binary data to a more useful format. The upshot is that you cannot do much more at this point than to display the numbers stored using code like this:

```
Sub ReadDataBack()
  Dim myFileStream As Stream, i As Integer
  Try
    myFileStream = New FileStream("C:\foo", FileMode.Open, FileAccess.Read)
    For i = 0 To 255
      Console.Write(myFileStream.ReadByte)
    Next
  Catch e As Exception
    MsgBox(e.Message)
  Finally
    If Not (myFileStream Is Nothing) Then myFileStream.Close()
  End Try
End Sub
```

You can always use the `Length` method in the base `Stream` class to set up a loop to read back the correct number of bytes, regardless of the file structure. For example, the following code does this one byte at a time. (It also throws back the exception to the calling code; in a more realistic program, you would probably create a new exception class):

```
Sub DisplayAFile(ByVal theFileName As String)
    Dim theFile As FileStream
    Dim i As Long
    Try
      theFile = New FileStream(theFileName, FileMode.Open, FileAccess.Read)
      For i = 0 To (theFile.Length - 1) 'one less since count starts at 0
        Console.Write(theFile.ReadByte)
      Next
    Catch
      Throw
    Finally
      If Not (theFile Is Nothing) Then theFile.Close()
    End Try
  End Sub
```

> **TIP** *If the file is small enough to fit in memory, reading it in one gulp via a single call to* `Read` *with the correct size byte array will be much faster.*

Another version of this kind of program that you will occasionally see depends on the `ReadByte` method returning –1 at the end of a stream. The core code then looks like this:

```
Dim i As Integer

i = theFile.ReadByte
Do Until i = -1
  Console.Write(i)
  i = theFile.ReadByte
Loop
```

Working with files on the byte level is not all that common; it is only necessary for low-level file manipulation. To work with files in a more useful way, the trick is to send the raw file stream to the constructor of a more capable stream. This is often called *layering streams*. For example, you can feed a raw file stream to a text reader stream that automatically understands text. We take up the various methods of layering streams in the next few sections. Still, before you move onto those sections we suggest looking over Table 9-10, which summarizes the most useful methods of the basic `FileStream` class. You will be using these members regardless of how you layer your basic file stream.

Table 9-10. Key Members of the `FileStream` *Class*

MEMBER	DESCRIPTION
`Handle` property	Gets the operating-system file handle for the file that the current `FileStream` object encapsulates.
`Length` property	Gets the size of the stream in bytes.
`Name` property	The full name of the file that was passed to the `FileStream` constructor.
`Position` property	Gets or sets the current position in the reading from or writing to this stream (zero-based).
`Close`	Closes the file stream and releases any resources associated with it.
`Flush`	Sends any buffered data to be written to the underlying device. `Close` calls `Flush`.
`Lock(ByVal position As Long, ByVal length As Long)`	Prevents access by other processes to all or part of a file (zero-based).

Table 9-10. Key Members of the `FileStream` *Class (Continued)*

MEMBER	DESCRIPTION
`Read(ByVal array() As Byte, ByVal offset As Integer, ByVal count As Integer)`	Reads the specified number of bytes in the array of bytes to the file stream starting from the specified position.
`ReadByte`	Reads a single byte from the file and advances the read position by one.
`Seek(ByVal offset As Long, ByVal origin As SeekOrigin)`	Sets the current position of this stream to the given value.
`Unlock(ByVal position As Long, ByVal length As Long)`	Unlocks the file stream that was previously locked (zero-based).
`Write(ByVal array() As Byte, ByVal offset As Integer, ByVal count As Integer)`	Writes the specified number of bytes in the array of bytes to the file stream starting from the specified position.
`WriteByte`	Writes a byte to the current position in the file stream.

Getting Binary Data into and out of Streams: `BinaryReader` *and* `BinaryWriter`

Reading and writing raw bytes is just too primitive to be very useful. The .NET Framework therefore gives you a couple of much more practical ways to read and write data to a file stream. In this section we show you how to use the `BinaryReader` and `BinaryWriter` classes to read and write encoded strings and primitive data types. These classes automatically convert primitive data types to and from an encoded binary format that you can store on a disk or send over a network.

Creating a `BinaryReader` or `BinaryWriter` involves layering stream constructors: you create one by passing an existing stream object into the binary reader-writer constructor, as shown in the following code. *You get an instance of them by passing an existing stream object variable into their constructor, not a string.* (This is why the process is called layering streams.) For example, look at the line in bold:

```
Dim aFileStream As FileStream
Try
  aFileStream = New FileStream("c:\data.txt", FileMode.OpenOrCreate, _
    FileAccess.Write)
  Dim myBinaryWriter As New BinaryWriter(aFileStream)
  myBinaryWriter.Write("Hello world")
  myBinaryWriter.Write(1)
Catch e as Exception
  Console.Writeline(e.stacktrace)
Finally
  If not(aFileStream is Nothing) Then  aFileStream.Close()
End Try
```

Notice that the code in bold passes the file stream object `aFileStream` into the `BinaryWriter` constructor. The result is a more capable stream, which lets you write text and numbers to the file in an encoded binary format. The lines following the creation of the `BinaryWriter`:

```
myBinaryWriter.Write("Hello world")
myBinaryWriter.Write(1)
```

depend on the key `Write` method in the more capable `BinaryWriter` class being overloaded to let you to easily write any basic data type to the stream. Here is a list of the most common overloads:

```
Sub Write(Byte)
Sub Write(Byte())
Sub Write(Char)
Sub Write(Char())
Sub Write(Decimal)
Sub Write(Double)
Sub Write(Short)
Sub Write(Integer)
Sub Write(Long)
Sub Write(Byte)
Sub Write(Single)
Sub Write(String)
```

The code in the preceding example gives the following file when viewed in a hex editor (see Figure 9-3). Notice that the string was encoded in the obvious fashion but the number one was encoded using four bytes.

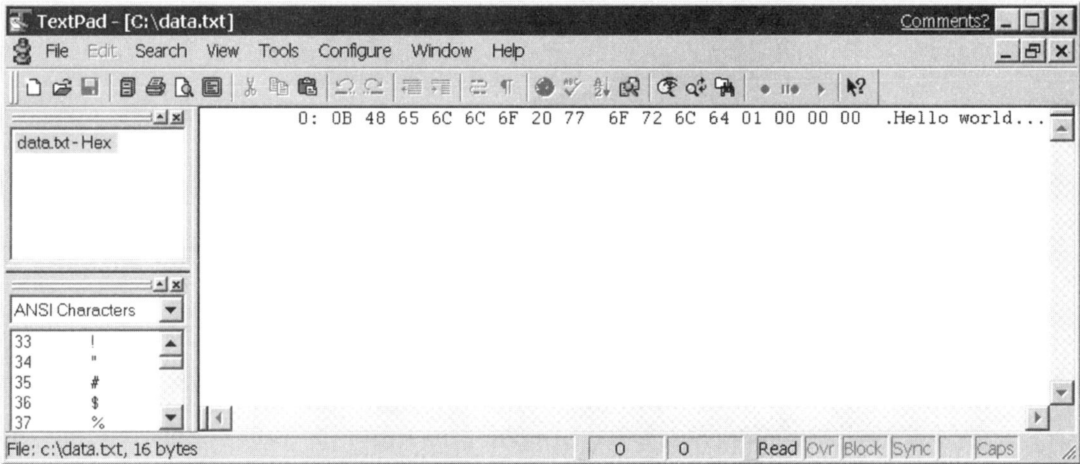

Figure 9-3. A binary writer file viewed in hex

Unfortunately, while the various `Write` methods are overloaded to let you store information in the stream, when you use a `BinaryReader` to read back the information stored with a `BinaryWriter`, the corresponding `Read` methods are not. Instead, there are different versions of `Read` for each data type; for example: `ReadString`, `ReadInt32` (for integers), `ReadChar`, and so on. You need to know what data is stored in the file and in the order in which it was stored, or you cannot undo the process. The following code shows you what you do in our example:

```
aFileStream = New FileStream("c:\data.txt", FileMode.Open, FileAccess.Read)
Dim myBinaryReader As New BinaryReader(aFileStream)
Console.WriteLine(myBinaryReader.ReadString)
Console.WriteLine(myBinaryReader.ReadInt32)
```

TIP *If you do need to write a general binary reader to display binary data without worrying about its underlying type, you can use the* `PeekChar` *method, which looks ahead to the next byte and determines if its value is –1 (the EOF marker in .NET), as in the following example code:*

```
While myBInaryReader.PeekChar() <> -1
   'read the next bit of stuff
Loop
```

NOTE *Because file streams automatically buffer input, there is no need in our example to layer the binary reader or writer classes by passing the binary reader to a* `BufferedStream` *constructor.*

`TextReader`, `TextWriter`, *and Their Derived Classes*

Knowing how the data is stored in a file in binary format, binary readers and writers are fine for programmers, but the resulting files are not always human readable. They are thus not the optimal classes to choose when you need to store ordinary text in a file. For this common situation, use the `StreamReader` and `StreamWriter` classes rather than the `BinaryReader-BinaryWriter` pair. Essentially, `StreamWriter` and `StreamReader` correspond to the traditional sequential files from earlier versions of VB, except that `StreamReader` and `StreamWriter` classes handle Unicode characters correctly. What is more, the `StreamReader` class not only has a convenient `ReadLine` method, it also has a `ReadToEnd` method that lets you get the whole file in one gulp.

Interestingly, these classes inherit from the abstract `TextReader` and `TextWriter` classes, not from `Stream`. These abstract (`MustInherit`) classes contain the common functionality for reading and writing text, as shown in Tables 9-11 and 9-12.

Table 9-11. Key Members of the `TextReader` *Class*

MEMBER	DESCRIPTION
`Close`	Closes an existing `TextReader` and releases any system resources it grabbed.
`Peek`	Returns the next character in the stream without actually moving the file pointer.
`Read`	Reads a single character from an input stream. An overloaded version lets you read a specified number of characters into an array of characters, starting from a specified position.
`ReadLine`	Reads a line of characters (up to the carriage return-line feed pair) and returns it as a string. Returns `Nothing` if you are at the end of the file.
`ReadToEnd`	This method reads all characters from the current position to the end of the `TextReader` and returns them as one string. (Very useful for relatively small files.)

Table 9-12. Key Members of the `TextWriter` *Class*

MEMBER	DESCRIPTION
`Close`	Closes an existing `TextWriter` and releases any system resources it grabbed
`Write`	Overloaded to let you write any basic data type to a text stream in text format
`WriteLine`	Overloaded to let you write any basic data type to a text stream in text format, but also follows the text written by a carriage return-line feed combination

TIP *The important* `Console.In` *and* `Console.Out` *classes used for keyboard input and output are actually instances of the* `TextWriter` *and* `TextReader` *classes. You can use the* `Console.SetIn` *and* `Console.SetOut` *methods to redirect standard input or output to any text reader or text writer class, respectively, from standard input and output.*

Of course, since the `TextReader` and `TextWriter` class are abstract `MustInherit` classes, you work with their concrete `StreamReader` and `StreamWriter` implementations. As with the `BinaryReader` and `BinaryWriter` classes, in order to create a `StreamReader` or `StreamWriter` object, you generally pass an existing stream object to its constructor, as in this example:

```
myFile = New FileStream(fileName, FileMode.Open, FileAccess.Read)
textFile = New StreamReader(myFile)
```

Another way to get a stream reader or writer is with methods of the `File` class. For example, this code would create the stream reader by implicitly creating a file stream:

```
Dim aStreamReader As StreamReader
aStreamReader = File.OpenText ("sample.txt");
```

Similarly, this would create a stream writer:

```
Dim aStreamWriter As StreamWriter
aStreamWriter = File.CreateText ("test.txt");
```

You write data to a stream writer object using the `Write` or `WriteLine` methods. To read data back you have two choices. The most common is to determine whether the data in a line that you tried to read back using `ReadLine` is `Nothing`, via code that looks like this:

```
Dim s As String
Do
  s = theStreamReader.ReadLine
  If Not s Is Nothing Then
    ' do stuff with s
    'for example Console.WriteLine(s)
  End If
Loop Until s Is Nothing
```

You can also use the `Peek` method to determine whether the next character to be read is –1 (the EOF marker):

```
Do Until theStreamReader.Peek = -1
```

As an example of using a `TextReader`, here is a simple procedure that displays text in a file on the screen. Notice in lines **5–17** how the relevant code is encased in a `Try-Catch-Finally` block. Like all file handling code, this block attempts to close the stream that was opened, no matter what happens. As you have seen before, this is done in line **16** by first determining whether the stream actually was successfully created before calling `Close`. Also notice in line **14** that we added a useful message to the exception that was thrown. In a more realistic program, you might want to create a new exception class as you saw in Chapter 7:

```
1  Sub DisplayTextFile(ByVal fName As String)
2      Dim myFile As FileStream
3      Dim textFile As StreamReader
4      Dim stuff As String
5      Try
6        myFile = New FileStream(fName, FileMode.Open, FileAccess.Read)
7        textFile = New StreamReader(myFile)
8        stuff = textFile.ReadLine()
9        Do Until stuff Is Nothing
10         Console.WriteLine(stuff)
11         stuff = textFile.ReadLine()
```

```
12        Loop
13      Catch e As Exception
14        Throw New Exception("If the file existed, it was closed")
15      Finally
16        If Not (myFile Is Nothing) Then myFile.Close()
17      End Try
18    End Sub
19  End Module
```

More generally, you might want to capture the individual lines of the file into an `ArrayList`, assuming there are not a large number of lines in the file. This requires only minor changes in the previous program. You change the header of the procedure to take the array list as a parameter:

```
Sub DisplayTextFile(ByVal fName As String, ByVal where As ArrayList)
```

and change line **10** to be:

```
where.Add(stuff)
```

Object Streams: Persisting Objects

Object-oriented programming would be pretty useless if there was not a way for you to store the current state of objects permanently and then have a way to restore them (*persistence* is the buzzword). The process of writing an object to a stream is called *serialization* and undoing it is called *deserialization*. In the next few sections we want to show you the basics of serialization and deserialization.

Before we start, it is worth noting that this turns out to be a somewhat more subtle and difficult problem to solve than one might think. Why? One reason is that, as in our `Manager` and `Secretary` classes from Chapter 5, objects may contain other objects. Thus, any storage process must automatically take into account potentially recursive procedures. Moreover, as in the `Secretary` and `Manager` classes, there may be cross references between the instance fields inside the classes, so we need some way to avoid duplication. After all, if 100 programmers share one lonely and frantic group assistant, then we do not want to store 100 copies of the poor group assistant's frantic state when one copy with some cross-referencing would suffice (much as databases avoid redundancy via the correct normal form).

Fortunately, the .NET Framework makes the process of efficiently storing objects almost effortless and the use of property bags in VB6 for object storage seem primitive. As you will soon see, you can even store objects using the human-readable XML-based SOAP (Simple Object Access Protocol) format.

Simple Serialization

First off, you will always want to import the `System.Runtime.Serialization` namespace to avoid a lot of typing. In the most common situation, all you have to do to enable serialization is to add an attribute to the header for the name of the class:

```
<Serializable()> Public Class Employee
```

Every child class of your class and every nested class that is contained in the class will also need the `<Serializable()>` attribute; otherwise, the necessary recursive process will break down with a `System.Runtime.Serialization.SerializationException` exception.

> **TIP** *Built-in classes that are serializable are those that implement the* `ISerializable` *interface.*

Once you have marked a class as serializable, you need to decide if you want to store the object in an XML format based on SOAP or a more compact binary format. The default binary format is automatically available. To use the XML-based SOAP format, you need to add a reference to the `System.Runtime.Serialization.Formatters.Soap` assembly.

Here is an example of the kind of code you can use to serialize an array. (Note that an array list is an object, which in turn can contain other objects—in this example, it will contain employee objects.) Because array lists are automatically serializable, all it takes is marking our various employee classes as serializable. The two lines in bold do the trick:

```
Sub SerializeToBinary(ByVal myEmployees As ArrayList, ByVal fName As String)
    Dim fStream As FileStream
    Dim myBinaryFormatter As New Formatters.Binary.BinaryFormatter()
    Try
      fStream = New FileStream(fName, FileMode.Create, FileAccess.Write)
      myBinaryFormatter.Serialize(fStream, myEmployees)
    Catch e As Exception
      Throw e
    Finally
      If Not (fStream Is Nothing) Then fStream.Close()
    End Try
  End Sub
```

To use the SOAP format, all you need to do is add a reference to the `System.Runtime.Serialization.Formatters.Soap` assembly (via the Project|References dialog box) and change the preceding lines in bold to:

```
Dim mySoapFormatter As New Formatters.Soap.SoapFormatter()
```

and

```
mySoapFormatter.Serialize(fStream, myEmployees)
```

The resulting file in SOAP format looks like Figure 9-4.

TIP *You can mark specific instance fields within a class with a* `<NonSerialized()>` *attribute. If you do this, the current state of that instance field will not be stored.*

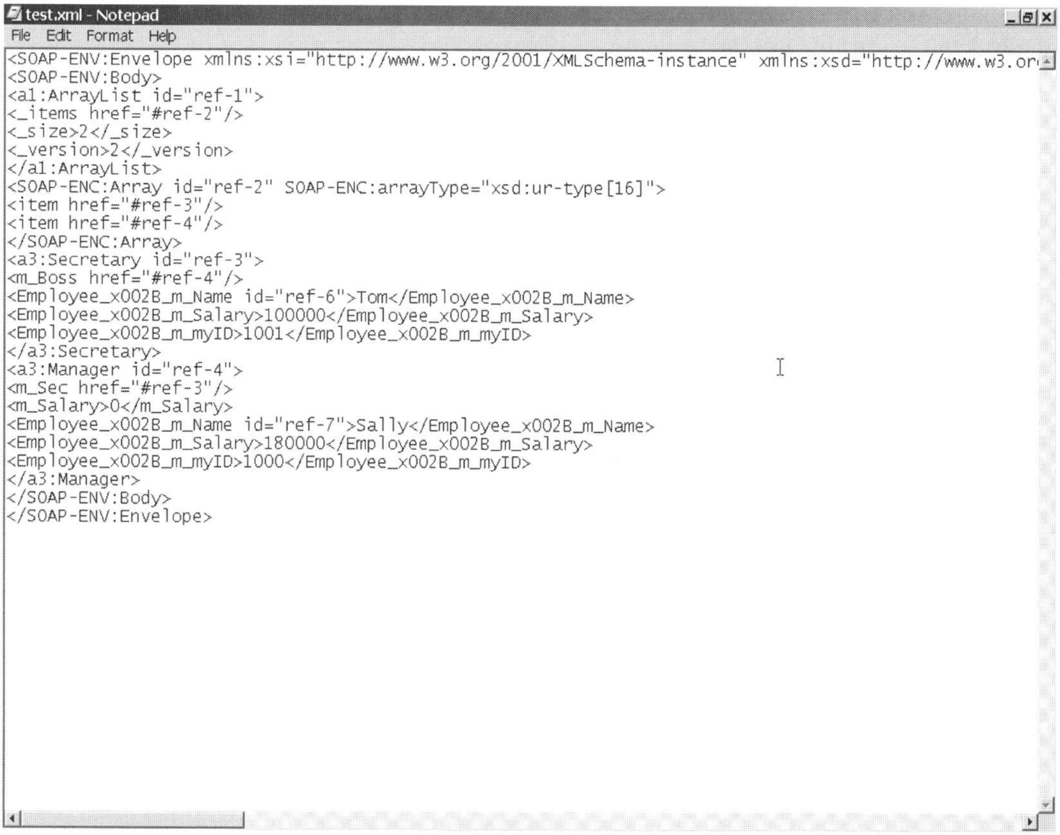

test.xml - Notepad

File Edit Format Help


```
<SOAP-ENV:Envelope xmlns:xsi="http://www.w3.org/2001/XMLSchema-instance" xmlns:xsd="http://www.w3.or
<SOAP-ENV:Body>
<a1:ArrayList id="ref-1">
<_items href="#ref-2"/>
<_size>2</_size>
<_version>2</_version>
</a1:ArrayList>
<SOAP-ENC:Array id="ref-2" SOAP-ENC:arrayType="xsd:ur-type[16]">
<item href="#ref-3"/>
<item href="#ref-4"/>
</SOAP-ENC:Array>
<a3:Secretary id="ref-3">
<m_Boss href="#ref-4"/>
<Employee_x002B_m_Name id="ref-6">Tom</Employee_x002B_m_Name>
<Employee_x002B_m_Salary>100000</Employee_x002B_m_Salary>
<Employee_x002B_m_myID>1001</Employee_x002B_m_myID>
</a3:Secretary>
<a3:Manager id="ref-4">
<m_Sec href="#ref-3"/>
<m_Salary>0</m_Salary>
<Employee_x002B_m_Name id="ref-7">Sally</Employee_x002B_m_Name>
<Employee_x002B_m_Salary>180000</Employee_x002B_m_Salary>
<Employee_x002B_m_myID>1000</Employee_x002B_m_myID>
</a3:Manager>
</SOAP-ENV:Body>
</SOAP-ENV:Envelope>
```


Figure 9-4. A SOAP-based serialization in NotePad

Simple Deserialization

Deserialization is a little trickier: because you get back an Object, you must convert it back to the correct type, as we did in the line in bold:

```
Function DeSerializeFromSoap(ByVal fName As String) As ArrayList
    Dim fStream As New FileStream(fName, FileMode.Open, FileAccess.Read)
    Dim mySoapFormatter As New Formatters.Soap.SoapFormatter()
    Try
      fStream = New FileStream("C:\test.xml", FileMode.Open, FileAccess.Read)
      Return CType(mySoapFormatter.Deserialize(fStream), ArrayList)
    Catch e As Exception
      Throw e
    Finally
      If Not (fStream Is Nothing) Then fStream.Close()
    End Try
End Function
```

Using Serialization to Clone Objects

One of the more nifty uses of serialization is for cloning complicated objects. The trick here is to serialize the object to a memory stream and then deserialize it. (Memory streams are a very useful convenience that allow you to use fast RAM for working with data by treating RAM like a disk file.). The prototype code inside your objects looks like this:

```
Public Function Clone() As Object Implements ICloneable.Clone
  Dim myBinaryFormatter As New Formatters.Binary.BinaryFormatter()
  Try
    SerializeToBinary()
    mSTream.Position = 0
    Return myBinaryFormatter.Deserialize(mSTream)
  Finally
    mSTream.Close()
  End Try
End Function
Sub SerializeToBinary()
  Dim myBinaryFormatter As New Formatters.Binary.BinaryFormatter()
  Try
    mSTream = New MemoryStream()
    myBinaryFormatter.Serialize(mSTream, Me)
  Catch
    Throw
  End Try
End Sub
```

Putting It All Together: A Persistent Employees Array List

Before we show you the complete code for this example, we want to alert you to a potential problem that will always occur when deserializing objects, but is a particular problem when you store objects in an array list. The problem is that, when you finish the deserialization process, you have a bunch of *objects* stored an array list. How do you know what type they really are, so that you can convert them back to their correct type? In the example that follows, we hardwire this information into the deserialization process, because we know the order that we added employees to the array list. In a more general situation, you may need to store this information in a separate file.

In the example, we create a manager named Sally and her secretary named Tom. The `Manager` class contains an embedded `Secretary` object as an instance field; the `Secretary` class contains a reference to the manager.

> **CAUTION** *Remember, you must add a reference to the* `System.Runtime.Serialization.Formatters.Soap` *assembly for this program to work.*

Here is the code for the testing portion of the program. The three key lines are in bold:

```
Option Strict On
'uses the System.Runtime.Serialization.Formatters.Soap assembly
Imports System.IO
Imports System.Runtime.Serialization
Imports System.Runtime.Serialization.Formatters
Module Module1
  Sub Main()
    Dim Sally As New Manager("Sally", 150000)
    Dim Tom As Secretary
    Tom = New Secretary("Tom", 100000, Sally)
    Sally.MySecretary = Tom

    Dim Employees As New ArrayList()
    Employees.Add(Tom)
    Employees.Add(Sally)

    Console.WriteLine(Tom.TheName & " is employee " & _
    Tom.TheID & " and has salary " & Tom.Salary)
    Console.WriteLine("Tom's boss is " & Tom.MyManager.TheName)
    Console.WriteLine("Sally's secretary is " & Sally.MySecretary.TheName)
    Console.WriteLine()
    Console.WriteLine(Sally.TheName & " is employee " & _
    Sally.TheID & " has salary " & Sally.Salary)
    Sally.RaiseSalary(0.1D)
    Console.WriteLine("After raise " & Sally.TheName & " has salary " _
& Sally.Salary)
    SerializeToSoap(Employees, "C:\test.xml")
    Console.WriteLine("Serializing and clearing employee array list!")
    Console.WriteLine()
    Employees.Clear()

    Console.WriteLine("DeSerializing and restoring employee array list!")
    Employees = DeSerializeFromSoap("C:\test.xml")
    Tom = CType(Employees(0), Secretary)
    Sally = CType(Employees(1), Manager)
```

```
    'Check that state was restored
    Console.WriteLine(Tom.TheName & " is employee " & _
    Tom.TheID & " and has salary " & Tom.Salary)
    Console.WriteLine("Tom's boss is " & Tom.MyManager.TheName)
    Console.WriteLine("Sally's secretary is " & Sally.MySecretary.TheName)
    Console.WriteLine()
    Console.WriteLine(Sally.TheName & " is employee " & _
    Sally.TheID & " has salary " & Sally.Salary)

    'check that functionality was restored
    Sally.RaiseSalary(0.1D)
    Console.WriteLine("After raise " & Sally.TheName & " has salary " _
      & Sally.Salary)
    Console.ReadLine()
  End Sub
```

Notice that in the first line in bold we clear the array list to be able to check that our program is actually working. In the other lines in bold we use our knowledge of how the data was stored to convert the objects stored in the array list back to the correct type. Figure 9-5 shows the results of running this program:

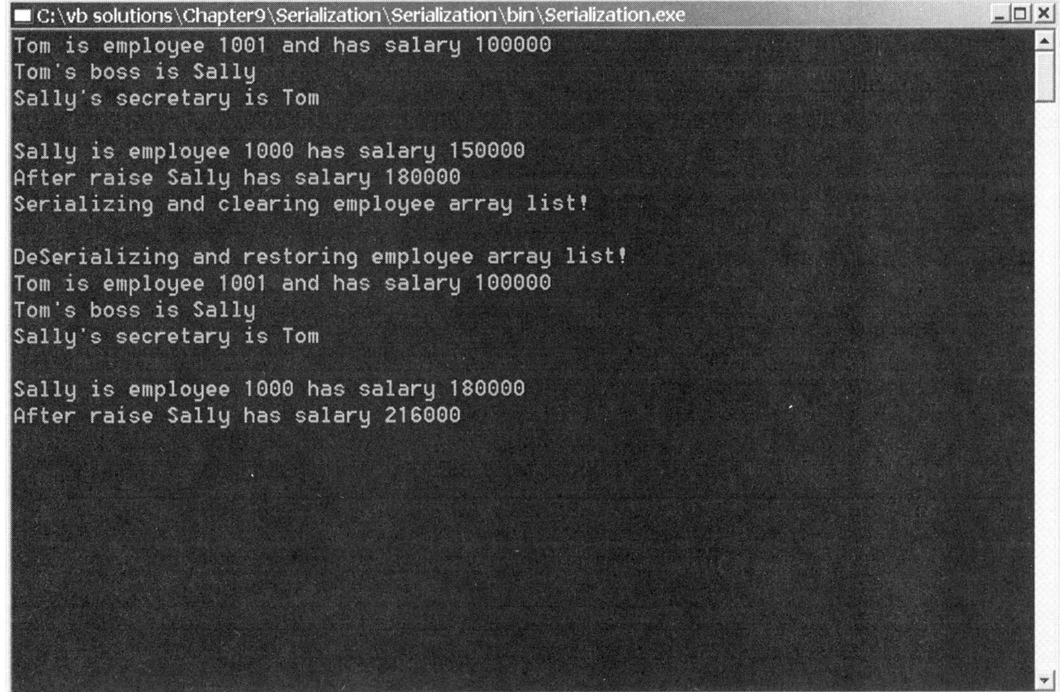

Figure 9-5. Results of the employee list serialization example

Here is the rest of the code for this example:

```
Sub SerializeToSoap(ByVal myEmployees As ArrayList, ByVal fName As String)
  Dim fStream As FileStream
  Dim mySoapFormatter As New Formatters.Soap.SoapFormatter()
  Try
    fStream = New FileStream(fName, FileMode.Create, FileAccess.Write)
    mySoapFormatter.Serialize(fStream, myEmployees)
  Catch
    Throw
  Finally
    If Not (fStream Is Nothing) Then fStream.Close()
  End Try
End Sub

Function DeSerializeFromSoap(ByVal fName As String) As ArrayList
  Dim fStream As New FileStream(fName, FileMode.Open, FileAccess.Read)
  Dim mySoapFormatter As New Formatters.Soap.SoapFormatter()
  Try
    fStream = New FileStream(fName, FileMode.Open, FileAccess.Read)
    Return CType(mySoapFormatter.Deserialize(fStream), ArrayList)
  Catch
    Throw
  Finally
    If Not (fStream Is Nothing) Then fStream.Close()
  End Try
End Function

End Module
<Serializable()> Public Class Employee
Private m_Name As String
Private m_Salary As Decimal
Private Const LIMIT As Decimal = 0.1D
Private Shared m_EmployeeId As Integer = 1000
Private m_myID As Integer
Public Sub New(ByVal sName As String, ByVal curSalary As Decimal)
  m_Name = sName
  m_Salary = curSalary
  m_myID = m_EmployeeId
  m_EmployeeId = m_EmployeeId + 1
End Sub
```

```
ReadOnly Property TheID() As Integer
  Get
    Return m_myID
  End Get
End Property
ReadOnly Property TheName() As String
  Get
    Return m_Name
  End Get
End Property
ReadOnly Property Salary() As Decimal
  Get
    Return MyClass.m_Salary
  End Get
End Property
Public Overridable Overloads Sub RaiseSalary(ByVal Percent As Decimal)
  If Percent > LIMIT Then
    'not allowed
    Console.WriteLine("MUST HAVE PASSWORD TO RAISE SALARY MORE THAN LIMIT!!!!")
  Else
    m_Salary = (1 + Percent) * m_Salary
  End If
End Sub
Public Overridable Overloads Sub RaiseSalary(ByVal Percent As Decimal, _
    ByVal Password As String)
  If Password = "special" Then
    m_Salary = (1 + Percent) * m_Salary
  End If
End Sub
End Class
<Serializable()> Public Class Manager
Inherits Employee
Private m_Sec As Secretary
Private m_Salary As Decimal
Public Sub New(ByVal sName As String, ByVal curSalary As Decimal)
  MyBase.New(sName, curSalary)
End Sub
Public Sub New(ByVal sName As String, ByVal curSalary As Decimal, _
    ByVal mySec As Secretary)
  MyBase.New(sName, curSalary)
  m_Sec = mySec
End Sub
```

```
Property MySecretary() As Secretary
  Get
    Return m_Sec
  End Get
  Set(ByVal Value As Secretary)
    m_Sec = Value
  End Set
End Property
Public Overloads Overrides Sub RaiseSalary(ByVal percent As Decimal)
  MyBase.RaiseSalary(2 * percent, "special")
End Sub
End Class
<Serializable()> Public Class Secretary
Inherits Employee
Private m_Boss As Manager
Public Sub New(ByVal sName As String, ByVal curSalary As Decimal, _
    ByVal myBoss As Manager)
  MyBase.New(sName, curSalary)
  m_Boss = myBoss
End Sub
Property MyManager() As Manager
  Get
    Return m_Boss
  End Get
  Set(ByVal Value As Manager)
    m_Boss = Value
  End Set
End Property
End Class
```

Network Streams

One place where abstracting out the idea of a stream shows its power is in working with information transmitted over the Internet: it makes working with raw HTML or raw XML almost effortless. While we can only introduce you to this important topic and the needed namespaces in this section, we at least want to show you an application of treating network data as a stream. The example we chose is usually called "screen scraping," or sending information to a Web site and getting the raw HTML of a new page as a result of the query. You then parse the raw HTML to get the data you want.

We cannot resist what is obviously an example of screen scraping at its best: a little application that goes to Amazon.com and returns the current sales rank for this book! The basic process carried out by our code is:

1. Get a `URI` (Universal Resource Indicator) object by passing the correct string to the `URI` constructor.

2. Pass this `URI` object to the `Create` member of a class called `HttpWebRequest` to initiate the http (hypertext transfer protocol) request.

3. Call the `GetResponse` method of the `HttpWebRequest` class to return a stream.

4. Parse the resulting stream, which contains the raw HTML to get the information we want. This requires understanding the structure of the page and points out an obvious reason why Web services are so much better than screen scraping as a way to get data: if Amazon changes the structure of the page, this application ceases to function.

The first step is to figure out what `URL` you need, this will determine the form of the `URI`. If you look at Figure 9-6 closely you can see that Amazon.com uses what is called the ISBN number in order to pull up the page for a book.

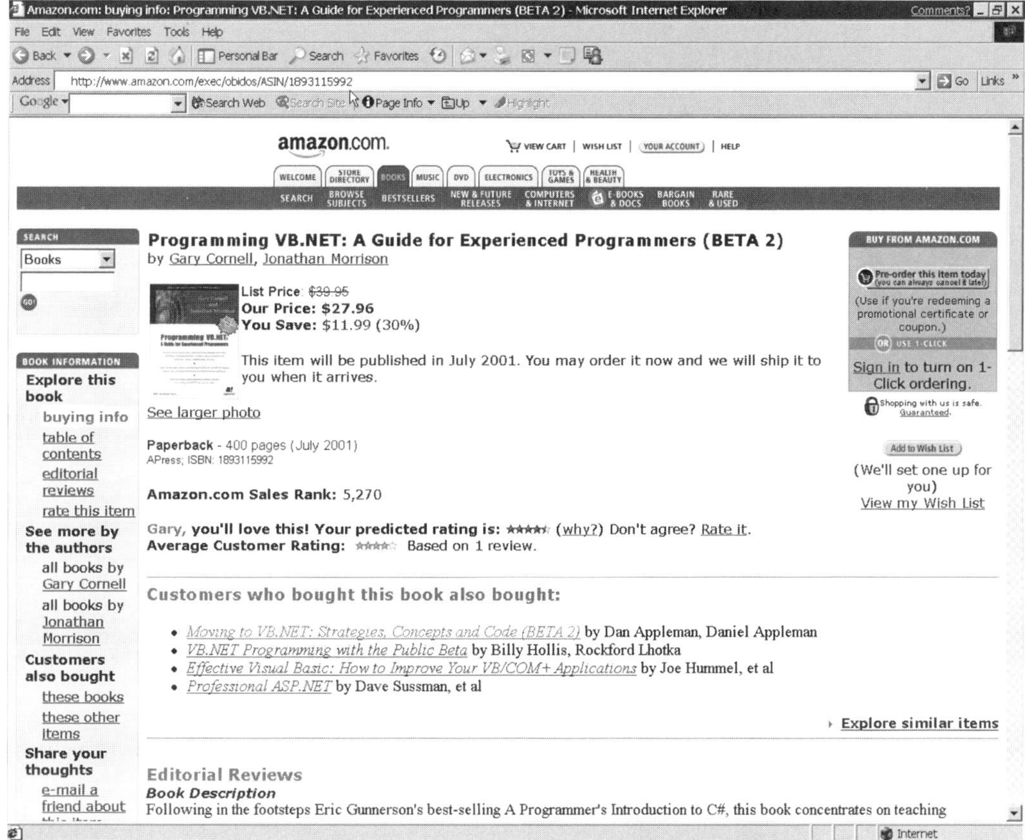

Figure 9-6. The Amazon page for our book

In our case, the page is generated through the following query string which will be our URI (the last part of the URI is the ISBN number of our book):

```
http://www.amazon.com/exec/obidos/ASIN/1893115992
```

In the following code, we create a class that encapsulates the ISBN string in an instance field in its constructor:

```
Public Sub New(ByVal ISBN As String)
    m_URL = "http://www.amazon.com/exec/obidos/ASIN/" & ISBN
End Sub
```

The read-only property GetRank in our class simply calls a private function whose key code is shown in the following eight lines:

```
1 Dim theURL As New URI(m_URL)
2 Dim theRequest As WebRequest
3 theRequest = WebRequest.Create(theURL)
4 Dim theResponse As WebResponse
5 theResponse = theRequest.GetResponse
6 Dim aReader As New StreamReader(theResponse.GetResponseStream())
7 Dim theData As String
8 theData = aReader.ReadToEnd
```

Line **1** creates the URI object. Lines **2** and **3** make the Web request to be sent to Amazon.com. Lines **4** and **5** get the response to the request and line **6** uses the GetResponseStream method of the Response class to construct a StreamReader from the response stream. At this point, the string variable theData contains the raw HTML of the Web page for our book. You can see a portion of this page in Figure 9-7.

You can see in Figure 9-7 that the ranking of the book is embedded in text that looks like this:

```
<font face=verdana,arial,helvetica size=-1>
<b>Amazon.com Sales Rank: </b>
5,776
</font><br>
```

We have only to parse the string theData in order to get this sales rank back. We do this in a helper function called Analyze:

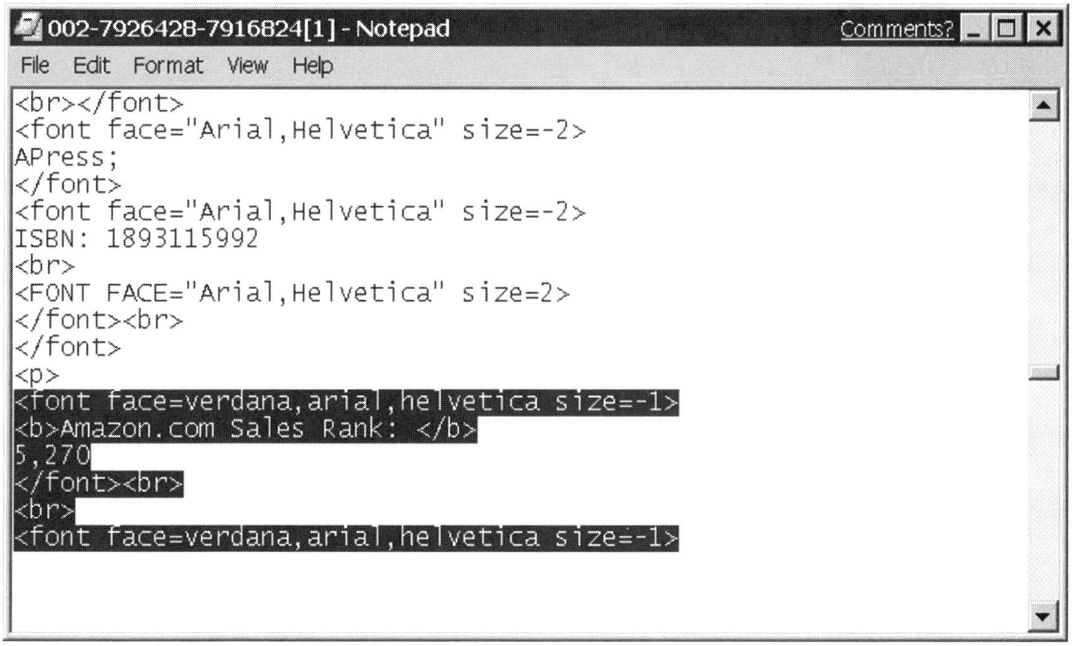

```
002-7926428-7916824[1] - Notepad
File Edit Format View Help
<br></font>
<font face="Arial,Helvetica" size=-2>
APress;
</font>
<font face="Arial,Helvetica" size=-2>
ISBN: 1893115992
<br>
<FONT FACE="Arial,Helvetica" size=2>
</font><br>
</font>
<p>
<font face=verdana,arial,helvetica size=-1>
<b>Amazon.com Sales Rank: </b>
5,270
</font><br>
<br>
<font face=verdana,arial,helvetica size=-1>
```

Figure 9-7. The raw HTML for our Amazon page

```
Private Function Analyze(ByVal theData As String) As Integer
Dim Location As Integer
Location = theData.IndexOf("<b>Amazon.com Sales Rank: </b>") _
  + "<b>Amazon.com Sales Rank: </b>".Length
Dim temp As String
Do Until theData.Substring(Location, 1) = "<"
  temp = temp & theData.Substring(Location, 1)
  Location += 1
Loop
Return CInt(temp)
End Function
```

> **TIP** *The Regular Expression Class in* `System.Text` *would give another way to parse this string.*

Here is the full code for a module that tests this class. (You will need a live Internet connection in order to use this program, of course.)

```
Option Strict On
Imports System.IO
Imports System.Net
Module Module1
  Sub Main()
    Dim myBook As New AmazonRanker("1893115992")
    MsgBox("This book's current rank is " & myBook.GetRank)
  End Sub
End Module

Public Class AmazonRanker
  Private m_URL As String
  Private m_Rank As Integer
  Public Sub New(ByVal ISBN As String)
    m_URL = "http://www.amazon.com/exec/obidos/ASIN/" & ISBN
  End Sub

  Public ReadOnly Property GetRank() As Integer
    Get
      Return ScrapeAmazon()
    End Get
  End Property

  Private Function ScrapeAmazon() As Integer
    Try
      Dim theURL As New URI(m_URL)
      Dim theRequest As WebRequest
      theRequest = WebRequest.Create(theURL)
      Dim theResponse As WebResponse
      theResponse = theRequest.GetResponse
      Dim aReader As New StreamReader(theResponse.GetResponseStream())
      Dim theData As String
      theData = aReader.ReadToEnd
      Return Analyze(theData)
    Catch E As Exception
      Console.WriteLine(E.StackTrace)
      Console.ReadLine()
    End Try
  End Function
```

```
  Private Function Analyze(ByVal theData As String) As Integer
    Dim Location As Integer
    Location = theData.IndexOf("<b>Amazon.com Sales Rank: </b>") _
    + "<b>Amazon.com Sales Rank: </b>".Length
    Dim temp As String
    Do Until theData.Substring(Location, 1) = "<"
      temp = temp & theData.Substring(Location, 1)
      Location += 1
    Loop
    Return CInt(temp)
  End Function
End Class
```

NOTE *Interestingly enough, this program shows you how subtle localization issues can be. When a friend of ours ran this program in Europe, the code would not work. The problem turned out to be that Amazon is of course using a U.S. number format, but the version of Windows the person was using on their machine was not. The result was that the "," was interpreted differently. By having the function return a string, you can avoid such problems, of course.*

Writing a File System Monitor

Among the many fundamentally new ideas in VB .NET, compared to earlier versions of VB, is the idea of doing for the server what VB has long done for the client: encapsulate common functionality in controls, thus making a little code go a long way. We want to conclude this chapter by showing you how to use the `FileSystemMonitor` class to write a program that monitors a specific directory for changes and then, of course, triggers an event. You put code in the procedure that handles the event.

You can watch the contents of an entire directory or a set of files inside the directory that satisfy some filter. You can even have the `FileSystemMonitor` control monitor recursively through the whole subdirectory structure of a given directory. The events that get triggered are shown in Table 9-13.

Table 9-13. File System Monitor Events

EVENT	DESCRIPTION
Changed	When there are changes to the size, system attributes, last write time, last access time, or security permissions of a subdirectory or file.
Created	When a subdirectory or file is created.
Deleted	When a subdirectory or file is deleted.
Renamed	When the name of a subdirectory or file is changed.

One thing you cannot do, however, is use the `FileSystemWatcher` component to watch changes in the directory itself. If someone renames a file in the directory, you will be notified, but if someone renames the directory itself you will not be. (Of course, you can monitor its parent directory to detect these kinds of changes.)

Like all components on the various toolboxes in VS .NET, the `FileSystemMonitor` component is the concrete realization of a class. In this case, it is the `FileSystemWatcher` class that inherits from the `Component` class. For example code like this:

```
FileSystemWatcher1.IncludeSubdirectories = True
```

tells the `FileSystemWatcher` to also monitor subdirectories.

Figure 9-8 shows what the Form window should look like. The `FileSystemWatcher` component which wraps this class is found on the Components tab and, because it is an invisible control, you see it in the tray (at the bottom of Figure 9-8) when you place it on a form.

This is the key code to activate this simple example:

```
Private Sub btnStart_Click(ByVal sender As System.Object, _
    ByVal e As System.EventArgs) Handles btnStart.Click
  If CheckPath() Then
    FileSystemWatcher1.Path = txtDirectory.Text
    FileSystemWatcher1.IncludeSubdirectories = chkRecursive.Checked
    FileSystemWatcher1.EnableRaisingEvents = True
  End If
End Sub
```

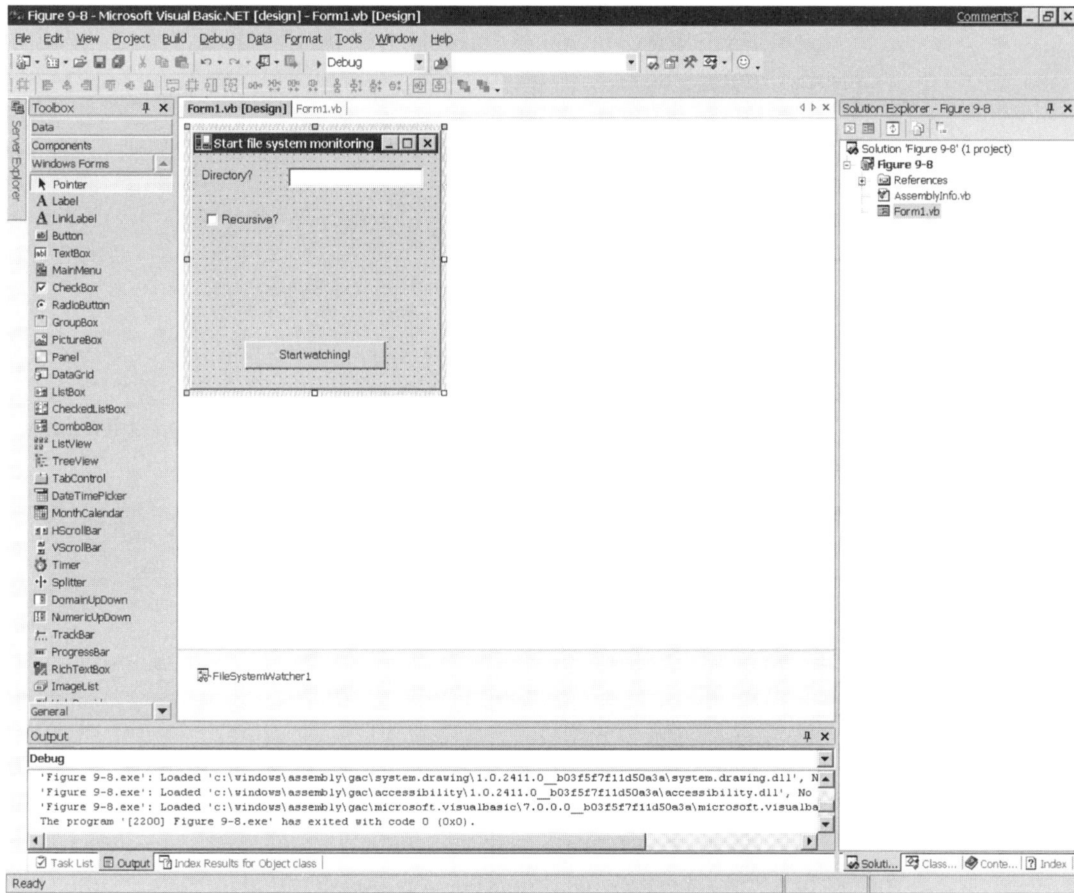

Figure 9-8. A `FileSystemWatcher` *example*

Just to reinforce what you have seen, we use the `Directory` class to check if the directory exists, so you need to import `System.IO` to use this code:

```
Function CheckPath() As Boolean
  If Directory.Exists(txtDirectory.Text) Then
    Return (True)
  Else
    txtDirectory.Text = ""
    txtDirectory.Focus()
    MsgBox("No directory by that name exists!")
    Return False
  End If
End Function
```

Then VB .NET automatically hooks up the correct event procedure, as shown here where we added the statement that displays a message box:

```
Private Sub FileSystemWatcher1_Changed(ByVal sender As Object, _
    ByVal e As System.IO.FileSystemEventArgs) Handles _
    FileSystemWatcher1.Changed
  MsgBox(txtDirectory.Text & " has changed!")
End Sub
```

Going Further with File Monitoring

Although we cannot cover this powerful component completely here, there are a couple of points you should be aware of before going further with it:

- You can use the `Filter` property to filter the names of the files and directories you want to monitor.
- Because there may be many different kinds of changes, you will want to specify which types of changes you are interested in watching more precisely. For example, if you only want to be notified when files are created, you would only handle the `Created` event.

If you need even more precise control, look at the online help for the `NotifyFilter` property, which uses an enum whose values can be combined via the `Or` operator to specify what properties you are interested in. For example, you can monitor for changes in an attribute, a filename, or a file size.

> **TIP** *Without use of the* `Filter` *and* `NotifyFilter` *properties, a program that recursively monitors an active directory or a root directory is almost unusable, because the* `Changed` *event may be triggered too frequently as Windows does its normal bookkeeping.*

CHAPTER 10

Multithreading

MULTITASKING IS A FEATURE of modern operating systems that we all take for granted.[1] After all, we expect to be able to run a word processor and an e-mail program at the same time and not have them be in conflict, or have the word processor stop working if e-mail needs to be downloaded. Of course, what actually happens is that the operating system rapidly switches between the programs that are running on the CPU (unless you have multiple CPUs of course). This gives the *impression* that multiple programs are running at the same time, because even the fastest typist (or for that matter, the fastest Internet connection) cannot keep up with the speed of even one modern CPU.

Multithreading, in a way, is the next level of multitasking: instead of having the operating system switch between different *programs*, multithreading asks the operating system to switch between different *parts* of the *same* program. Multithreading allows an e-mail program to download new messages while you are reading or composing another message. Multithreading, too, is a feature we all seem to take for granted.

VB has never really done multithreading. It is true that, starting with VB5, it did get a form of multithreading, called *apartment* threading. As you will soon see, apartment threading is multithreading on training wheels. And, like training wheels, apartment threading gives you some of the benefits of multithreading, but prevents you from accessing its full power in an attempt to keep you safe. We all need to remove the training wheels sooner or later, and VB .NET is the first version of VB that does so.

However, multithreading is not an easy feature to fully implement in a programming language or for programmers to master. Why?

- Because multithreading can cause extraordinarily subtle bugs in your code that seem to occur randomly (the most frustrating kind of bugs!).

We therefore need to give you fair warning: multithreading is the most sophisticated form of programming. If you are not exceedingly careful, you can create bugs that are almost impossible to find and cost a fortune to fix. For this reason, some of the programs in this chapter are *bad* programs—we purposefully

1. Interestingly enough, prior to the release of Apple's OS X, the Macintosh lacked a modern multitasking operating system. A true multitasking operating system is extremely difficult to design properly, and Apple was eventually forced to use Unix as the basis of its OS X!

designed them in order to show you how things can go *wrong*. We think the safest approach to learning multithreaded programming is to see what can go wrong even when, on the surface, a program looks like it should work. You must become more aware of potential problems and ways of avoiding them if you want to use multithreaded programming techniques.

> **NOTE** *While we hope we give you a firm foundation, we cannot cover all the ins and outs of multithreading here—just printing the documentation for the classes in the* `Threading` *namespace takes more than 100 pages. If you want to go further with multithreading, you will need to study specialized books.*

Still, as dangerous as it can be, multithreading is *required* if you are to solve certain programming problems in a professional way. If your programs do not use multithreading when it is called for, users will be seriously disappointed and will choose someone else's program. For example, it was not until Eudora's fourth version that the popular e-mail program had the multithreaded features that modern e-mail programs must have if they are not to seriously frustrate users. By the time Eudora implemented multithreading, many people had moved on to other products. (One of us who was using Eudora as his primary e-mail program stopped using it because a multithreaded version was not available then.)

Finally, there is no escaping multithreading in .NET: *all* .NET programs are multithreaded, since the garbage collector runs as a low priority thread in the background. And as you will soon learn, serious GUI programming in .NET depends on using threads correctly in order to keep GUI programs responsive when parts of your code are running time-consuming processes.

Getting Started with Multithreading

The term *thread* comes from "thread of execution," which is used to mean that every program is running in a certain *context*. The context describes how the thread is using memory for storing its code and data. If you store the context, you essentially store a thread of execution within your program.

Taking a snapshot of the thread's context takes time. The operating system has to freeze the thread's context and store it somewhere when it passes control to another thread. When the program wants to restart the stopped thread, it has to restore the thread's context, which takes more time. You should use multithreading only when the benefit outweighs the cost. Here are some typical examples of when this is true:

- When there is a natural division of the users handling the program, as in the example of downloading e-mail while composing new e-mail

- When you need to do a complicated calculation in a GUI-intensive program and do not want your GUI to become unresponsive

- When you need to take full advantage of a multiprocessor computer running an operating system that can use multiple processors (in this case, as long as you keep the number of active threads to be less than the number of CPUs, you should incur little or no thread overhead)

Before we delve into the mechanics of writing multithreaded programs, we want to clear up one common source of confusion amongst people new to multithreaded programming:

- A thread runs a *procedure*, not an object.

We are not sure what "running an object" means, but one of us often teaches multithreading programming, and this question seems to be the uppermost in many people's minds. Perhaps they are thinking that a thread should start only by calling the `New` method of a class, and then that thread then runs any messages sent to that object. This is *completely* wrong. A single object can have multiple threads running different (or even the same) methods, so different threads are sending and responding to specific messages sent to the object. (This, as you will see, is one of the reasons thread programming is so hard: to debug a program, you have to know which thread is running which procedure at the moment!)

Because a thread is created from a method of an object, you usually must have previously created the object. After you build the object, you create the thread by passing it the address of the method inside the object, and *then* you tell the thread to start running that method. Of course, a procedure that a thread was created to run, like all procedures, can create new objects or manipulate existing objects. It can also call other procedures or functions that are visible to it. A The

> **NOTE** *Threads can also run shared methods of classes, in which case no object instance is needed.*

The other vital point to keep in mind is:

- A thread ends when the procedure that you used to create it ends *and will not end normally until this procedure ends.*

> **NOTE** *It is possible to end a thread abnormally without letting it end itself. This is usually a very bad idea. See the section on "Ending/Interrupting a Thread" for more on this.*

.NET keeps most of the functionality you call upon to use threads with in the `Threading` namespace. Most programs that use threads therefore begin with:

```
Imports System.Threading
```

to simplify typing and to make IntelliSense most useful.

Next, as you might expect, *delegates* (Chapter 6) figure prominently into the picture, since threads run procedures. In particular, the .NET Framework comes with a `ThreadStart` delegate in the `Threading` namespace that you usually use to start a thread. Here is the syntax for using this delegate:

```
Public Delegate Sub ThreadStart()
```

The procedure a `ThreadStart` delegate calls must be a parameterless subprocedure. Thus, you cannot build a thread using a function (since this returns a value) or a procedure that takes parameters. What is more, you must have alternative methods to get information out of a thread, because the methods they run do not have return values, nor can they use `ByRef` parameters. For example, if `ThreadMethod` sits inside a class called `WillUseThread`, then you can have the `ThreadMethod` affect the properties of instances of the `WillUseThread` class to pass information out of the `ThreadMethod` procedure.

Application Domains

Threads in .NET run in an *application domain* (usually abbreviated as *app domain*), which the documentation defines as "an isolated environment where applications execute." Think of app domains as lightweight analogues of Win 32 processes; a single Win32 process can host multiple app domains. This is because the main difference between an app domain and a process is that a Win32 process needs to have a distinct memory address space. (The documentation also describes an app domain as a logical process occurring inside a physical process.) Because the .NET runtime manages memory, many application domains can run in a single Win 32 process. (One advantage is that this allows much better scaling.) The application domain is encapsulated in the `AppDomain` class (the class's documentation is worth examining). The `AppDomain` class lets you drill down into the environment your program is running. For example, you can use it to do reflection on the .NET system classes. This code lets you look at the assemblies loaded at run time:

```
Imports System.Reflection
Module Module1
  Sub Main()
    Dim theDomain As AppDomain
    theDomain = AppDomain.CurrentDomain
    Dim Assemblies() As [Assembly]
    Assemblies = theDomain.GetAssemblies
    Dim anAssembly As [Assembly]
    For Each anAssembly In Assemblies
      Console.WriteLine(anAssembly.FullName)
    Next
    Console.ReadLine()
  End Sub
End Module
```

The Mechanics of Thread Creation

Let us start with a trivial example: suppose you want to run, in a separate thread, a procedure that simply decrements a counter forever. Here is the class that contains the procedure:

```
Public Class WillUseThreads
  Public Sub SubtractFromCounter()
    Dim count As Integer
    Do While True
      count -= 1
      Console.WriteLine("Am in another thread and counter  =" _
      & count)
    Loop
  End Sub
End Class
```

Because the test `Do Loop` is always true, you would think that the `SubtractFromCounter` sub would run without interruption. However, through the magic of threads, this will not quite happen.

Here is the `Sub Main` and the `Imports` statement we need to get the thread to run:

```
Option Strict On
Imports System.Threading
Module Module1
  Sub Main()
1     Dim myTest As New WillUseThreads()
2     Dim bThreadStart As New ThreadStart(AddressOf _
      myTest.SubtractFromCounter)
3     Dim bThread As New Thread(bThreadStart)
4     bThread.Start()
      Dim i As Integer
5     Do While True
         Console.WriteLine("In main thread and count is " & i)
         i += 1
     Loop
  End Sub
End Module
```

Let us go over the key points one by one. First, `Sub Main` always runs in what is called the *main* thread. A .NET program always has at least two threads running: the main thread and the garbage collection thread. In line **1** we make a new instance of the test class. In line **2** we create a `ThreadStart` delegate by passing to it the address of the parameterless sub named `SubtractFromCounter` in the instance of the test class we created in line **1**. Because we import the `Threading` namespace, we do not need to use the long form `ThreadMethod`. We actually create the thread in line **3**. Notice that the constructor for the `Thread` class requires a `ThreadStart` delegate. Some people like to combine the two lines into one (logical) line:

```
Dim bThread As New Thread(New ThreadStart(AddressOf _
myTest.SubtractFromCounter))
```

Finally, line **4** "starts" the thread by calling the `Start` method on the instance of the `Thread` class you created with a `ThreadStart` delegate. This tells the system to run the `Subtract` function on its own thread.

CAUTION *We put quotes around starts in the preceding paragraph, because this line is where you first encounter one of the many strange features of thread programming: the* `Start` *method does not actually start a thread! What it does do is tell the operating system to schedule that thread to be started—and you have only very crude control over when this happens. In particular, you have no way to force a thread to start running at your convenience, because threads always run at the convenience of the operating system. (See the following section on priority levels for details on how to nudge the operating system to think about starting your thread more rapidly.)*

Figure 10-1 is an example of what might happen after you run this program for a while and then stop it with Ctrl+Break. In our case, the counter got up to 341 in the main thread before it decided to actually run the new thread!

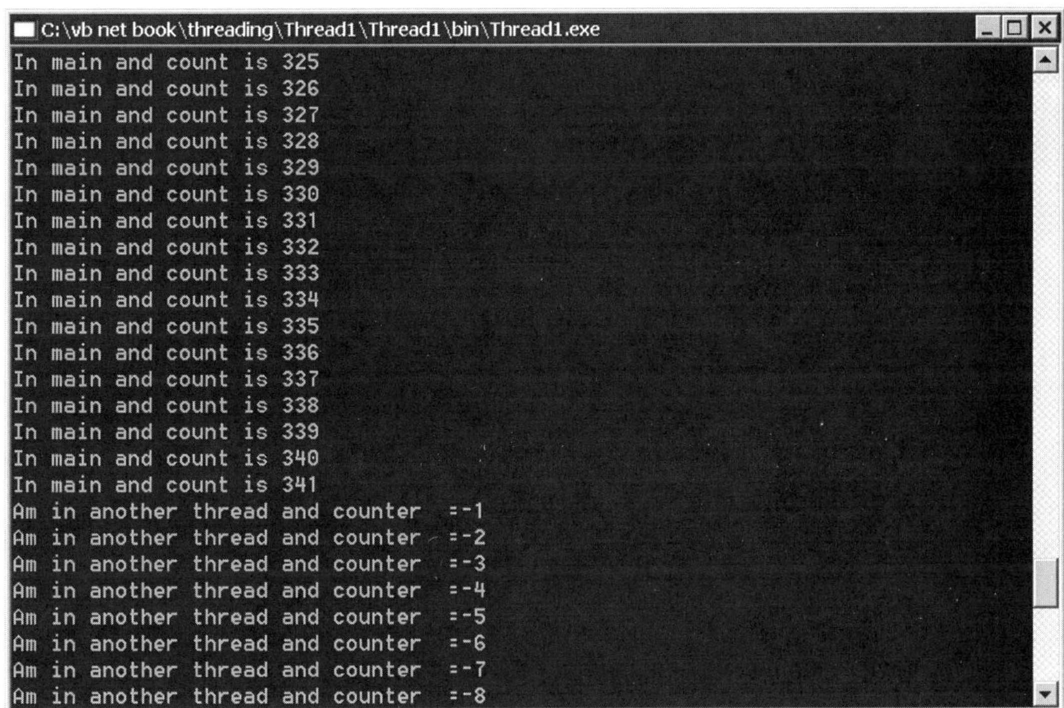

Figure 10-1. A simple mutithreaded program stopped while running

If you run the program a little longer, you will see something like Figure 10-2, which shows that the separate thread was put on hold while the main thread got to run again. What happens is called *preemptive multithreading through time slicing* and we take up what this mouthful means next.

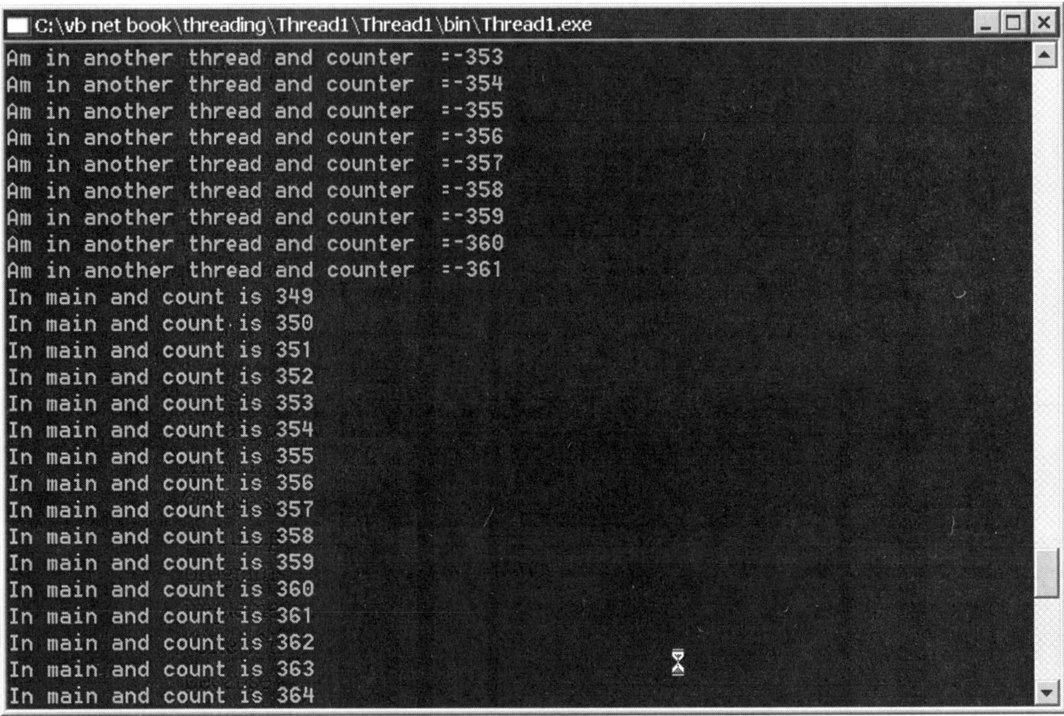

Figure 10-2. Switching between threads in a simple multithreaded program

The operating system uses what is known as preemptive multithreading through time slicing, to interrupt threads and give other threads time to run. Certain ways of doing time slicing also solve one of the more common troubles with multithreading programs—a phenomenon called *starvation,* which occurs when you have one thread that takes up all the CPU cycles and never releases control to the other threads. (Typically, this is the result of using tight loops like the ones in our example program). To prevent starvation, make sure your threads give up some time to the other threads. The next best solution is to have an operating system that always preempts running threads, no matter how high their priority, so that every thread gets at least a small slice of time to work in.

CAUTION *Because all versions of Windows that .NET runs on use time slicing that gives every thread a minimum amount of time, starvation is usually not that serious an issue in .NET programming. If .NET is ever ported to other operating systems, however, this may no longer be true.*

By adding this line to the example thread program, right before the call to start the thread, even low priority threads get a chance at some CPU time:

```
bThread.Priority=ThreadPriority.Highest
```

This tells Windows to run the new thread with its highest priority and makes the main thread a lower priority. Figure 10-3 shows that the new thread starts running sooner than it did previously, but Figure 10-4 shows that the main thread still gets some time (admittedly, only a very small amount of time, and only after the subtracting thread ran for a long while). The results you get when you run the program will be similar to those shown in Figures 10-3 and 10-4, but because of differences between your system and ours, they will not be identical.

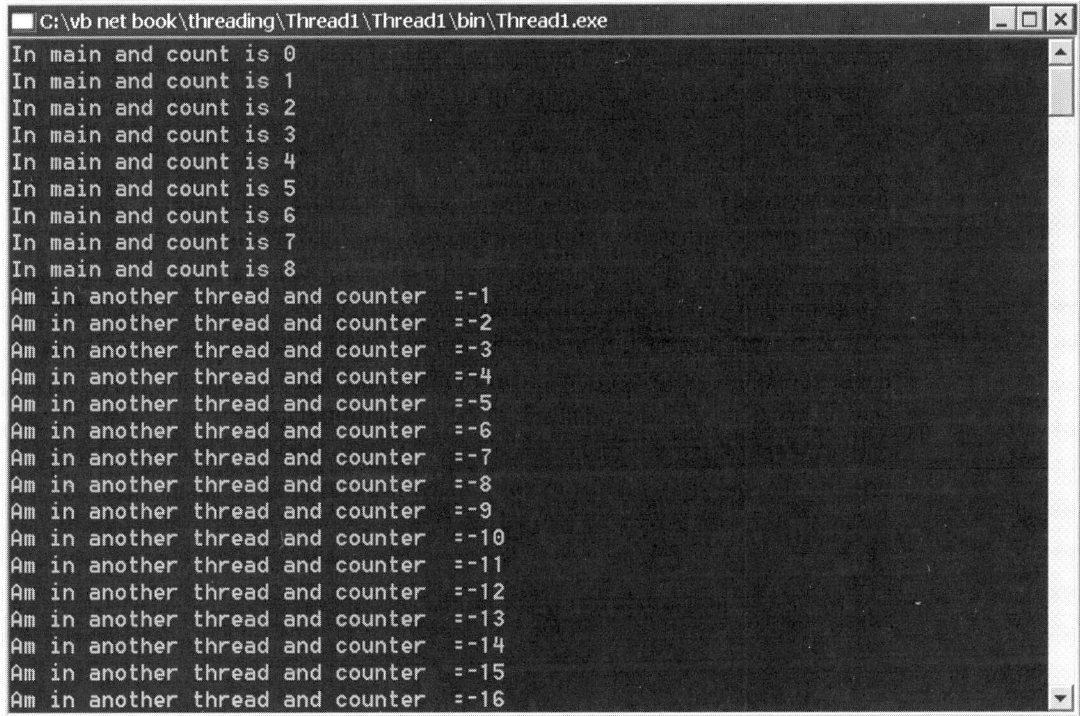

Figure 10-3. Highest priority thread (usually) starts up quicker

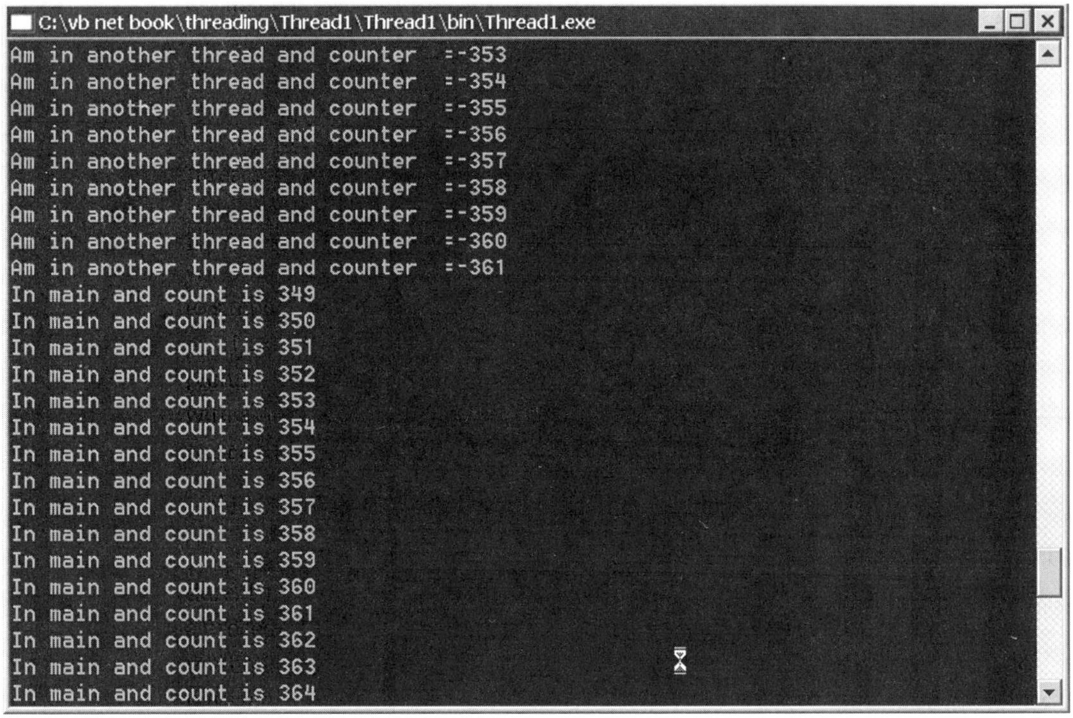

```
C:\vb net book\threading\Thread1\Thread1\bin\Thread1.exe
Am in another thread and counter  =-353
Am in another thread and counter  =-354
Am in another thread and counter  =-355
Am in another thread and counter  =-356
Am in another thread and counter  =-357
Am in another thread and counter  =-358
Am in another thread and counter  =-359
Am in another thread and counter  =-360
Am in another thread and counter  =-361
In main and count is 349
In main and count is 350
In main and count is 351
In main and count is 352
In main and count is 353
In main and count is 354
In main and count is 355
In main and count is 356
In main and count is 357
In main and count is 358
In main and count is 359
In main and count is 360
In main and count is 361
In main and count is 362
In main and count is 363
In main and count is 364
```

Figure 10-4. Lower priority thread is still not starved.

The `ThreadPriority` enumeration has five levels:

```
ThreadPriority.Highest
ThreadPriority.AboveNormal
ThreadPriority.Normal
ThreadPriority.BelowNormal
ThreadPriority.Lowest
```

Join

You sometimes need to stop a thread until another thread has finished doing some work. For example, you may want thread 1 to wait until computations in thread 2 are finished. You set this up by calling the `Join` method on thread 2 *while running thread 1.* In other words, code like this:

```
thread2.Join()
```

puts the current thread to sleep and it waits until thread 2 is over. Thread 1 is now a *blocked* thread.

If you join thread 1 to thread 2, the operating system will (eventually) start thread 1 once thread 2 ends. (The jargon says it is now *unblocked*.) Keep in mind that this process is *nondeterministic*: you cannot know exactly how soon after thread 2 finishes will thread 1 start up again.

There is another version of `Join` that returns a Boolean value:

```
thread2.Join(Integer)
```

This method either waits for the thread 2 to die or waits for a specified time in milliseconds to expire before thread 2 is unblocked, so that it will be scheduled to run again by the operating system. This method returns true if thread 2 dies before the timeout specified, and false if it does not.

> **CAUTION** *Always keep in mind that, even if the timeout has elapsed or the second thread has ended, you have no control over how soon after that thread 1 will wake up.*

Thread Names, CurrentThread, *and* ThreadState

Get into the habit of giving each of your threads a name before you start them. This helps a great deal when debugging programs involving threads. You do this via the `Name` property of thread objects with code like this:

```
bThread.Name = "Subtracting thread"
```

Also, you can always get a reference to the thread that is running a piece of code by using `Thread.CurrentThread`, which returns a reference to the currently running thread.

> **TIP** *Even with the fancy features of the Threads window, which you will soon see, we cannot tell you how often we have been saved by a line of code like this:*
>
> ```
> MsgBox(Thread.CurrentThread.Name)
> ```
>
> *which made it clear that the thread we thought was running a piece of code, was not.*

Again, saying that threads are scheduled in a nondeterministic manner is a fancy way of saying you have very little control over what scheduling the operating system is doing. For this reason, you will occasionally want to make a call to the `ThreadState` property, which returns a value that indicates the current state of a thread.

The Threads Window

Visual Studio .NET's Threads window is a great help in dealing with threaded programs. You make this window active when you are in break mode by going to the Debug|Windows submenu. Suppose, for example, you name `bThread` via a call to:

```
bThread.Name = "Subtracting thread"
```

After you use Ctrl+Break (or some other method) to stop the program, your Threads window will look something like Figure 10-5.

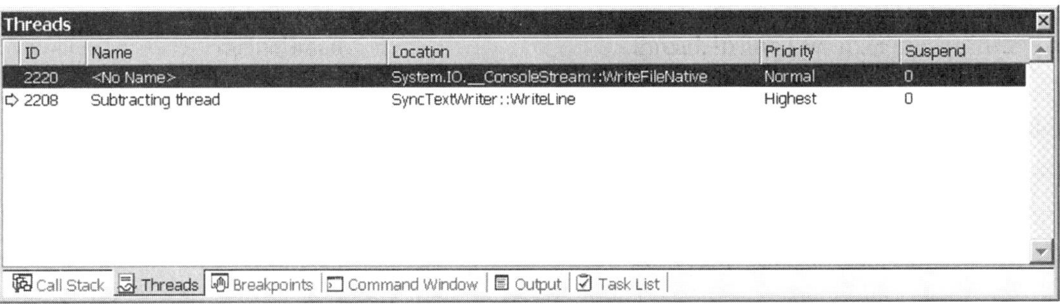

Figure 10-5. The Threads window

The arrow in the first column marks the active thread, the same thread you get by calling `Thread.CurrentThread`. The ID column merely lists a number that identifies each thread. The next column gives the name of the thread (if you assigned it one). The next column identifies the code currently running. (For example, the `WriteLine` procedure in the `Console` class, as shown in Figure 10-5). The remaining columns indicate the priority level and whether the thread is suspended (see the next section).

The Threads window lets you—and not the operating system—control threads in your program via the context menu for each item. For example, you can freeze the current thread by right-clicking on its line and choosing Freeze (you can later unfreeze it). Because the operating system cannot run a frozen thread, this can be a useful in debugging when you need to isolate a misbehaving thread. You can also make another (nonfrozen) thread active by right-clicking on its line and choosing Switch to Thread (double-clicking the thread also works). This is extremely useful when analyzing a program for possible deadlocks, as you see later in this chapter.

Putting a Thread to Sleep

You may occasionally want to tell a thread to `Sleep` when it is not needed. A sleeping thread is another example of a blocked thread. When you put a thread to sleep, the other threads in the program obviously have more CPU cycles to play with. A common syntax for `Sleep` is:

```
Thread.Sleep(Number of milliseconds)
```

which tells the currently active thread to sleep for at least the specified number of milliseconds. (It may not wake up exactly at that moment, however.) Notice the lack of a reference to a specific thread—you can only tell the currently executing thread to sleep.

This version of `Sleep` makes the current thread relinquish the rest of its time slice:

```
Thread.Sleep(0)
```

This version tells the current thread to go to sleep indefinitely (only a call to `Interrupt` can waken it):

```
Thread.Sleep(Timeout.Infinite)
```

Because you can interrupt a sleeping thread (even if it is sleeping indefinitely) with a call to the `Interrupt` method, which throws a `ThreadInterruptedException`, you should use `Sleep` only in a `Try-Catch` block, as in this framework:

```
Try
  Thread.Sleep(200)
Catch tIe As ThreadInterruptedException
   'thread interrupted
Catch e As Exception
  'other exception
End Try
```

> **TIP** *Because every .NET program runs in a thread, you can use the* `Sleep` *method to pause a program. (If you do not import the* `Threading` *namespace, you need to use the long form:* `Threading.Thread.Sleep`.*)*

Ending or Interrupting a Thread

A thread ends when you get to the end of the method used to create it in the `ThreadStart` delegate, but you may need a way to end the method (and thus the thread) when certain events occur. It is occasionally useful to direct a thread to check a *condition variable* to decide if it should end abnormally. Creating a framework for using a condition variable involves placing code that tests the condition variable and then exits the `Sub` if the condition variable exists. The most common way to do this is to have an enclosing `Do-While` loop in your `Sub`:

```
Sub ThreadedMethod()
'you need to have a way to poll the condition variable
'for example, it can be a property of a class that you have a reference to
Do While conditionVariable = False And MoreWorkToDo
   'all the code goes here
Loop
End Sub
```

> **TIP** *Polling takes time. use it only if you expect to have to end a thread prematurely.*

If you need to check the condition variable at a special place, use an `If-Then` with the `Exit Sub` keywords inside an infinite loop.

> **CAUTION** *A condition variable must be synchronized, so that is not affected by other threads in a way that interferes with its operation. See the section on "The Solution: Synchronization" for more on this important concept.*

Unfortunately, code in a sleeping thread (or one that is otherwise blocked) is not running, so polling the condition variable will not work. In this case, you need to:

- Call the `Interrupt` method on an object variable that references the thread.

You can call `Interrupt` only on a thread in a `Wait`, `Sleep`, or `Join` thread state. If you do call interrupt on a thread in one of these states, then (eventually) the thread will start up again, and the runtime will trigger a `ThreadInterruptedException` in the thread. This happens even if the thread has been put to sleep indefinitely via a call to `Thread.Sleep(Timeout.Infinite)`. (We say eventually, because of the nondeterministic nature of thread scheduling.) In this case, you `Catch` the `ThreadInterruptedException` and write cleanup code in the `Catch` clause. However, the `Catch` clause is not required to end the thread in response to an interruption—that is up to the thread itself!

> **NOTE** *In .NET you can even interrupt a nonblocked thread. The thread will be interrupted the next time it is blocked.*

Suspending or Killing a Thread

Two other methods in the threading namespace interrupt the normal functioning of a thread:

- `Suspend`
- `Abort`

We are not sure why these methods were included in .NET, because using either `Suspend` or `Abort` is likely to leave your programs in an unstable state. Neither method gives a thread a reasonable chance to do any cleanup. If you call `Suspend` or `Abort`, you have no way of knowing the state the thread leaves objects in when it suspends itself or when it is aborted.

Calling `Abort` throws a `ThreadAbortException`, but, to stress how bad an idea relying on this rather strange exception is, we quote the documentation for the .NET SDK:

> *When a call is made to* `Abort` *to destroy a thread, the common language runtime throws a* `ThreadAbortException`. `ThreadAbortException` *is a special exception that is not catchable. When this exception is raised, the runtime executes all the finally blocks before killing the thread. Since the thread can do an unbounded computation in the finally blocks, you must call* `Join` *to guarantee that the thread has died.*

The moral is: do not use `Abort` or `Suspend`. (If you do use `Suspend`, you must use `Resume` to wake up the suspended thread.) Hence:

- The only safe method to use to end a thread is to poll a (synchronized) condition variable or use the `Interrupt` method we just showed you.

Daemon (Background) Threads

Some threads that run in the background automatically stop when nothing else in the program is running. The garbage collector, for instance, runs in one of these background threads. You usually create a background thread if you want to have a thread that listens for data, but you want this to happen only as long as there is some code that can process the data running in other threads. The syntax is:

```
NameOfThread.IsBackground = True
```

> **CAUTION** *When the only remaining threads in an application are daemon (background) threads, the application automatically ends.*

A More Serious Example: Screen Scraping Redux

We recommend using threads when there are natural breaks in what your program does. A good example of this comes from an improved version of the screen scraping program we showed you in the I/O chapter. That class had two parts: data gathering from Amazon's site and then data processing. This is a perfect example of where multithreading can bring benefits. We create the various classes and then do the analysis in separate threads. By spawning new threads for each book, you maximize the efficiency of the program, because one thread can gather new data (which may involve waiting for Amazon's server) while the other thread processes data it has already received.

> **NOTE** *This program will be more efficient than the single-threaded version only if you have multiple processors, or the time it takes to download additional data can be used profitably by the analysis routine.*

Because you can start a thread only with a parameterless subprocedure, you need to make minor modifications to the code. For example, here is the key `Sub` rewritten to be parameterless:

```
Public Sub FindRank()
  m_Rank = ScrapeAmazon()
  Console.WriteLine("the rank of " & m_Name & " is " & GetRank)
End Sub
```

Because we cannot yet use a combo box to store or get the information (see the last section of this chapter for how to write multithreaded GUI programs), the program hardwires the four books into an array whose code begins as follows:

```
Dim theBook(3, 1) As String
theBook(0, 0) = "1893115992"
theBook(0, 1) = "Programming VB .NET"
'etc.
```

We then create four threads inside the same loop that makes the objects themselves:

```
For i = 0 To 3
  Try
    theRanker = New AmazonRanker(theBook(i, 0), theBook(i, 1))
    aThreadStart = New ThreadStart(AddressOf theRanker.FindRank)
    aThread = New Thread(aThreadStart)
    aThread.Name = theBook(i, 1)
    aThread.Start()
  Catch e As Exception
    Console.WriteLine(e.Message)
  End Try
Next
```

That is it. Here is the full code:

```
Option Strict On
Imports System.IO
Imports System.Net
Imports System.ThreadIng
Module Module1
  Sub Main()
    Dim theBook(3, 1) As String
    theBook(0, 0) = "1893115992"
    theBook(0, 1) = "Programming VB .NET"
    theBook(1, 0) = "1893115291"
    theBook(1, 1) = "Database Programming VB .NET"
    theBook(2, 0) = "1893115623"
    theBook(2, 1) = "Programmer's Introduction to C#, "
    theBook(3, 0) = "1893115593"
    theBook(3, 1) = "C# and the .Net Platform "
    Dim i As Integer
    Dim theRanker As AmazonRanker
    Dim aThreadStart As Threading.ThreadStart
    Dim aThread As Threading.Thread
```

```
    For i = 0 To 3
      Try
        theRanker = New AmazonRanker(theBook(i, 0), theBook(i, 1))
        aThreadStart = New ThreadStart(AddressOf theRanker.FindRank)
        aThread = New Thread(aThreadStart)
        aThread.Name = theBook(i, 1)
        aThread.Start()
      Catch e As Exception
        Console.WriteLine(e.Message)
      End Try
    Next
    Console.ReadLine()
  End Sub
End Module
Public Class AmazonRanker
  Private m_URL As String
  Private m_Rank As Integer
  Private m_Name As String
  Public Sub New(ByVal ISBN As String, ByVal theName As String)
    m_URL = "http://www.amazon.com/exec/obidos/ASIN/" & ISBN
    m_Name = theName
  End Sub
  Public Sub FindRank()
    m_Rank = ScrapeAmazon()
    Console.WriteLine("the rank of " & m_Name & " is " _
    & GetRank)
  End Sub
  Public ReadOnly Property GetRank() As String
    Get
      If m_Rank <> 0 Then
        Return CStr(m_Rank)
      Else
        'problems
      End If
    End Get
  End Property
  Public ReadOnly Property GetName() As String
    Get
      Return m_Name
    End Get
  End Property
```

```
  Private Function ScrapeAmazon() As Integer
    Try
      Dim theURL As New Uri(m_URL)
      Dim theRequest As WebRequest
      theRequest = WebRequest.Create(theURL)
      Dim theResponse As WebResponse
      theResponse = theRequest.GetResponse
      Dim aReader As New StreamReader(theResponse.GetResponseStream())
      Dim theData As String
      theData = aReader.ReadToEnd
      Return Analyze(theData)
    Catch E As Exception
      Console.WriteLine(E.Message)
      Console.WriteLine(E.StackTrace)
      Console.ReadLine()
    End Try
  End Function
  Private Function Analyze(ByVal theData As String) As Integer
    Dim Location As Integer
    Location = theData.IndexOf("<b>Amazon.com Sales Rank: </b>") _
    + "<b>Amazon.com Sales Rank: </b>".Length
    Dim temp As String
    Do Until theData.Substring(Location, 1) = "<"
      temp = temp & theData.Substring(Location, 1)
      Location += 1
    Loop
    Return CInt(temp)
  End Function
End Class
```

NOTE *Because multithreading with the .NET and I/O namespaces is so common, the Framework's library gives you special methods (called asynchronous calls) to deal with this common situation. For example, look at the documentation for the* `BeginGetResponse` *and* `EndGetResponse` *in the* `HTTPWebRequest` *class to learn more about using asynchronous calls to write multithreaded programs.*

The Big Danger: Shared Data

Up to this point, we have dealt with the only safe place to use threads: when the threads *do not change shared data.* When you allow threads to change shared data, the potential for bugs starts to multiply and ridding your programs of them becomes much more difficult. On the other hand, thread programming in .NET would be no more powerful than thread programming in VB6 if it were not possible to modify shared data from different threads.

To demonstrate the potential problems and yet not bog down our example program in extraneous details, we created an example called the “House You Get Cooked In.” Here is the idea: imagine modeling a house in code. Each room has a thermostat. If the thermostat is 5 or more degrees Fahrenheit (about 2.77 degrees Celsius) less than the target setting, we tell the house's heating unit to increase its temperature by 5 degrees; otherwise, we tell it to increase the temperature by 1 degree. Each room's temperature-adjusting code runs in a separate thread, with a 200-millisecond delay each time we change the temperature, to mirror lag time. For example, we use code like this:

```
If mHouse.HouseTemp < mHouse.MAX_TEMP - 5 Then
  Try
    Thread.Sleep(200)
  Catch tie As ThreadInterruptedException
     'thread interrupted
  Catch e As Exception
    'other exception
  End Try
mHouse.HouseTemp += 5
'etc.
```

Here is the full code for this example. Figure 10-6 shows you the (unfortunate) output of this program: a house temperature of 105°F (40.5°C)!

```
Option Strict On
Imports System.Threading
Module Module1
  Sub Main()
    Dim myHouse As New House(10)
    Console.ReadLine()
  End Sub
End Module

Public Class House
  Public Const MAX_TEMP As Integer = 75
  Private mCurTemp As Integer = 55
  Private mRooms() As Room
  Public Sub New(ByVal numOfRooms As Integer)
    ReDim mRooms(numOfRooms - 1)
    Dim i As Integer
    Dim aThreadStart As Threading.ThreadStart
    Dim aThread As Thread
```

```
    For i = 0 To numOfRooms - 1
      Try
        mRooms(i) = New Room(Me, mCurTemp, CStr(i) & "'th room")
        aThreadStart = New ThreadStart(AddressOf mRooms(i).CheckTempInRoom)
        aThread = New Thread(aThreadStart)
        aThread.Start()
      Catch E As Exception
        Console.WriteLine(E.StackTrace)
      End Try
    Next
  End Sub
  Public Property HouseTemp() As Integer
    Get
      Return mCurTemp
    End Get
    Set(ByVal Value As Integer)
      mCurTemp = Value
    End Set
  End Property
End Class

Public Class Room
  Private mCurTemp As Integer
  Private mName As String
  Private mHouse As House
  Public Sub New(ByVal theHouse As House, ByVal temp As Integer, _
  ByVal roomName As String)
    mHouse = theHouse
    mCurTemp = temp
    mName = roomName
  End Sub
  Public Sub CheckTempInRoom()
    ChangeTemperature()
  End Sub
  Private Sub ChangeTemperature()
    Try
      If mHouse.HouseTemp < mHouse.MAX_TEMP - 5 Then
        Thread.Sleep(200)
        mHouse.HouseTemp += 5
        Console.WriteLine("Am in " & Me.mName & _
      ".  Current temperature is " & mHouse.HouseTemp)
```

```
57          ElseIf mHouse.HouseTemp < mHouse.MAX_TEMP Then
58            Thread.Sleep(200)
59            mHouse.HouseTemp += 1
60            Console.WriteLine("Am in " & Me.mName & _
61          ".  Current temperature is " & mHouse.HouseTemp)
62          Else
63            Console.WriteLine("Am in " & Me.mName & _
64         ".  Current temperature is " & mHouse.HouseTemp)
65            'Do nothing temp OK
66          End If
67        Catch tae As ThreadInterruptedException
68          'thread interrupted
69        Catch e As Exception
70          'other exception
71        End Try
72      End Sub
73    End Class
```

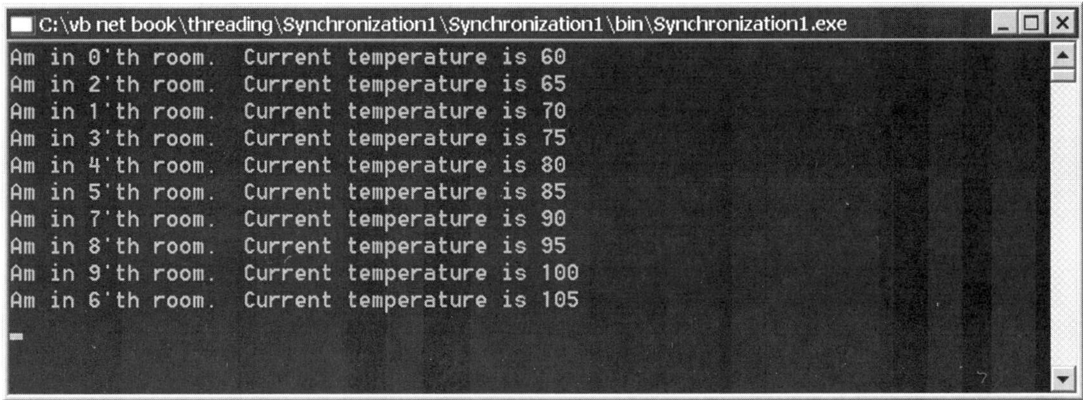

Figure 10-6. Threading problems, or "you're cooked"

The `Sub Main` (lines **4–7**) creates a house with ten "rooms." The `House` class sets up a maximum temperature of 75°F (about 24°C). Lines **13–28** are the somewhat complicated constructor of the house. Lines **18–27** are the key to this program. Line **20** eventually sets up ten rooms, passing a reference to the house so that the rooms can refer back to the house. Lines **21–23** set up the temperature adjustment for each room in ten individual threads. The code for the `Room` class is in lines **38–73**. Notice how we cache a reference to the `House` by assigning to the `mHouse` instance field in the constructor (line **43**) of the `Room` class. The code to check and adjust the temperature (lines **50–66**) seems straightforward, but as you soon see, it is hardly that! Finally, notice how this code is surrounded by a `Try-Catch` block, because we use a call to `Sleep`.

A house temperature of 105°F (40.5°C) is not a good thing! What went wrong? The problem is the line:

```
If mHouse.HouseTemp < mHouse.MAX_TEMP - 5 Then
```

Here is what probably happened: Thread 1 is running and it checks the temperature. It sees that the temperature is way too low, so it raises the temperature 5 degrees. Unfortunately, before it can do that, thread 1 is interrupted and thread 2 starts running. Thread 2 checks the same (shared) variable which was *not yet* changed by thread 1. So thread 2 prepares to raise the temperature 5 degrees as well. However, before it can do so it to is put to sleep. The process continues until thread 1 eventually wakes up and proceeds to move onto its next instruction: raising the temperature another 5 degrees. Do this for ten rooms and you are well and truly cooked.

The Solution: Synchronization

The house program encountered a *race condition* in which the results depend on the order in which thread code runs. The solution to race conditions is to make sure statements like this:

```
If mHouse.HouseTemp < mHouse.MAX_TEMP - 5 Then …
```

are completely executed by a running thread before they can be interrupted. The feature we need is called *atomicity*: you need to make sure a block of code is treated by each thread as an atomic unit. This gives you a way to make multiple statements uninterruptible by the thread scheduler until they are finished. All multithreaded programming languages have ways to enforce atomicity. The easiest way in VB .NET is to use the `SyncLock` statement, which takes an object or object variable. If you modify the house program to look like this (the key lines are bolded), it will run just fine:

```
Private Sub ChangeTemperature()
  SyncLock (mHouse)
       Try
         If mHouse.HouseTemp < mHouse.MAX_TEMP - 5 Then
        Thread.Sleep(200)
        mHouse.HouseTemp += 5
        Console.WriteLine("Am in " & Me.mName & _
      ".  Current temperature is " & mHouse.HouseTemp)
```

```
      ElseIf mHouse.HouseTemp < mHouse.MAX_TEMP Then
        Thread.Sleep(200)
        mHouse.HouseTemp += 1
        Console.WriteLine("Am in " & Me.mName & _
      ".  Current temperature is " & mHouse.HouseTemp)
      Else
        Console.WriteLine("Am in " & Me.mName & _
     ".  Current temperature is " & mHouse.HouseTemp)
        'Do nothing temp OK
      End If
    Catch tie As ThreadInterruptedException
      'thread interrupted
    Catch e As Exception
      'other exception
    End Try
  End SyncLock
End Sub
```

The code in a `SyncLock` block is treated atomically. No other thread will be let into this code until the first thread relinquishes the lock by executing the `End SyncLock` statement. Note that if the thread is sleeping in a synchronized block, it holds the lock until it wakes up or is interrupted.

CAUTION *The proper use of* `SyncLock` *makes your code thread safe. Unfortunately, the overuse of* `SyncLock` *can lead to performance problems. When you synchronize a block of code in a multithreaded program, that code runs many times slower. Lock only the code that must be locked, and release the lock as soon as possible.*

TIP *Working with the basic collection classes is not thread safe, but the .NET Framework comes with thread-safe versions of most of the collection classes. These classes wrap the code for the various dangerous methods with* `SyncLocks`*. Use the thread-safe versions of the collection classes in your multithreaded programs whenever there is a danger of data corruption.*

Finally, you can easily use the SyncLock statement to create a condition variable. Merely set up a shared read-write Boolean property in a synchronized property, as in this code:

```
Public Class ConditionVariable
Private Shared locker As Object = New Object()
  Private Shared mOK As Boolean
  Shared Property TheConditionVariable() As Boolean
    Get
      Return mOK
    End Get
    Set(ByVal Value As Boolean)
      SyncLock (locker)
        mOK = Value
      End SyncLock
    End Set
  End Property
End Class
```

More on SyncLock *and the* Monitor *Class*

The SyncLock statement is quite a bit more subtle then its use in the simple example above shows. The key is your choice of object reference to lock. Before we explain why, rerun the code with the following SyncLock statement:

```
SyncLock (Me)
```

instead of:

```
SyncLock (mHouse)
```

The result: cooked again!

The point you have to keep in mind is that a lock is associated with the *object* used as the parameter in the SyncLock statement, and not with a piece of code. It is as if the object used as the parameter in the SyncLock statement is acting as a door to the other threads. When you used SyncLock(Me) you were, in effect, providing ten different doors to the code—which was exactly what you did not want to do. In other words:

- To guard shared data, the threads accessing the shared data must SyncLock on the *same* object.

Because a lock is associated with an object, it is possible to inadvertently lock down multiple blocks of code. For example, suppose you have two synchronized methods called `first` and `second`, and both are locked down by a `bigLock` object. When thread 1 enters the `first` method and grabs `bigLock`, no other thread can enter the second method, because its lock is already owned by the first thread!

The `SyncLock` statement is a shorthand means of gaining access to the basic power of the `Monitor` class, which lets you fine-tune synchronization and helps you handle more sophisticated synchronization problems. Using `SyncLock` is roughly equivalent to using the `Enter` and `Exit` methods in the `Monitor` class, like this:

```
Try
  Monitor.Enter(theObject)
Finally
  Monitor.Exit(theObject)
End Try
```

> **TIP** *For the common situations where you are either incrementing or decrementing a variable or exchanging the contents of two variables, the .NET Framework provides the* `Interlocked` *class, whose methods do these common operations atomically. Using the* `Interlocked` *class is much faster than using a* `SyncLock`.

Deadlock: The Danger of Synchronization

Because locks belong to objects and not to code, you may encounter some very subtle problems if you use *different* objects to lock down *different* pieces of code. (Which, unfortunately, is sometimes necessary—threads will be blocked too often if too many pieces of synchronized code are locked by the same object.)

Here is a deadlock situation stripped down to its barest essentials: Imagine two programmers sitting down to eat a meal. Unfortunately, there is only one knife and one fork. Assuming you must have both a fork and a knife to eat, then there are two possible situations:

- One person manages to grab both the fork and the knife before the other person does and gets to eat some food. When that person is finished, he puts both utensils down and the other person can grab them and eat.
- Each person grabs one utensil. This means nobody can eat until one person relinquishes a utensil.

In a multithreaded program, this situation is called a *deadlock* (or a *deadly embrace*). You have two synchronized methods locked by *different* objects. Thread A grabs a lock on object 1 by entering the code it guards. Unfortunately, it also needs to run the code guarded by another `SyncLock` block that uses a different object. Before it can enter the code guarded by the second object, thread B enters the code and grabs that lock. Now thread A cannot enter the second piece of code, thread B cannot enter the first piece of code, and both sit around waiting forever. Neither thread can continue, because the lock each needs never gets released.

CAUTION *One of the problems with detecting deadlocks is that they may not happen very often. Deadlocks always depend on the order in which threads are scheduled. It may be that, most of the time, the locks are not grabbed in the order that causes a deadlock.*

Here is an implementation of the deadlock situation we described. After discussing the key points, we will show you how the Threads window helps you recognize the deadlock we cause here:

```
Option Strict On
Imports System.Threading
Module Module1
  Sub Main()
    Dim Tom As New Programmer("Tom")
    Dim Bob As New Programmer("Bob")
    Dim aThreadStart As New ThreadStart(AddressOf Tom.Eat)
    Dim aThread As New Thread(aThreadStart)
    aThread.Name = "Tom"
    Dim bThreadStart As New ThreadStart(AddressOf Bob.Eat)
    Dim bThread As New Thread(bThreadStart)
    bThread.Name = "Bob"
    aThread.Start()
    bThread.Start()
  End Sub
End Module

Public Class Fork
  Private Shared mForkAvailable As Boolean = True
  Private Shared mOwner As String = "Nobody"
```

```
  Private ReadOnly Property OwnsUtensil() As String
    Get
      Return mOwner
    End Get
  End Property

  Public Sub GrabFork(ByVal a As Programmer)
    Console.WriteLine(Thread.CurrentThread.Name & _
    " trying to grab the fork.")
    Console.WriteLine(Me.OwnsUtensil & " has the fork.")
    Monitor.Enter(Me) 'SyncLock (aFork) '
    If mForkAvailable Then
      a.HasFork = True
      mOwner = a.MyName
      mForkAvailable = False
      Console.WriteLine(a.MyName & " just got the fork, waiting")
      Try
           Thread.Sleep(100)
       Catch e As Exception
           Console.WriteLine (e.StackTrace)
        End Try
    End If
    Monitor.Exit(Me) 'End SyncLock
  End Sub
End Class

Public Class Knife
  Private Shared mKnifeAvailable As Boolean = True
  Private Shared mOwner As String = "Nobody"

  Private ReadOnly Property OwnsUtensil() As String
    Get
      Return mOwner
    End Get
  End Property
```

```
  Public Sub GrabKnife(ByVal a As Programmer)
    Console.WriteLine(Thread.CurrentThread.Name & _
    " trying to grab the knife.")
    Console.WriteLine(Me.OwnsUtensil & " has the knife.")
    Monitor.Enter(Me) 'SyncLock (aKnife) '
    If mKnifeAvailable Then
      mKnifeAvailable = False
      a.HasKnife = True
      mOwner = a.MyName
      Console.WriteLine(a.MyName & " just got the knife, waiting")
      Try
           Thread.Sleep(100)
       Catch e As Exception
           Console.WriteLine (e.StackTrace)
        End Try
    End If
    Monitor.Exit(Me)
  End Sub
End Class

Public Class Programmer
  Private mName As String
  Private Shared mFork As Fork
  Private Shared mKnife As Knife
  Private mHasKnife As Boolean
  Private mHasFork As Boolean

  Shared Sub New()
    mFork = New Fork()
    mKnife = New Knife()
  End Sub

  Public Sub New(ByVal theName As String)
    mName = theName
  End Sub

  Public ReadOnly Property MyName() As String
    Get
      Return mName
    End Get
  End Property
```

```
79    Public Property HasKnife() As Boolean
80      Get
81        Return mHasKnife
82      End Get
83      Set(ByVal Value As Boolean)
84        mHasKnife = Value
85      End Set
86    End Property

87    Public Property HasFork() As Boolean
88      Get
89        Return mHasFork
90      End Get
91      Set(ByVal Value As Boolean)
92        mHasFork = Value
93      End Set
94    End Property

95    Public Sub Eat()
96      Do Until Me.HasKnife And Me.HasFork
97        Console.WriteLine(Thread.CurrentThread.Name & " is in the thread.")
98        If Rnd() < 0.5 Then
99          mFork.GrabFork(Me)
100        Else
101          mKnife.GrabKnife(Me)
102        End If
103     Loop
104     MsgBox(Me.MyName & " can eat!")
105     mKnife = New Knife()
106     mFork = New Fork()
107   End Sub
108 End Class
```

Our `Main` method (lines **4–16**) sets up two instances of the `Programmer` class and then starts up two separate threads to run the crucial `Eat` method contained in the `Programmer` class (lines **95–108**), which we discuss shortly. This code names and starts the threads and should be familiar to you by now.

The more interesting code is contained in the similar `Fork` (lines **17–38**) and `Knife` classes (lines **39–60**). For example, in lines **18** and **19** we set up shared instance fields to let us know if the utensil is available and who has it if it is not. The read-only `OwnsUtensil` property (lines **20–24**) is a straightforward reporting property. The key method is the one that grabs the utensil (lines **25–27**).

Lines **26** and **27** merely report on what is happening. In the vital synchronized code (lines **28–36**), we guard the fork using the `Me` object variable. Because we wrote this program so that there is only one fork, this has the effect of making sure two threads cannot grab the fork at the same time. The `Sleep` command (the block defined on line **34**) imitates the lag that one might expect after grabbing the utensil. Keep in mind that `Sleep` does not release any lock being held and thereby increases the speed at which a program deadlocks!

The most interesting code is, of course, contained in the `Programmer` class (lines **61–108**). In lines **67–70** we use a *shared* constructor to ensure that there is only one fork and one knife in this program. The code for the properties (lines **74–94**) is straightforward. The `Eat` method is where all the action is, because this method is run by the two separate threads. The loop allows the process to continue until somebody can eat with both a knife and a fork. The call to `Rnd` in lines **98–102** models someone randomly picking up a utensil—this is actually what *causes* the deadlock. It goes like this:

1. The thread for Tom's `Eat` method wakes up and starts the loop. It then grabs the knife and the lock for the knife and goes to sleep.

2. Then the thread for Bob's `Eat` method wakes up and starts the loop. It cannot grab the knife but it can grab the fork and the lock for the fork.

3. The thread for Tom's `Eat` method wakes up and continues the loop. It tries to grab the fork but it is already grabbed by Bob so it goes to sleep.

4. The thread for Bob's `Eat` method wakes up and continues the loop. It tries to grab the knife but it is already grabbed by Tom so it goes to sleep.

This continues forever and we have a deadlock. (And if you actually run the code you will see that nobody gets to eat.)

The Threads window helps confirm the deadlock: run the program and then use Ctrl+Break to stop the program. Add a watch for the `Me` variable and open up the Threads window. The result should look like Figure 10-7. As you can see, the Bob thread is running and Bob has the knife but does not have the fork. Now right-click in the Threads window on the Tom thread and choose Switch to Thread. You can see that the Watch window shows that Tom has the fork but not the knife. While this is not conclusive proof of a deadlock, this kind of behavior should make you very suspicious that this is the problem!

> **TIP** *The best way to avoid deadlock in multithreaded code (if you cannot lock on a single object such as our house object in the first synchronization example), is to somehow number the locks and acquire the locks in the same order that you use them. For example, continuing the meal analogy, if somebody must always have the knife before they can grab the fork, then there is no problem. Whoever grabs the knife first gets to eat. Translating this to the language of threads, you cannot grab the lock on object 2 unless you already have the lock on object 1.*

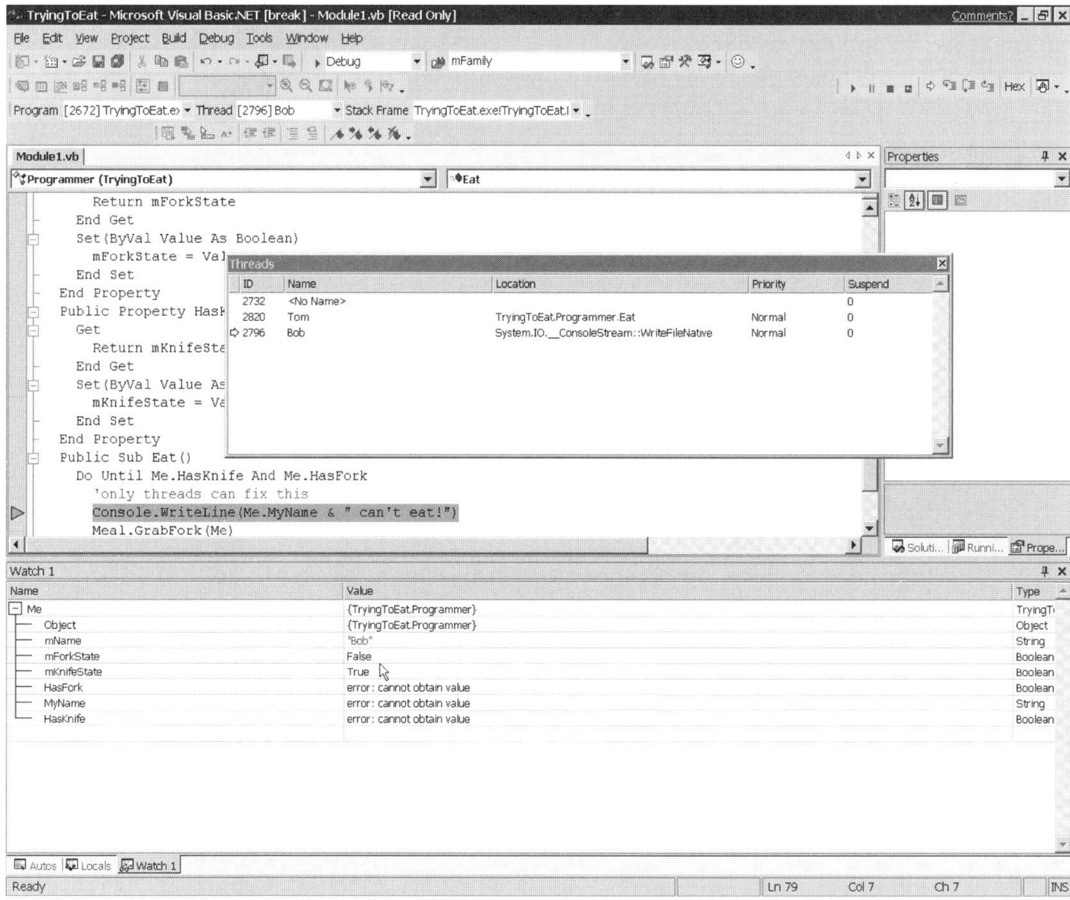

Figure 10-7. Analyzing a deadlock

Interestingly, the preceding tip means that if we did not have the call to `Rnd` in line **98** and instead used this code:

```
mFork.GrabFork(Me)
mKnife.GrabKnife(Me)
```

there would have been no deadlock!

Sharing Data as It Is Produced

One common problem in thread programming arises when you have a program where not only is the data shared, but you *have* to wait for it to be produced by thread 1 before thread 2 can use it. Because the data is shared, you must synchronize in order to avoid data corruption. You also need a way to provide notification to the other threads when the data is produced.

This situation is often called the *producer-consumer problem.* A thread tries to work with data but it is not there yet, so it must yield to another thread that produces what it needs. To solve this, you need to write code to perform this process:

- The consumer thread, thread 1, wakes up, enters a synchronized method, looks for data, does not find it, and so waits. But it must release its lock to the producer thread for any progress to be made.
- The producer thread, thread 2, enters the (now unlocked) synchronized method, *produces* the data needed by thread 1, and (somehow) notifies thread 1 that it produced the data. It must then yield the lock to thread 1 so thread 1 can consume the data.

> **CAUTION** *Do not attempt to solve this problem by constantly waking up thread 1 in order to check the status of a condition variable set by thread 2, which in turn is constantly being put to sleep. If you choose this approach, the performance of your code will suffer, because most of the time thread 1 will have woken up for no good reason and thread 2 will be asleep so often that it won't have time to produce the data.*

Because a producer-consumer relationship is so common, multithreaded programming frameworks come with primitives for dealing with this situation. In .NET, the primitives are called `Wait` and `Pulse-PulseAll`, and are part of the `Monitor` class. Figure 10-8 describes the idiom we will soon be coding. Notice in Figure 10-8 that there are three queues for the threads involved in this kind of program: a "wait" queue, a "blocked" queue and a "runnable" queue for threads that are just waiting but not blocked. (They would get blocked if they try to enter the sync locked code, of course.) Threads in the wait queue are not given any time by the thread scheduler: they must move to the blocked but runnable queue before the scheduler can give them time. This makes the whole process much more efficient than polling a condition variable.

The pseudo code for the consumer idiom looks like this:

```
'Enters Synchronized Block which should be of this form
While no data;
  go to wait queue
Loop
  if the data is there, consume the data.
End of Synchronized Block
```

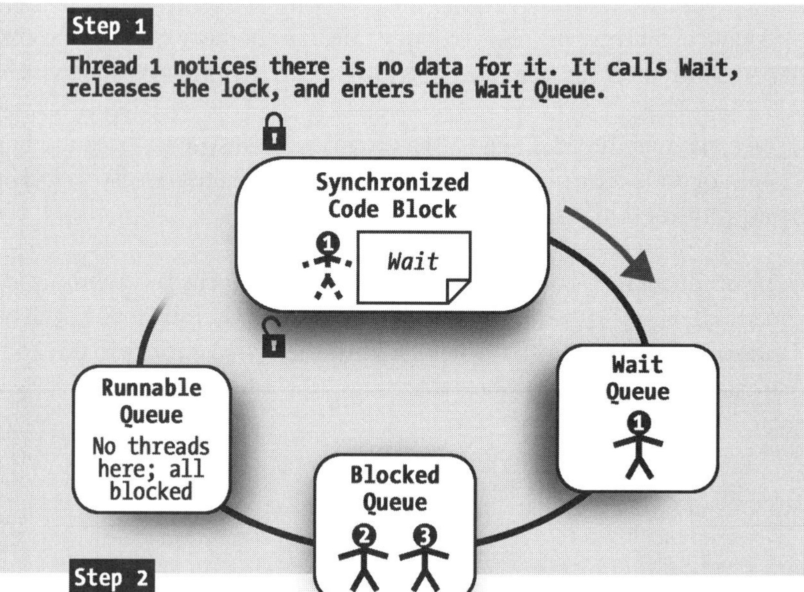
Step 1
Thread 1 notices there is no data for it. It calls Wait, releases the lock, and enters the Wait Queue.
Synchronized Code Block
Wait
Wait Queue
Runnable Queue
No threads here; all blocked
Blocked Queue
Step 2
When the lock is released, either threads 2 or 3 can leave the blocked queue and enter the code block, grabbing the lock.

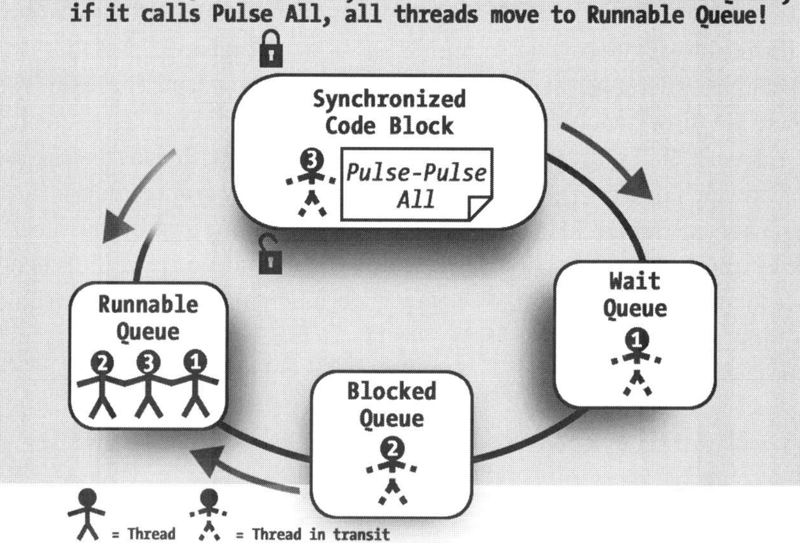
Step 3
Suppose thread 3 enters the code block and produces data and then calls to Pulse-Pulse All. As soon as it leaves the block this opens the lock and moves thread 1 to the Runnable Queue. If thread 3 calls Pulse, one thread moves to Runnable Queue; if it calls Pulse All, all threads move to Runnable Queue!
Synchronized Code Block
Pulse-Pulse All
Wait Queue
Runnable Queue
Blocked Queue
= Thread
= Thread in transit

Figure 10-8. The producer-consumer problem

As soon as the Wait command is processed, the thread is suspended, the lock is released, and the thread goes to the wait queue. Once the lock is released, a thread in the runnable queue eventually gets a chance to run. Presumably, one or more of the blocked but now runnable threads will produce the data needed by the thread that is now in the wait queue. Also notice that, by testing for the data in a loop, we get to the line to consume the data (the line after the loop) only when data is available to be consumed.

The pseudo code for the producer idiom looks like this:

```
'Enters Synchronized Block which should be of this form
While data is NOT needed
     wait (go to wait queue)
else produce data
When the data is produced call to Pulse-PulseAll to move one or all of the threads
in the "wait queue" from the blocked queue to the runnable queue
Leave synchronized block (and then go back to the runnable queue)
```

For our code example, imagine modeling a family with one parent who produces all the money and a child who spends all the money produced. Of course, once the money is gone, the child has to wait until there is more money to spend. Here is the code:

```
Option Strict On
Imports System.Threading
Module Module1
  Sub Main()
    Dim theFamily As New Family()
    theFamily.StartItsLife()
  End Sub
End Module

Public Class Family
  Private mMoney As Integer
  Private mWeek As Integer = 1
  Public Sub StartItsLife()
    Dim aThreadStart As New ThreadStart(AddressOf Me.Produce)
    Dim bThreadStart As New ThreadStart(AddressOf Me.Consume)
    Dim aThread As New Thread(aThreadStart)
    Dim bThread As New Thread(bThreadStart)
    aThread.Name = "Produce"
    aThread.Start()
    bThread.Name = "Consume"
    bThread.Start()
  End Sub
```

```
  Public Property TheWeek() As Integer
    Get
      Return mWeek
    End Get
    Set(ByVal Value As Integer)
      mWeek = Value
    End Set
  End Property
  Public Property OurMoney() As Integer
    Get
      Return mMoney
    End Get
    Set(ByVal Value As Integer)
      mMoney = Value
    End Set
  End Property
  Public Sub Produce()
    Thread.Sleep(500)
    Do
      Monitor.Enter(Me)
      Do While Me.OurMoney > 0
        Monitor.Wait(Me)
      Loop
      Me.OurMoney = 1000
      Monitor.PulseAll(Me)
      Monitor.Exit(Me)
    Loop
  End Sub
  Public Sub Consume()
    MsgBox("Am in consume thread")
    Do
      Monitor.Enter(Me)
      Do While Me.OurMoney = 0
        Monitor.Wait(Me)
      Loop
      Console.WriteLine("Dear parent I just spent all your money in week " _
      & TheWeek)
      TheWeek += 1
      If TheWeek = 21 * 52 Then System.Environment.Exit(0)
      Me.OurMoney = 0
      Monitor.PulseAll(Me)
      Monitor.Exit(Me)
    Loop
  End Sub
End Class
```

The StartItsLife method (lines **13–22**) does the bookkeeping needed to start up the Produce and Consume threads. The key behavior occurs in the Produce (lines **39–50**) and Consume (lines **51–65**) threads themselves. The Produce Sub determines whether money is available, and if there is, it goes to the wait queue. If not, the parent generates some more money (line **46**) and then notifies the objects in the wait queue that it has changed the situation. Note that a Pulse-PulseAll has no effect until the Monitor.Exit command (which releases the lock) is processed. Conversely, the Consume Sub waits if there is no money to be spent and notifies the waiting parent when he or she has spent all the money. Line **60** is merely a cute way to end the program after the equivalent of 21 years: System.Environment.Exit(0) is the .NET equivalent of End (which you can also use, although End does not return a value to the OS as System.Environment.Exit does.)

CAUTION *Once you put threads in the wait queue, another part of your program must release them. This is why we prefer using* PulseAll *instead of* Pulse. *Because you cannot be sure what thread* Pulse *wakes up,*[2] *you might as well use* PulseAll *if you do not have too many threads waiting in the queue.*

Multithreading a GUI Program

To get started with multithreading a GUI application, we want to show you why they are often needed. Create a form with two buttons, Start (btnStart) and Cancel (btnCancel), as in Figure 10-9. When you click on the start button, you create a class that encapsulates a random string with ten million characters, and which also has the ability to count the number of E's in the ten million character string. Notice the use of the StringBuilder utility class to increase the efficiency of creating a ten million character string).

2. Some people say that Pulse uses a first-in, first-out notification scheme. This is unusual, so we asked a person who handles threads on Microsoft's .NET team and were told in no uncertain terms that this is *not* guaranteed.

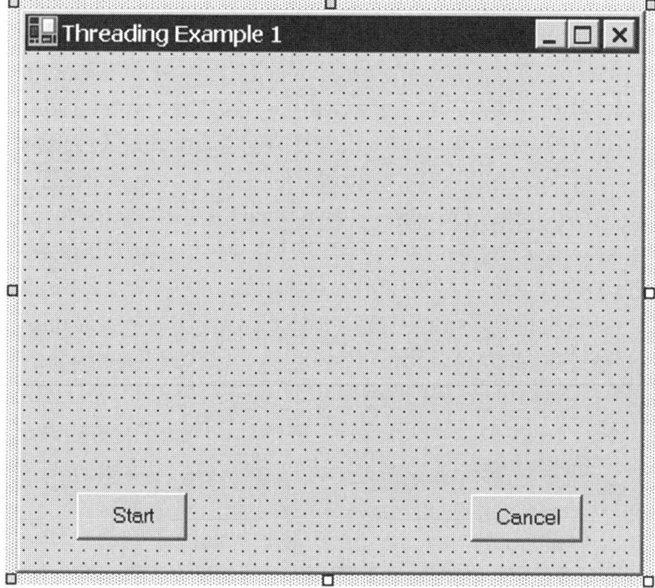

Figure 10-9. Multithreading a simple GUI application

```
Imports System.Text
Public Class RandomCharacters
  Private m_Data As StringBuilder
  Private m_CountDone As Boolean
  Private m_length, m_count As Integer
  Public Sub New(ByVal n As Integer)
    m_length = n - 1
    m_Data = New StringBuilder(m_length)
    MakeString()
  End Sub
  Private Sub MakeString()
    Dim i As Integer
    Dim myRnd As New Random()
    For i = 0 To m_length
'get a random number between 65 and 90, convert it to a capital letter
'add it to the string builder object
      m_Data.Append(Chr(myRnd.Next(65, 90)))
    Next
  End Sub
  Public Sub StartCount()
    GetEes()
  End Sub
```

```
  Private Sub GetEes()
    Dim i As Integer
    For i = 0 To m_length
      If m_Data.Chars(i) = CChar("E") Then
        m_count += 1
      End If
    Next
    m_CountDone = True
  End Sub
  Public ReadOnly Property GetCount() As Integer
    Get
      If Not (m_CountDone) Then
        Throw New Exception("Count not yet done")
      Else
        Return m_count
      End If
    End Get
  End Property
  Public ReadOnly Property IsDone() As Boolean
    Get
      Return m_CountDone
    End Get
  End Property
End Class
```

The GUI code for the two buttons is straightforward. In the `btnStart_Click` procedure, we create an instance of the previous class encapsulating the ten million character string:

```
Private Sub btnStart_Click(ByVal sender As System.Object, _
ByVal e As System.EventArgs) Handles btnSTart.Click
  Dim RC As New RandomCharacters(10000000)
  RC.StartCount()
  MsgBox("The number of e's is " & RC.GetCount)
End Sub
```

and the cancel button displays a message box:

```
Private Sub btnCancel_Click(ByVal sender As System.Object, _
ByVal e As System.EventArgs) Handles btnCancel.Click
  MsgBox("Count Interrupted!")
End Sub
```

If you run the code, you will find that the cancel button is unresponsive. This is because the tight counting loop is preventing the event from being passed onto the button. This is unacceptable behavior in a modern program!

There are two solutions. The first, which avoids multithreading, is to do what you did in earlier versions of VB: add a call to `DoEvents` in the counting code that uses the big loop. It takes this form in .NET:

```
Application.DoEvents()
```

This is overkill—you do not want ten million calls to `DoEvents` slowing down your code! Instead, if you make the class that counts the code work in a *separate* thread, the operating system switches back and forth and your cancel button stays responsive. Here is the code that spins everything off to a different thread. To make it clear that the Cancel button really is working, we have it end the program:

```
Private Sub btnStart_Click(ByVal sender As System.Object, _
ByVal e As System.EventArgs) Handles btnStart.Click
    Dim RC As New RandomCharacters(10000000)
    Dim aThreadStart As New ThreadStart(AddressOf RC.StartCount)
    Dim aThread As New Thread(aThreadStart)
    aThread.Priority = ThreadPriority.BelowNormal
    aThread.Start()
  End Sub
  Private Sub btnCancel_Click(ByVal sender As System.Object, _
  ByVal e As System.EventArgs) Handles btnCancel.Click
    System.Environment.Exit(0)
  End Sub
End Class
```

The Next Step: Adding a Show Count Button

Suppose you decide to get a little fancy by making your form look like Figure 10-9. Notice how the Show Count button is disabled.

You need to have the thread do the counting and enable the button when it finishes the count. This is certainly possible and in fact is quite a common desire. Unfortunately, what you cannot do is proceed in the obvious fashion of having the secondary thread communicate back to the GUI thread by keeping a reference to the `ShowCount` button in its constructor or even use a standard delegate. In other words, you should *never* use code like this (the key *bad* lines are in bold):

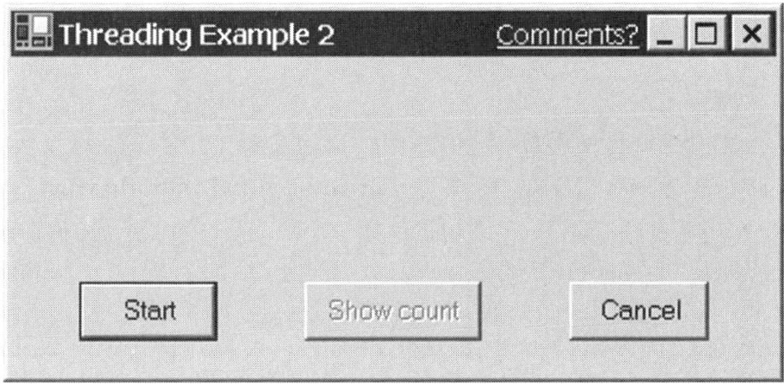

Figure 10-10. A form with a disabled button

```
Public Class RandomCharacters
  Private m_Data As StringBuilder
  Private m_CountDone As Boolean
  Private m_length, m_count As Integer
  Private m_Button As Windows.Forms.Button
  Public Sub New(ByVal n As Integer, ByVal b As Windows.Forms.Button)
    m_length = n - 1
    m_Data = New StringBuilder(m_length)
    m_Button = b
    MakeString()
  End Sub
  Private Sub MakeString()
    Dim I As Integer
    Dim myRnd As New Random()
    For I = 0 To m_length
      m_Data.Append(Chr(myRnd.Next(65, 90)))
    Next
  End Sub
  Public Sub StartCount()
    GetEes()
  End Sub
  Private Sub GetEes()
    Dim I As Integer
    For I = 0 To m_length
      If m_Data.Chars(I) = CChar("E") Then
        m_count += 1
      End If
    Next
    m_CountDone = True
    m_Button.Enabled = True
  End Sub
```

```
  Public ReadOnly Property GetCount() As Integer
    Get
      If Not (m_CountDone) Then
        Throw New Exception("Count not yet done")
      Else
        Return m_count
      End If
    End Get
  End Property
  Public ReadOnly Property IsDone() As Boolean
    Get
      Return m_CountDone
    End Get
  End Property
End Class
```

Here is the problem:

- This code may run most of the time.

However:

- You cannot use any *obvious* method of communicating from a secondary thread back into a thread that created a GUI.

- *Never* write code that modifies controls in a GUI-based program from a thread different than the one that created the GUI.

If you violate this rule:

- We *guarantee* that your multithreaded GUI-based programs will be filled with subtle, almost undetectable bugs.

> **NOTE** *When an event is raised from one object to another object, the event handler executes on the same thread that the* `RaiseEvent` *occurred in, so events will not help you either.*

Still, you obviously have to have a way to communicate to a GUI-based application from a thread different than the one that created it. The .NET Framework gives you a thread-safe way to call into a GUI application from another thread. You do this using a special kind of delegate called `MethodInvoker`, which is part of the `System.Windows.Forms` namespace. This code modifies the `GetEes` method (the lines in bold indicate what you have to do):

```
Private Sub GetEes()
  Dim I As Integer
  For I = 0 To m_length
    If m_Data.Chars(I) = CChar("E") Then
      m_count += 1
    End If
  Next
  m_CountDone = True
  Try
    Dim myInvoker As New MethodInvoker(AddressOf UpDateButton)
    myInvoker.Invoke()
  Catch e As ThreadInterruptedException
    'oops
  End Try
  End Sub
  Public Sub UpDateButton()
  m_Button.Enabled = True
End Sub
```

The call to the GUI button made across threads is done with a `MethodInvoker`, rather than being done directly. The framework guarantees that this is thread-safe.

Why Is Multithreading Programming *So* Confusing?

Now that you have played a little with multithreading programming and have been warned so often about its potential problems, we thought it fitting to end this chapter with our answer to this question.

One reason is that multithreading is a nonlinear process, and we are much more comfortable with linear programming models. The idea of code execution being interrupted randomly so that other code can run is just plain hard to absorb.

But there is a more fundamental reason for the confusion caused by multithreaded programming: Most of us rarely program in assembly language anymore or, for that matter, even look very often at the assembly language output of the compilers we use! If we did, then it would be easier for all of us to keep in mind that:

- A single instruction in a high-level language like VB .NET can correspond to *dozens* of assembly language instructions. Thus, a thread can be interrupted after *any* one of these instructions and hence during a high-level instruction.

It gets worse: Modern compilers are designed to optimize performance, and hardware can manage memory as well. A consequence of this is that:

- The order of your original source code may, in effect, be *rearranged* by the compiler or the hardware without you knowing it.[3]

We think both these points go a long way toward explaining why multithreading programming is so confusing and so hard to think about correctly. But if you keep these two points in mind, then you will at least be *less* surprised at the behavior of your multithreaded programs!

---

3. Many compilers rearrange instructions like the ones in this loop for copying arrays : for `i = 0` to `n:b(i) = a(i):next`. A compiler (or even special purpose memory management hardware) may simply create the first array and then copy it with one block copy instead of multiple individual copies!

CHAPTER 11

A Brief Introduction to Database Access with VB .NET

THIS BRIEF CHAPTER IS DESIGNED to orient you only; it is impossible in the space we have to even briefly survey, let alone discuss, *all* the power that VB .NET brings to database access. To go further with this important topic, we recommend Carsten Thomsen's *Database Programming with Visual Basic .NET* (Apress, 2001. ISBN: 1-893115-29-1). We think Thomsen's book is the natural continuation of this book—it is roughly the same length and written at about the same level. We also think it covers all the essential topics you will need to know about programming database access using VB .NET. Thomsen covers the advantages and disadvantages of using data-bound controls to access a database, which is an interesting topic that we do not have the space to address here. To see how to best combine classic ADO with ADO .NET, we recommend the second edition of Bill Vaughn's *ADO Examples and Best Practices* (also from Apress) which should be available in early 2002.

> **TIP** *To see the data bound controls at work, we recommend running the Data Form wizard. Also, looking at the code this wizard generates is a useful way to understand more about the power VB .NET supplies in the database arena.*

Why ADO .NET Is Not ADO++

With each version of VB came a different model for accessing a database. VB .NET follows in this tradition with a whole new way of accessing data: ADO .NET. This means ADO .NET is horribly misnamed. Why? Because it is hardly the next generation of ADO! In fact, it is a completely different model for accessing data than classic ADO. In particular, you must learn a new object model based on a `DataSet` object for your results. (Because they are not tied to a single table, ADO .NET `DataSet` objects are far more capable than ADO `RecordSet` objects, for example.)

In addition, ADO .NET:

- Is designed as a completely disconnected architecture (although the `DataAdapter`, `Connection`, `Command`, and `DataReader` classes are still connection-oriented).
- Does not support server-side cursors. ADO's dynamic cursors are no longer available.
- Is XML-based[1] (which lets you work over the Internet, even if the client sits behind a firewall).
- Is part of the .NET `System.Data.DLL` assembly, rather than being language-based.
- Is unlikely to support legacy Windows 95 clients.

The other interesting point is that in order to have essential features such as two-phase commit, you need to use Enterprise Services (which is basically COM+/MTS with a .NET wrapper).

Disconnected Data Sets: The New Way to Use Databases

In VB6, a typical database application opened a connection to the database and then used that connection for all queries for the life of the program. In VB .NET, database access through ADO .NET usually depends on *disconnected* (detached) data access. This is a fancy way of saying that you most often ask for the data from a database and then, after your program retrieves the data, the connection is dropped. With ADO .NET, you are very unlikely to have a persistent connection to a data source. (You can continue to use persistent connections through "classic" ADO using the COM/Interop facilities of .NET with the attendant scalability problems that classic ADO always had.)

Because data is usually disconnected, a typical .NET database application has to reconnect to the database for each query it executes. At first, this seems like a big step backward, but it really is not. The old way of maintaining a connection is not really practical for a distributed world: if your application opens a connection to a database and then *leaves it open*, the server has to maintain that connection until the client closes it. With heavily loaded servers pushing googles of bits of data, maintaining all those per-client connections is very costly in terms of bandwidth.

1. Internally, ADO .NET data classes use an optimized format, but XML is used for all data exchange.

Furthermore, a different computer may handle each query you make of a Web farm. (A *Web farm* is group of computers that handle traffic for a single URL—most large sites use Web farms so they can be scalable.) Persistent connections to a Web farm are useless, because you do not know which server you will be hitting for subsequent requests.

The Classes in System.Data.DLL

The `System.Data.DLL` assembly contains a huge number of classes divided into five data namespaces plus the `System.Xml` namespace. The `System.Data.SqlTypes` is a utility namespace that contains the value types that correspond to the data types in SQL Server, such as `SqlMoney` or `SqlDateTime`.

> **NOTE** *Because SQL data types are implemented as value types, translation back and forth into SQL is quite efficient compared to languages such as Java, in which the corresponding SQL types are implemented as reference types.*

The other utility namespace, `System.Data.Common`, contains the common classes you use to access a data source. In this chapter, we focus on the `System.Data.OleDb` and `System.Data.SqlClient` namespaces, which actually do the work They access functionality in `System.Data.Common`, such as the `DataAdapter` class. The `DataAdapter` class represents the data commands and the database connection used to fill data sets or update the data source.

> **NOTE** `System.Data.OleDb` *and* `System.Data.SqlClient` *are similar in functionality, except that the classes in the* `System.Data.OleDb` *namespace connect to OLE DB data sources, whereas the ones in* `System.Data.SqlClient` *namespace are for use with Microsoft SQL Server 7.0 or later.*

System.Data.OleDb

The `System.Data.OleDb` namespace contains the classes needed to communicate with an OLE DB–compliant database, such as Microsoft Access or Microsoft Fox Pro. Your program will usually work with the `OleDbConnection`, `OleDbCommand`, and `OleDbDataReader` classes in this namespace. Here are brief descriptions of these important classes:

`OleDbConnection` class: Think of this class as representing a connection to an OLE DB data source, including any properties necessary to connect to the database, such as the OLE DB provider, username, and password. Once connected, the instance of this class contains additional metadata about the database to which it has been connected.

`OleDbCommand` class: This class represents SQL statements that you execute against the OLE DB database, including the SQL statement itself plus any parameters or additional information about how to execute the query.

`OleDbDataReader` class: This class is useful only after you have retrieved the data from the data source using the two classes just described. It is a specialized form of read-only reader (see Chapter 9 on I/O) that knows how to read data returned from an `OleDbCommand` object. Think of a `DataReader` object as a read-only, forward movement only, server-side recordset in ADO.

Here is an example of these three classes in a simple application that connects to the Northwind example database supplied with Access and current versions of SQL Server:

```
Imports System.Data.OleDb
Module Module1
  Sub Main()
    Dim myAccessConn As OleDbConnection
    Dim dbReader As OleDbDataReader
    Dim dbCmd As OleDbCommand = New OleDbCommand( _
"SELECT Employees.FirstName, Employees.LastName FROM Employees")
    Try
      'open the connection
      myAccessConn = New OleDbConnection( _
 "Provider=Microsoft.Jet.OLEDB.4.0;" & _
 "Data Source=C:\Program Files\Microsoft _
  Office\Office\Samples\Northwind.mdb")
      myAccessConn.Open()
      dbCmd.Connection = myAccessConn
      dbReader = dbCmd.ExecuteReader(CommandBehavior.SingleResult)
      Do While dbReader.Read()
        Console.WriteLine(dbReader.GetString(0) & " " & _
        dbReader.GetString(1))
      Loop
      Console.ReadLine()
    Catch e As Exception
      MsgBox(e.Message)
    End Try
  End Sub
End Module
```

After running this application, you will see the results shown in Figure 11-1.

Figure 11-1. Results of a simple SQL query

Although this application merely lists the employees at Northwind, the code is typical of connecting to a database using the OleDb .NET provider supplied with VB .NET. We first `Import` the `System.Data.OleDb` namespace to simplify typing. Lines **4** and **5** declare two object variables. An `OleDbConnection` object encapsulates the current connection to the `OleDb` provider and thus eventually to the database (lines **10–12**). The `OleDbDataReader` object encapsulates the actual data. Unlike `Recordset` objects, these need not be a single table, although that is, in effect, what we get in this example. Line **6** sets up the SQL query, which is encapsulated in an `OleDbCommand` object. The particular constructor we are using for this object takes a `String` parameter, which is a SQL statement—in our case, about the simplest query possible.

We open the connection to the database in line **10**. Notice that we have to pass the name of the OleDb provider for the database into the constructor. This value is referenced in the Windows Registry and is not part of .NET. (The one we are using here is for the standard provider for Access.) Note that we hardwired the location of the Northwind database using the default location for an Office installation—change this line if your Northwind database is in a different location.

Next, we open the connection. Because this connection could fail for various reasons, we enclose the code that opens and reads from the database in a `Try-Catch` block. Once the call to `Open()` is successful (line **13**), we have a valid connection to the database. (You can also do these steps in the constructor and save a few lines of code.) We then set the connection property for the `OleDbCommand` object to the newly opened database connection in line **14**, because the `OleDbCommand` object has no idea which connection to use until we give it one. One advantage to this approach is that you can reuse the same command object with several connections.

We execute the command using the `ExecuteReader()` method of the `OleDbCommand` object (line **15**). We use the `ExecuteReader` method because the other `Execute` methods allow you to return data as XML and traditional record sets, which is less efficient. In line **15** we pass the enum value `CommandBehavior.SingleResult` as a parameter to the `ExecuteReader` method. The `SingleResult` flag tells the command to get all of the results at once from the database. Other flags let you get a few rows or only one row. We loop through all of the retrieved rows in lines **16–18**.

NOTE *The code we use is analogous to the VB6/ADO code:*

```
Do While Not rs.EOF
  Print rs(0)
  rs.MoveNext()
Loop
```

Notice that the way the data reader uses the `Read()` method prevents the common mistake VB6 ADO programmers often made: forgetting to advance the recordset with the `MoveNext()`. You always work on the same record between calls to `Read()`, which means that once you call `Read()`, you cannot go back to the previous record.

Next, inside the loop, we call a version of the various `GetXXX()` methods on the `OleDbDataReader` object. These calls are used to retrieve the value in the column at the specified index (which is zero-based). This is why

```
dbReader.GetString(1)
```

gets the *second* column's value as a `String`. You can also use the column name instead of the position in the call to `GetString()`, but using the ordinal position is likely to be more efficient.

CAUTION *You must specify the correct column type before you can retrieve its value. This is because we always program with* `Option Strict On` *so lossy type conversions will not be done without a call to a conversion function.*

System.Data.SqlClient

Retrieving data from a SQL Server database is similar: the syntax for the `OleDb` and `SqlClient` namespaces is almost identical. Here is a version of the preceding program that assumes we are working through SQL Server:

```
Imports System.Data.SqlClient
Module Module1
  Sub Main()
    Dim mySQLConnString As String
    Dim mySQLConn As SqlConnection
    Dim dbReader As SqlDataReader
    Dim dbCmd As SqlCommand = New SqlCommand( _
  "SELECT Employees.FirstName, Employees.LastName FROM Employees")
    Try
      mySQLConnString = _
      "uid=test;password=apress;database=northwind;server=Apress"
      mySQLConn = New SqlConnection(mySQLConnString)
      mySQLConn.Open()
      dbCmd.Connection = mySQLConn
      dbReader = dbCmd.ExecuteReader(CommandBehavior.SingleResult)
      Do While dbReader.Read()
        'write the data to the screen
        Console.WriteLine(dbReader.GetString(0) & "," & _
                          dbReader.GetString(1))
      Loop
    Catch e As Exception
      MsgBox(e.Message)
    End Try
    Console.ReadLine()
  End Sub
End Module
```

The key difference (aside from the different class names) is the form of the connection string, which assumes there is a test account with a password of `apress` on a server named `Apress`. The SQL Server connection string requires the user ID, password, server, and database name. We pass the connection string to get a connection object. Finally, as you can imagine, more complicated SQL queries are easy to construct: just build up the query string one piece at a time.

> **TIP** *Although the connection strings are different, the coding model in ADO .NET is the same for both SQL and OLE DB applications—an important advantage. In particular, because of common interfaces such as* `IDbCOnnection`, `IdbCommand`, *and so on, writing generic code is pretty easy in ADO .NET.*

Calling a Stored Procedure

Here is an example of how to use a stored procedure named `getalbumbyname` that takes one parameter, the name of an album, to retrieve from a database we call `albums`:

```
create procedure getalbumbyname
    @albumname varchar(255)
As
    select * from albums where albumname = @albumname
```

We call this using code similar to what we used for querying the Northwind database:

```
Dim dbCmd As SqlCommand = New SqlCommand( _
"execute getalbumbyname 'Operation Mindcrime'")
Try
  mySQLConn = New SqlConnection(
"user id=sa;password=password;" & _
"database=albums;server=i-ri3")
  mySQLConn.Open()
  dbCmd.Connection = mySQLConn
  dbReader = dbCmd.ExecuteReader(CommandBehavior.SingleResult)
'more code
End Try
```

As you can see, the code is pretty much the same as before, except the SQL statement we use to create our `SQLCommand` object is an `execute` statement that calls the `getalbumbyname` stored procedure and passes as a parameter the name of the album we want to get information about. Of course, we need no loop after the call to `ExecuteReader()`, because we know that there will only be one record returned.

> **NOTE** *Instead of passing the parameter for the stored procedure in the statement, you can use the* `Parameters` *collection of the* `SQLCommand` *object to load the parameters. We find it much easier to pass them in the SQL statement itself. Of course, this is only possible if you know the value when you write your code otherwise you need to use the* `Parameters` *collection.*

A More Complete VB .NET Database Application

In this section, we present a GUI application that lets users connect to the SQL database of their choice, execute a query on that database, and display the results of their query in a listbox. For the sake of brevity, we ignore validation of user entries. We use three separate files: two forms (`frmMain` and `frmResults`, shown in Figures 11-2 and 11-3, respectively), and a standard module named `Module1`.

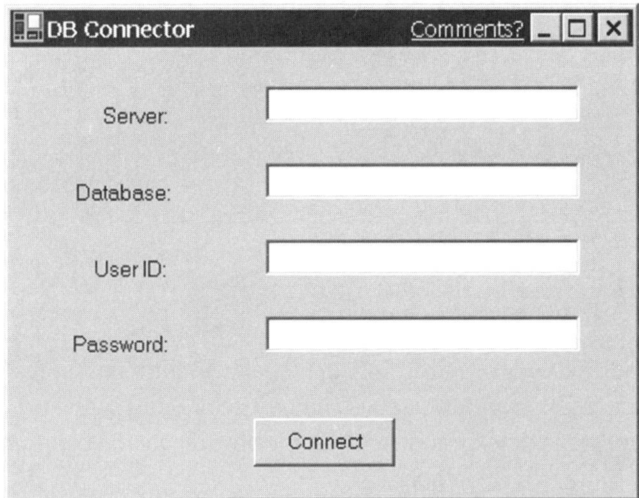

Figure 11-2. The Main form for our database application

Figure 11-3. The Result form for our database application

Although longwinded, this code uses nothing new. The main form has four textboxes that let users enter server name, database name, user ID, and password. When they click the Connect button, the code to dynamically execute the command string is built in the lines shown in bold:

```
'frmMain.vb
Imports System.Data.SqlClient
Public Class frmMain
  Inherits System.Windows.Forms.Form
#Region " Windows Form Designer generated code "
  Public Sub New()
    MyBase.New()
    'This call is required by the Windows Form Designer.
    InitializeComponent()
    'Add any initialization after the InitializeComponent() call
  End Sub
```

```
'Form overrides dispose to clean up the component list.
Protected Overloads Overrides Sub Dispose(ByVal disposing As Boolean)
  If Disposing Then
    If Not (components Is Nothing) Then
      components.Dispose()
    End If
  End If
  MyBase.Dispose(Disposing)
End Sub
Private WithEvents Label1 As System.Windows.Forms.Label
Private WithEvents Label2 As System.Windows.Forms.Label
Private WithEvents Label3 As System.Windows.Forms.Label
Private WithEvents Label4 As System.Windows.Forms.Label
Private WithEvents btnConnect As System.Windows.Forms.Button
Private WithEvents txtUID As System.Windows.Forms.TextBox
Private WithEvents txtPassword As System.Windows.Forms.TextBox
Private WithEvents txtDatabase As System.Windows.Forms.TextBox
Private WithEvents txtServer As System.Windows.Forms.TextBox
'Required by the Windows Form Designer
Private components As System.ComponentModel.Container
'NOTE: The following procedure is required by the Windows Form Designer
'It can be modified using the Windows Form Designer.
'Do not modify it using the code editor.
<System.Diagnostics.DebuggerStepThrough()> Private Sub InitializeComponent()
  Me.Label4 = New System.Windows.Forms.Label()
  Me.txtPassword = New System.Windows.Forms.TextBox()
  Me.Label1 = New System.Windows.Forms.Label()
  Me.txtServer = New System.Windows.Forms.TextBox()
  Me.Label2 = New System.Windows.Forms.Label()
  Me.Label3 = New System.Windows.Forms.Label()
  Me.txtUID = New System.Windows.Forms.TextBox()
  Me.txtDatabase = New System.Windows.Forms.TextBox()
  Me.btnConnect = New System.Windows.Forms.Button()
  Me.SuspendLayout()
  '
  'Label4
  Me.Label4.Location = New System.Drawing.Point(24, 176)
  Me.Label4.Name = "Label4"
  Me.Label4.Size = New System.Drawing.Size(82, 19)
  Me.Label4.TabIndex = 0
  Me.Label4.Text = "Password:"
  Me.Label4.TextAlign = System.Drawing.ContentAlignment.MiddleRight
  '
```

```
'txtPassword
Me.txtPassword.Location = New System.Drawing.Point(168, 168)
Me.txtPassword.Name = "txtPassword"
Me.txtPassword.PasswordChar = ChrW(42)
Me.txtPassword.Size = New System.Drawing.Size(205, 22)
Me.txtPassword.TabIndex = 3
Me.txtPassword.Text = ""
'
'Label1
Me.Label1.Location = New System.Drawing.Point(24, 32)
Me.Label1.Name = "Label1"
Me.Label1.Size = New System.Drawing.Size(82, 20)
Me.Label1.TabIndex = 0
Me.Label1.Text = "Server:"
Me.Label1.TextAlign = System.Drawing.ContentAlignment.MiddleRight
'
'txtServer
Me.txtServer.Location = New System.Drawing.Point(168, 24)
Me.txtServer.Name = "txtServer"
Me.txtServer.Size = New System.Drawing.Size(205, 22)
Me.txtServer.TabIndex = 0
Me.txtServer.Text = ""
'
'Label2
Me.Label2.Location = New System.Drawing.Point(24, 80)
Me.Label2.Name = "Label2"
Me.Label2.Size = New System.Drawing.Size(82, 20)
Me.Label2.TabIndex = 0
Me.Label2.Text = "Database:"
Me.Label2.TextAlign = System.Drawing.ContentAlignment.MiddleRight
'
'Label3
Me.Label3.Anchor = System.Windows.Forms.AnchorStyles.None
Me.Label3.Location = New System.Drawing.Point(24, 128)
Me.Label3.Name = "Label3"
Me.Label3.Size = New System.Drawing.Size(82, 20)
Me.Label3.TabIndex = 0
Me.Label3.Text = "User ID:"
Me.Label3.TextAlign = System.Drawing.ContentAlignment.MiddleRight
'
```

```
    'txtUID
    Me.txtUID.Location = New System.Drawing.Point(168, 120)
    Me.txtUID.Name = "txtUID"
    Me.txtUID.Size = New System.Drawing.Size(205, 22)
    Me.txtUID.TabIndex = 2
    Me.txtUID.Text = ""
    '
    'txtDatabase
    Me.txtDatabase.Location = New System.Drawing.Point(168, 72)
    Me.txtDatabase.Name = "txtDatabase"
    Me.txtDatabase.Size = New System.Drawing.Size(205, 22)
    Me.txtDatabase.TabIndex = 1
    Me.txtDatabase.Text = ""
    '
    'btnConnect
    Me.btnConnect.Location = New System.Drawing.Point(160, 232)
    Me.btnConnect.Name = "btnConnect"
    Me.btnConnect.Size = New System.Drawing.Size(92, 30)
    Me.btnConnect.TabIndex = 4
    Me.btnConnect.Text = "&Connect"
    '
    'frmMain
    Me.AutoScaleBaseSize = New System.Drawing.Size(6, 15)
    Me.ClientSize = New System.Drawing.Size(408, 280)
    Me.Controls.AddRange(New System.Windows.Forms.Control() {Me.btnConnect, _
    Me.txtPassword, Me.txtUID, Me.txtDatabase, Me.txtServer, Me.Label4, _
    Me.Label3, Me.Label2, Me.Label1})
    Me.Name = "frmMain"
    Me.Text = "DB Connector"
    Me.ResumeLayout(False)
  End Sub
#End Region
  Private Sub btnConnect_Click(ByVal sender As System.Object, _
  ByVal e As System.EventArgs) Handles btnConnect.Click
    Try
      mySQLConn = New SqlConnection("user id=" & txtUID.Text & _
                                    ";password=" & txtPassword.Text & _
                                    ";database=" & txtDatabase.Text & _
                                    ";server=" & txtServer.Text)
      mySQLConn.Open()
      dbCmd.Connection = mySQLConn
      Dim frmChild As New frmResults()
      frmChild.Show()
```

```
    Catch except As Exception
      MsgBox( _
"Failed to connect for the following reason: <" & _
except.Message & ">")
    End Try
  End Sub
End Class
```

The `Module` looks like this:

```
Imports System.Data.SqlClient
Module main
    'Global definitions
    Public mySQLConn As SqlConnection
    Public dbReader As SqlDataReader
    Public dbCmd As SqlCommand = New SqlCommand()
End Module
```

> **NOTE** `Module1` *contains only global definitions for the various SQL objects that we want to make available to both forms. Although you usually would not use global data this way in production code, making these SQL objects global lets several forms share them and lets you concentrate on the database part of this code.*

The `frmResults` form is probably the most interesting. Here is the code, which we explain after you have a chance to look at it. The key code is the `btnQuery_Click()`, shown in bold:

```
'frmResults.vb
Imports System.Data.SqlClient
Public Class frmResults
  Inherits System.Windows.Forms.Form
#Region " Windows Form Designer generated code "
   Public Sub New()
  MyBase.New()
   'This call is required by the Windows Form Designer.
  InitializeComponent()
   'Add any initialization after the InitializeComponent() call
   End Sub
```

```
'Form overrides dispose to clean up the component list.
Public Overrides Sub Dispose()
MyBase.Dispose()
If Not (components Is Nothing) Then
components.Dispose()
End If
End Sub
Private WithEvents txtQuery As System.Windows.Forms.TextBox
Private WithEvents btnQuery As System.Windows.Forms.Button
Private WithEvents lstData As System.Windows.Forms.ListBox
'Required by the Windows Form Designer
Private components As System.ComponentModel.Container
'NOTE: The following procedure is required by the Windows Form Designer
'It can be modified using the Windows Form Designer.
'Do not modify it using the code editor.
<System.Diagnostics.DebuggerStepThrough()> Private Sub InitializeComponent()
Me.btnQuery = New System.Windows.Forms.Button()
Me.txtQuery = New System.Windows.Forms.TextBox()
Me.lstData = New System.Windows.Forms.ListBox()
Me.SuspendLayout()
'
'btnQuery
Me.btnQuery.Font = New System.Drawing.Font("Microsoft Sans Serif", _
8.5!, System.Drawing.FontStyle.Regular, _
System.Drawing.GraphicsUnit.Point, CType(0, Byte))
Me.btnQuery.Location = New System.Drawing.Point(440, 0)
Me.btnQuery.Name = "btnQuery"
Me.btnQuery.Size = New System.Drawing.Size(56, 24)
Me.btnQuery.TabIndex = 2
Me.btnQuery.Text = "&Execute"
'
'txtQuery
Me.txtQuery.Font = New System.Drawing.Font("Microsoft Sans Serif", _
8.5!, System.Drawing.FontStyle.Regular, _
System.Drawing.GraphicsUnit.Point, CType(0, Byte))
Me.txtQuery.Location = New System.Drawing.Point(8, 0)
Me.txtQuery.Name = "txtQuery"
Me.txtQuery.Size = New System.Drawing.Size(432, 20)
Me.txtQuery.TabIndex = 1
Me.txtQuery.Text = "TextBox1"
'
```

```
'lstData
Me.lstData.ColumnWidth = 120
Me.lstData.Location = New System.Drawing.Point(8, 32)
Me.lstData.MultiColumn = True
Me.lstData.Name = "lstData"
Me.lstData.Size = New System.Drawing.Size(488, 355)
Me.lstData.TabIndex = 3
'
'frmResults
Me.AutoScaleBaseSize = New System.Drawing.Size(5, 13)
Me.ClientSize = New System.Drawing.Size(504, 397)
Me.Controls.AddRange(New System.Windows.Forms.Control() _
{Me.lstData, Me.btnQuery, Me.txtQuery})
Me.Name = "frmResults"
Me.Text = "Query Window"
Me.ResumeLayout(False)
End Sub
#End Region
Private Sub btnQuery_Click(ByVal sender As System.Object, _
ByVal e As System.EventArgs) Handles btnQuery.Click
Try
dbCmd.CommandText = txtQuery.Text
dbReader = dbCmd.ExecuteReader(CommandBehavior.SingleResult)
 'get the schema of the table
Dim dtblInfo As DataTable = dbReader.GetSchemaTable()
 'place holder variable while iterating rows
Dim rwRow As DataRow
Dim strHeaders As System.Text.StringBuilder = _
New System.Text.StringBuilder()
Dim strData As System.Text.StringBuilder = New  _
System.Text.StringBuilder()
Dim typTypes(dtblInfo.Columns.Count) As Type
Dim intCounter As Integer = 0
 'loop through each row in the metadata
For Each rwRow In dtblInfo.Rows
    'get the type of the value in the row
    typTypes(intCounter) = rwRow("DataType")
    intCounter += 1
   'add the column heading to the string
    strHeaders.Append("<" & rwRow(0) & ">" & vbTab)
Next
 'write the header to the listbox
lstData.Items.Add(strHeaders.ToString())
 'loop through the rows of data that we really care about
```

```
  Do While dbReader.Read()
      'read once for each column
      For intCounter = 0 To (dbReader.FieldCount - 1)
          'add the column data to the output string
          strData.Append(GetProperType(dbReader,  intCounter, _
 typTypes(intCounter)) &  vbTab)
      Next
     'write the data to the listbox
      lstData.Items.Add(strData.ToString())
     'clear the string builder
      strData = New System.Text.StringBuilder()
  Loop
  Catch except As Exception
  MsgBox("Error: " & except.Message)
  End Try
End Sub
   'this function gets the value of a specific column
  Private Function GetProperType(ByVal dr As SqlDataReader, _
  ByVal intPos As Integer, ByVal typType As Type) As Object
  'get the type of the field - then get the value
  Select Case typType.Name
  Case "String"
      'cast and return
      Return CType(dr.GetString(intPos), String)
   Case "Int32"
      'cast and return
      Return CType(dr.GetInt32(intPos), Int32)
     'here is where you could check for all other
      'types and return them as necessary. I just go the easy
      'route and check for the most common 2
  Case Else
      Return "<Unsupported Type>"
  End Select
  End Function
End Class
```

What we do in response to the button click is set the text of our SQL command to what is supplied by the user from a textbox via:

```
dbCmd.CommandText = txtQuery.Text
```

(In this example, we ignore the validation that would be necessary in a full-featured program.)

The next few lines include declarations to retrieve and display the database column names and values:

```
Dim dtblInfo As DataTable = dbReader.GetSchemaTable()
Dim rwRow As DataRow
Dim strHeaders As System.Text.StringBuilder = New System.Text.StringBuilder()
Dim strData As System.Text.StringBuilder = New System.Text.StringBuilder()
Dim typTypes(dtblInfo.Columns.Count) As Type
```

For this application, because we cannot know the structure of the database ahead of time, we make a call to `GetSchemaTable()` to tell us the structure of the database. The `GetSchemaTable()` method returns a `DataTable` object that describes the columns that make up each row in the retrieved data set. Having the metadata lets us discover the number of columns in a row, the name of each column, and the type of the data stored in each column. With these three pieces of information, we can query and display data from any database to which we can connect. (Remember, you need type information to call the proper `GetXXX()` function on the `DataReader` when `Option Strict` is on (as it should be). We use the two `StringBuilder` variables for efficiency, as we explain next.

This loop gives us the information we need to be able to present the data in the listbox:

```
Dim intCounter As Integer = 0
For Each rwRow In dtblInfo.Rows
    typTypes(intCounter) = rwRow("DataType")
    intCounter += 1
    strHeaders.Append("<" & rwRow(0) & ">" & vbTab)
Next
```

Notice that we use the `For Each` construct to iterate all of the rows in the `DataTable`. We also store the type of the column's value in the `typTypes` array, and then append the column's name to the `StringBuilder` so we can write all of the column names to the listbox at one time. (It is always faster to update a property once.) Also, notice that we use the name of the column in the call to `rwRow("DataType")` instead of the ordinal, because the structure of that table could change, and that would change the column number for the `DataType` field. After the loop completes, we have all of the column's names and types stored, and we can move on to displaying the records the user wants to see, using this slightly complicated looking nested loop:

```
Do While dbReader.Read()
    For intCounter = 0 To (dbReader.FieldCount - 1)
        strData.Append(GetProperType(dbReader, intCounter, _
        typTypes(intCounter)) & vbTab)
    Nextp
    lstData.Items.Add(strData.ToString())
    strData = New System.Text.StringBuilder()
Loop
```

The first part of the loop is exactly like the ones in the preceding examples, except that we loop once for each column in the row to discover the type of the column and retrieve it, before making the next call to `Read()`.We created the `GetProperType()` helper function to accomplish this task.

Figure 11-4 shows the results of querying the Northwind database.

Figure 11-4. The results of querying the Northwind database

We have tried to give you a taste of what you can do with ADO .NET. But we have to reiterate that this chapter is only the briefest of surveys. We did not show you how to use stored procedures to update data nor did we discuss data-bound controls or the `DataAdapter/DataSet` objects. For all this and more, please consult Thomsen's book, which we mentioned in the introduction to this chapter.

CHAPTER 12

A Brief Overview of ASP .NET

ON THE SURFACE IT MAY SEEM as if ASP .NET is nothing more then yet another way to serve up Web pages dynamically, but it goes far beyond what could be done with traditional ASP pages. Although ASP code will run under ASP .NET, ASP .NET is really a totally different animal that was rebuilt from the ground up. For example, ASP .NET comes with Web Form controls that promise to make browser-based delivery as easy as the original VB controls made Windows development, *whether the client is a PC browser or a handheld device.* ASP .NET is compiled so that it runs much faster on the server. It scales well. It can use the security model of .NET. It allows for multiple forms of authentication and much more.

We think it is fair to say that ASP .NET will be the first part of .NET that will be used extensively in commercial applications. In fact, Microsoft is so proud of what they have accomplished with ASP .NET that, in addition to running parts of their own Web site on ASP .NET, they have made the unprecedented move of allowing companies to deploy commercial ASP .NET apps based on beta 2!

This brief chapter is designed to give you a sense of what ASP .NET can do if you have some familiarity with traditional ASP. It is not intended to replace any of the thick books on ASP .NET that are already available.

Some History

ASP was introduced in 1997 to give Internet Information Server (IIS) a way to serve up Web pages dynamically. The idea was that you wrote a combination of HTML and script code, which was interpreted by IIS in response to client requests. The end result was an HTML page that got sent back to the user. The trouble with ASP was that it was:

- Slower than it had to be because it relied on server-side code that was interpreted.
- Harder to develop and maintain, because it did not separate the presentation of the page from the code that drove the page.

- Hard to scale because ASP pages essentially could not maintain state when you tried to scale to multiple servers in a Web farm or after a restart.
- Did not have a good security model.

ASP .NET solves all these problems and more.

A Simple ASP .NET Web Application

We suggest starting up a new ASP .NET application from the New Project dialog box so you can follow along with us.

After a short delay, the VS IDE will create a page with the default name of `WebForms1.aspx`. This page contains the display code for an ASP .NET application. The VS .NET IDE will look like Figure 12-1. Notice how many files have been created to back up this simple page in Figure 12-1's Solution Explorer. For example, there is a cascading style sheet that determines the look and feel of the page that you can modify. Next, notice that the designer looks very similar to the Windows Forms designer shown in Chapter 8. There is a toolbox with controls on it and you can drag and drop controls onto this Web page. (Of course, Web pages do not have quite as much flexibility at design time as do Windows Form–based pages since they ultimately must run inside a browser.)

Now add a label and a button to the page. Stretch the label to be the size of the page and place the button centered directly below the label. Doing this generates instances of classes that lie in the `System.Web.UI.WebControl` namespace. This namespace is automatically referenced when you ask the IDE to create a new ASP .NET application. Change the `Text` property of the label to be blank, and change the `Text` property of the button to "Click me!". These property changes will be saved to the HTML contained in the .aspx page. You can see the underlying HTML by choosing View|HTML Source (Ctrl+Page Down) or choosing the HTML tab in the IDE. It looks something like this with the key lines in bold:

```
<%@ Page Language="vb" AutoEventWireup="false"
Codebehind="WebForm1.aspx.vb" Inherits="WebApplication1.WebForm1"%>
<!DOCTYPE HTML PUBLIC "-//W3C//DTD HTML 4.0 Transitional//EN">
<HTML>
<HEAD>
  <title></title>
  <meta name="GENERATOR" content="Microsoft Visual Studio.NET 7.0">
  <meta name="CODE_LANGUAGE" content="Visual Basic 7.0">
  <meta name="vs_defaultClientScript" content="JavaScript">
  <meta name="vs_targetSchema" content=
"http://schemas.microsoft.com/intellisense/ie5">
```

```
</HEAD>
 <body MS_POSITIONING="GridLayout">
  <form id="Form1" method="post" runat="server">
    <asp:Button id="Button1" style="Z-INDEX: 101; LEFT: 311px;
POSITION: absolute; TOP: 212px" runat="server" Text="Click me!"
Width="123px" Height="67px"></asp:Button>
    <asp:Label id="Label1" style="Z-INDEX: 102; LEFT: 15px; POSITION: absolute;
TOP: 40px" runat="server" Width="631px" Height="132px"></asp:Label>
  </form>
 </body>
</HTML>
```

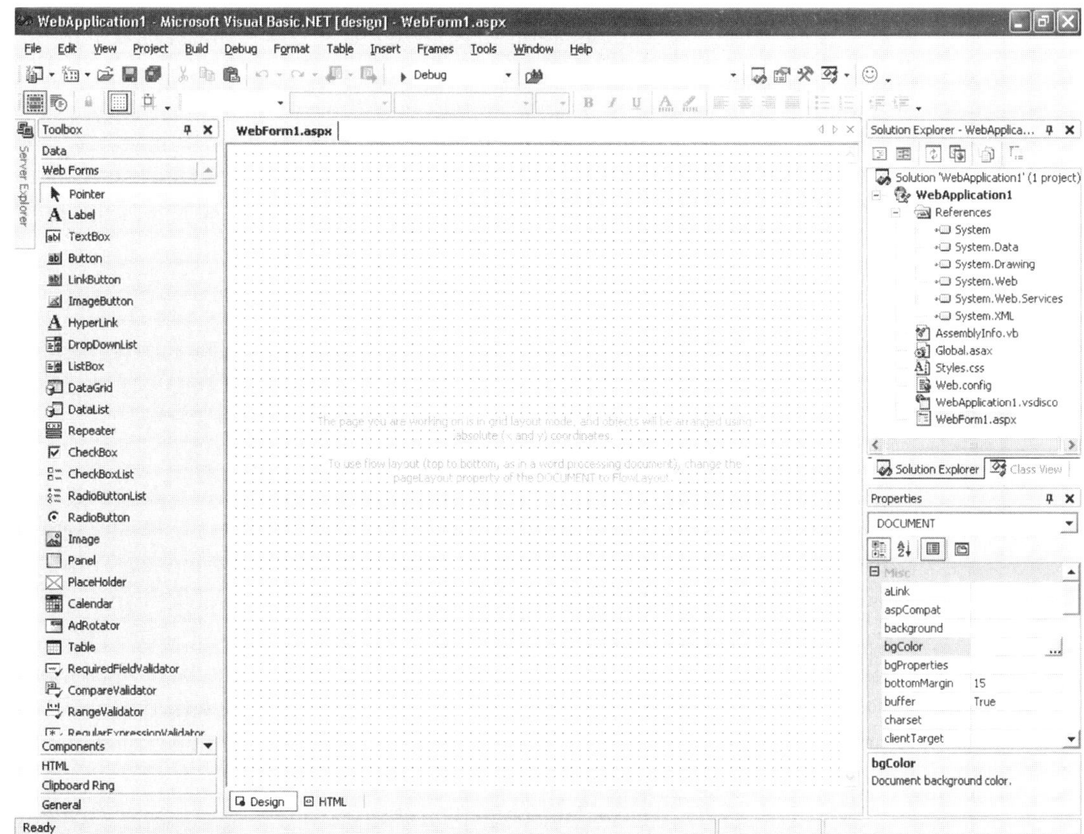

Figure 12-1. A simple ASP .NET application in the IDE

Notice that the first bold line in the preceding code includes the `runat` attribute with the `server` value, indicating that the control and its code will run on the server rather than on the client. It is possible to run ASP .NET code on the client, but this is very unusual and you lose a lot of the capabilities of ASP .NET if you do so.

(Essentially, if you do this you are running a client-side script that has nothing to do with ASP .NET.)

Next, notice that the controls on this page are all prefixed by `<asp:`. This is because ASP .NET controls are *not* HTML controls. They lie on the server and only the pages that get sent to the client use ordinary HTML-based controls (where appropriate). For example, there are no HTML counterparts to ASP .NET controls, such as the range valuator or the calendar. In this case, ASP .NET uses a necessary combination of ordinary HTML controls, scripting, and server-side code to achieve the effect you want.

Next, double-click on the button to go to the `Click` event in the code window. Notice how you are taken to a page that looks just like the code behind a Windows Form application, replete with lots of automatically generated code that we explain shortly. ASP .NET applications usually keep the code separate from the presentation layer via a feature Microsoft calls *code behind*. This is a fancy way of saying you can separate your programming logic contained in the .aspx page from the (HTML) code to display the page. The code behind an ASP .NET page is stored in a separate file with a double extension of .aspx.vb.

Now add the following code to the `Click` event procedure so that it looks like this:

```
Private Sub Button1_Click(ByVal sender As System.Object, _
ByVal e As System.EventArgs) Handles Button1.Click
  Me.Label1.Font.Size = FontUnit.XLarge
  Me.Label1.Text = "Welcome to ASP .NET @" & Now
End Sub
```

Notice how similar this code is to the code you would place in a Window Form's click event, complete with `sender` and `EventArgs` parameters. Next, notice how the `Font` property is a little different for Web controls than for Windows Forms. This is natural because of the limitation on the fonts that HTML pages can display compared to Windows Forms. Finally, notice how we can use a built-in function of .NET, such as `Now`, in our ASP .NET code. An ASP .NET application has total access to the .NET Framework. This means you can, for example, use all the database controls or database code available to you from .NET and briefly described in Chapter 11 to access data via ASP .NET.

If you have specified the default page, then after you hit F5, the VS .NET IDE will generate a Web page and automatically run it in Internet Explorer. After you click on the button, the results should look something like what you see in Figure 12-2.

> **NOTE** *An ASP .NET application is compiled into a DLL just like any .NET application. The IDE will generate the assembly info file for the DLL, which will live on the server. The ASP .NET application will also include an .aspx page and associated other files as well.*

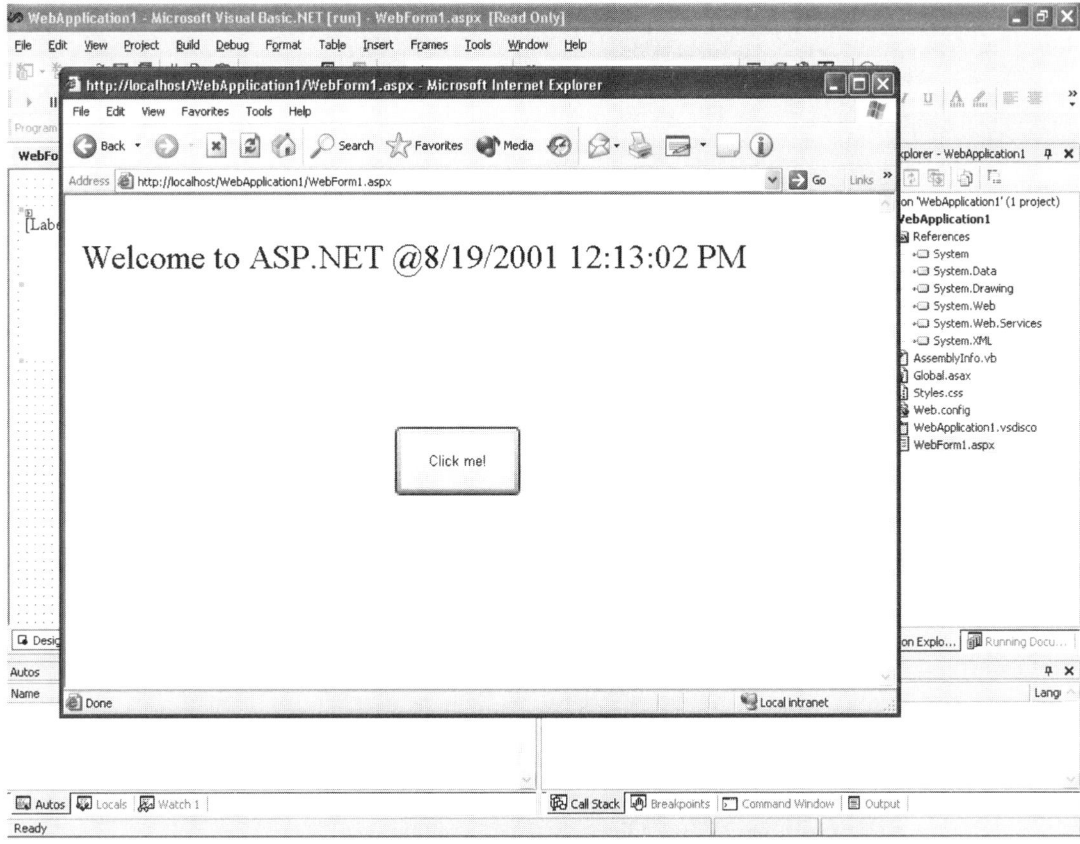

Figure 12-2. The result of a simple ASP .NET page

Here is the full code behind this page with all regions expanded:

```
Public Class WebForm1
  Inherits System.Web.UI.Page
  Protected WithEvents Label1 As System.Web.UI.WebControls.Label
  Protected WithEvents Button1 As System.Web.UI.WebControls.Button
#Region " Web Form Designer Generated Code "
  'This call is required by the Web Form Designer.
  <System.Diagnostics.DebuggerStepThrough()> Private Sub InitializeComponent()
  End Sub
  Private Sub Page_Init(ByVal sender As System.Object, _
ByVal e As System.EventArgs)
Handles MyBase.Init
    'CODEGEN: This method call is required by the Web Form Designer
    'Do not modify it using the code editor.
    InitializeComponent()
  End Sub
```

```
#End Region
  Private Sub Page_Load(ByVal sender As System.Object,
ByVal e As System.EventArgs)
Handles MyBase.Load
    'Put user code to initialize the page here
  End Sub
  Private Sub Button1_Click(ByVal sender As System.Object, ByVal e As
 System.EventArgs) Handles Button1.Click
    Me.Label1.Font.Size = FontUnit.XLarge
    Me.Label1.Text = "Welcome to ASP .NET @" & Now
  End Sub
End Class
```

Finally, ASP .NET uses a file called `global.asax`, which works similarly to the `global.asa` file used in ASP. The main differences are that the `global.asax` file is called:

- At the beginning of each request
- When an error occurs
- When an attempt is made to authenticate a user (more on authentication later in this chapter)

> **NOTE** *If you want to add any application initialization code to* `global.asax`, *you will need to put it in the* `InitializeComponent()` *function, because this is what is called when the application is first loaded.*

What Gets Sent to the Client?

The magic of ASP .NET is that although you write in normal VB .NET style, different kinds of HTML get generated, *depending on the nature of the browser client.* If the browser is a late version of Internet Explorer, you will get a lot of dynamic HTML with client-state validation for things like the built-in range validation control. However, if the browser is a WAP (Wireless Application Protocol)-enabled mobile phone, then you will get WML, the version of HTML that works on this platform, and any verifications needed will be done by the server. All of this is transparent to the programmer![1]

1. Except of course if you want to write custom Web Form controls; then you have a lot of work ahead of you. It is the job of the Web Form control to know how to render HTML for different platforms.

For example, on the version of Internet Explorer running on Windows XP, the HTML generated for the client in the preceding example looks like this with the most important lines in bold:

```
<!DOCTYPE HTML PUBLIC "-//W3C//DTD HTML 4.0 Transitional//EN">
<HTML>
  <HEAD>
    <title></title>
    <meta name="GENERATOR" content="Microsoft Visual Studio.NET 7.0">
    <meta name="CODE_LANGUAGE" content="Visual Basic 7.0">
    <meta name="vs_defaultClientScript" content="JavaScript">
    <meta name="vs_targetSchema"
content="http://schemas.microsoft.com/intellisense/ie5">
  </HEAD>
  <body MS_POSITIONING="GridLayout">
    <form name="Form1" method="post" action="WebForm1.aspx" id="Form1">
<input type="hidden" name="__VIEWSTATE" value="dDwxMDA3MzE2MzEyOzs+" />
   <input type="submit" name="Button1" value="Click me!" id="Button1"
style="height:67px;width:123px;Z-INDEX: 101; LEFT: 311px;
POSITION: absolute; TOP: 212px" />
      <span id="Label1" style="height:132px;width:631px;Z-INDEX: 102;
LEFT: 15px; POSITION: absolute; TOP: 40px"></span>
    </form>
  </body>
</HTML>
```

As the bold lines in the code indicate, the client-side HTML that was automatically generated includes an HTML form with a `post` attribute and a hidden field named `__VIEWSTATE`. These lines enable ASP .NET to maintain state without needing any direct storage of the state by the client. The `post` attribute tells the server which page it should view on subsequent requests. The hidden `__VIEWSTATE` holds the data in an encrypted form. ASP .NET can use this data to regenerate the page and its state. Essentially, it is a specialized form of serialization that you can turn off by setting a control's `EnableViewState` property to be `False`.

The best way to see all this at work is to click on the button and then look at the source again. If you do, the key lines in the HTML source you get will now look something like this:

```
<form name="Form1" method="post" action="WebForm1.aspx" id="Form1">
<input type="hidden" name="__VIEWSTATE"
value="dDwxMDA3MzE2MzEyO3Q8O2w8aTwxPjs+O2w8dDw7bDxpPDM+Oz47bDxOPHA
8cDxsPEZvbnRfU2l6ZTtUZXhOO18hUOI7PjtsPFN5c3RlbS5XZWIuVUkuV2ViQ29udHJvbH
MuRm9udFVuaXQsIFN5c3RlbS5XZWIsIFZlcnNpb249MS4wLjIOMTEuMCwgQ3VsdHVyZT
1uZXVOcmFsLCBQdWJsaWNLZXlUb2tlbj1iMDNmNWY3ZjExZDUwYTNhPFgtTGFyZ2U+O
1dlbGNvbWUgdG8gQVNQLk5FVCBAOC8xOS8yMDAxIDEyOjM2OjAwIFBNO2k8MTQwOT
47Pj47Pjs7Pjs+Pjs+Pjs+" />
```

Although the underlying .aspx page given in the `<form>` attribute is unchanged, the `__VIEWSTATE` hidden variable has changed quite a bit. In fact, the data in this field is a compressed representation of the *complete* state of the HTML controls and data. One benefit to this approach to maintaining state is that it is now transparent to the ASP .NET developer. All you have to worry about is making sure the `EnableViewState` property is true and writing the VB code for the underlying logic. The minor drawback is that extra data has to be sent with every page. In most cases, this is a relatively small amount of data and so the negatives are few.

> **NOTE** *Input controls on the client side always remember their current state, even after a trip to the server and back. You cannot turn off the automatic maintaining of state for input controls on the client that is done in ASP .NET.*

Finally, each .aspx page has a property called `Session` that returns a `Session` object that encapsulates information about the user of the current page. We like to think of a `Session` object is a sort of a super cookie on the server that you can use like a hashtable to store information via keys. For example:

```
Session("user name") = TextBox1.Text
```

would store the contents of `TextBox1` in a item indexed by the string `"user name"`.

> **TIP** *Although we do not have space to cover it here, we do want to point out that for complicated situations where you do not want to store everything in the* `Session` *object in server memory, you can store session state in a SQL server database. You can even specify that this information be stored on a specific machine when your Web site is being served up by a Web farm. Both these features greatly increase the scalability of ASP .NET!*

The Web.config File

Configuration files under Windows have always been in flux: first there were various kind of .ini files, then we went to a globally maintained Registry. An ASP .NET application essentially returns to the era of text-based .ini files by using a text file called "Web.config" in its application directory for its configuration information. This file controls the environment that the ASP .NET application runs in, such as debug settings and security. Configuration files are quite complex. Here is what the Web.config file looks like for the simple example given previously; we explain its major pieces after you have a chance to look over the whole thing:

```
<?xml version="1.0" encoding="utf-8" ?>
<configuration>
 <system.web>
 <!--  DYNAMIC DEBUG COMPILATION
  Set compilation debug="true" to insert debugging symbols (.pdb
  information) into the compiled page. Because this creates a larger file
  that executes more slowly, you should set this value to true only when
  debugging, and to false at all other times. For more information, refer
  to the documentation about debugging ASP .NET files.
    -->
   <compilation defaultLanguage="vb" debug="true" />
   <!--  CUSTOM ERROR MESSAGES
   Set customErrors mode="On" or "RemoteOnly" to enable custom error
   messages,  "Off" to disable. Add <error> tags for each of the errors
   you want to handle.
    -->
   <customErrors mode="RemoteOnly" />
   <!--  AUTHENTICATION
    This section sets the authentication policies of the application.
    Possible modes are "Windows", "Forms", "Passport" and "None"
     -->
     <authentication mode="Windows" />
     <!--  AUTHORIZATION
   This section sets the authorization policies of the application. You can
   allow or deny access to application resources by user or role.
   Wildcards: "*" mean everyone, "?"  means anonymous  (unauthenticated)
   users.
     -->
```

```
    <authorization>
     <allow users="*" /> <!-- Allow all users -->
       <!--  <allow    users="[comma separated list of users]"
                  roles="[comma separated list of roles]"/>
          <deny    users="[comma separated list of users]"
                  roles="[comma separated list of roles]"/>
       -->
   </authorization>
   <!--  APPLICATION-LEVEL TRACE LOGGING
    Application-level tracing enables trace log output for every page within
    an application. Set trace enabled="true" to enable application trace
    logging. If pageOutput="true", the trace information will be displayed at
    the bottom of each page. Otherwise, you can view the application trace
    log by browsing the "trace.axd" page from your Web application root.
     -->
    <trace enabled="false" requestLimit="10"
    pageOutput="false"traceMode="SortByTime"
 localOnly="true" />
   !--  SESSION STATE SETTINGS
   By default ASP .NET uses cookies to identify which requests belong to a
   particular session. If cookies are not available, a session can be
   tracked by adding a session identifier session. To disable cookies, set
   sessionState cookieless="true".
    -->
    <sessionState
       mode="InProc"
       stateConnectionString="tcpip=127.0.0.1:42424"
       sqlConnectionString="data source=127.0.0.1;user id=sa;password="
       cookieless="false"
       timeout="20"
    />
    <!--  PREVENT SOURCE CODE DOWNLOAD
      This section sets the types of files that will not be downloaded. As
      well as entering a httphandler for a file type, you must also
      associate that file type with the xspisapi.dll in the App Mappings
      property of the Web site, or the file can be downloaded. It is
      recommended that you use this section to prevent your sources from
      being downloaded.
    -->
```

```
68      <httpHandlers>
69         <add verb="*" path="*.vb"
70         type="System.Web.HttpNotFoundHandler,System.Web" />
71         <add verb="*" path="*.cs"
72         type="System.Web.HttpNotFoundHandler,System.Web" />
73         <add verb="*" path="*.vbproj"
74         type="System.Web.HttpNotFoundHandler,System.Web" />
75         <add verb="*" path="*.csproj"
76         type="System.Web.HttpNotFoundHandler,System.Web" />
77         <add verb="*" path="*.webinfo"
78         type="System.Web.HttpNotFoundHandler,System.Web" />
79      </httpHandlers>
80      <!--  GLOBALIZATION
81        This section sets the globalization settings of the application.
82      -->
83      <globalization requestEncoding="utf-8" responseEncoding="utf-8" />
84    </system.web>
85  </configuration>
```

Line **1** shows that, like many things in .NET, ASP .NET pages are built on XML. Lines **2–11** comprise the section of the config file that controls the language and determines whether this page is used for testing and development or for production. This part of the file also gives the languages being used for the page. (VB in our case, as you can see in line **11**.)

> **TIP** *Set* `debug=false` *in the Web.config file when you deploy the application. Although having it on is vital when developing an application, leaving it on during the production phase can lead to serious degradation of your ASP .NET application performance—sometimes by as much as an order of magnitude.*

The next interesting section is the authorization section contained in lines **18–36**. We currently have authorization set to "*", which allows any user to use the application. As you can see in the automatically generated comments in this section, you can also specify or deny a group of people access using the `allow` or `deny` keywords.

A good authentication scheme is a key to programming in a distributed world: How does a page know who you are? There are three type of authentication schemes possible in ASP .NET, as shown in Table 12-1.

Table 12-1. Authentication Schemes for ASP .NET

AUTHENTICATION SCHEME	DESCRIPTION
Windows	Uses the authentication built into IIS (pops up a dialog box that accepts a username and password). Requires the user to have an account on the machine.
Forms	Is the most common form of authentication. After a successful login, the server generates a cookie that will be included as a header sent to the server for the duration. You set up forms-based authentication by giving the name of the login form and the ASP .NET page that will control it.
Passport	This is the new authentication scheme championed by Microsoft.

> **NOTE** *The first two authentication schemes are standard; only the third is controversial. A search on Google shows that, as we write this, there are many thousands of Web pages devoted to the pros and cons of Microsoft's Passport authentication system—we will leave it to you to make up your mind about its worth!*

Keep in mind that, regardless of the authentication scheme you choose, because HTTP is a text-based protocol, the information sent back to the client is "in the clear" and can be retrieved via packet sniffing. You need to use a secure socket layer (SSL) transport mechanism to stop this.

> **TIP** *The built-in* `WebRequest` *and* `WebResponse` *classes in .NET automatically use SSL if the URL begins with "https."*

Lines **47–59** control session state, and most of the time you will want to leave this to ASP .NET default mechanisms because they are so robust. Lines **60** to the end of this file implement a nifty feature of ASP .NET that is of great interest if you want to keep your intellectual property secure. This section allows you to add a list of file types that can never be downloaded from the server.

A Simple Web Service

As we mention in Chapter 9, using screen scraping to get information from Web pages is slow (because the whole page must be parsed) and potentially problematic (because of the way the layout of the page may change). The solution is for a Web site to provide this kind of useful information is a *Web Service.* This is a fancy way of saying that Web sites will expose their functionality in way we can program against. (VB programmers should just shut their eyes an imagine that an Internet rich with Web Services means every site that uses Web Services is potentially a component with which you can program!)

> **NOTE** *More precisely, a* Web Service *is functionality exposed by a server that can be called by a client using HTML, XML, and standard Web protocols.*

In .NET, creating a Web Service that clients can program against is almost trivial. Essentially, all you have to do is build a .NET class and mark the members you want to be usable as a Web Service with the `<WebMethod()>` attribute. As a simple example, suppose we want to build a Web Service that can expose weather data.

> **NOTE** *Because we are not the weather service, we will simply hardwire example text into the code as the value of a function we call* `GetWeather`.

To follow along with us, simply start up a new Web Service project by choosing ASP .NET Web Service in the New Project dialog box. The screen is shown in Figure 12-3.

Double-click on the designer and notice the code behind starts out by displaying:

```
Public Class Service1
    Inherits System.Web.Services.WebService
```

because the `System.Web.Services.WebService` class is the base class for all .NET Web Services. Through the magic of inheritance, you get all the functionality, such as the `Context` property, which allows you to retrieve the http request that was used to request your service via the Web.

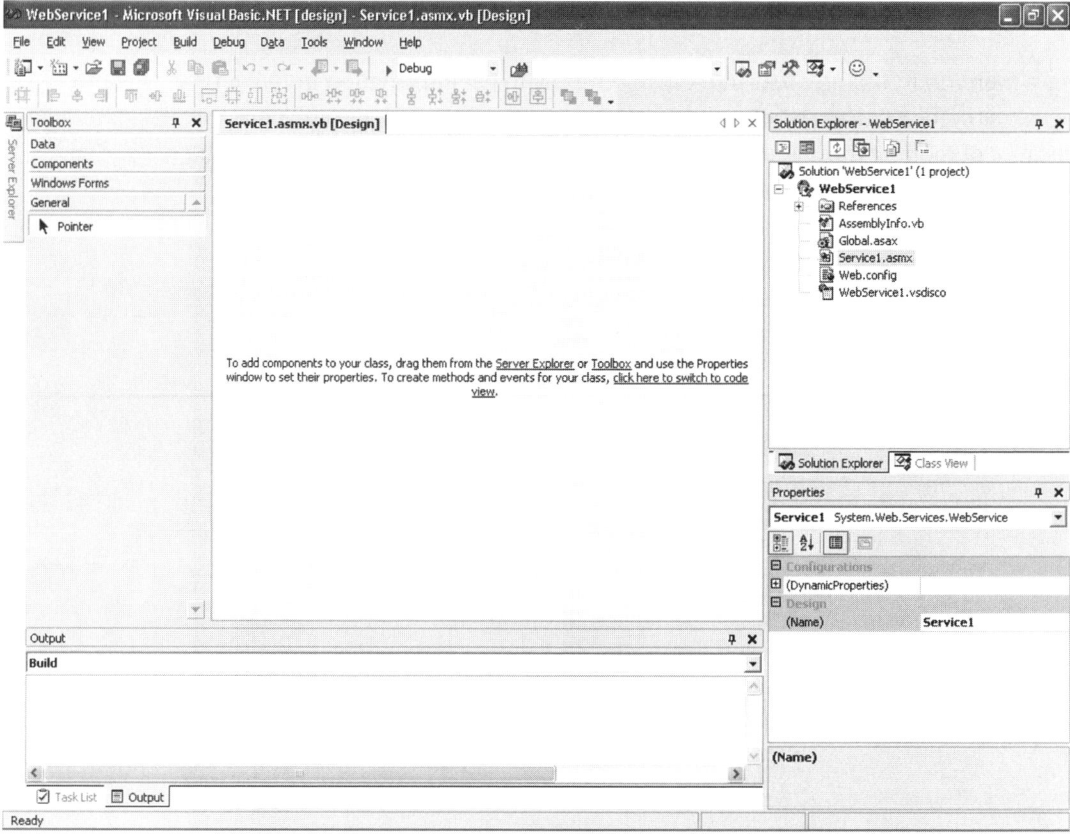

Figure 12-3. The IDE for a Web Service

Now add the following code right before the `End Class` statement:

```
<WebMethod()>Public Function GetWeather(ByVal City As String) As String
   Select Case City
     'get the weather for seattle
     Case "Seattle"
       Return "The current temperature is 64 degrees, and raining of course."
     Case Else
       Return "Can't find data for " & City & "."
   End Select
End Function
```

If you hit F5, the VS .NET IDE will automatically generate a Web page like the one in Figure 12-4. This Web page tells us which Web Service we are supporting.

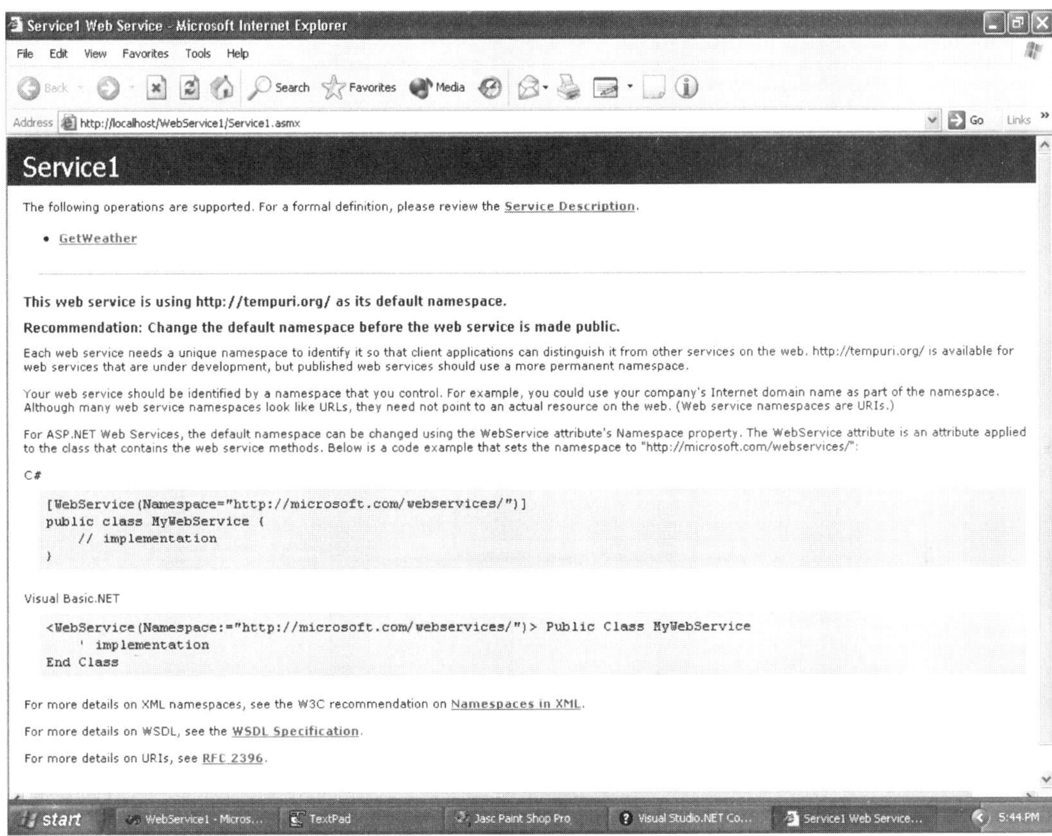

Figure 12-4. The automatically generated discover page for a Web Service

> **NOTE** *Every time you build a Web Service, the VS .NET IDE automatically generates an XML file that is written in the Web Services Descriptor Language (WSDL). These files use XML to describe which services you are exposing. (COM programmers should think of them as analogous to type libraries.) These descriptor files can even be stored in repositories unattached to your site if you so choose. You can control what the WSDL tells about your Web Service by working with the .vsdisco file that is automatically generated. Figure 12-4 is generated from the WSDL code.*

Client-Side Use of a Web Service

If you click on the `GetWeather` link in Figure 12-4, you are taken to a page that looks like Figure 12-5. This page contains the code you can use to access this Web Service. The first item listed in the figure describes how to use the XML-based SOAP protocol, which is the most flexible protocol, although it is also somewhat complicated to implement. The simplest way to use this Web Service is to use a simple HTTP GET whose prototype code looks like this:

```
/WebService1/Service1.asmx/GetWeather?city=string HTTP/1.1
Host: LocalHost
```

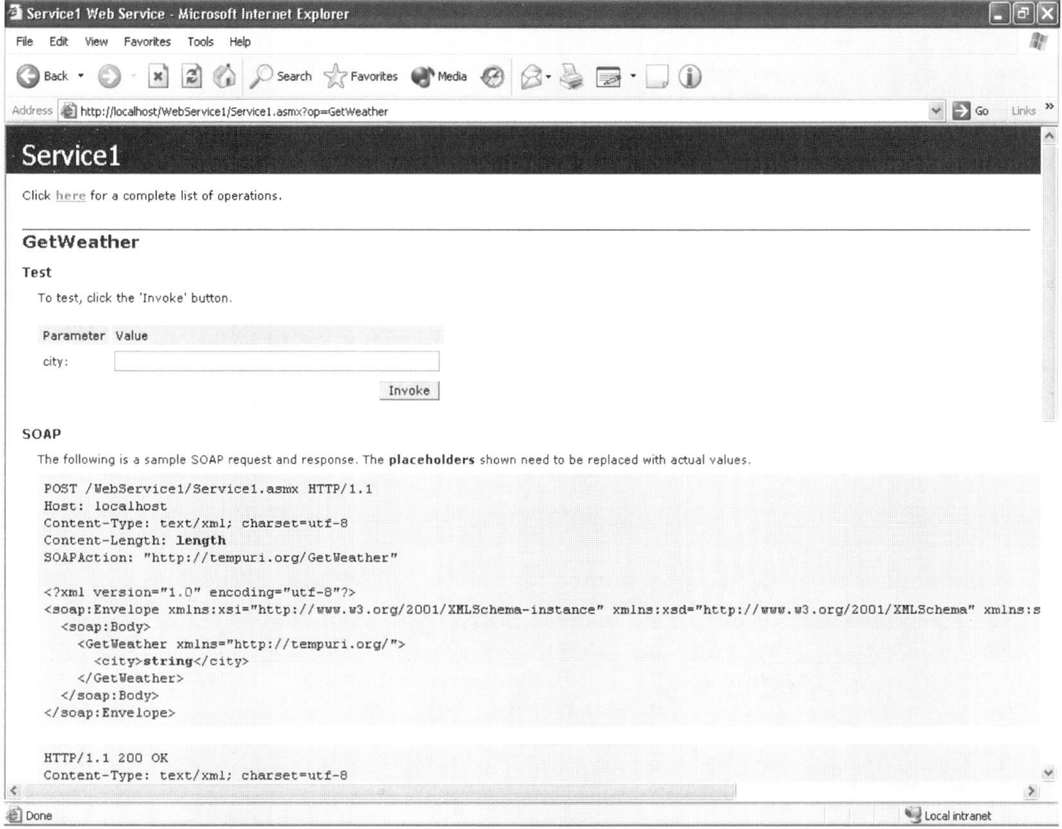

Figure 12-5. The simplest way to use our Web Service

For example, if you type **Seattle** into the textbox and click on the Invoke button, you will see something like Figure 12-6.

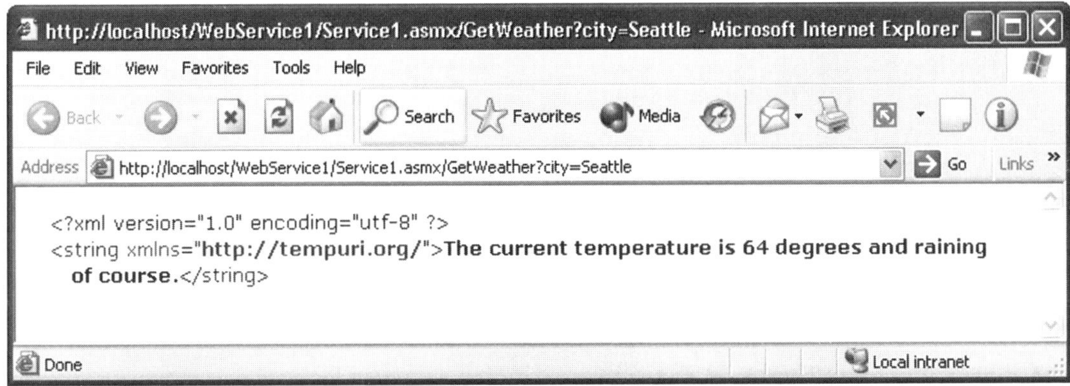

Figure 12-6. The results of using our simple Web Service

Notice that the result is XML, so you can easily write code to parse it. Finally, notice that the automatically generated code shows you how to programmatically access Web functionality away from the IDE. All you need to do is to generate the correct GET or SOAP request. Here is how to generate the GET programmatically with a simple console application that uses the `WebRequest` and `WebResponse` classes in `System.Net` to send the correct GET request:

```
Imports System.Net
Imports System.IO
Module Module1
  Sub Main()
    Dim myResponse As WebResponse
    Try
      Dim myWebServiceRequest As WebRequest
      myWebServiceRequest = WebRequest.Create _
      ("http://localhost/WebService1/Service1.asmx/GetWeather?city=Seattle")
       myResponse = _
       myWebServiceRequest.GetResponse()
       Dim theAnswer As String
       Dim aStream As New StreamReader(myResponse.GetResponseStream)
       theAnswer = aStream.ReadToEnd
       MsgBox(theAnswer)
```

```
16      Catch e As Exception
17        Console.WriteLine(e.Message)
18      Finally
19        myResponse.Close()
20      End Try
21    End Sub
22  End Module
```

Line **8** (which continues onto line **9**) is the key. We simply send the correct GET string to the server. The result, as you saw in Chapter 9, is a stream that we pipe into a `StreamReader` (line **13**). Line **14** picks up all the text in the stream. Line **19** closes the HTTP request to release any resources we were using. (By the way, if you are wondering why we declared the `myResponse` variable in line **5**, it is because declaring it in the `Try` block in lines **6–15** would have made it invisible to the `Finally` clause.) The result of this little program is shown in Figure 12-7.

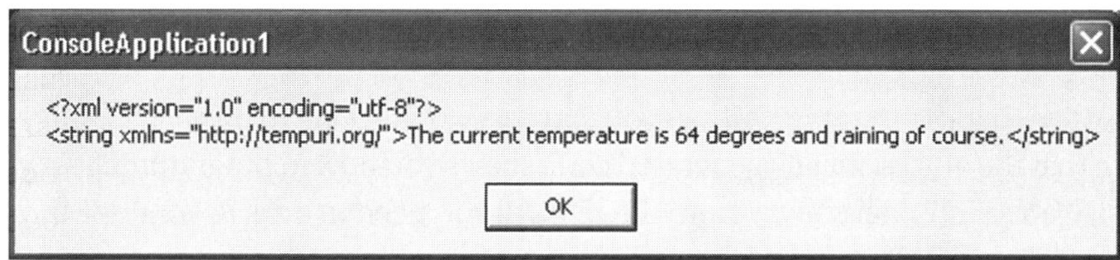

Figure 12-7. Result of calling a simple Web Service via a GET

Generating a SOAP request by hand is not something that one would really do willingly. Instead, you have two choices, choose Project|Add Web Reference or use a command line tool called wsdl.exe, which is supplied with the .NET Framework. Both give you the same result: a proxy class that you can code against.

We find the command line tool a little more flexible. In our case, the command line call to use this tool looks like this (we broke it up into two lines but you need to type it on one):

```
"C:\Program Files\Microsoft.NET\FrameworkSDK\Bin\wsdl” /language:VB"
http://localhost/WebService1/Service1.asmx?wsdl
```

Using this tool with the `/language` switch set to VB generates the code for a VB proxy class with the name `Service1.vb`, which by default is stored in the same directory as wsdl.exe. (Use the `out` flag to change the output directory.) The working parts of the proxy class look like this with the key lines in bold:

```
Option Strict Off
Option Explicit On
Imports System
Imports System.Diagnostics
Imports System.Web.Services
Imports System.Web.Services.Protocols
Imports System.Xml.Serialization

'This source code was auto-generated by wsdl, Version=1.0.2914.16.
<System.Web.Services.WebServiceBindingAttribute(Name:="Service1Soap",
[Namespace]:="http://tempuri.org/")>  _
Public Class Service1
  Inherits System.Web.Services.Protocols.SoapHttpClientProtocol
  <System.Diagnostics.DebuggerStepThroughAttribute()>  _
  Public Sub New()
    MyBase.New
    Me.Url = "http://localhost/WebService1/Service1.asmx"
  End Sub
  <System.Diagnostics.DebuggerStepThroughAttribute(),  _
System.Web.Services.Protocols.SoapDocumentMethodAttribute _
("http://tempuri.org/GetWeather",  _
Use:=System.Web.Services.Description.SoapBindingUse.Literal,  _
ParameterStyle:=System.Web.Services.Protocols.SoapParameterStyle.Wrapped)>  _
  Public Function GetWeather(ByVal city As String) As String
    Dim results() As Object = Me.Invoke("GetWeather", New Object() {city})
    Return CType(results(0),String)
  End Function
  <System.Diagnostics.DebuggerStepThroughAttribute()>  _
  Public Function BeginGetWeather(ByVal city As String, ByVal callback As
System.AsyncCallback, ByVal asyncState As Object) As System.IAsyncResult
    Return Me.BeginInvoke("GetWeather", New Object() {city}, callback, asyncState)
  End Function
  <System.Diagnostics.DebuggerStepThroughAttribute()>  _
  Public Function EndGetWeather(ByVal asyncResult As System.IAsyncResult) As
String
    Dim results() As Object = Me.EndInvoke(asyncResult)
    Return CType(results(0),String)
  End Function
End Class
```

At this point, you can add or reference this class in your project and add references to the `System.Web`, `System.XML`, and `System.Web.Services` assemblies. Once you do this, you can make objects from this proxy class. Once you have an instance of this proxy class, just call the `GetWeather` function!

Finally, we want to end this chapter by pointing out that now that you know how to grab the result of a Web Service request, we hope that it is an easy step to imagine:

- Aggregating the results of many Web Service calls into one file.
- Applying a custom XSL transform against the result to generate a new page of HTML whose data is based on the services exposed by multiple sites.

This is precisely the vision that Microsoft is pushing: an interconnected world where you can mine data stored on the Web almost effortlessly.

CHAPTER 13

.NET Assemblies, Deployment, and COM Interop

IT SEEMS TO US THAT the right way to end the book is to explain a little bit more about deployment and the use of the existing legacy, Component Object Model (COM) code. It is possible to write a whole book on these topics but we hope this short survey is enough to get you started!

For most .NET applications you build, deploying it can be as simple as copying the directory that contains the files for the applications to any user's machine that has the .NET runtime installed. The user can just double-click on the .exe filename in Explorer to run the program.

> **TIP** *By choosing Setup and Deployment Projects in the New Project dialog box you will have access to some pretty sophisticated installation options. The Setup Wizard option is both powerful enough for most situations and ridiculously easy to use.*

Still, there are times even under .NET when this kind of XCopy deployment of an application will not work and using a Wizard is too restrictive. To go further with .NET deployment you have to have an idea of what goes on under the hood in .NET assemblies. This is because .NET applications are ultimately packaged for deployment using assemblies.

Many applications you deploy will use traditional COM objects for at least some of their work, so we also want to explain briefly how you can use COM objects under .NET.[1] And since .NET was developed in part in an attempt to make

1. You can actually use .NET objects under COM as well but we find that combination strange at best.

a better COM, we will start with a brief overview of how COM works and what its problems are.[2]

How COM Works

COM makes it easier to create software that is compatible across various versions of the Windows platform in a more or less language-independent way. COM components can be created in languages including plain vanilla C (if you are a masochist), C++, Delphi, and VB5 and 6. COM allows objects such as VB OCX controls to be created with packaged functionality in a wildly successful way.

COM was introduced as a way for software components to discover the capabilities of other components and then request services from them without ever having to worry about implementation details.[3] It did this by coming up with a standard way for components to discover the interfaces that the other components supported, along with a standardized way to call the specific implementation of an interface inside an object instance.

However, COM has its problems. First, COM as implemented in Windows requires the Registry to hold pretty much *all* of the information about *all* of the components on a system. You have to register components in order to install programs and unregister them to remove the programs. When you try to uninstall a program, you run the risk that the changes the uninstaller might make to the Registry might affect lots of other programs. If you trash the Registry, nothing works. Also, if someone registers a different version of the component, it can (and way too often did) break programs that depend on earlier versions of the component.

NOTE *Windows 98 introduced the idea of side-by-side execution, which meant that an application could use a local copy of a COM component in the application's directory instead of one that was already registered. It is fair to say, however, that side-by-side execution never really took off as a solution to DLL hell. (And in any case, it works only under Windows 98, 2000, and XP—and only if the vendor takes extra care.)*

2. VB programmers who want more information on COM should run, not walk, to their bookstore and buy a copy of Dan Appleman's book *Dan Appleman's Developing COM/ActiveX Components with Visual Basic 6* from Sams.

3. Although many competing approaches to discovering and reusing code such as CORBA were attempted, COM was the most successful by far.

Still, it is worth going a little deeper into what happens at the Registry level when you register a COM component:

1. The developer creates a Globally Unique Identifier (GUID) for the component.

2. The developer creates a Programmatic Identifier (ProgID) for the component.

3. A registration tool associates the component's ProgID with its GUID by putting an entry in the Registry.

4. The registration tool lists the full path of the binary file that implements the component into the Registry and also associates it with the component's GUID.

5. The registration tool can put additional information about the component in the Registry, such as the component's threading model.

Now consider what happens when someone wants to use the component:

1. The application developer creates an instance of the component using the ProgID.

2. COM looks up the GUID for the component in the Registry.

3. COM finds the binary file that implements the component.

4. COM creates an instance of the component.

Although this is a lot of work, the problems really arise when a new version of the binary file that implements the component somehow gets copied onto a system without the Registry being updated, or if you change the GUID for the ProgID. Your previously working application just stops. This is because COM installation is ultimately order-dependent and has no good way to version its components.

.NET Assemblies

One of the marketing phrases for .NET is *XCopy deployment* which, as we mentioned in the introduction to this chapter, is a fancy way of saying you simply copy files and the program runs. Delete the files and only that program stops working. There are no Registry entries and no dependencies. To make XCopy deployment work .NET uses the idea of an assembly to make programs self-contained and self-describing.

Technically, an *assembly* in .NET is nothing more the smallest deployable unit of code in .NET.[4] An assembly will function either as a standalone EXE or as a DLL you can reference and use in other .NET applications. But an assembly contains a lot more than MSIL code that will be compiled and run by the .NET runtime. At its absolute minimum, an assembly is one or more modules and classes compiled into MSIL and *metadata* (or data about data[5]) that describes the assembly itself, as well as the functionality of the classes in the assembly. The metadata contained in an assembly is why the documentation says assemblies are *self-describing*. Often, an assembly will be a single file, but assemblies can be made up of several files. For example, an assembly can contain resource files or images. An assembly can even span multiple EXEs and DLLs. In any case, an assembly is the smallest .NET object where you can define types, do versioning, or set permissions.

NOTE *Most of the time, you will create single file assemblies that will reside in a single DLL or EXE file.*[6]

Assemblies are either private or shared. *Private* assemblies are always located in either the application's directory or a subdirectory. *Shared* assemblies are more complicated, and are stored in the *global assembly cache* (GAC). We discuss private assemblies first because they are the default for solutions built into the VS .NET IDE. Shared assemblies are quite a bit more complicated, and we survey them later in this chapter.

Generally speaking, private assemblies have much better versioning but can require more hard disk space to deploy if you end up having multiple copies of files sitting in different directories.[7] When you reference an assembly using Project|Add Reference, by default you get a copy in your own application directory as a private assembly! We recommend that you use private assemblies in most cases.

---

4. Assemblies have nothing to do with assembly language.
5. As best we can tell, the prefix *meta* for this kind of second order abstraction comes from *metamathematics*, which is an area of mathematics that talks about mathematics objects themselves.
6. As we write this, VS .NET can only create single file assemblies.
7. Hard disk space is so cheap that we think the convenience of using private assemblies is worth the wasted space.

> **NOTE** *Assemblies can also be controlled by an XML-based config file. This file must be in the same directory as the entry point for the assembly. The config file can be used to control permissions, search directories for dependent DLLs, as well as search pretty for much any information needed for loading of the assembly. Consult Andrew Troelsen's book,* VB .NET and the .NET Platform *(Apress, 2002. ISBN: 1-893115-26-7) for more on using a config file, or check the online documentation.*

The Manifest

An assembly is a potentially complicated beast. Therefore, an assembly contains a *manifest*, which contains all the information the CLR needs to know about the assembly. The manifest is what gives the runtime (CLR) the information it needs to load, compile (if necessary), and run the assembly. The manifest includes:

- Information needed to locate the code upon which the assembly depends
- The names of all of the files that make up the assembly
- The names and metadata of all assemblies and files on which the current assembly depends
- Version information for the assembly
- Type information that the runtime uses to export types from the assembly (much like the information found in a COM type library)

The manifest is what ultimately makes it possible for an assembly to be made up of multiple files. The manifest also takes the place of a complicated registry-based deployment system. The first window you have into an assembly and its manifest is the AssemblyInfo.vb file, which you can look at by double-clicking on it in VS .NET's Solution Explorer. As you can see in the following code, this text file contains numerous attributes, such as company name, which you can customize directly. (You can also usually set these via dialog boxes in the various project Property dialog boxes in the IDE.)

```
Imports System.Reflection
Imports System.Runtime.InteropServices

' General Information about an assembly is controlled through the following
' set of attributes. Change these attribute values to modify the information
' associated with an assembly.

' Review the values of the assembly attributes

<Assembly: AssemblyTitle("Sample")>
<Assembly: AssemblyDescription("")>
<Assembly: AssemblyCompany("Apress")>
<Assembly: AssemblyProduct("")>
<Assembly: AssemblyCopyright("2001")>
<Assembly: AssemblyTrademark("")>
<Assembly: CLSCompliant(True)>

'The following GUID is for the ID of the typelib if this project is exposed to COM
<Assembly: Guid("5D7BAFDE-EACA-4653-9C55-BA619E13D447")>

' Version information for an assembly consists of the following four values:
'
'      Major Version
'      Minor Version
'      Build Number
'      Revision
'
' You can specify all the values or you can default the Build and Revision Numbers
' by using the '*' as shown below:
<Assembly: AssemblyVersion("1.0.*")>
```

> **NOTE** *If you set these properties and then build the assembly you can see this information from Windows Explorer. For this, right-click on the EXE in Windows Explorer, choose Properties from the context menu, and go to the Version tab.*

The ILDASM program found in the SDK's `\bin` directory is a useful tool that you can use to drill down into an assembly and its manifest. Figure 13-1 shows you what you get running ILDASM on the Employee program from Chapter 4.

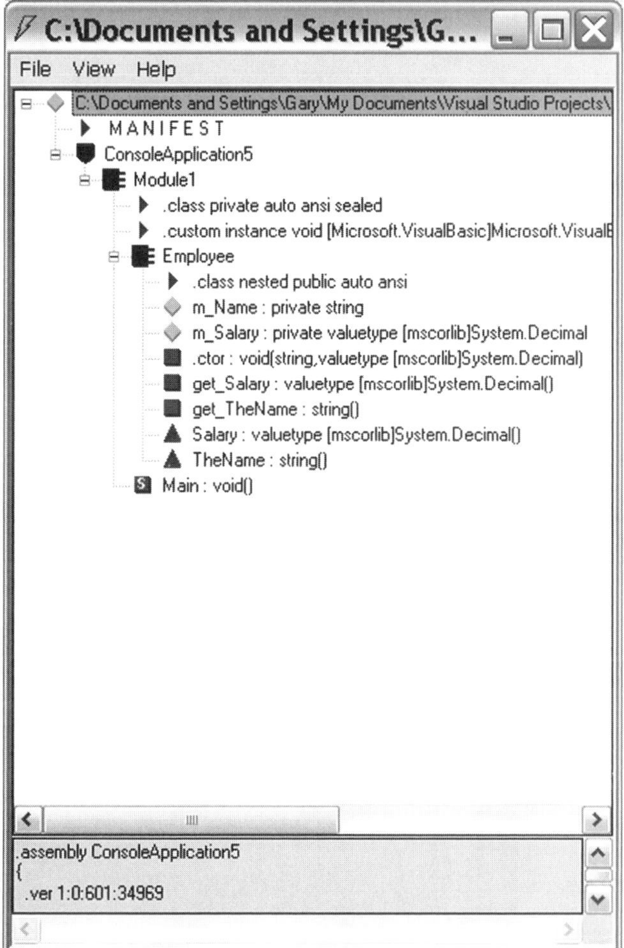

Figure 13-1. ILDASM at work

Drilling Down into a Manifest

If you double-click on the line marked Manifest in Figure 13-1, you should see something similar to Figure 13-2. Notice how all the assemblies on which this application depends are here, as well as description of the employee class.

An assembly manifest always has two required pieces. You can see these toward the bottom of Figure 13-2. The required pieces are the:

- Assembly name
- Major and minor version numbers

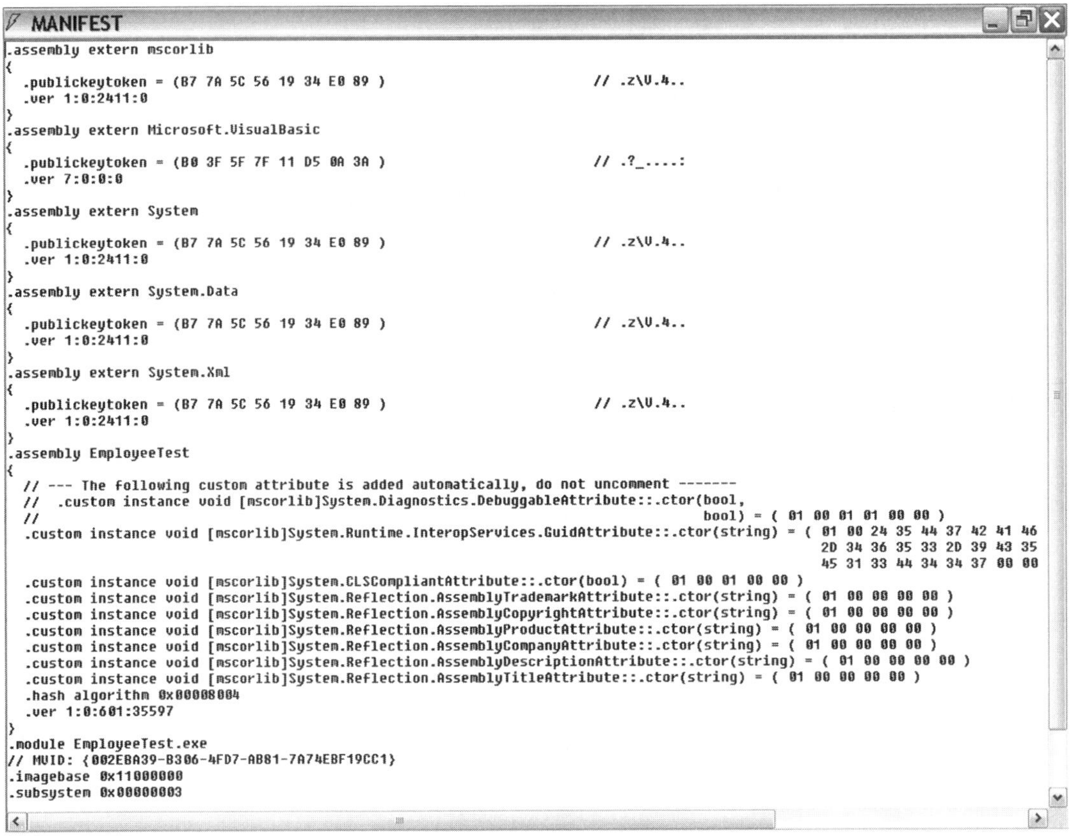

```
MANIFEST
.assembly extern mscorlib
{
  .publickeytoken = (B7 7A 5C 56 19 34 E0 89 )                         // .z\V.4..
  .ver 1:0:2411:0
}
.assembly extern Microsoft.VisualBasic
{
  .publickeytoken = (B0 3F 5F 7F 11 D5 0A 3A )                         // .?_....:
  .ver 7:0:0:0
}
.assembly extern System
{
  .publickeytoken = (B7 7A 5C 56 19 34 E0 89 )                         // .z\V.4..
  .ver 1:0:2411:0
}
.assembly extern System.Data
{
  .publickeytoken = (B7 7A 5C 56 19 34 E0 89 )                         // .z\V.4..
  .ver 1:0:2411:0
}
.assembly extern System.Xml
{
  .publickeytoken = (B7 7A 5C 56 19 34 E0 89 )                         // .z\V.4..
  .ver 1:0:2411:0
}
.assembly EmployeeTest
{
  // --- The following custom attribute is added automatically, do not uncomment -------
  //  .custom instance void [mscorlib]System.Diagnostics.DebuggableAttribute::.ctor(bool,
  //                                                                                bool) = ( 01 00 01 01 00 00 )
  .custom instance void [mscorlib]System.Runtime.InteropServices.GuidAttribute::.ctor(string) = ( 01 00 24 35 44 37 42 41 46
                                                                                                   2D 34 36 35 33 2D 39 43 35
                                                                                                   45 31 33 44 34 34 37 00 00
  .custom instance void [mscorlib]System.CLSCompliantAttribute::.ctor(bool) = ( 01 00 01 00 00 )
  .custom instance void [mscorlib]System.Reflection.AssemblyTrademarkAttribute::.ctor(string) = ( 01 00 00 00 00 )
  .custom instance void [mscorlib]System.Reflection.AssemblyCopyrightAttribute::.ctor(string) = ( 01 00 00 00 00 )
  .custom instance void [mscorlib]System.Reflection.AssemblyProductAttribute::.ctor(string) = ( 01 00 00 00 00 )
  .custom instance void [mscorlib]System.Reflection.AssemblyCompanyAttribute::.ctor(string) = ( 01 00 00 00 00 )
  .custom instance void [mscorlib]System.Reflection.AssemblyDescriptionAttribute::.ctor(string) = ( 01 00 00 00 00 )
  .custom instance void [mscorlib]System.Reflection.AssemblyTitleAttribute::.ctor(string) = ( 01 00 00 00 00 )
  .hash algorithm 0x00008004
  .ver 1:0:601:35597
}
.module EmployeeTest.exe
// MVID: {002EBA39-B306-4FD7-AB81-7A74EBF19CC1}
.imagebase 0x11000000
.subsystem 0x00000003
```

Figure 13-2. The manifest for the employee class

The assembly name is any legal filename. You usually set this by choosing Project Properties and then working with the General Property page under Common Properties.

The major, minor, revision, and build numbers are stored in the form:

<MajorVersion>.<MinorVersion>.<RevisionNumber>.<BuildNumber>.

You can set these directly in the `AssemblyInfo.vb` file. To activate the autoincrement, feature, leave the version as `x.y.*`, where the `*` indicates to VS that it should generate the build and revision number automatically.

> **NOTE** *Version checking is not done on private assemblies, only on shared assemblies.*

Two optional pieces that many assemblies have that are also stored in the Manifest are the:

- Culture of the assembly
- Strong name information

The *culture* of an assembly is information about the locales that the assembly supports. Note that locales are not languages. For example, both Britain and the U.S. use English, but they have different cultures in both a real and a .NET sense, and an assembly can be set to reflect these differences. (For example, differences in how dates or currency are displayed.)

Think of a *strong name* as roughly equivalent to a GUID, although it is quite a bit more sophisticated. They are only required if the assembly is going to be shared. We explain more about strong names in the following section.

Multiple File Assemblies

As we write this, no development environment supports creating assemblies with multiple file assemblies. If you want to create them, you will have to consult the documentation and then use the appropriate .NET SDK utilities. All of the .NET command line compilers are capable of creating multiple file assemblies. Although we will not cover multiple file assemblies in this book, we do want to point out one cool thing about them: multiple file assemblies can *still* work via XCopy deployment, only you do not have to load all of the files in the assembly onto the end user's computer at the same time—you can actually load components as they are needed. This makes them potentially very useful for Internet-based deployment, where bandwidth is an issue. For example, in a multiple file assembly, you could delay the download of the Help file component until the user asks for help.

Shared Assemblies and the GAC

The GAC (Global Assembly Cache) is where shared .NET assemblies live. It has the advantage of saving both hard disk space and real memory, because only one copy needs to be stored on the disk or in memory at runtime. This sharing of course can potentially lead to some of the disadvantages of the old registry-based solution to sharing DLLs. Luckily, the versioning capabilities of .NET mean that you can have multiple copies of different versions of the same assembly in the

GAC, and each application will use the correct one. We strongly suggest not using the GAC unless you absolutely must. The GAC is best used for those assemblies that either:

- Absolutely must be shared amongst several applications; yet for space reasons, keeping multiple local copies is impractical, or
- Need special protection (because only administrators can remove assemblies from the GAC).

The GAC, as its name suggests, is essentially a cache of the currently loaded and shared assemblies. You can view a list of assemblies in the GAC by using the gacutil.exe program found in the `\bin` directory of the .NET SDK. The command line is:

```
gacutil.exe -l
```

Here is the beginning of the GAC list on one of our boxes (it is actually quite large, even at this stage of .NET it runs to around three pages):

```
Microsoft (R) .NET Global Assembly Cache Utility.  Version 1.0.2914.16
Copyright (C) Microsoft Corp. 1998-2001. All rights reserved.

The Global Assembly Cache contains the following assemblies:
    Accessibility, Version=1.0.2411.0, Culture=neutral,
PublicKeyToken=b03f5f7f11d50a3a, Custom=null
    ADODB, Version=2.7.0.0, Culture=neutral, PublicKeyToken=b03f5f7f11d50a3a,
Custom=null
    CRVsPackageLib, Version=1.0.0.0, Culture=neutral,
PublicKeyToken=4f3430cff154c24c, Custom=null
    CrystalDecisions.CrystalReports.Engine, Version=9.1.0.0, Culture=neutral,
PublicKeyToken=4f3430cff154c24c, Custom=null
```

Versioning is much more important for GAC assemblies than for private assemblies, and you can see the version number indicated in the GAC. Reading from right to left, the last of the four numbers in the version number is for daily builds, which are assumed to be nonbreaking changes. Next is a revision number change, which presumably is used to indicate a larger change than a build change. This number is also presumed to be nonbreaking. The next two numbers are for minor and major changes, and both are presumed to be breaking. What all this means is that if you request version 2.0.0.0 and the GAC has version 2.5.0.0 only, your program will not run unless you override this with a config file.[8] On the other

8. See Andrew Troelsen's, *VB .NET and the .NET Platform* (Apress, 2002. ISBN: 1-893115-26-7), for more on how to do this.

hand, a version 2.0.0/37 is assumed to be compatible with a version 2.0.0.0 and will be loaded.

> **NOTE** *Only strongly named assemblies (see following section on "Strong Names = Shared Names") can be added to the GAC. This is because the GAC can have two different versions of the same assembly stored. The strong name is what helps the GAC differentiate between the two versions.*

Adding and Removing Assemblies from the GAC

The best way to add an assembly to the GAC when you deploy a shared assembly is to use a GAC-friendly installer such as the latest version of the Microsoft Installer (MSI) package. Explaining the installer is beyond the scope of this book but we do want to point out it is a free download from Microsoft's MSDN site (`http://msdn.microsoft.com/`).

During development, however, you will usually not use an installer but `gacutil` instead. The syntax is

```
gacutil -i <assembly_name>
```

This will add the named assembly to the GAC.

Strong Names = Shared Names

A strong name, such as a GUID, is supposed to be a name that is unique throughout all space and time. Unlike GUIDs, which in theory can be stolen, strong names use public key cryptography to ensure[9] that the strong name is secure from spoofing. The math behind a specific version of public key cryptography (PKC) can be pretty sophisticated, but the idea behind basic public key cryptography is actually pretty simple.[10]

Although there are many forms of public key cryptography, they each depend on the fact that in certain circumstances getting the parts from the whole can be really, really difficult.

---

9. Well, as long as you keep the private key secure.

10. Look at the end of the book *The Code Book : The Science of Secrecy from Ancient Egypt to Quantum Cryptography* by Simon Singh for a popular account. If you know C, you can look at the book *Cryptography in C and C++* by Michael Welschenbach (Apress, 2001. ISBN: 1-893115-95-X) for implementations and details on, for example, the RSA algorithm, which was recently released from patent protection and is among the most popular public key systems.

More precisely, they all depend on *trap door* functions. With these functions, it is easy to go one direction but really hard to go back (as with an ordinary trap door), at least without special knowledge. For example, with current knowledge it is really easy to multiply two large integers together to make a really big number; but once you have the really big number, getting the two pieces that were multiplied together is practically impossible, unless you know one of the pieces (factors).[11] The trap door is sprung after the multiplication is done.

All versions of PKC have the keys coming in pairs, one public and one private. The *public key* can be made public because without knowledge of the private key, you cannot undo the encryption done with the private key to encrypt in a reasonable amount of time. For example, you can *sign* and *verify* data by applying your private key to the data in your manifest. Others can then use the public key to verify that you are the source of the assembly provided. And, through something like Verisign, they even have a way of knowing that the public key belongs to you and not to someone else. (PKC can protect the integrity of data, but an external agency is needed to verify from whom the public key comes from.)

> **NOTE** *Actually, what goes on under the hood is that .NET calculates a number (called a hash) in a standard way from all the information in your assembly. It then applies the private key you generated to that hash number to obtain an encrypted hash. Since the point of PKC is to allow the reversal of encryption using the opposite key, the published public key can then be used to decrypt the encrypted hash to get back the original hash. The final step is to recompute the hash from the information contained in the manifest to see if the numbers match. If they do not then .NET knows the files have been tampered with and will not load the assembly.*

Generating a Key Pair

In .NET you do not have to worry about which PKC algorithm others choose.[12] You most often get a public and private key pair using the sn.exe (sn =strong name) utility that comes with the .NET SDK.

---

11. This is the basis of RSA, the popular public key algorithm. RSA also depends on raising numbers to a power and a few other bits of number theory, because multiplication alone is not secure. (You can always get the first factor from the second factor and the answer by dividing.)

12. It seems to be a version of the industry standard (and now off patent) RSA algorithm (`www.rsa.com`).

The keys are stored in a binary file. The command line syntax to generate the pair is:

```
sn -k <filename>
```

These files should have a .snk extension, so we created a key pair with the following command line:

```
sn -k c:\keys\pair.snk
```

which creates a file like the one shown in Figure 13-3. As you can see, this file is basically unreadable (although at the very top you can see the cursor pointing to the keyword `RSA`, which probably indicates that RSA is the algorithm used). In any case, the .snk file does contain a private and public key pair.

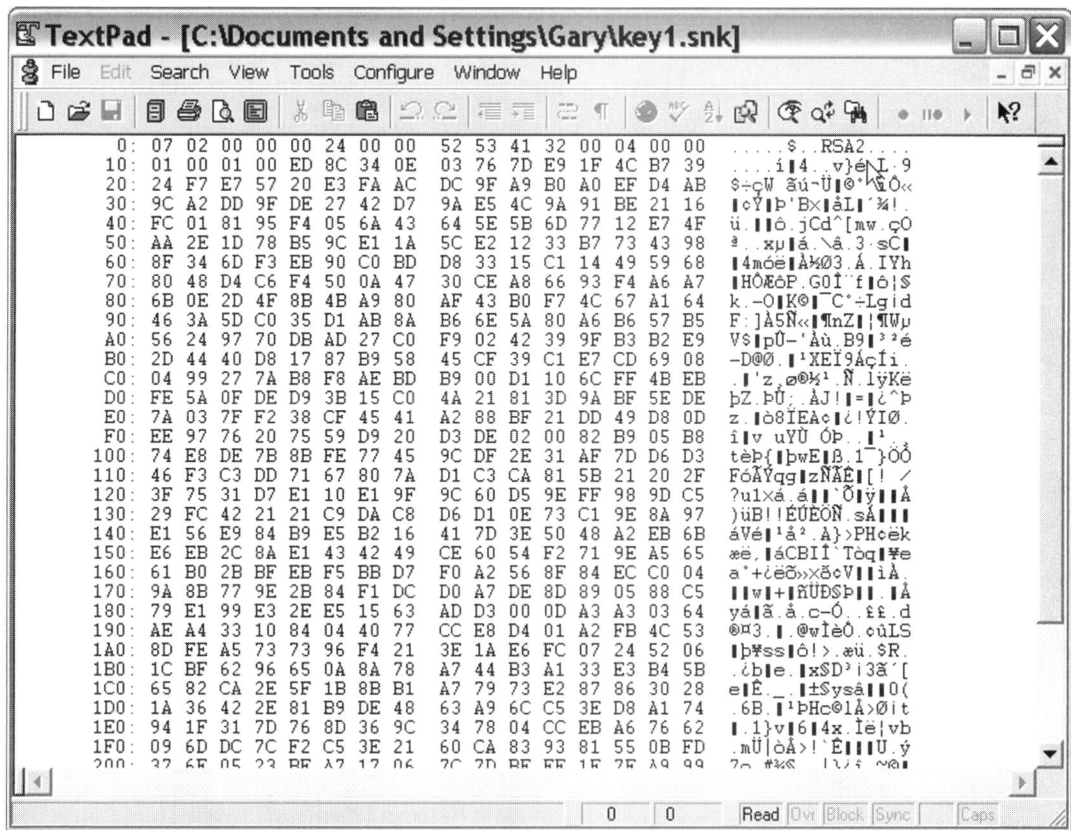

Figure 13-3. A public and private key .snk file

NOTE *You can also use the VS .NET IDE to generate a .snk file by looking under Strong Name in the Project Properties dialog box, but most people prefer to generate keys as a separate process done only under tight security. You must keep the .snk file secure from unauthorized access; the private key must remain unknown or it is useless. (The IDE suggests using a Key Container to avoid having the .snk file as part of your project.)*

Signing an Assembly

Once you have a public and private key pair in the form of a `.snk` file, you can sign your assembly using the private key. When you do this, .NET will essentially publish the public key[13] in the assembly manifest and use your private key to create a hash from all the information in the assembly and then publish that. This creates a way for other assemblies that use our code to verify that they are getting exactly what they expect, and that no one has tampered with the assembly. This is done by applying the public key to the encrypted hash and checking the result against what the manifest is advertising.

To sign an assembly, use the `AssemblyKeyFileAttribute` attribute in your source code with the name of the .snk file after any imports, or use the Sharing tab in Project Settings dialog box. Here is an example:

```
Imports System.Reflection
<Assembly: AssemblyKeyFileAttribute("c:\keys\pair.snk")> \
```

CAUTION *Many companies do not give people access to their private key, so .NET has a way to delay signing assemblies to allow for this. (For more on this please see the documentation.)*

COM Interoperability and Native DLL Function Calls

Legacy COM code is not going away and luckily the interoperability layer for COM code works very well. Using it can cause both performance and maintenance problems so we do not think you will want to mix legacy COM code into a .NET

13. Actually, what it publishes is a hashed version of it which .NET calls the *public key token*. It uses a hashed version to save space presumably, although we think they should simply publish the public key.

application unless you have to! Still, COM interoperability is almost automatic in Visual Studio .NET. Simply choose COM objects from the COM tab in the References dialog box, and this will allow you to treat COM objects as if they were .NET classes. The IDE does this by reading the COM type library, and then creating a .NET wrapper class. The wrapper class exposes as public members all the public members of the COM object, and IntelliSense will work on objects you instantiate from these wrappers.

> **NOTE** *The tlbimp.exe tool that ships with the .NET SDK also creates this wrapper class for you. This is useful if you want to create a bunch of .NET wrappers via a script at one time for future use.*

DLL Function Calls

Although you can still use the older `Declare` syntax to use functions in a DLL, the preferred way in .NET is to use the `DllImport` attribute since it allows you to create shared entry points. To use the `DllImport` attribute, define an empty function that has the signature of the API that you want to call. Here is an example of how to use the `DllImport` attribute:

```
Imports System.Drawing
Imports System.Runtime.InteropServices
Module Module1
    'import the CreateDC function from the Win32 API
    <DllImport("gdi32.dll")> Public Function CreateDC( ByVal strDriver As String, _
                                              ByVal strDeviceName As String, _
                                              ByVal strOutput As String, _
                                              ByVal nullDEVICE As Integer _
                                              ) As IntPtr
    End Function
    Sub Main()
        'create a rectangle
        Dim rctWindow As Rectangle = New Rectangle(100, 100, 200, 200)
        Dim penBlack As Pen = New Pen(Color.Black)
        penBlack.Brush = Brushes.DarkKhaki
        Dim grfx As Graphics
        Dim hDC As IntPtr = CreateDC("DISPLAY", vbNullString, _
```

```
vbNullString, vbNullString)
        grfx = Graphics.FromHdc(hDC)
        Do While (True)
            grfx.FillRectangle(penBlack.Brush, rctWindow)
            System.Threading.Thread.Sleep(0)
        Loop
    End Sub
End Module
```

The other main difference between using `DllImport` and the `Declare` keyword is that with `DllImport`, you have finer control over certain parts of the call. For instance, you can pass the calling convention that you want to use when you call the function, and you can control the character set that is used to marshal strings to the function.

Index

Symbols

A

B

D

H

I

J

K

L

M

P

Q

R

T

U

V

W

X

Z

Apress Titles

ISBN	PRICE	AUTHOR	TITLE
1-893115-01-1	$39.95	Appleman	Appleman's Win32 API Puzzle Book and Tutorial for Visual Basic Programmers
1-893115-23-2	$29.95	Appleman	How Computer Programming Works
1-893115-97-6	$39.95	Appleman	Moving to VB. NET: Strategies, Concepts, and Code
1-893115-09-7	$29.95	Baum	Dave Baum's Definitive Guide to LEGO MINDSTORMS
1-893115-84-4	$29.95	Baum, Gasperi, Hempel, and Villa	Extreme MINDSTORMS
1-893115-82-8	$59.95	Ben-Gan/Moreau	Advanced Transact-SQL for SQL Server 2000
1-893115-99-2	$39.95	Cornell/Morrison	Programming VB .NET: A Guide for Experienced Programmers
1-893115-71-2	$39.95	Ferguson	Mobile .NET
1-893115-90-9	$44.95	Finsel	The Handbook for Reluctant Database Administrators
1-893115-85-2	$34.95	Gilmore	A Programmer's Introduction to PHP 4.0
1-893115-17-8	$59.95	Gross	A Programmer's Introduction to Windows DNA
1-893115-62-3	$39.95	Gunnerson	A Programmer's Introduction to C#, Second Edition
1-893115-10-0	$34.95	Holub	Taming Java Threads
1-893115-04-6	$34.95	Hyman/Vaddadi	Mike and Phani's Essential C++ Techniques
1-893115-50-X	$34.95	Knudsen	Wireless Java: Developing with Java 2, Micro Edition
1-893115-79-8	$49.95	Kofler	Definitive Guide to Excel VBA
1-893115-56-9	$39.95	Kofler	MySQL
1-893115-87-9	$39.95	Kurata	Doing Web Development: Client-Side Techniques
1-893115-75-5	$44.95	Kurniawan	Internet Programming with VB
1-893115-19-4	$49.95	Macdonald	Serious ADO: Universal Data Access with Visual Basic

ISBN	PRICE	AUTHOR	TITLE
1-893115-06-2	$39.95	Marquis/Smith	A Visual Basic 6.0 Programmer's Toolkit
1-893115-22-4	$27.95	McCarter	David McCarter's VB Tips and Techniques
1-893115-76-3	$49.95	Morrison	C++ For VB Programmers
1-893115-80-1	$39.95	Newmarch	A Programmer's Guide to Jini Technology
1-893115-58-5	$49.95	Oellermann	Architecting Web Services
1-893115-81-X	$39.95	Pike	SQL Server: Common Problems, Tested Solutions
1-893115-20-8	$34.95	Rischpater	Wireless Web Development
1-893115-93-3	$34.95	Rischpater	Wireless Web Development with PHP and WAP
1-893115-24-0	$49.95	Sinclair	From Access to SQL Server
1-893115-94-1	$29.95	Spolsky	User Interface Design for Programmers
1-893115-53-4	$39.95	Sweeney	Visual Basic for Testers
1-893115-29-1	$44.95	Thomsen	Database Programming with Visual Basic .NET
1-893115-65-8	$39.95	Tiffany	Pocket PC Database Development with eMbedded Visual Basic
1-893115-59-3	$59.95	Troelsen	C# and the .NET Platform
1-893115-26-7	Troelsen	Visual Basic .NET and the .NET Platform	
1-893115-54-2	$49.95	Trueblood/Lovett	Data Mining and Statistical Analysis Using SQL
1-893115-16-X	$49.95	Vaughn	ADO Examples and Best Practices
1-893115-83-6	$44.95	Wells	Code Centric: T-SQL Programming with Stored Procedures and Triggers
1-893115-95-X	$49.95	Welschenbach	Cryptography in C and C++
1-893115-05-4	$39.95	Williamson	Writing Cross-Browser Dynamic HTML
1-893115-78-X	$49.95	Zukowski	Definitive Guide to Swing for Java 2, Second Edition
1-893115-92-5	$49.95	Zukowski	Java Collections

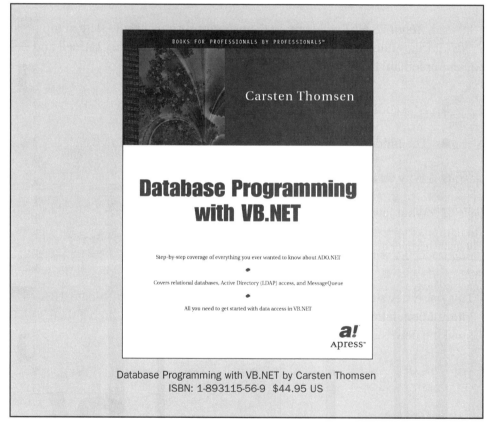

books for professionals by professionals™

About Apress

Apress, located in Berkeley, CA, is an innovative publishing company devoted to meeting the needs of existing and potential programming professionals. Simply put, the "A" in Apress stands for the "Author's Press™." Apress' unique author-centric approach to publishing grew from conversations between Dan Appleman and Gary Cornell, authors of best-selling, highly regarded computer books. In 1998, they set out to create a publishing company that emphasized quality above all else, a company with books that would be considered the best in their market. Dan and Gary's vision has resulted in over 30 widely acclaimed titles by some of the industry's leading software professionals.

Do You Have What It Takes to Write for Apress?

Apress is rapidly expanding its publishing program. If you can write and refuse to compromise on the quality of your work, if you believe in doing more then rehashing existing documentation, and if you're looking for opportunities and rewards that go far beyond those offered by traditional publishing houses, we want to hear from you!

Consider these innovations that we offer all of our authors:

- **Top royalties with *no* hidden switch statements**
  Authors typically only receive half of their normal royalty rate on foreign sales. In contrast, Apress' royalty rate remains the same for both foreign and domestic sales.
- **A mechanism for authors to obtain equity in Apress**
  Unlike the software industry, where stock options are essential to motivate and retain software professionals, the publishing industry has adhered to an outdated compensation model based on royalties alone. In the spirit of most software companies, Apress reserves a significant portion of its equity for authors.
- **Serious treatment of the technical review process**
  Each Apress book has a technical reviewing team whose remuneration depends in part on the success of the book since they too receive royalties.

Moreover, through a partnership with Springer-Verlag, one of the world's major publishing houses, Apress has significant venture capital behind it. Thus, we have the resources to produce the highest quality books *and* market them aggressively.

If you fit the model of the Apress author who can write a book that gives the "professional what he or she needs to know™," then please contact one of our Editorial Directors, Gary Cornell (gary_cornell@apress.com), Dan Appleman (dan_appleman@apress.com), Karen Watterson (karen_watterson@apress.com) or Jason Gilmore (jason_gilmore@apress.com) for more information.